Sociology and Visual Repr

Our culture has become far more visual. Recent technological developments have engendered a transformation. Visual representation now concerns a wide spectrum of social scientists: no longer is it the province of a mere handful interested in visual art. This book is concerned with still images, diagrams, and the visual presentation of the written text. It is particularly aimed at postgraduate students, and provides a selective historical survey of texts whose authors have contributed to the development of the social analysis of visual representation. It focuses, especially, on those recent texts which have changed the relationship of analysis to topic by incorporating visual representation *into* the analysis itself.

The first section of the book focuses on 'critical' accounts. It charts the history of critical theories and critical analyses of visual art from the propositions of antiquity to the present day. The author shows that photography, critical post-modernism and, above all, feminism have each played a part in blurring the distinction between art and non-art visual representations and in questioning the assumption that the verbal does the analysing while the visual merely constitutes the object of analysis. Chaplin argues that critical analyses of society are powerful when both verbal and visual dimensions are consciously activated and coordinated. The second section charts the history of empirical social analyses of visual art, scientific and other depictions. Again, it highlights those works that make *use* of the visual dimension, especially in the field of anthropology; and it includes an account of Elizabeth Chaplin's own photographic project. The section ends by examining social science accounts which take new literary forms, for these indicate that attention to the visual dimension of textual presentation reaches to the heart of current methodological issues.

Chaplin demonstrates that while depictions can contribute to social science analysis things that words alone cannot, unconventional typography and page layout can also add sociological meaning and contribute to a sound methodological stance. She urges social scientists to make more conscious use of visual representation in their analyses. And she suggests that such a course offers social scientists who are women the opportunity to develop a distinctive women's approach to social analysis.

Elizabeth Chaplin is a tutor/counsellor for the Open University in London and a visiting lecturer in sociology at the University of York.

Sociology and Visual Representation

Elizabeth Chaplin

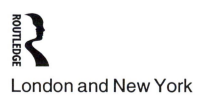

London and New York

First published 1994
by Routledge
11 New Fetter Lane, London EC4P 4EE

Simultaneously published in the USA and Canada
by Routledge
29 West 35th Street, New York, NY 10001

© 1994 Elizabeth Chaplin

Typeset in Garamond by LaserScript, Mitcham, Surrey
Printed and bound in Great Britain by
Biddles Ltd, Guildford and King's Lynn

British Library Cataloguing in Publication Data

A catalogue record for this book is available from the British Library

Library of Congress Cataloging in Publication Data

Chaplin, Elizabeth, 1939–
  Sociology and visual representation / Elizabeth Chaplin.
     p. cm.
  Includes bibliographic references and index.
  1. Art and society—History—20th century.
  2. Visual communication.   I. Title.
N72.S6C34   1994
306.4'7—dc20   94–5590
                                                                    CIP

ISBN 0–415–07362–6 (hbk)
      0–415–07363–4 (pbk)

For Stephen

Contents

Figures

Acknowledgements

Thanks are due to individual artists and authors, museums, scholarly institutions and journals, publishers, and other commercial concerns, for permission to reproduce material.

Figure 1 is courtesy of Dimplex UK Ltd.
Figure 2 is courtesy of Malcolm Hughes.
Figure 3 is courtesy of the following: Griselda Pollock; the Kelmscott Management Committee; Ashmolean Museum, Oxford; Fitzwilliam Museum, Cambridge; Birmingham Museum and Art Gallery; the Board of Trustees of the Victoria & Albert Museum.
Figures 4–8 are courtesy of the following: Victor Burgin; Basil Blackwell/ Institute of Contemporary Arts, London, 1986.
Figure 9 is courtesy of Val Green.
Figure 10 is courtesy of Lisa Williamson.
Figure 11 is courtesy of Violet Hendrickson.
Figure 12 is courtesy of Rachael Field.
Figure 13 is courtesy of Bamforth and Company Ltd, Holmfirth.
Figure 14 is courtesy of the following: Cindy Sherman; Fotofolio, Inc., New York; Metro Pictures, New York.
Figure 15 is courtesy of Nina Edge.
Figure 16 is courtesy of Barbara Weinberger and Charles Madge.
Figure 17b is courtesy of Gordon Fyfe.
Figure 18 is courtesy of the following: Geof Bowker; Bruno Latour; *Proselec*, Ecole des Mines, Paris.
Figure 19 is courtesy of Nigel Gilbert and Michael Mulkay.
Figure 19a is from A. L. Lehninger, E. Carafoli and C. S. Rossi, 'Energy-linked ion movements in mitochondrial systems', *Advances in Enzymology* 29 (1967). Copyright © John Wiley & Sons, Inc., Interscience, New York. Figure 19b is from P. Hinkle and R. McCarty, 'How Cells Make ATP'. Copyright © 1978 by *Scientific American*, Inc. All rights reserved.
Figure 20 is courtesy of the editors of *Sociology*.
Figure 21c is courtesy of the Royal Anthropological Institute.

Figure 22. The cooperation of the *American Journal of Sociology* and the University of Chicago Press is acknowledged.

Figure 23 is courtesy of the New York Academy of Sciences.

Figure 24. The drawings are made for this book by Stephen Chaplin, and are his copyright. They are based on slides of advertisements made by John Casey and Lee Ann Draud for the book *Gender Advertisements* by Erving Goffman, published by Macmillan.

Figure 25 is courtesy of Douglas Harper.

Figure 27 is courtesy of Pluto Press.

Figure 28 is courtesy of the following: Quartet Books Ltd; The Library of Congress, Washington; Mr Badr El-Hage; the Freya Stark collection, The Middle East Centre, St Antony's College, Oxford; Maynard Owen Williams, © National Geographic Society.

Figure 29 is courtesy of Malcolm Ashmore, Michael Mulkay and Trevor Pinch.

Figure 31 is courtesy of the following: Sage Publications; Anna Wynne; Steve Woolgar.

Figure 32 is courtesy of Jonathan Barnbrook and Tomoko Yoneda.

All efforts have been made to trace copyright holders. The author and publisher would be happy to hear from those we were not able to locate.

Personal acknowledgements

Many people have contributed to this book; and in particular, I am thinking of discussions with seminar groups of sociology postgraduate students at the University of York, with Michael Mulkay, and with the Countervail group of artists. There are three people, however, without whose help this project simply would not have been possible. They are Malcolm Hughes, Jean Spencer and Stephen Chaplin: I am deeply indebted to each of them.

Introduction

When we represent our world verbally to one another, we are using what has long been our most familiar and powerful form of communication. Indeed, language is sometimes referred to as 'natural language'.[1] Sociologists habitually focus on talk and texts, which they also use to communicate their own kind of understanding, or specialist knowledge. However, we do not rely on words alone – on the semantic character of language – to accomplish the task of representing our realities to each other. We communicate in a variety of different ways. For example, we represent our world visually: through artefacts, still pictures, television, video, and via the typescript and layout of verbal text itself. Furthermore, visual representation is acknowledged to be increasingly influential in shaping our views of the world. It thus concerns sociologists both as a topic of social analysis and in terms of its communicative potential.

'Representation' is a complex term, and since it occupies a key position in this book, I will explain what I mean by it before proceeding further.[2] It implies that images and texts – and here I am concerned primarily with *still* images and texts – do not reflect their sources but refashion them according to pictorial or textual codes, so that they are quite separate from, and other than, those sources. Further than this, 'representation' can be understood as articulating and contributing to social processes. These social processes determine the representation but are also consequently influenced and altered by it. Thus representations articulate not only visual or verbal codes and conventions but also the social practices and forces which underlie them, with which we interpret the world. Finally, a recipient is implied: someone to whom the representation and its realisation is addressed.

Sociological knowledge, or understanding, is itself a representation of reality, and it is routinely conveyed through textual codes. Yet most sociological research involves the visual domain, because in large part we

---

1 For example, Umberto Eco (1984: 172–7) talks about the power of natural language.
2 Here I have drawn upon the very useful characterisation of the term made by Griselda Pollock (1988).

theorise what we *see*.[3] social contexts, spatial arrangements, people's appearances and their actions; although the huge visual dimension of the social world and the fact that we transpose this into words are not much remarked upon.[4] Visual art works have long been subjected to sociological analysis, and more recently, other still visual representations such as advertisements and scientific depictions have also been treated as analytical data by sociologists. A few of these texts discuss the translation process involved when visual representation is analysed in verbal terms. But there is still a widely held assumption that though sociologists may study and analyse visual representation, the resultant analysis itself is separate from the visual domain: the verbal analyses the visual. In this book I shall discuss sociologies *of* visual representation – as implied in that assumption. But in addition, I will examine the proposition that the distinction between social analysis and visual representation is becoming less clear-cut, and that social analysis is beginning to make more use of visual representation, and indeed *should* make more use of visual depictions, unconventional typography and page layout in its analysis. These ideas will be examined in the light of current methodological and epistemological concerns, technological changes and advances, and recent work from areas as apparently diverse as feminist art theory and practice and the sociology of scientific knowledge.

With this project in mind, I have drawn together material which, when arranged roughly in historical order, shows the changing relationship between social analysis and visual representation. As indicated, some of the literature comes from areas outside sociology; much of the early material is in fact drawn from political writings and from the social history of art. In effect, an equally important project in this book has been to bring together texts and ideas from various sources for the benefit of the growing number of students of sociology who are becoming interested in visual representation (and the book is written particularly for university students who are thinking of pursuing their interest in sociology and visual representation at postgraduate level). However, to have attempted to include all or most of the relevant literature would have been impossible. I have instead selected certain key authors, and have analysed their ideas and their most relevant texts in some detail, in the hope that students will subsequently be tempted to explore the topic of sociology and visual representation further.[5] I have

---

3 And, in turn, how we see is shaped by theory.
4 However, Michael Ball and Gregory Smith note that 'in disciplines of words, language does the work of the eyes' (Ball and Smith 1992: 68).
5 At the start of each chapter is a list of the principal authors and/or works discussed in that chapter. The lists in the earlier chapters of Part I contain only authors' names. This is because I am not concerned to undertake a detailed analysis of famous 'historical' texts (these have, in any case, already been subjected to the scrutiny of many distinguished scholars), but simply to discuss the acknowledged theoretical positions of certain key philosophers and social philosophers. Details of the works in which these theories are set out are listed in the bibliography. As my survey comes closer to the present day, however, it no longer makes sense to discuss an author's ideas or 'acknowledged theoretical position' because these are as

divided the material into two basic categories, or paradigms, so that there are two roughly historical sequences, one following the other. The first part of the book is devoted to the 'critical' paradigm, and the second to the 'empirical' paradigm. Each paradigm constitutes a distinct tradition of sociological thought. This categorisation allows us to chart the different ways in which social analysis has engaged with visual representation within each paradigm, and to compare the two paradigms in a more general sense. Although many of the authors, ideas and texts in the critical paradigm antedate most of the material in the empirical paradigm, these two sections of the book can be seen as running in parallel, and need not necessarily be read in the order in which they are set out.

We tend to take for granted the pre-eminence of the written text in almost all areas of knowledge, and to regard any accompanying visual material as subsidiary to it. We talk about 'illustrations', and regard the written text as transmitting the argument or message to recipients. However, depictions and other visual forms in which discourse is represented on the page always play a much more positive part than this, because they do not merely reflect the reality referred to in the written text, but refashion their sources according to pictorial codes and the social practices and forces underlying them. They thus contribute social argument in their own right. And in cases such as Figure 1, which shows instructions for the installation of Dimplex storage heaters, visual representation clearly makes a very prominent contribution. The main pictorial codes used in Figure 1 are those of figurative imagery and the scientific diagram. A combination of these codes produces the distinctive visual convention associated with the installation of electrical appliances; and such conventions – generated by a specific set of social practices – contribute much to our knowledge of a given topic. Furthermore, depicted images, fashioned according to pictorial codes, tend to impress themselves on us at a deep subliminal level (as advertisers know well), and to stay with us, influencing our thoughts and actions as much – if not more – than words do.[6] However, a combination of image *and* text constitutes one of the most effective means of communication (though it is important to stress that written text itself includes the visual dimensions of typography and page layout, and that these are also constructed according to codes and

yet relatively unfixed and unacknowledged. Instead, there is a need to focus on specific *texts* since these may not have been subjected to very much scrutiny, interpretation of them is relatively unsettled and my readings of them may not be endorsed by others; and in any case, some of the authors are still writing, and modifying their ideas in each subsequent publication. (Indeed, as I move increasingly towards analyses which contain *visual* representation, so it becomes necessary to attend to the visual-textual construction of a particular page.) The 'lists' at the start of the later chapters therefore contain authors' names *and* the specific works by them which I discuss in those chapters.

6 Stuart Hall (1987) observes that images are more powerful vote-getters than political ideas and prescriptions.

Assembly of heater

1. Remove feet and accessories bag from corner fittings (accessories bag is located within one of the feet). Using screws (provided) secure each foot to base with the lug engaging the slot in the front panel. (On Model XT12 it will be necessary to remove base corner packaging pieces to locate feet in position.) The foot fixing screws are 'Taptite' thread cutting screws. **APPLY END PRESSURE WHILST TURNING SCREWS SO THAT THEY FORM THEIR OWN THREAD IN THE PLUNGED HOLES IN THE BASE.** Stand heater on feet and remove all packaging pieces.

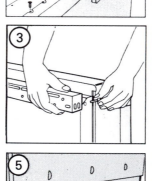

2. Place heater in its intended final position and mark off the wall fixing member location on the wall at each corner.

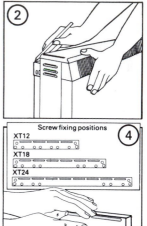

Screw fixing positions
XT12
XT18
XT24

3. Remove the wall fixing member by removing the screws and spacer bushes at each end.

4. Hold the wall fixing bracket in its position on the wall and mark the positions of the 2 lower short end fixing slots. Make these two wall fixings as described under the heading ''Special Instructions for Fitting the Heater to the Wall'', adjusting as necessary to make level. Mark off and fix the remaining screws with the wall bracket held in position by these two end screws.

5. If left hand cable connection is required, feed supply cable through cable support straps at rear of heater, leaving sufficient spare cable free to make connection easier later on.

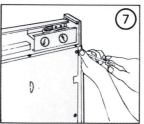

6. Secure heater to wall fixing member using both screws and spacer bushes. Remove the screws from the top rear flange of the heater and pull top forward and lift top and front panel from the heater body.

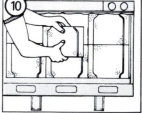

7. Remove the protective polystyrene packing attached to the front inner skin panel and discard. Remove screws from front inner skin.

8. Carefully remove front inner skin with insulation panel in position.

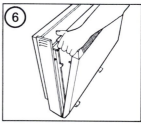

9. Carefully remove internal packing containing the heating elements.

10. Position bottom rear layer of bricks with the airways to the centre and restrictions coinciding with the air slots in the base insulation slabs. Position top rear layer of bricks with the airways to the centre and with the restrictions uppermost.

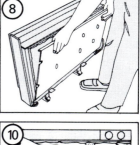

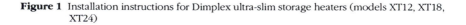

Figure 1 Installation instructions for Dimplex ultra-slim storage heaters (models XT12, XT18, XT24)

11. Fit the heating elements to the terminals in the base ensuring that the insulators are in contact with the upper face of the terminal blocks.

12. Fit front bricks in the same manner as the rear bricks.

13. Re-fit the front inner skin/insulation panel, (see diagram 7 and 8). Introduce mains supply cable through the cable clamp into the terminal area, and connect in accordance with the terminal markings. HEAT RESISTING CABLE MUST BE USED. Ensure that the cable is clamped such that there is no excess cable in the terminal area. ON NO ACCOUNT SHOULD ANY SURPLUS CABLE BE PUSHED INSIDE OR BEHIND THE HEATER.
WARNING: THIS APPLIANCE MUST BE EARTHED.
Check all electrical connections for tightness.

14. Check that the damper mechanism functions freely by rotating the left-hand control knob with the aid of a coin. Leave knob on maximum setting to ensure mechanism is not damaged when front panel is re-fitted. Similarly, check the rotation of the charge-controller, right hand control knob.

15. Position slots in bottom flange of front panel over locating lugs on feet and ensure that the locating pegs on rear flanges of front panel are located in the receiving holes in front flange of each side panel. Secure panel assembly to the top rear flange of the heater.

16. Disconnect electricity supply and connect free end of cable to a suitable double pole switch adjacent to the appliance. The heater is now ready for operation and the electricity supply can be reinstated.

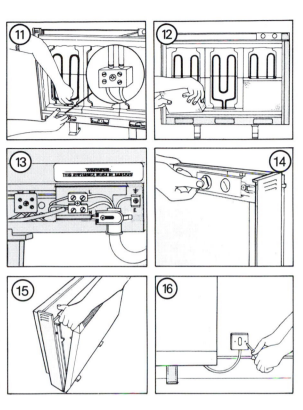

Circuit Diagram

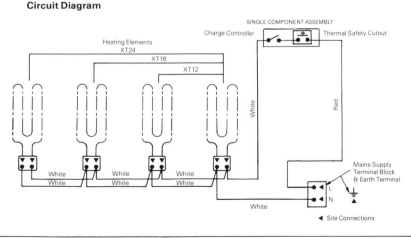

conventions generated by social practices and forces). A carefully crafted combinatory package of images and text such as scripto-visual feminist art practice,[7] or the Dimplex storage heater installation instructions in Figure 1, is a powerful didactic tool. How the combination of images and text is crafted is all important; and this topic will be explored in subsequent chapters.

In the case of visual art, the verbal/visual hierarchy is formally, and by definition, reversed. In art contexts, respondents focus on the visual art works, and treat the labels as supportive, or subsidiary. (Even so, people tend to go straight for labels in art galleries because they are more confident with verbal than with visual information. But the point is that they hope the verbal information will help to explain and give meaning to the visual works.) Visual art works were for many years virtually the only type of visual representation which social analysts addressed. Hence, in the early chapters of each part of this book – and particularly those concerned with the critical paradigm – social analyses of visual art are what I discuss. However, my experience of the visual art world extends beyond a concern with social analyses of it. For some years I have been associated with a network of artists; one of whom, Malcolm Hughes, became my research partner. I will tell the story of my involvement with these artists since it has generated methodological issues which are at the heart of this book. It has also influenced the manner in which the material in it is organised. In adopting the story-telling format, I associate myself with the feminist claim that the personal is not only political but also theoretical.

Michael Mulkay (1979) demonstrated that scientific knowledge is not a special case, but is socially constructed like other kinds of knowledge. In my doctoral thesis (1982), I adopted a similar approach to 'art knowledge' through a case study of all the responses that were made to the work of the American Abstract Expressionist artist Jackson Pollock before the year 1960. In an analysis of these responses I showed the different ways in which aesthetic discourse and responses to visual art works are socially constructed. But I eventually became dissatisfied with two crucial limitations of the brief I had originally set myself. First, analysis was solely of *verbal* accounts, and it consequently bypassed the *visual* art itself, which I was coming to realise did indeed constitute a type of knowledge, or understanding. Second, Pollock was already dead, and this meant that the material available for analysis consisted almost entirely of formal accounts of his work. I had no opportunity to observe the culture of a living art world, and to see how art knowledge is constructed and negotiated informally between art world personnel. In a future project, I resolved to become involved with practising artists.

---

7 Scripto-visual feminist art practice is discussed in Chapter 2.

I discussed these ideas with the artist Malcolm Hughes, explaining the parallel project in the field of scientific knowledge. He expressed an interest in reading the relevant sociology of science literature. I made this available to him; and in return, he told me about his own art practice, Systematic Constructivism, and about other British artists who work along similar lines. I learned that Systematic Constructive Art Practice (SCAP) is formal and abstract, and that it is descended in part from Russian Constructivism, which forged links at both practical and theoretical levels with Marxism, and with the scientific ideas and industrial technology of its day;[8] hence Hughes's interest in recent developments in the sociology of science.[9] I also learned that the British SCAP artists constitute a loosely associating network in the sense that each acknowledges a similar overlapping lineage; and that their work is envisaged as a form of theoretical collaborative practice. This is unusual; most other artists in Britain have a more individualistic approach.

SCAP in the 1970s was based, in the context of contemporary scientific theory, on developing generative systems such as syntactical, formal and mathematical structures. From one such structure, the artist would generate a series of paintings or reliefs. Some claimed that these works were objective in a positivistic sense since they were precisely rooted in a formal notation, and therefore by implication the generative system was recoverable. Others put more emphasis on the social context in which the work was seen; they stressed their own accountability and the importance of demystifying the work, and thus its accessibility. These two viewpoints formed the basis of a dialogue between the artists in the early 1980s when Hughes and I were exchanging information about our respective worlds.

As Hughes read the recent literature on the sociology of scientific knowledge, he saw that it proposed a far more convincing parallel with how visual art knowledge is constructed than that indicated by the positivist view of science. Previously SCAP had claimed objective status for its art works on the grounds that in their systematic approach, the artists made huge efforts to achieve rigour and precision in the measurement of formal relationships; for it was that rigour and precision of measurement that the formal accounts of science claimed made science objective and true. However, recent studies within the sociology of science show that however precise scientists make their measurements, an experiment is always contingent upon the situation in which it is carried out; and Hughes realised that this had implications for SCAP's former rigorous approach to the measurement of formal relations, and required it to reposition itself in relation to positivism. For if science

---

8 That is, in the period c. 1918–28. On this point see Lodder (1983: 74).

9 SCAP's roots also lie in Polish Constructivism and the Dutch de Stijl movement; and Systematic Constructivists in Britain can trace their lineage to all three of these movements via the Swiss Concrete artists. For an account of these various schools and the way they separately 'feed into' and form the lineage of the SCAP network of artists, see the introduction, by Stephen Bann, to the catalogue of the art exhibition, *Systems* (1972–3); and in particular, the chart on page 4 of the catalogue.

never actually achieves perfect objectivity, then it would surely be misguided for SCAP to endeavour to do so. Instead, the artists could emphasise that their link with science lay rather in their systematic approach – compared with the idiosyncratic one adopted by most other artists. In addition, he saw that the generative system (the content of the work) could be made to communicate the contingent nature of the situation in which it was produced or, indeed, viewed. While it is fair to say that postmodernism was already beginning to permeate the theory and practice of some of these artists, recent developments in the sociology of scientific knowledge now began to influence it as well. Figure 2a shows a double unit painting by Malcolm Hughes which is primarily concerned with the clarity and exactness with which the systematic permutation of a given set of numerical/geometric relationships can be displayed. This work was made prior to an awareness of recent developments in the sociology of scientific knowledge. However, the work by Hughes in Figure 2b suggests an awareness of these developments. While it is also fairly evidently concerned with system, it indicates the presence of the artist, via the brushstrokes in the uneven/layered painted surfaces of the canvas; and it invites the viewer to speculate about the relationship of the taped square to the two painted square canvases, to speculate about the positioning of the three elements of the art work in relation to each other and to the wall/architectual space, and also to speculate about the function of the wall – which is at the same time an integral part of the art work and an element of the specific context in which that work is placed.

We formed a research partnership, and Hughes introduced me to twenty-three British SCAP artists. Over a period of six years (1984–9), we conducted two series of interviews with the artists in their studios. The topics that we covered in the interviews reflected our respective interests. For example, from a position on the edge of their culture I wanted to find out how the artists theorised the relationship between their visual work and their political ideas and beliefs; whereas Hughes wished to explore how the various conceptions of science that they held influenced their art practice. And from what started as a practical arrangement which was mutually beneficial, we began to think more about the *idea* of working collaboratively. For example, we came to acknowledge that what we could actually *do* together was itself problematic; and we speculated about the wider implications of working *with* participants, rather than working *on* them.

Quite early in my period of involvement with the artists, I had the idea of producing visual work myself. For I realised that however much I familiar-ised myself with the artists' culture, I remained an outsider to the extent that I did not have a formal visual project. And without such a project, the whole informal area of craft and tacit craft knowledge could only be talked about at second-hand;[10] which was a serious problem, since the technical and craft

10 See Ravetz (1971: 75–108), for a discussion of the importance of craft and tacit craft knowledge in the construction of scientific knowledge.

Figure 2 Malcolm Hughes.
a) Double unit painting (1982–3). Oil on canvas. Each part 50.5 × 50.8 cms. Painting made prior to awareness of recent developments in the sociology of scientific knowledge.
b) Three elements (1990–1). Oil on canvas, acrylic tape. Each element 76 × 76 cms. Painting made in the context of critical debate about postmodernist theory, and in an awareness of recent developments in the sociology of scientific knowledge.

aspects of constructing the work are an integral part of the art project as
theoretical project.[11] I decided to take a photograph each day; in effect, to
keep a visual diary. Eventually I learned to process my own film, I exhibited
some of the work, and I am still continuing with the photographic project,
though in a slightly modified form. The daily attempt to 'look sociologically',
to frame and caption my subject matter, and to process the film, have all
helped me to conceptualise a closer relationship between sociological understanding and visual art practice, and have probably increased the bond
between sociologist and artists as well. In addition, the visual diary includes
photographs of the artists and their work; and excerpts from this document
of their culture have been used in the catalogue for the exhibition,
Countervail (1992–3; see below).

I have also collaborated with the SCAP artists more directly. One such
venture involved an attempt to combine both 'perspectives' – sociological
analysis and Systematic Constructive art practice – in an integrated, shared
project. I worked with Judith Dean, one of the younger artists, on an
undergraduate teaching programme in a university sociology department.
Our joint theme was the social use of space. Judith installed some site-
specific work in the corridors of the department, and the system on which
this work was based interacted systematically with the modular system of the
architecture. Her work was continually interfered with: some of it was
repositioned and some torn down – though we never discovered who the
perpetrators were. Several people called this vandalism; so the students were
invited to make a study of this situation, itself a by-product of the original
project.

Another collaborative project had its origin in the interview discussions,
where several artists raised the issue of gender. SCAP artists are bound to be
concerned by the inequalities arising from gender, race and other minority
group divisions since their work has a critical dimension; but its abstract
character and consequent lack of subject matter make problematic its relationship with the various forms of feminist art practice. Most feminist art is
figurative, or scripto-visual, because works of this type have proved to be
very effective in the short term as a means of confronting viewers with
feminist ideas. The discussions that Hughes and I had with the other Systematic
Constructive artists revealed a variety of views about how their work related
to gender issues, and a great deal of interest in this subject. However, none
of the artists were concerned with the short-term didactic effects of their
visual work; they were more interested in a longer-term project.

The women associated with SCAP, including myself, were given the
opportunity to explore this problematic area in more depth. Michael Tooby,
then curator of the Mappin Art Gallery in Sheffield, offered us an exhibition,

11 Artists increasingly regard theory and practice as integrated; and not as belonging in separate,
adjacent spheres.

as one in a sequence of three shows by women abstract artists.[12] We called our exhibition *Countervail*. Preparation for it entailed a series of meetings; and in these we discussed our various attitudes to art practice and to sociological understanding, and we compared the different ways in which each one of us was committed to feminism. It is clear that these discussions brought out another sense of 'working with' participants, since both artists and sociologist were addressing the question of the empowerment and the emancipation of women. In my contribution to the project, in which I began, tentatively, to theorise the relationship between SCAP and gender divisions, I drew on certain ideas of Evelyn Fox Keller.

Keller (1985) claims that science is a male body of knowledge, which constantly re-enacts the Cartesian mind/body divide in its most basic methodological moves. She argues that its ideology of 'objectivity' divides the knower (mind) from the known (nature), subject from object; and having divided the world into two halves, it then genders them, with the knower/ mind/subject cast as male, and the known/nature/object cast as female. She wants to abolish this situation in which the relationship between gender and science is concealed, and women are excluded from science. She argues that women scientists must strive to overturn this dichotomy by producing science which is '*for* women' rather than 'about women'; that is, science which casts women in the role of active producers of their own lives. Keller envisages a slow process, generated from within the scientific community itself, in which a network of women scientists gradually change what has come to count as science through the character of their social interactions and researches. In so doing, they produce change whose effect is felt beyond the confines of science. I sensed that her ideas were relevant to the Countervail collective because we want women's art works to assist in the development of a non-patriarchal art practice, and in particular we want to change SCAP from within. Our 'Countervail' exhibition, shown at Sheffield and subsequently at the Mead Gallery, University of Warwick, is a beginning. But we recognise that this is a long-term process, and that SCAP contrasts markedly with interventionary figurative feminist art practice which aims to produce an immediate effect on viewers. However, we hope that the long-term process of change from *within* SCAP, towards which we continue to work, will produce repercussions which eventually reach well beyond the confines of art practice.[13]

The collaborative projects I have described are markedly unlike the conventional approach in which the sociologist works *on* his or her research subjects ('the natives'). That distancing of researcher from research participants has its roots in the positivist philosophy which most sociologists have now rejected. The concept of 'working with' can therefore be seen as a

---

12 Michael Tooby was subsequently appointed Director of the Tate in the West, St Ives, Cornwall.
13 In another context, similar hopes are expressed by Klein (1983: 95).

methodological characteristic of post-positivism, in which the distinction between sociology and the topic area it studies becomes much less rigid. From this viewpoint, it no longer really makes sense to talk about the sociology *of* visual representation. Rather, we should expect to see a situation in which an interdependence between the two topic areas is increasingly acknowledged by a methodology and practice which reflect this. And we can consequently expect that the distinction between *verbal* sociology and *visual* art may not remain as clear-cut as when positivist methods were the norm.

A similar set of ideas is expressed by Griselda Pollock (1988). She argues that because society is an historical process, not a static entity, history cannot be reduced to a manageable block of information; it has itself to be grasped as a complex of processes and relationships. She suggests that we have to abandon all formulations such as 'art *and* society', 'art *and* its historical background', etc., because in those 'ands' reside the real difficulties which are not being confronted.

> What we have to deal with is the interplay of multiple histories – of the codes of art, of ideologies of the art world, of institutions of art, of forms of production . . . whose mutual determinations and independences have to be mapped together in precise and heterogeneous configurations.
>
> (Pollock 1988: 30)

This book is called *Sociology and Visual Representation*, but that 'and' is *not* used in the same way as in the titles that Pollock criticises. In an argument parallel to Pollock's, I wish to avoid the title 'sociology *of*' anything, because this formulation implies a distancing of sociology from its subject matter, and a static relationship between the two. As might be expected, the earlier texts I examine in both critical and empirical paradigms (in Chapters 1 and 4) do tend to have titles of the 'sociology *of* visual art' variety; and this reflects an approach derived from positivist philosophy which treats visual art as a static social entity and history as a manageable block of information. But I have shown that sociological understanding is now related to visual art in a much more complex fashion. Methodologically, the two areas are not so easy to separate; and it can be argued (for example, from a feminist viewpoint) that an attempt to do so is morally and politically undesirable. And if sociology and visual art are crossing over each other – as may also be the case between sociology and other areas – then we cannot assume that our 'discipline' will continue to communicate overwhelmingly via textual conventions that derive from an approach which puts a clear distance between social researchers and the areas of social life that they analyse.

These ideas might be countered by the claim that I have simply turned 'native' – or at any rate semi-native, as a result of my prolonged association with a number of visual artists. But the concept of 'working with' works *against* this conventional warning to anthropologists, and again raises questions about its underlying assumptions. And in case the concept of a more visual sociology is difficult to grasp, it is worth recalling that other authors have shown that the dominant form of communication has not always been verbal. Both Michel Foucault (Gutting 1989) and Svetlana Alpers (1983) discuss times and places when visual cultures predominated. Alpers argues that the culture of seventeenth-century Holland was fundamentally visual rather than verbal. She shows that pictorial and craft traditions already established by the seventeenth century were reinforced by the new experimental science and technology, which confirmed seeing and representing over reading and interpretation as the means to new knowledge of the world. Yet even reading and interpretation involve visual representation. Writing is originally drawn, as small children, primary school teachers, graphic designers, graphologists and those connected with book design and publication know well. Chinese and Japanese cultures place considerable emphasis on the drawing of the characters in their languages. However, in the West, where typography and page layout tend to be more standardised, we attend primarily to the semantic property of words rather than to how they are delineated and arranged on the page. But unconventional typography and layout can dispel this taken-for-grantedness, and inject a fresh dimension of meaning into a text.

And despite the dominance of language in our own culture, images are now ubiquitous. Photographs have long been commonplace in advertisements and other public situations. 'Popular' photography is increasingly popular, due to the range of cheap automatic cameras and the proliferation of quick colour processing stores. The centenary of photography's invention in 1989 led to many photographic exhibitions[14] and articles about photography, which have increased its stature. The National Museum of Photography, fairly recently established at Bradford, was named 'Museum of the Year' in 1991 and hailed as the most popular provincial museum in Britain. Furthermore, photography has proved an excellent means by which minority group members can record their lives and critique the culture of the majority, as I shall show in Chapter 3.

A detailed consideration of moving images is regretfully outside the scope of this book. These seem to entail a different kind of looking and therefore a different kind of analysis. Moreover, they have already generated a vast specialist literature; and in focusing on still images and social analyses which deploy or respond to them, I am following an existing line of bifurcation between these two very different types of visual representation.[15] However, we should note that most people spend far more time grazing through

---

14 For example, 'Photography Now' (1989). This exhibition, held at the Victoria and Albert Museum, London, marked the 150th anniversary of the first public announcement of the invention of photography. See also *Through the Looking Glass: Photographic Art in Britain 1945–1989* (1989), London: Barbican Art Gallery.

15 In relation to this point, it has been suggested, for example, that the still photographic image provides a point of emotional contact with viewers that the moving image still hasn't achieved.

television channels and watching videos than reading books, and that modern visual technologies relating to both moving and still images have consequently had a huge impact on cultural production. Visual artists are increasingly using Fax and Electronic Computer Transfer.[16] And most writers, including sociologists, now use word-processors or computers, with the result that the type of linear thinking entailed in writing by hand is being superseded by thinking 'straight onto the keyboard', where the computer allows the author to work on more than one passage at a time, to move blocks of text around, and to make innumerable alterations with ease. Working with a computer also promotes visual skills, particularly those associated with desktop publishing. Typography and page-design can be made to contribute meaning to a text – including sociological meaning. This topic is explored in Chapter 6, where I look at some of the new literary forms now being used to present research within the empirical paradigm.

There is also plenty of evidence from within the critical paradigm of an increased interest in visual representation.[17] I have already indicated that most Systematic Constructive artists, through their work, adopt a critical approach to society. My involvement with these artists has led to the decision to divide the material in this book into two sections, reflecting the empirical and critical approaches in sociology. In order to explain this, I return to the story of that experience once again.

In the sociology department of the university where I teach, the MA course in Contemporary Cultural Studies is divided into two parts: a programme of critical theory seminars is paralleled by a series of empirical workshops. I contribute to the latter. Every year I have introduced students to my project with the SCAP artists, and have discussed with them my aim to work with participants rather than on them.[18] However, I found that the more closely I became involved with the artists, the more I was getting the students to consider the theoretical basis of Systematic Constructive art. Thus, they were being increasingly directed towards texts on critical aesthetic theory, while they were *also* studying these texts in the critical theory seminars. Unlike other people's research participants, 'my' artists were proving to be curiously close to home. Indeed some of them could have made sound contributions to the critical theory course.

But my training was as an empirical sociologist. Whereas the critical paradigm constitutes a theoretical analysis of the inequalities existing between social strata based on its vision of a more equitable future, the

---

16 For example, Richard Hamilton and David Hockney. In an interview with Eamon McCabe, David Hockney (1991) explains that it is important to him to use the latest technology in his work.

17 For example, see Baudrillard (1983); Lyotard (1984); Jameson (1991).

18 My research partner, Malcolm Hughes, has produced art work for the course: work which is both site-specific and 'event-specific'. He contributes to seminars on a regular basis, and we discuss his work, theory and practice with the students.

empirical paradigm has classically not been concerned with what should be, and has argued that far from assuming 'inequalities' in society, these have first to be empirically established through fieldwork: its practitioners want to *find out* what human society is actually like in all its detail, here and now. Erving Goffman sums up these two positions in the following passage, while making his own relationship to them clear:

> I make no claim whatsoever to be talking about the core matters of sociology – social organization and social structure. . . . I am not addressing the structure of social life but the structure of experience individuals have at any moment of their social lives. I personally hold society to be first in every way and any individual's current involvement to be second; this report deals only with matters that are second. . . . The analysis developed does not catch at the differences between the advantaged and disadvantaged classes. . . . I can only suggest that he who would combat false consciousness and awaken people to their true interests has much to do, because the sleep is very deep. And I do not intend here to provide a lullaby but merely to sneak in and watch the way people snore.
>
> (Goffman 1974: 13–14)

As an empirical sociologist involved with the Systematic Constructive artists, I was also involved in their debates about critical theory and its relationship to their art practice; and I increasingly experienced the clear division between these two types of sociology, and felt as though I was a buffer between them. (This is probably similar to the experience of anthropologists, who classically lead a somewhat schizophrenic existence between two cultures.) In my experience, representatives of the two sociological traditions rarely discuss their differences in outlook; indeed, for the most part, they have hardly acknowledged each other's existence. References of the type made by Goffman to the two positions are rare. The best way of organising the sociological texts in this book seemed to be to reflect this bifurcation which I have experienced; but by showing both kinds of sociology running in parallel, I want to help increase the possibility that in the future we can draw from both traditions.

In summary, a central theme of this book is that the relationship of sociological understanding to visual representation is complex, and is itself changing. While social scientists have long studied visual art works, an interest in the social analysis of visual representation outside the field of visual art has recently been gathering pace. This interest can in part be attributed to the enormous changes being wrought by advances in visual technologies, which affect our daily lives. And there is evidence of a growing appreciation among social scientists of the role played by visual representation (depictions, typography, layout) in textual argument and analysis. While I shall show that feminist art practice, anthropology and the sociology of scientific knowledge can teach us a good deal about the ways in which visual representation can enhance the presentation of sociology texts, and thus sociological understanding, I argue that post-positivist and feminist methodological approaches in themselves suggest the desirability of a visually enriched sociology. For these approaches indicate that the sociology *of* a topic be replaced by a sociology which puts less distance between itself and the topic area, or data, that it studies; and this in turn implies that the distinction between verbal analysis and visual representation-as-data should become less clear-cut. These sets of ideas emerge and are developed during the course of my historical survey of the relationship of social analysis to visual representation in both critical and empirical paradigms. They are intended to support my belief that sociological analysis should make more conscious use of visual representation in its own textual presentation.

Part I

The Critical Paradigm

Chapter 1

Critical writing about visual art

Art criticism has remained a hazardous combination of subjective judgment and formal analysis.

(Herbert Read, *Art and Alienation*, 1967)

1 INTRODUCTION AND EARLY WRITINGS

| Thucydides; Pliny the Elder; Plutarch; Ghiberti; Vasari; Kant; Hegel

Chapters 1, 2 and 3 are concerned with the changing relationship between critical analysis and visual representation. Critical analysis operates on the assumption that its data are ideologically constructed and positioned,[1] whereas the notion of ideology is usually absent in empirical analysis. Traditionally, critical analysis has been overwhelmingly verbal, and, when applied to the field of visual representation, its theoretical object has been visual art.[2] My review and discussion of the critical literature in Chapter 1 centres on texts where some form of *class* analysis is applied to the field of visual art; and since the chapter focuses *on* verbal texts as such, it contains no visual material. There is a brief and selective historical introduction, which is followed by a section on Marx and subsequent Marxist writings on visual art. The second part of Chapter 1 focuses on connoisseurial art history. The reason for this diversion is that it would be difficult to discuss the work of recent critical writers without first considering this major target of their critique. The final section of this chapter looks at some of those class

---

1 In this context 'critical analysis' should be distinguished from 'critical theory', which is frequently associated with the intellectual tradition of the Frankfurt School. I use the term 'critical' in a wider sense, to encompass Marxist and Marxist-related analyses which are not necessarily related to the Frankfurt School's particular tradition of social analysis.

My use of the term is also distinguished from the sense in which it is deployed in Michael Podro's *The Critical Historians of Art* (1982), where 'critical' denotes a certain type of nineteenth century German perspective on art. I refer to this text in the third part of this chapter.

2 More recently, this has included photographs.

analyses which come under the label of 'The New Art History',[3] and it also examines concurrent texts from the sociology of art. This review of verbal class analyses of visual art is not intended to be comprehensive, but it nevertheless aims to discuss those writers and their texts which are most significant for the present project.

Thucydides' *History of the Peloponnesian War* (1972), written around 410 BC, established history as a distinct written discipline, and its influence on all subsequent historical accounts has been incalculable. The author's hope that an understanding of the past might help to clarify present and future situations was the reason he gave for writing the *History*; and its reliability is reinforced in contemporary political comedies. In the introduction, he says this about his aims and methods:

> Either I was present myself at the events which I have described or else I heard of them from eye-witnesses whose reports I have checked with as much thoroughness as possible. Not that even so the truth was easy to discover: different eye-witnesses give different accounts of the same events, speaking out of partiality for one side or the other or else from imperfect memories. And it may well be that my history will seem less easy to read because of the absence in it of a romantic element. It will be enough for me, however, if these words of mine are judged useful by those who want to understand clearly the events which happened in the past and which (human nature being what it is) will, at some time or other and in much the same ways, be repeated in the future.
>
> (Thucydides 1972: 48)

While Thucydides' work was a blueprint for future historians, Pliny the Elder left the first written account of art in relation to the society he described. His *Natural History* (1991), completed in AD 77, was an encyclopaedic coverage of scientific matters. In describing the uses that Greek and Roman craftsmen made of minerals, precious stones and metals, he makes what is thought to be the earliest known reference to famous artists and their creations, to schools of art and to Roman architectural styles and technology. In the Middle Ages several of the larger monastic libraries had copies of this work; so that it was assured of a place in European literature, and thus came to influence the intellectual development of Western Europe.

Plutarch's *Vitae Parallelae* (1972–3) [c. AD 100] has also had a profound influence on that development, and for similar reasons: it was known in Europe by the sixteenth century, and was subsequently very popular for several centuries.[4] It consists of twenty-two pairs of biographies of Greek and Roman soldiers, legislators, orators and statesmen. These biographies were designed to encourage mutual respect between Greeks and Romans. By exhibiting noble deeds and characters, the biographies were also intended to provide model patterns of behaviour for the future. Each pair of biographies

---

3 This label probably derives from the title of a book edited by A. L. Rees and F. Borzello: *The New Art History* (1986)
4 Pliny the Elder was Roman, whereas Plutarch was Greek. They were near contemporaries.

was chosen as far as possible for the similarity of the character or career of its two subjects, and each was followed by a formal comparison. Much of what is important to know about the Parthenon has been acquired from Plutarch's story of Pericles. But even more significantly, Plutarch's *Vitae Parallelae* has been the influential source of several methods for conceptualising and writing about material: first, the idea of writing individual biographies; second, the idea of treating character according to ethical principles; third, the idea of analysis by comparison; and fourth – as with Thucydides – the idea of the patterning of events.

Very broadly speaking, then, it can be argued that from these three ancient writers we have inherited the following: the very idea of history and of the patterning of events; the concept of art styles – associated with places and famous artists; the notion of individual biographies of the great and good; and the comparative method of analysis. In fifteenth-century Florence some of these areas were developed into the first 'modern' history of art: Lorenzo Ghiberti's *I Commentarii* (1958).[5] This was directly influenced by fourteenth century humanist works such as Villani's *De Famosis Civibus*, continued as *Quatuor Uomini Famosi* (1955), but both ultimately took Plutarch's *Vitae Parallelae* as a model for writing about the lives of famous artists. It has been suggested that one purpose of *I Commentarii* was to give status to Ghiberti's own work: he had the idea of attaching himself to aspects of history, antiquity and theory with the hope that this would make him seem learned, and worthy of respect.

However, just as Thucydides' *History of the Peleponesian Wars* established history as a discipline, Georgio Vasari's *The Lives of the Painters, Sculptors and Architects* (1927) which was completed in 1547, is argued to have done the same for art history. Vasari hoped that by writing about the work of artists of the present, and disseminating knowledge about them, this might help prevent the arts from falling 'to a like ruin and disorder' (a reference to the fall of the Greek and Roman civilizations) and would thereby establish a steady advance towards ultimate perfection. Progress in the arts is the underlying theme of his preface; but he cannot really account for a second flowering of the arts in Tuscany, and puts it down tentatively to a change in the air. The preface is followed by three main sections, each one of which, he tells us, represents a distinct school of artists, rather than a chronological arrangement. Each of these sections consists of a group of artistic biographies. Giotto and his work are positioned at the centre of the first section, Masaccio occupies the dominant position in the second section, and the high point of the third is the work of Leonardo. This basic manner of categorising Renaissance art has never changed. Vasari goes through the œuvre of each of the artists whose life and work he describes. In doing so, he makes a whole series of attributions, thereby setting future art historians

---

5 According to the staff of the Courtauld Institute of Art in their translation of Ghiberti's *Commentaries* (1958).

the task of assessing their accuracy. And he even records studio conversation. Here is the start of connoisseurial art history, where focus is on the famous individual artist to whom work is attributed by experts and categorised according to its style. Vasari evaluates the artist's œuvre in relation to the work of other artists who have been placed in the same stylistic category, and then assesses it according to a notion of progress towards the highest point of stylistic attainment in the arts. In all of this, he has apparently supplied both the content and an influential method of structuring Renaissance art history.

Immanuel Kant was eventually to use Vasari's account of studio processes in his writings on aesthetics. These writings have had a seminal influence; for although some of Kant's ideas on aesthetics had been anticipated, by Baumgarten and Addison for example, no one before had so thoroughly systematised the subject matter of philosophy.[6] Consequently, his work has affected the basic assumptions of all those who read it and who subsequently aimed to supersede his approach. In the first place, in his reflections on the conditions of possible knowledge, Kant wished to locate the range of inevitable subjective conditions which make any theory in natural science possible and place limits upon that theory. His analysis led him to argue that embedded in the human subject, and constituted by basic faculties of the brain, are three *a priori* categories according to which our 'perception' decisively organises the incoherent profusion of sensations and impressions that bombard us from without. According to Kant, knowledge is constituted, perceived and organised according to the discrete spheres of scientific knowledge, aesthetics[7] and morals. Subsequent writers have often used these three categories as the organisational framework for their own ideas, though they may not concede the *a priori* status of the categories. This categorisation leads to a drastic differentiation between kinds of thought – the scientific, the conceptual, and the intuitive thought associated with artistic genius; and it prepared the way for the distinction which has been made between facts and values.

The implications of making aesthetic thought into a separate category or faculty of the mind are immense, and lead to the idea that art is autonomous and therefore has an immanent development. It has led to the development of art theory in its own right, and has provided the theoretical underpinning for connoisseurship, theories of art for art's sake, and the modernist art theory of Clement Greenberg (1986) [1940]. In addition, Kant's notion that the artist has creative, intuitive, expressive powers (which unlike scientific understanding, are not susceptible of discursive exposition) underpins the

---

6 This section on Kant relates, principally, to ideas which originate in his three Critiques: *The Critique of Pure Reason* (1986) [1781], *The Critique of Practical Reason* (1956) [1788], *The Critique of Judgment* (1961) [1792].

7 His analysis led him to argue that aesthetic value exhibits itself in a sort of pleasure. However, it was a very special sort of pleasure. In order to attain to beauty, the pleasure must be 1) disinterested, 2) universal, 3) necessary in a uniquely specified way, and 4) must give the effect of purposiveness without actually being the satisfaction of a purpose.

Romantic notion of the artist, and the idea that art is ineffable; both of which are still widely accepted.

Furthermore, in his systematic scheme, Kant accorded aesthetics a pivotal position *between* the categories of science and morality. And he claimed that each type of knowledge – the aesthetic, the ethical and the scientific – is at the same time contributing to something larger and transcendent, in the sense that on this higher plane, aesthetics, morals and science are all linked in an ultimately 'pure knowledge'. His proposition that aesthetics occupies a position in the overall system between ethics and scientific knowledge prepared the ground for subsequent theories which have addressed the relationship between art and science as separate and autonomous forms of knowledge. This proposition also generated debates, still current, about the relationship between art and politics, and about the moral function of art.[8]

The idea of critique is a product of the Enlightenment, though the term is older still. It was first used by the Humanists and Reformers to describe the art of informed judgement, appropriate to the study of ancient texts. By Kant's time, the process of critique had acquired public force. To Kant, critique meant oppositional thinking in the sense of reflecting on the conditions of possible knowledge. But the term critique, as commonly used today, contains another meaning. It implies reflection on a system of constraints which are humanly produced: those distorting pressures to which individuals, or a group of individuals, or the human race as a whole, succumb in their process of self-formation. Critique in this sense has its root in the philosophical writings of Hegel.

Whereas Kant's statements are often hedged around with qualifications, Hegel seems to have had a vision of absolute truth, and he expounded it with confidence.[9] The Hegelian system(s) claimed to provide a unitary solution to all of the problems of philosophy. It is a kind of spiritual monism which held that the *speculative* point of view, which transcends all particular and separate perspectives, must grasp the *one* truth, bringing back to its proper centre all of the problems of logic, metaphysics, and the philosophies of nature, law, history and culture (artistic, religious and philosophical). According to Hegel, this attitude is more than a formal method that remains extraneous to its own content. Rather, it represents the actual development of the Absolute, the all-embracing totality of reality, considered 'as Subject and not merely as Substance'. This Absolute first puts forth itself in the immediacy of its own inner consciousness and then negates this positing. It is thus now alienated

---

8 For example, a group of British philosophers (including Peter Dews, Andrew Bowie, Jay Bernstein, Andrew Benjamin and Peter Osborne) is re-negotiating Kant's categories, especially the category of morals, in the light of developments in postmodern theory which signal the demise of the dominance of reason. Hence his presence is still felt in the basic organisation of thought. See, for example, A. Benjamin (1989), and J. Bernstein (1992).

9 This section on Hegel relates, principally, to ideas which originate in *Phenomenology of Spirit* (1977) [1807], *Encyclopaedia of the Philosophical Sciences in Outline* (1970) [1817], and *Aesthetics: Lectures on Fine Art,* (1975) [1720–9].

from its absolute self by its expression in the particularity and determinateness of the factual elements of life and culture. The Absolute finally regains itself, through the negation of the former negation that had constituted the finite world.

However, the formal *method* of exposition, dialectics, proved to be Hegel's signal contribution to subsequent developments in critical theory. To explain this in an everyday context, it often happens that in a discussion two people who at first present diametrically opposed points of view ultimately agree to reject their own partial views and to accept a new and broader view that does justice to the substance of each – the 'highest common denominator', as it were. Hegel believed that thinking always proceeds according to this pattern: positive thesis, antithesis, synthesis of the two former positions. Thus, thinking itself, as a process, has negativity as one of its constituent moments; and for Hegel, though not for most subsequent dialecticians, the finite is, as God's self-manifestation, part and parcel of the infinite itself.

Although Hegel's panoramic system had the merit of engaging philosophy in the consideration of all the problems of history and culture, it deprived each of the implicated elements and problems of its autonomy and particular authenticity; reducing them to symbolic manifestations of the one process, that of the Absolute Spirit's quest for and conquest of its own self. Such a speculative dialectical mediation between opposites, when directed to the more impending problems of the time, such as religion and politics, led ultimately to the evasion of the most urgent and imperious ideological demands, and was not easily able to escape the charge of ambiguity and opportunism.

At the specific level of Hegel's aesthetic philosophy, the same kind of criticism can be applied. He rejected rationalistic approaches and, like Kant, argued for a rigorous observance of the uniqueness and autonomy of art, ranking it with the highest of spiritual activities. However, he also rejected the idea that art leads towards a *future* transcendental perfection, since the spirit is (already) wholly immersed in reality, materialised in history. So how was art to be located within the overall speculative system? Hegel argued that in nature the spirit is not perfectly manifested, but that via the creative impulse of the artist's mind which possesses a god-like strength, the brutishness of raw nature is transformed and takes on the plasticity and harmony of Spirit: 'Art is nature twice-begotten, nature born again in the inventions of genius.' Thus art's source in the poetic imagination ensures its exaltation above crude, common, given facts. Considered in its relationship to earlier thought, Hegel's aesthetic is, and is intended to be, consummation. There is no want of art in his perfect cosmos, and as a consequence, no striving after new aims. Art is viewed as a phenomenon of the past: the history of art has no future.

In one way or another subsequent philosophers felt that the harmony of Hegel's system was too easily obtained. Yet his successors, each emphasising one or another of the strands in his thought (conservative, revolutionary, religious, atheistic) have interpreted him variously and drawn inspiration from him. Marx, for example, took over the Hegelian notion of critique (and entailed in this, his method of dialectics), but turned idealism on its head and rooted the method in the real historical material world. And to take a more recent but less well-known example, the distinguished art and architectural historian, Nikolaus Pevsner, offers the following clue to the philosophical perspective which, he gives us to understand, underpins his approach to the history of architecture:

> The birth of a civilisation coincides with the moment when a leading idea, a *leitmotiv*, emerges for the first time, the idea which will in the course of the centuries to follow gather strength, spread, mature, mellow, and ultimately – this is fate, and must be faced – abandon the civilisation whose soul it had been. When this happens the civilisation dies, and another, somewhere else or from the same soil, grows up, starting out of its own prehistory into its own primitive dark age, and then developing its own essentially new ideology.
>
> (Pevsner 1943: xi)

The great historical figures whose ideas I have briefly discussed in these opening pages, have – through their work – had a profound influence on the subsequent development of both the discipline of art history and critical theories of art. The next section focuses on the writings and ideas of some of the principal critical art theorists of the nineteenth and early twentieth centuries.

2 CRITICAL WRITINGS ABOUT VISUAL ART: CLASS ANALYSES I

Karl Marx; Georg Lukács; Antonio Gramsci; Louis Althusser; Max Raphael; Theodor Adorno; Walter Benjamin; Arnold Hauser; Herbert Read

> The great figures of early sociology . . . did not use photographs. From the beginning sociologists produced abstract images of society rather than literal renderings of particular social processes. It would have been just as reasonable, however, to use photographs to pursue certain research questions as it was to use descriptive surveys or statistics to pursue others. Karl Marx, for example, used Engels's descriptions of the English working class to provide detail and descriptive substance to his analyses of capitalism. Photographs such as were produced by Lewis Hine and Jacob Riis a few decades later would show the conditions of the working class (as well as the capitalist class), the urban squalor of the industrial city, the working conditions of children, and many other subjects that play a predominant role in Marx's analyses.
>
> (Douglas Harper, 'Visual Sociology: Expanding Sociological Vision', *The American Sociologist*, 1988)

Karl Marx completed none of his major system-building works, and this can, in a sense, be seen as a reaction against the grandiose attempt by Hegel to systematise knowledge. Thus Marx and Engels left no formal aesthetic system, no single extended work on the theory of art, no major analysis of an artist's œuvre nor of an individual art work; so there is no 'original' Marxist aesthetics for later Marxists to apply. The history of Marxist aesthetics has been the history of the unfolding of the possible applications of Marxist ideas and categories to the arts and to the theory of art. However, Marx's own writings, which include a body of brief comments and writings on art and literature, stand as crucial correctives to the tendency of subsequent writers to equate art with ideology or to insist on an exact parallel between class interest and artistic expression.

Marx and Engels' general emphasis, drawn from the Enlightenment rather than from the Romanticism which Hegel espoused, was on the artist as thinker, as educator, as unfolder of social truths, as one who reveals the inner workings of society, as ideologist who pierces the veil of false consciousness. This conception of the artist is entailed in Marx's general political theory, which I therefore now outline. Overturning Hegel's philosophy, Marx declared that: 'It is not the consciousness of men that determines their existence, but on the contrary their social existence that determines their consciousness' (Marx 1968: 181). His reasoning started from the economistic premise that men (sic) originally had to work on nature in order to survive. This, in turn, entailed social negotiation since survival could not be achieved alone. And as men struggled together to survive, they changed their socio-economic circumstances, and, as a consequence their thoughts changed too. Marx further argued that these negotiations produced unequal social relationships, which in turn became patterned, and then solidified into mutually antagonistic socio-economic relations. The specific character of these relations gave rise to the specific socio-economic structure of society itself. However, since individual relationships were always changing, so society correspondingly changed. Eventually its specific structure would collapse, at the same time giving rise to another historical stage in its development. Society would eventually – and inevitably – pass through a series of such historical stages. Each stage, Marx argued, is characterised by a different specific socio-economic structure. In the present stage, capitalism, two mutually dependent classes – the owners of the means of production and the workers (i.e. those who have to sell their labour in order to survive) – are locked in conflict over who has the right to the increased value of the goods produced for sale by the workers whose own labours have transformed raw materials into finished products. But of course the owners are the winners of this conflict because they have ultimate control over the work situation. The finished goods are exchanged for money, and a minimal proportion of this is allocated to the workers as wages, whilst the owners appropriate any profit from the exchange. They re-invest a sufficient amount of this profit to ensure the survival of the firm in a situation of increased competition between firms, and pocket the remainder for their own private consumption. Each class gives rise to its own form of consciousness, yet the working class is alienated from its true consciousness. This is because the economically dominating class generates a set of ideas which also dominate, and these consequently impose a false ideology on the working class. But contained within the specific social system of capitalism (as in the case with all historical stages) are the seeds of its own destruction. Forced together in increasingly large numbers in the factory, workers become aware of their collective strength as a class which can act *for* itself. Their false consciousness is thus gradually shattered by their growing ability to demystify the present, to see the real beneath the apparent. Put differently, the human relations which underlie commodity relations in capitalism become exposed, and the true motivations of historical movement are revealed. Ultimately, according to Marx, an understanding of the true economic-dialectical interpretation of history, which gives 'knowledge of the real motivations and substance of a period, and of the actual contents within the shell', will enable this once oppressed class to overthrow the capitalist system and create the socialist state.

But Marx argues that the workers' realisation of this potential to change society is crucially helped to fruition by an anticipatory element which comes from the highest level of consciousness of the most advanced members of the ruling class, who, through their various critical theorisings, seek to avoid the painful realities of social existence and to transcend their awareness of impending extinction as a class. Their ideas penetrate various strata of society through the mediation of the art forms and theoretical writings in which they are expressed, and in this way these ideas become part of the consciousness of the oppressed class, crystallizing as Utopian, revolutionary, system-sharing goals. Art, poetry, and philosophy feed and sustain the imagination, and thereby help to supply the necessary motor of the labour process and of history itself. But the mechanism and impulse of the dialectic is such that art is at one and the same time the product of socio-economic divisions, *and* the manifestation of a desire to transform those divisions. So art simultaneously reflects and transcends, is created by history and creates history; it points toward the future by reference to the past, aiming to liberate latent tendencies in the present. Thus Marxism, unlike Hegel's theory, is concerned with the future path of art as well as with its sources; and art's ability to transcend the historical moment was of special concern and interest to Marx himself.

For Marx, then, art is not an economic category, nor is it to be confused with false consciousness. Art is (like Marxism itself) a strategy of demystification, and it is a distinct form of the labour process in which is kept alive the materialised imagery of man's hope for a future society. Art is, in another sense, man's mode of mediation between the sense and the intellect, between cognition and feeling; it is a means of educating men's senses, their sensibility, and their consciousness; and it is a mode of human expression which provides both the commitment and the enthusiasm to permit the activity of transforming the latent into the actual, the present into beyond the present.

It is within this framework that Marxist theorists, with their passionate involvement in humanity, 'Utopianism', and desire to make the irrational rational, can be situated. They take as their starting point the 'Eleventh Thesis on Feuerbach': 'The philosophers have only *interpreted* the world, in various ways; the point, however, is to *change* it' (Marx 1968: 30). Marxist artists and critics also aim to improve it.

Georg Lukács (born 1885) abandoned his initial researches into aesthetics and the arts when he joined the Communist Party in 1918 and became active in politics. But after retiring from the inner party, he began to write again; and this time, he wrote as a Marxist literary historian and aesthetician from a centrist, orthodox position. That is, he applied the generally accepted categories of Soviet Communist aesthetics to a vast realm of literary and philosophical subject matter. Lukács was a firm adherent of the view that ideologies and art works reflect the class which produced them, but at the same time he was intensely aware that the reflection theory downgrades the revolutionary potential of both art and ideology. Throughout his work he was beset by this contradiction, and he was forced in practice to combat the inertia it produces by proposing that:

> Great artists have ever been pioneers in the advance of the human race. By their creative work they uncover previously unknown interconnections between things – interconnections which science and philosophy are able to put into exact form only much later.
>
> (Lukács 1950: 114)

Thus, Lukács does not allow art or ideology to transcend its historical-class genesis, but in practice he appears to fall for simple idealism by proposing that art reflects future historical events. However, Benjamin, Adorno, Marcuse and more recent critical writers have been influenced by his ability to pose fundamental questions for Marxist art history, and in a crucial sense this is where his importance lies. For example, T. H. Clark's influential article 'The Conditions of Artistic Creation', which helped to shape a new, social approach to art history in the 1970s, refocuses the minds of contemporary art historians on the fundamental questions which Lukács originally raised.[10] Maynard Solomon comments: 'If we cannot always agree with his answers,

---

10 Clark quotes the following passage from Lukács' 'Reification and the Consciousness of the Proletariat' (1971a) [1922] in support of his own project:

> And yet, as the really important historians of the nineteenth century such as Riegl, Dilthey and Dvorak could not fail to notice, the essence of history lies precisely in the changes undergone by those *structural forms* which are the focal points of man's interaction with environment at any given moment and which determine the objective nature of both his inner and outer life. But this only becomes objectively possible (and hence can only be adequately comprehended) when the individuality, the uniqueness of an epoch or an historical figure, etc. *is* grounded in the character of these structural forms, when it is discovered and exhibited in them and through them.
>
> (Clark 1974: 526)

we are constantly aware that he knows all the questions – and on a level not surpassed by any other Marxist critic of the twentieth century' (Solomon 1979: 396).

By contrast, Antonio Gramsci (born 1891) came to reject economic determinism. This was as a result of re-examining the early works of Marx which have a utopian–socialist emphasis, a humanist and psychological dimension, in contrast to the later works which were fundamental to orthodox Communist thought. He then re-read these later works in the light of his understanding of the earlier ones, and came to the conclusion that what can be extrapolated from Marx's writings is that ideas have political power in their own right, and consequent upon this that the 'superstructure' is not just a reflection of the economic base.[11] He therefore argued that in order to overturn capitalism, revolutionary socialists had to do more than seize power – they had to build a counter-culture of their own. For they had to recognise that the contradiction of interests between social classes which capitalism generated in its economic base could be ameliorated by political and ideological initiatives in its superstructure. Capitalism was given stability, Gramsci argued, by its acceptance and articulation of a dominant set of pro-capitalist ideas put about by social institutions such as the media, education and trade unions; and it was this hegemony that had to be broken down. Two major tasks were entailed for socialism: 'To combat modern ideologies in their most refined form in order to create its own core of independent intellectuals; and to educate the masses of the people whose level of culture was medieval' (Solomon 1979: 266).

He observed that efforts had so far been directed almost exclusively towards the latter task, with the result that the general intellectual level at which Marxists were operating was crude. In order to break the hegemony of the capitalist class, the first of these task needed urgent attention. Accordingly, Marxists must attend to the development and refinement of their own intellectual arguments.

Gramsci's emphasis on the political importance and therefore relative independence of ideas has considerable implications for the status and role of the visual arts. The visual artist, like other intellectuals, can be seen as a potential contributor to the task of refining Marxist ideas in the combat against capitalist ideology. Gramsci's insistence that this task of countering capitalist hegemony is a general cultural matter gives visual art itself a certain critical status, and lends an urgency to critical visual art projects in the building of a counter-culture. It is at this point, perhaps, that we can first see the potential for a class analysis which is not confined to the verbal text.

---

11 For these ideas, and those subsequently laid out in this section, see Gramsci (1971: especially 123–205).

In the late 1960s, Louis Althusser (born 1918) also took up the theme of the importance and power of ideas.[12] But unlike Gramsci, who emphasised the humanist aspect of Marxist theory, Althusser's perspective was an anti-humanist one. It focused, in part, on the structural relations of the various parts of the superstructure to each other and ultimately to the economic base. He argued that each part of the superstructure – the education system, the family, the legal system, the arts – is relatively autonomous in relation to the others and to the economic base; and that what joins them together, precluding their complete autonomy, and ensuring capitalist reproduction, is its ideology. Thus the notion of ideology occupies a key position in Althusser's thought. It is the glue which binds the different cultural compon-ents of society into an overall capitalist structure. But Althusser suggested that, at the same time, ideology represents the imaginary relationship of individuals to their real conditions of existence. It constructs identities or subject positions for us, and calls us into them in such a way that we then recognise these subject positions as our own. Thus he treated ideology as 'social relations', displacing notions of ideas or consciousness which had hitherto reduced ideology to a (mis)representation of the social in thought. 'Ideology' now appeared as the effect of definite institutions, practices and forms of subjection, and as an indispensable mode of the organisation and conduct of social relations.

Althusser's theory also has considerable implications for the arts because the concept of the relative autonomy of superstructural components suggests that the arts exert ideological influence on behalf of capitalism. But whereas Gramsci's perspective indicates the artist as cultural producer, Althusser's anti-humanist perspective focuses on the work of art in the context of its reception; and he indicates that art works make us 'see', 'perceive' or 'feel' the reality of the ideology of the world they describe. During the course of an essay entitled 'Cremonini, Painter of the Abstract', he says:

> Perhaps one might even suggest the following proposition, that as the specific function of the work of art is to make *visible (donner à voir)*, by establishing a distance from it, the reality of the existing ideology (of any one of its forms), the work of art *cannot fail to exercise* a directly ideological effect, that it therefore maintains far closer relations with ideology than any other *object*, and that it is impossible to think of the work of art, in its specifically aesthetic existence, without taking into account the privileged relation between it and ideology, i.e. *its direct and inevitable ideological effect.*
>
> (Althusser 1971: 291)

Thus, the *critical* visual art work has a specific and vital function to perform on behalf of the Marxist counter-culture. It prises us away from the existing ideology by opening our eyes to the identity which capitalism has con-structed for us through the manner in which its visual structure and content annouce their distance from that ideology.

---

12 See, in particular, his essay, 'Ideology and Ideological State Apparatuses' (1984).

However, critical writers on art have long been puzzled by Marx's question as to why Greek art often stands as a norm against which the quality of other art is measured, long after the demise of Greek society itself.[13] Is art an opiate, a form of ideology like religion, which the ruling class uses to subdue the masses? Or does that scenario represent the reverse of art's 'true' essence, which is its liberatory potential? Max Raphael (born 1889) believed that Marx's most important declaration about art is that ' . . . it is well known that some of its peaks by no means correspond to the general development of society; nor do they therefore to the material substructure, the skeleton as it were of its organisation' (Marx 1970: 149). Rather than building on the historicism of Marxism – its alleged revelation of an inevitable historical pattern – he focused on that aspect of it which enables concrete individuals to be sited within a general historical process. A classicist at heart, Raphael argued that, at the same time, we must historically analyse the conditions in which Greek art has been able to re-emerge at certain critical stages in the development of Christian art and assume a normative status. His writings constitute a critical sociology on *behalf* of visual art – a sociology which seeks to justify visual art's unique liberatory potential.

His theory, outlined below, is at the same time a practical plan. He aimed to place an improved critical apparatus at our disposal which would bring us into contact with the processes of conceptual production, turning us from readers or spectators into collaborators, turning our struggle to understand art into 'the struggle for a social order in which everyone will have the fullest opportunity to develop their creative capacities' (Raphael 1968: 204). Raphael's method was designed to be used by everyone.[14] And it was intended to be applied minutely in single, particular, concrete instances. In his own analyses of prehistoric cave paintings, Rembrandt drawings, Picasso's *Guernica* and other works, he is considered by many to be a dialectical thinker of the first order. The following outline of Raphael's method draws extensively on John Tagg's article: 'The Method of Criticism and Its Objects in Max Raphael's Theory of Art' (1980).

Raphael was dissatisfied with the primitive state of art theory as he found it, but he maintained that art is not inherently opaque to scientific under-standing; rather, he claimed that art theorists had imposed intellectual and theoretical limitations upon themselves which prevented them from encom-passing the very complex situation which art presented for their analysis. His aim was to construct a scientific method of establishing – in the most general abstract terms – the artist's way of working. According to Raphael, this entailed a sociology of art which would relate the art work to the external socio-economic stage of the society in which it was constructed, and also –

---

13 This is posed in Marx's *Introduction to a Contribution to the Critique of Political Economy* (1970).

14 For example, by the working men and women of the Berlin Volkshochschule, to whom he taught his method of analysis for a short period.

dialectically interrelated with this sociology – a 'science' of art which would provide a systematic analysis of the internal nature of the art work.

In addressing the problem of the general rules by which an art work is created, he made use of Husserl's phenomenological method of 'annihilating' the work of art, then asking what must be done to reconstitute it. In this way he aimed to recreate in consciousness the constituent stages by which it was made: that is, the artistic method. As Tagg puts it, the critic had to find a route from the created work to the way in which it had come about. Objectively, the method could be viewed as the life of content in the process of achieving form; subjectively, as the life of form in the process of acquiring a content.

Tagg explains that the manner in which this phenomenological analysis was to proceed was systematic and extended, passing though certain well-defined stages which correspond to stages in the process of artistic creation. In this process, the relatively constant elements had to be brought together or differentiated according to some given method, to give birth to an artistic form. The concrete mode of this process would depend on the economic basis, previous artistic development and other ideologies, and 'harmonious systematisation' (a concept deriving from Engels' treatment of the relationship of legal structures to the economic base) which lends the work relative autonomy.

To take the last of these factors first, Raphael argued that it is the task of the science of art to undertake the fullest (immanent) analysis of this tendency towards relative autonomy. In doing so it reveals three levels in works of art: the creation of form from its ultimate elements; the connection among forms according to compositional laws appropriate to the particular type of structural unity; and the unfolding of individual and total form from the abstract to concrete appearance. All these levels are closely interconnected. When the science of art has established the nature of a particular work's relative autonomy, the analyst next makes a systematic comparison of works of art from all periods and cultures, and this leads to an ideal type of work, as it were, in terms of its three constituent levels.

However, the resultant analysis would lead to formalism if this were not now dialectically interrelated with a sociology of art, giving a study of the economic and social conditions and the creative methods which were prevalent in any given era. And in addition, there remained those problems concerned with the variations in time undergone by the structures identified in the 'science of art'; and also the problem of assigning these structures a precise place within a scale of values. Raphael argued that the first of these problems was the concern of art history, and the second that of art criticism.

He considered that art history is never more than auxiliary to the sociology of art (though in a definite and definable relation with it). The reason for this is that the sociology of art rests on a material basis extraneous to art, and can account for the concrete particularity of each work of art, the interaction of art with other ideologies, and art's reciprocal influence on the material basis; whereas art history, together with the 'science' of art and art criticism are all immanent studies: the studies of essence, evolution and value, respectively. Art criticism was to be concerned with values attributed to art of the past by a given epoch, with the values given as the norm for an epoch, and with what should be assimilated and reproduced. Art criticism thus shows the mistakes an epoch makes; it draws a division between true and 'sham' art. This dividing line changes and can be accounted for sociologically, but art criticism addresses what criteria divide true from sham art. Thus, Raphael believed that whereas some criteria belong only to a given period in history, others have a significance which transcends time. Art criticism therefore elucidates the relative and absolute elements in each work of art, empirically establishing the nature of their integration in it – so that a hierarchical order may be disclosed: 'an order which extends over an infinite path toward the goal of perfect congruence of form and content with what is concrete and abstract, relative and absolute in every given epoch'[15] (Raphael 1933: 139). Raphael's belief in absolute values stands as a critique of the 'positionless position' of scepticism, as he terms it, 'which has no commitments'; and indeed of modern liberalism. Tagg points out that Raphael based his views, in this context, on his understanding of the Marxist theory of knowledge: what holds for truth holds for art, and what holds for totalities holds for individual creations. Lenin had previously argued that truth is at once relative and absolute, in the sense that the sum of relative truths is absolute truth; and Raphael introduced into this conception the idea that there are different degrees of approximation to an 'absolute' final value, and that within these limits we may speak of a hierarchy of values. More specifically:

> Absolute signifies not only a fact's repeated action on the historical process, but also progressive development toward a goal ever closer to reality. And yet this goal, were it ever to be attained, would amount to a total congruence between reality and consciousness.
>
> (Raphael 1933: 180–1)

This explains the sense in which Raphael could regard such a hierarchy of values as a reality beyond personal taste and the historically conditioned view of any single era. For he claimed that to deny the existence of universally valid criteria in evaluating art was not only to eschew one of the most self-evident problems but to destroy the world of values.

We are now led to ask: what are the relations between the relative independence of artistic creation (together with a scientific theory of art interpreting it) and economic conditions (together with a sociology of art elucidating these conditions)? In Raphael's *total* method, the dialectical

---

15 Malcolm Hughes points out that this area of values has since been developed via Freud and a theory of the subject. See, for example, Lyotard (1984).

materialist method grasps all social facts with a single method but leaves the specificity of each domain relatively autonomous, subject only to the most general materialist dialectics. Here, Tagg notes that the fruitfulness of Marx's demonstration that economic facts are the ultimate but not the sole found-ation of ideologies 'does not lie in its universality. It is disclosed only in the course of a specific analysis' (Raphael 1933: 126). So it is with Raphael's empirical science of art.

Raphael agreed with Lenin that workers should not reject the culture and knowledge of the bourgeois era; instead, they should be selective – being directed only towards those parts of our heritage which were currently helpful and useful to them. Raphael's method of analysis would help them find out which works of art were relevant for them; that is, those which they could interpret as materialist or dialectical. In fact, Raphael distinguished three categories of materialist, dialectical and socially critical works. Each of these categories he derived from the extensive application of his dialectical method to specific works.

For Raphael, a *materialist* work is one in which the artist views the ruled class at a given period from its own historical viewpoint, and represents it by means of expression which corresponds to the nature of that class. Thus materialist works were and are unusual. Raphael gave the example of *The Peasant Family* by Le Nain, as a result of analysing the work.

The *dialectical* work of art is one in which there is a total interrelationship of the parts, and parts with the whole: a cosmic system of forms corres-ponding to the content. Here, Raphael cites some of Cézanne's paintings, some examples of Greek art and architecture, and Poussin's Apollo and Daphne. There is no prior definition of the nature of the dialectical work of art (unlike the materialist one) but

> In a dialectical work contradictions which are at first internal exteriorize them-selves and then, having confronted one another, cancel one another out to create a higher unity; and . . . this is continued until a totality is established as regards both form and content.
>
> (Raphael 1975: 40–1)

Those works which Raphael termed *socially critical* contain criticism of the class depicted in the work, finding new effective forms for social criticism. The greatest dialectical work of art is *Autonomous, Organic or Self-Positing*.

> In it, every form is qualified by its adjacent parts and subordinated to the purpose of the whole. No external factors condition its self-sufficient structure which is as independent of the artist's subjectivity as of the world outside. In the process of creation of the Organic work, causality and finality, logical thought and spon-taneous growth, are conjoined in an autonomous entity which is both musical and archtectonic.
>
> (Tagg 1980: 12)

Certain paintings by Cézanne and Poussin, and some examples of Chinese, Buddhist, Gothic and Greek art were found, on analysis, to be organic. They also have the synthesising dialectical method in common. The organic work embodies Raphael's theory of knowledge or 'intellectual creation', his methodological analysis of art and his concept of a hierarchy of values applicable to all works of art, to the Self, and to the State – all interrelated with the others. This dialectical fusion, according to Raphael, is what artists must comprehend if they are to produce the art of the future; for dialectical art is inimitable, while academic art is by definition imitative.

In *The Demands of Art* (1968), Raphael puts his method into practice, demonstrating the power of his dialectical analysis of specific art works. And while the strictly scientific nature of his enterprise may now be questioned, what he did achieve was a complete reversal of the positivistic emphasis in philosophy since the early nineteenth century: instead of putting science at the centre, he took the work of art as his model for a theory of intellectual creation. Furthermore, he persisted throughout his career in extending his analyses to modern works of art – as unusual a project then as it is today; and this, in conjunction with his belief in the crucial function of a radical art practice, has made him an important theorist for some present-day critical artists.

The Frankfurt Institute of Social Research, the so-called Frankfurt School, was founded in 1923, and Max Horkheimer became its director in 1930.[16] Its original programme of a 'Critical Theory' was for a materialist reunification of philosophy with the empirical sciences. Its members rejected Hegel's idea that progress, however defined, is guaranteed by a logic of history, but they also rejected Marx's idea that the truth of their theory would be confirmed primarily in the historical action of the proletariat.[17] However, they kept the enlightenment myth that history is one all-embracing process in which a historical subject attains its essence. Their theory envisages a rational society,

16 Horkheimer was responsible for the fact that the school maintained an unbroken institutional continuity throughout its history in Weimar Germany, in the United States during the Second World War, and thereafter in the Federal German Republic as part of the University of Frankfurt. For an account of the early development of the Frankfurt School and the various contributions made by its members, see Jay (1973).

17 On the second point, see a remark made by Adorno at the German Sociological Association conference, Tubingen, 1961:

> ... in the first place, the theory developed by Marx and Engels has itself, in the meantime, taken on a completely dogmatic form. Secondly, because in this dogmatized and fossilized form of the theory, the notion of the transformation of the world has itself become an atrocious ideology which serves to justify the most wretched practice of the suppression of mankind. Thirdly, however, and this is perhaps the most serious – because the notion that through the theory, and through the enunciation of the theory, one can immediately stir people and arouse them to action has become doubly impossible. This results from the disposition of men who, as is well known, can no longer be aroused by theory in any way, and results from the form of reality which excludes the possibility of such actions which for Marx seemed to be just around the corner. If today one behaved as if one could change the world tomorrow, then one would be a liar.
>
> (Adorno, in Adorno *et al.* 1976: 128–9)

located in a possible future, whose goal is claimed to be 'really invested in every man' and whose attainment could be the concrete transformation of chaos into rational order. Horkheimer, looking back in 1971, said that reflecting on political systems taught us 'that it was necessary, as Adorno has expressed it, "not to think of claims to the Absolute as certain and yet, not to deduct anything from the appeal to the emphatic concept of the truth"' (Jay 1973: xii).

The Frankfurt School's concerns were very wide, and included the development of a critical sociology of the arts. Theodor Adorno, Herbert Marcuse and Walter Benjamin (who was for a time associated with the group) all saw aesthetic imagination as a utopian and therefore liberating faculty. Theodor Adorno (born 1903), to whom I now turn, was also a musician and a composer; and many of his writings on aesthetics relate specifically to music and musicians,[18] although he also wrote extensively about the visual arts, and his theory is, for the most part, broad enough in scope to be entirely relevant to this field. However, in considering his approach, a sharp distinction must be made between the idea of history as an all-embracing process in which, via aesthetic imagination, the historical subject has the potential to contribute towards the attainment of a future rational society, and a more pessimistic view of that process as a constant struggle by the subject *against* the effects of the increasing instrumental rationality of monopoly capitalism, in which, as time goes on, s/he is more and more likely to be the loser. Adorno proposed this second view, having been deeply depressed by the encroachment of fascism in Germany in the 1930s, and by the increasing imposition of monopoly capitalism and its concomitant bureaucracy in the United States in the 1950s. And, as a neo-Hegelian, the notion of the guarantee of the logic of the dialectical process theoretically reinforced his view that capitalism was on its inexorable trajectory towards rationality and conformity. He set out to combat what he saw as the deadening hand of capitalism, with its anti-liberational ideology of conformity arising out of the commodification process; seeing evidence of this in the products of the US culture industry, the most highly developed and hegemonic mass culture in the West.

His writings on aesthetics indicate that we should counter the spreading conformity entailed in the logic of capitalist expansion by focusing on the potential of particularising actions within the framework of specialisation. The world of avant-garde music and art was his concern: he argued that it is only through the struggles of particular 'high' art – artists – in their works for autonomy against the pull of the common, debasing standards demanded by the potential market commodification process of these works – that ground can be temporarily regained for the artist and his/her audience. Thus Adorno's is an elitist aesthetic theory, which focuses on the ever-threatened

---

18 In particular to the work of Arnold Schoenberg, who had been one of his teachers.

and thus precarious autonomy of the avant-garde artwork in bourgeois society. As a *sociological* theory, it sees that autonomy, moreover, as one which bourgeois society has itself constructed. John Tagg (1975) has suggested that in the works of Max Raphael we find the most thoroughgoing analyses of artworks yet provided. It is worth noting, in parallel, that many contemporary writers hold Adorno's *Aesthetic Theory* (1984) in the very highest regard.[19]

His loathing of the generalising tendency of monopoly capitalist industrial production, and the concomitant totalising tendency of Positivist philosophy (in the name of enlightened reason), led him to deploy discursive strategies which would combat those established linguistic and conceptual conventions which were used to promote commodities and to articulate the positivist philosophy. The fragmentary nature of his writing is intended to counter the domination in written scholarship of linear, 'coherent' prose, whose arguments are linked together cumulatively by 'therefores' and 'becauses' to produce a 'compelling' thesis. His strong sense of the unique specificity of things, his partisanship for the individual, and for that which is not or cannot be integrated, gives a force to his often epigrammatic style; and this theme will be taken up again in later chapters. By the same token, Adorno's writing is also intended to make the reader *work* to grasp its meaning, in contrast to the 'easy' style of popular culture, which, he would contend, lulls the consumer into an unthinking, uncritical state.

In *Aesthetic Theory*, Adorno presents his aesthetic theory along the following lines. In Western society before the rise of capitalism, art works performed a religion-enhancing function, and their production was tied to the social construction of a God-centred society. But the specific form of commodification of art within which the system of artistic production was embedded altered as the social relations of feudalism themselves began to decay. With the coming of capitalist society, the art work became a marketable commodity. Members of the bourgeoisie needed to establish their social status, an important aspect of which was to be seen to have the time and money for leisure. They were prepared to pay money for art because the contemplation of beauty in art was an activity that admirably fulfilled this requirement, reinforcing the leisured status. Thus, under capitalism, art works as commodities came to acquire value purely as objects of contemplation; they had no straightforward capitalist use-value. This development created a vacuum: there was now a need to patrol art values in order to

---

19 For example, Peter Osborne says:

> *Aesthetic Theory* contains the most philosophically sophisticated and aesthetically comprehensive framework yet developed in response to the set of problems posed by the idea of art works being socially determined and at the same time 'autonomous'.
>
> (Osborne 1989: footnote 25)

And John Roberts states that 'Theodor Adorno's *Asthetische Theorie* is probably the most important book written on aesthetics this century' (Roberts 1984: 27).

establish the contemplative value of individual art works in relation to each other, and thus to provide guidelines for a speculative market for them. In the eighteenth century, the vacuum was filled by the creation of aesthetics. So there arose the situation in which the art work – 'a social reality' as Adorno puts it – is constructed by capitalist society, and aesthetic theory establishes and legitimates its value.

It is important to add to this story of the development of the art work as capitalist commodity that for Adorno it has a fetishistic status. That is to say, the art work as a piece of painted canvas, for example, has come to evoke devotion and respect over and above its use-value as painted canvas. And it is this fetishistic quality of the painting which lends it artistic autonomy. But Adorno reminds us that under capitalism, the art work is constructed and institutionalised both as social commodity *and* as 'autonomous'. It thus has 'a dual essence'.

The artist is 'structured into society' as the agent for the production of an 'autonomous' work, and therefore comes to see and to know him/herself as that agent. To the artist, however, an art work is not autonomous because capitalist society has deemed it so. From his/her (and Adorno's) standpoint, the artwork s/he is creating strains towards autonomy as it strives to create for itself an *independence* from society and its system of aesthetic values. And in distancing itself from society, it comes to constitute a criticism of it. But the artist only has the *potential* to fulfil the role of producer of autonomous art object since art has a *dual* essence. The fact that as *commodity* the art work has an exchange value means that market forces continually exert pressure on the artist to produce a work that will sell well *as* a commodity and thus establish its exchange value. This pressure pulls the artist in the opposite direction from that in which s/he strains to produce an autonomous work, because to be autonomous, the work must refuse to conform with the requirements of the market. If the demands of the market are met, the art work's potential for distancing itself from capitalist society is lost. Moreover, the artist, having been constructed by capitalist society, is dependent on market forces and on his/her art work's relationship to the mechanism of exchange value in order to define the work's distance from it and therefore its relative autonomy.

But how does the artist set about achieving a degree of autonomy in the face of the threat of commodification? Adorno insists it is *not* by illustrating the social relations of capitalism; nor even by visually displaying some political critique of these relations. It is, at root, by transforming 'artistic material'. This is a key concept in Adorno's theory. Artistic material refers to 'all that the artist is confronted by, all that he must make a decision about, and that includes forms as well' (Adorno 1984: 213). It includes 'the stuff the artist controls and manipulates: words, colours, sounds – all the way up to connections of any kind and to the highly developed methods of integration he might use' (Adorno 1984: 213). It is the decisions that the artist makes about how artistic materials are to be used, and the subsequent transformation of a specific set of ideas, paint, and so forth into a new work, which determine the critical power of that work. Such a transformation is, however, constrained by and contingent upon the particular social character of the materials used; for material is 'always historical, never natural, irrespective of what artists themselves might think' (Adorno 1984: 214), and 'just as dependent upon technical changes as technique is upon materials worked upon by it' (Adorno 1984: 214). The artist must therefore tackle the problem of transforming the current socio/historical meanings and status of those materials in such a way that, in their new combination and use, they are now distanced from and point to the conventional nature of their deployment in previous art work. Here, Adorno stresses, we are, in effect, focusing on the work's *form*. Form is the key to understanding social content because 'the unresolved antagonisms of reality reappear in art in the guise of immanent problems of aesthetic form' (Adorno 1984: 8). Thus the artist attempts to produce a work whose form, in an intimate yet dialectical relationship with its content, stands as critique of the form of previous art; and this is *analogous* to the manner in which a radical social movement critiques capitalism. Adorno argues that an important strategy in the artist's struggle to attain autonomy for his/her work is to transform artistic material in such a way that the work becomes unintelligible to the masses, and thus resistant to exchange value (to market forces). And the dialectic between the pull of exchange value and the counter-pull of autonomy (embodied in the artist's transformation of artistic materials according to the logic of the production of the artwork itself) is the driving motor of modernism.

Adorno's work addressed the distancing of art from popular culture. For him, art represented the last vestiges of freedom for the individual in a situation where rapid totalisation threatened. Although, in a sense, that distance between popular and high art still remains, we cannot now identify with Adorno's stance, which was, of course, a theoretical response to the specific events of the time in which he lived. As John Roberts says: 'Instead of being on the outside looking in, we are now on the inside looking out; mass culture is less something we enter under duress than the ground of our social being' (Roberts 1984: 28). Yet, in many ways, Adorno's aesthetic theory remains extremely powerful. Not least is the sense in which his emancipated, struggling 'high artist' can be interpreted as setting an example for all 'consciousness-raised' individuals who live their lives amidst the contradictions of capitalism. Furthermore, in the light of events taking place in the 1980s and 1990s in Eastern Europe and the demise of many aspects of socialism and of concepts entailed in the *idea* of socialism such as central planning, revolution, and 'the false consciousness of the masses', Adorno's particular critical attitude towards capitalism would seem to be far more appropriate than the utopian views held by some of his contemporaries. Finally, Adorno's work has subsequently proved to be of great importance in current philosophical debates about the problem of modernity and the relationship of modernism to postmodernism.[20]

Walter Benjamin (born 1892) has become one of the best known critical writers on the arts, though he was known only to a few other intellectuals in his lifetime. His work was very much influenced by the political theory and practice of his friend Bertolt Brecht, who insisted on the revolutionary role of art, the artist, and, by implication, the art critic. Benjamin's idea of the true revolutionary author is one who instructs in criticism, placing an improved critical apparatus at our disposal. Whereas Raphael thought that everyone has the potential, the critical intelligence, to analyse works of art and to assess their liberatory potential, Benjamin believed that critical intelligence resides in the always-threatened keeping of the very few. Here he was on common ground with Adorno and Horkheimer; though they did not share his and Brecht's view that 'not criticism but revolution is the driving force of history' (as Marx and Engels wrote in *The German Ideology*, 1970). However, Horkheimer paid Benjamin a small stipend after the death of his parents and the termination of private financial means; and in return, Benjamin submitted work for the Frankfurt School's *Feschtschrift für Sozialforschung*, which Horkheimer and Adorno edited. The young Adorno was an extraordinarily acute, perceptive critic of Benjamin's work (for example, foreseeing a potential collision between his surrealistic, dream, fairytale images and the material basis of artistic production); although Adorno's remarks were sometimes damaging since he required Benjamin's work to fit in with the Frankfurt School emphasis on dialectics, and this tended to weaken it. Yet the correspondence between Adorno and Benjamin remains a document of utmost intellectual and literary interest today.[21]

Both writers shared an aversion to the concept of system and to the mode of discourse used to generate systematic works of grand theory. Benjamin's writings have been called labyrinthine, surpassing even Adorno's epigrammatic aphorisms in their brevity. In these writings, he acted almost like a medium for the transmission of ideas. He focused the insights of Marx and Engels, Brecht and Lukács, Freud and Valery, Surrealism and Dada, Baudelaire and Fourier, Bergson and Proust upon the nature of art and the discrete art object. In a sense, his work arrived at a position analogous to the totality of Marx's and Engels' comments on art and literature – an aesthetics in process of 'becoming' but never quite 'arrived'.

Like Adorno, Benjamin was concerned that focusing on the art work as such tended to absolutise it, thereby concealing its character as a historical artefact born of specific social pressures and responding to specific social needs; and that this in turn produced the bourgeois viewpoint, which fetishised the art work, making it appear as a cultural monument. On the

---

20 This is clearly shown, for example, in A. Benjamin (1989).
21 See Bloch, E., Lukács, G., Brecht, B., Benjamin, W., and Adorno, T. (1977: 110–34).

other hand, like Raphael, they both saw that a sociology of the arts bracketed out the problem of artistic quality, and did not address the work's internal dynamics and its manner of embodying social information. I have outlined Adorno's dialectical theory of the dual essence of art. Benjamin saw the task of art to be 'the creation of a *demand* which could be fully satisfied only later' (my emphasis) (Benjamin 1973: 239); and he wrote (following Breton) that every fundamentally new, pioneering creation of demands will carry beyond its goal. In other words, his vision of the role of art in society was utopian, but unlike Adorno's pessimistic view and elitist theory of the relationship of capitalist society to art's utopian potential, he saw art as bound up in a positive, practical sense with class relations: art's function was to lead society by awakening demands in the proletariat – demands which would impel that society toward a better organisation of their needs.

Benjamin's vision of the radical artist is indicated in 'The Author as Producer' (1934). Here he discusses the potential of photography to serve either ruling-class or working-class interests.[22] He argues that the photographer all too often creates an object of enjoyment and consumption for 'modish commerce'; and that in order to produce work with a revolutionary use-value, the photographer-as-artist must attempt to transcend the limits imposed by specialisation in the capitalist process of production by devising new, alienative techniques capable of serving the interests of socialism and of countering the ruling class productive apparatus. When the photographer-as-artist produces work whose innovatory 'political line and quality' is perceived by the proletariat, then they cannot but react to it, and in reacting to it they are *using* the work: that is, such a work awakens in them the realisation that they can demand the altered social conditions which it intimates. In his now well-known essay, 'The Work of Art in the Age of Mechanical Reproduction' (1973), Benjamin continues his discussion of modern techniques and their potential for achieving revolutionary change. He notes that advances in techniques of mechanical reproduction, especially in the areas of photography and film, have had the effect of replacing the unique art object by a plurality of copies. And in reproduction, the work's presence in time and space is lost, so that it loses its 'aura', its authority as a unique art object. (This all-important concept of 'aura' stems from Benjamin's preoccupation with Marx's concept of the 'fetishism of commodities'. Aura is commodity fetishism – it creates distance, mystifies, veils, invests with ritual content.) With the decay of the work's aura, Benjamin argues, 'tradition' is shattered, and with it the traditional values of the cultural heritage. Benjamin was a keen collector of fine objects and claimed that the collector always retains some traces of the fetishist, and by owning the work of art, shares in its ritual power. So for him personally, this decay of the work's aura was, in a sense, a matter of regret. But he gives more emphasis to the idea that with

22 'The Author as Producer' originated as a lecture delivered at the Institute for the Study of Fascism in Paris on 27 April 1934.

the passing of the work's aura goes the destruction of the basis in ritual for making art, and this opens up the possibility of making art on a different, political, basis. In sum, the defetishising of the art object as a result of technological change heralds the possibility of the politicisation of art; and in the context of Europe of the 1930s, Benjamin saw such attempts to politicise art as a necessary defence against the fascist aestheticising of war and the racial myth.

'The Work of Art in the Age of Mechanical Reproduction' was closely criticised by Adorno in his capacity as co-editor of the Frankfurt School *Zeitschrift für Sozialforschung*, although he eventually published it in a modified form (1936: V, 1). Yet this essay – which seeks to explain how the artist as producer plays a key part in awakening the frozen consciousness by re-presenting works of art, those petrified objects, from a revolutionary perspective – has become a key text in art criticism.

With the coming of the Second World War, many European Jewish intellectuals – including Adorno – emigrated either to Britain or to America, and this has had a profound and lasting effect on the scholarship of the two countries. Arnold Hauser was among those émigrés. A member of an influential Hungarian Marxist school,[23] he started to write *The Social History of Art* (1951) in the 1920s, but by the start of the Second World War it was still incomplete. He became a naturalised British subject in 1948, and the book was finally completed, translated into English and published in 1951. It was reissued in paperback in 1968, and this gave it a new lease of life, especially among younger British scholars.

The Social History of Art is an extraordinary work in its historical scope and in the breadth of its subject matter. Hauser treats the general origins and history of visual art in the West from 'Prehistoric Times' to 'The Film Age'. In addition, he frequently compares the visual art of a particular period with other art forms – theatre, the novel, poetry – thus giving a broad view of the general cultural life of the time. But it is the work's macro-Marxist sociological approach which constituted its most definitive contribution to the intellectual life of the 1950s in Britain, when the work was first published. This approach influenced the thinking of many artists and art historians at a time when British art history, more or less in its infancy, favoured the monograph and tended to be connoisseurial. Hauser's text thus offered students of art and art history a critical approach, and it also allowed them to situate their specialist studies in a wider historical context.

Having said this, it may be apparent to the present-day reader that positivism, which was widespread in the 1950s, pervades Hauser's writings. Statements in the third-person passive conceal Hauser's opinions, and his prose style now seems assertive. Often, the simple labelling of art styles

---

23 Which produced (amongst others) Georg Lukács, Zoltan Kodaly, Frederick Antal, and had a considerable influence on the work of Karl Mannheim.

transforms them into objective certainties; and there are no debates as to what counts as good or bad art; merely an assumption that we know quality when we see it. There is no introductory discussion of Hauser's methodology. Chapter 1 plunges straight in with the Old Stone Age. However, the first footnote lays out two opposing theories about the origins of art. The first, proposed by Gottfried Semper in 1860 and apparently favoured by conservatives at the time Hauser was writing, claimed that art is a by-product of craft, and that geometrically stylised forms which decorated domestic ware evolved into the earliest kind of art. Opposing this 'transfer of Darwinism to a field of cultural life', as Hauser puts it, was Alois Riegl, who proposed in 1893 that man had always had within him an urge to make art, and that artistic forms are found and achieved precisely in the struggle of purposive 'artistic intention' against our material conditions. Riegl argued that the earliest art must have been imitative of nature. Hauser strongly believes that Riegl's radical theory is correct, and that art is not a chance offshoot of practical necessity but that, on the contrary, it has an essential, eternal quality. And he sees Riegl's account as compatible with Marx's basic anthropology: the social production of art is a part of man's original socio-economic struggle against material conditions to achieve survival in society. Using this historical materialist account of man's desire and drive to produce art, Hauser proposes a dialectic between the mental and the material, between content and the means of expression, between the will and the substratum of the will.[24] Other remarks made during the course of the book help to clarify Hauser's Marxist approach. For instance, he suggests that Engels formulated one of the most important heuristic principles in the sociology of art when he claimed that artistic progressiveness and political conservatism are perfectly compatible and that every honest artist who describes reality faithfully and sincerely has an enlightening and emancipating influence on his age. This enables Hauser to avoid the problem of selecting or deselecting artists according to their apparent political intentions or choice of subject matter. And in response to Marx's puzzle about the paradox of historicity and timelessness in art, he argues that every work of art, even the most naturalistic, is an idealisation of reality – a legend, a kind of Utopia.

Hauser organises his data historically in relation to what he sees as important themes or periods, but from today's vantage point it seems that some topics are treated to the exclusion of others. For example, Impressionism and the Film are very fully discussed, but there is virtually no mention of the Russian Revolution, nor of Constructivist art. For a Marxist sociological history of art, these omissions are hard to understand. However, in respect to the periods and artists that Hauser does include, his macro-sociological perpective on art is consistently illuminating. For example, he says:

---

24 This last pair of opposites shows Hauser's very high regard for Freud, whose theoretical approach he considers has much in common with that of Marx.

> A continuous line can be traced from the Gothic to Impressionism comparable to the line leading from the late medieval economy to high capitalism; and modern man, who regards his whole existence as a struggle and a competition, who translates all being into motion and change, for whom experience of the world increasingly becomes experience of time, is the product of this bilateral, but fundamentally uniform development.
>
> (Hauser 1951: 872)

Indeed, his detailed account of the age of Impressionism and how it enmeshes with the development of European capitalism in a sense prefigures the project of Marshall Berman's *All That Is Solid Melts into Air* (1982).

Hauser's attitude to twentieth century art is reluctantly elitist. He has no faith in the opinions of the masses:

> Success with them is completely divorced from qualitative criteria. They do not react to what is artistically good or bad, but to impressions by which they feel themselves reassured or alarmed in their own sphere of existence . . . subject matter has to be attractive.
>
> (Hauser 1951: 951)

And he notes that the more progressive and ambitious an artistic work, the less popular it is with contemporary audiences. Yet he puzzles about the fact that, as he sees it, only a young art can be fully appreciated, for as soon as it grows older, we need to be acquainted with the earlier stages in its development in order to understand it, and this is only available to other artists and specialists. He also explores the implications of contemporary responses to art works, noting that what initially appears optically strange can later develop into a visual convention. These topics continue to occupy sociologists and other writers on visual art.

While Arnold Hauser brought a Marxist approach to the entire history of Western art, the work of Herbert Read – roughly Hauser's contemporary – demonstrates the coming together of European critical thinking and the British empiricism of his day which was also permeated by positivist philosophy. In Read's writings, psychologistic, humanist and other strands temper his critical approach to the visual arts; strands which are characteristics of the non-critical approaches discussed in the next section of this chapter. Yet Max Raphael was sufficiently impressed by Read's publications to send him his own manuscripts for safe-keeping during the Second World War; and leftist British artists in the 1940–50s held him in very high esteem. Read published a great deal during his long life, during which time his theoretical approach to visual art gradually altered and developed. In the following discussion, certain key works are presented in chronological order.

The dramatic political events which were taking place when Read first wrote about art (1930–40s) inevitably influenced his ideas. However, in *Art Now* (1933) he vehemently denies that developments in art are directly influenced by developments in a political regime, and he claims that modern art is evolving independently of social and political forces.

> The Nazi regime dismissed artists and museum directors from their posts, modern paintings and sculpture were relegated to the cellars or suffered worse in-dignities. This was entirely the result of a rash and inconsiderate identification of modernism in art and communism in politics. . . . The revolutionary artist is not . . . to be identified with the revolutionary politician. He works on another plane where his activities are determined by that wider destiny which governs all the activities of the human spirit.
>
> (Read 1933: 10)

In *Art and Society* (1937) Read claims that art is 'a mode of knowledge at once its own reality and its own end' (Read 1937: xiii) but argues that at the same time it 'contributes in its own right to that process of integration which we call a civilisation or a culture' (Read 1937: xiii). In a dialogue with the philosophies of Hegel and Marx, he now acknowledges that art is influenced by the material conditions of existence but argues that it is not merely a product of society in the economic and political sense. He claims that the ideology of each period is 'readymade', and mainly formed by religion. Thus art cannot straightforwardly contribute to or be influenced by ideologies, yet there is a certain give and take between ideology and artist. This is a dialectical process: 'Actually it is like a spark springing, at the right moment, between two opposite poles, one of which is the individual [artist], the other the society' (Read 1937: xiv). Like Hauser, he maintains that the typical art of a period is the art of the elite, but this does not depress him. He draws on Marx's conception of a classless society where elites have a place because they reflect the natural differentiation in people's talents and abilities, and should not therefore be suppressed. From this, he is able to argue that the artist is endowed with exceptional sensibilities and faculties of apprehension which set him apart, psychologically, from the majority of the population. Though many critical artists and sociologists today might baulk at his essentialist psychology, they would surely admire his belief that

> Art is a mode of expression . . . and the world of art is a system of knowledge as valuable to man – indeed more valuable – than the world of philosophy or the world of science. It is only when we have clearly recognised the function of art as a mode of knowledge parallel to the other modes by which man arrives at an understanding of his environment that we can begin to appreciate its significance in the history of mankind.
>
> (Read 1937: xix)

The critical strand in Read's approach to art is rather lost in *Education through Art* (1943). In this positivist work, Read aims to show that the production and reception of works of art are linked to laws of nature. Drawing on publications by contemporary psychologists, he suggests that four different types of mental activity can be associated with four distinct types of personality, giving rise to four basic 'natural' styles in art. He establishes a chain which links form in art to beauty, and then to nature, to mathematics, to universal laws, and finally to objectivity. Subjectivity is also linked into this chain via Eysenck's work which connects feelings with physiological features of the human body. By contrast with Hauser's critical approach, which although also positivistic in tone, entails a historical dimension and a utopianism, Read's current attempt to show that the creation and the understanding of different types of art are bound up with natural laws and scientific certainty would seem to weaken a historical approach, and it heavily reinforces his previous reluctance to associate the development of visual art in any direct fashion with economic and political change or progress.

Twenty-four years later, Read's *Art and Alienation* (1967) engages with more recent European critical thinking. One of the essays in this book is a response to two works by Herbert Marcuse: *Eros and Civilization* (1955) and *One-dimensional Man* (1964). In the essay, Read's mature ideas about the relationship of art to modern society are set out against those of Marcuse and, in a more general sense, the Frankfurt School. Unlike Benjamin, Marcuse holds a fundamentally pessimistic view of capitalism's developing technologies. He argues that they will undermine the very basis of artistic alienation and will subsume art into a one-dimensional culture of harmonising commercialism, ultimately threatening to overpower the struggles of critical thinkers in their task to create the (Hegelian) new Subject. Read is also critical of modern society and of the position it accords to art, but he emphasises the effect on the *individual* psyche of increased technological specialisation and also of the demise of religion. He argues that the mass of the population is being forced into dreary occupations which dull the imagination and cause the individual to experience himself as alienated (and here, he uses the term 'alienation' in a psychologistic rather than a structural Marxist sense). And while Marcuse presents a general theoretical view of the arts in our technological civilisation, Read tends towards empiricism: in his finest writings, he addresses specific art works, often contemporary abstract ones, and informs an art-historical interpretation with his particular political viewpoint. For he believed that through the correct understanding of great works of art, which such interpretations help us to achieve, we become empowered to perceive fundamental truths about ourselves. He consequently argued that we must produce a society which will be sure to nurture those exceptional individuals who have the artistic imagination to show us that truth. For Read, art is not directly about the struggle against capitalism as such; it is concerned, in a wider, humanist and even metaphysical sense, with the mystery of existence. Art is bound up with the individual psyche.

A major centenary exhibition, entitled 'Herbert Read: A British Vision of World Art' (Leeds City Art Galleries 1992–3) focused on the art and design promoted by Read during his long lifetime. The event, and responses to it, provides a postscript to this section. The accompanying catalogue begins to set Read's work in a different political context: it suggests that his insistence that modern art contributed to a new humanist order stemmed from an effort not to be identified with the communist cause, nor – on the other hand – with fascism. While the Leeds project is largely celebratory, critics of the exhibition (e.g., James Hall, *Guardian*, 6 December 1992) suggest that, in retrospect, the manner in which Read's theoretical approach altered during his lifetime can now be seen not so much as a 'development' but a hedging of bets resulting from a basic lack of critical discrimination and commitment, a desire to be accepted as intellectually and politically correct.

In this section, I have briefly examined the theoretical writings of Marx and several other critical theorists whose subsequent developments of his class analysis of capitalism either directly or indirectly address the area of visual art. In the next section, I present the ideas of some 'liberal' – non-Marxist – writers on art, who were working roughly between 1880 and 1980. Their ideas were to become a major target of criticism for those theorists of art who are represented in the final section of this chapter.

3 NON-CRITICAL WRITINGS ABOUT VISUAL ART: CONNOISSEURSHIP, HUMANISM

Heinrich Wölfflin; Bernard Berenson; Erwin Panofsky; The Courtauld Institute of Art (c. 1950–70); Ernst Gombrich

The writings of Heinrich Wölfflin (born 1864) have had considerable influence on several generations of art historians. Herbert Read, in his introduction to the English translation (1953) of Wölfflin's *Classic Art* [1899], suggested that when Wölfflin died in 1945, aged 81, it could be said of him that he had found art criticism a subjective chaos and left it a science. In 1893, Wölfflin succeeded Jacob Burckhardt in the chair of art history at the University of Basle. Though Burckhardt's generalisations about paintings appeared convincing, later art historians objected that he had no *method* by which he could classify the phenomena of art; no measure by which his personal prejudices might be controlled. During his lifetime, Wölfflin went a long way towards establishing such a systematic method in art-historical criticism. According to Read, he kept his eye steadily fixed on the work of art and began to analyse what he saw, and to classify the results of such visual analysis. He was searching for a conception of art history which would avoid both the superficiality of a subjective interpretation of art and the aridity of a purely formalistic type of art criticism. He started this task in *Classic Art* and completed it in *Principles of Art History* (1950) [1915]. His formalistic 'principles', based on the analysis of the visual experience of works of art, consist of a set of five contrary concepts: linear and painterly, plane and recession, closed and open form, multiplicity and unity, absolute and relative clarity of subject matter. When applied to works of art, Wölfflin claimed that this set of concepts elicited the specifics of their composition, which could thus be explained and classified. In addition, he argued that by using these five categories, or principles, the analyst could perceive the way in which the technique or style of a drawing or painting drew upon, responded to and developed the technique or style of a previous work. Thus the idea of a consequential visual development, via the artist's hand – as it were – underpins his approach.

The descriptive skill, the economy and perspicacity of Wölfflin's schemata or ideal types are still admired by many art historians. However, Read argues that they are based on, and applicable to, one kind of art only – the figurative art of the humanist tradition; and that they have no application to earlier traditions such as the Byzantine or the Egyptian, and even less to various types of modern art. The theoretical force or status of Wölfflin's concepts has also been challenged. For he claimed that this categorisation shows the nature of the artist's *own* achievement, his own contribution, as opposed to the impact of cultural conditions on his work; and that this contribution on the part of the artist accounts for the historical transformation of art. Michael Podro, in *The Critical Historians of Art* (1982) argues that a quasi-immanent visual (art) development of this kind cannot be possible, since the effect of the contingent and non-visual cultural factors on the production of a visual art work cannot be ignored. A similar position is adopted by sociologists of science when arguing against the claim that scientific knowledge has an immanent development. However, Podro comments that though the painter's exercise of his medium may be more complex than the aligning of his material to the world which is suggested by Wölfflin's five categories, nevertheless the kind of factors he defines are central to the painter's project, and are relatively less variable than the other complexities which may be involved.

Read informs us that Bernhard Berenson (born 1865) was much influenced by Wölfflin's categories. As a result of reading Wölfflin, Berenson was persuaded to look extremely carefully at a painting, and to analyse what he saw. He was also influenced by the work of Morelli, a trained comparative anatomist who made morphological comparisons in pictures between details of parts of the sitters' bodies – in particular their ears – which seemed to Morelli to offer objective criteria for authorship, and to justify his method as scientific. Berenson, however, suggested that such details as legs and arms were significant only so far as they were not vehicles of expression. He became increasingly concerned with 'level' and 'type' of quality, and with an analysis of style.

After Berenson's first visit to Italy, he published *The Italian Painters of the Renaissance* (1948) [1930]. In it he argued that his epoch was instinctively in sympathy with that of the Renaissance, and that painters currently working could learn a great deal from fifteenth century art. He distinguishes many different Italian Renaissance painters, and each is judged from 'genius' through to 'mediocre'; for example: 'We must judge Moroni, then, as a portrait painter pure and simple; although even here his place is not with the highest' (Berenson 1948: 315). Berenson thus emphasises the artist's individuality. In general, he presents it as those essential qualities considered specific to that artist and revealed by his entire production; while the social contextualisation of that œuvre is entirely ignored. Berenson's contribution to art theory is largely based on his concept of 'tactile values', or plasticity, by which he meant the ability to make a two-dimensional representation of a three-dimensional object look rounded, touchable, possessing depth. He argued that paintings of the Renaissance possessed this quality in various degrees (following Vasari, he claimed, for example, that Giotto was a man of genius), although in his opinion Italy has subsequently failed to produce a single great artist.

The Italian Painters of the Renaissance was accompanied by the famous 'Lists' of those pictures that Berenson accepted as authentic. It is on these lists, in part, that his reputation as a connoisseur is based. The origins of connoisseurship lie in the Renaissance, but the term has been particularly associated with *Berenson's* professional pursuits.[25] In general terms, connoisseurship consists in part of establishing the authorship of a work of art on the basis of comparison with known works; and it is also concerned with establishing the authenticity of such a work. In addition, the connoisseur may go on to assess the work's quality or intrinsic value, again by comparison with other objects of the same kind. The role that Berenson played in the history of taste and collecting is remarkable, and as a result, the concept of connoisseurship became particularly associated with his activities. By the early twentieth century, American millionaires were beginning to acquire masterpieces – or so they hoped – of Italian art. Berenson stimulated and guided this interest in Italian art; and, as the leading expert on it, he authenticated paintings for dealers and collectors. He appears to have regarded it as his mission to send to the United States as many Italian works of art as he could persuade collectors to acquire. Aided by the Payne-Aldrich Tariff Act of 1909, which allowed for duty-free import of works of art over twenty years old, Berenson's success may be measured by the fact that there are now more Italian Renaissance paintings in America than anywhere else except for their place of origin. His mission was also aided by the political interests of American capitalism. The American businessmen Samuel and Russ Kress sponsored the republication of *The Italian Painters of the Renaissance* in illustrated editions, with the intention that this should regenerate the interest of the American public in traditional as opposed to radical values.[26]

25 See Brown (1979: 13–29).
26 Ibid.: 23.

Mid-nineteenth century photographers had begun to make a systematic record of works of art, for at the time – and for many years subsequently – photographs were believed to be objective reproductions of the originals that they depicted.[27] This helps to explain why Berenson made much use of black and white photographs in his attributions, saying they were excellent for comparative purposes.[28] His custom was to inscribe an artist's name on the back of a photograph of an art work, which was sometimes accompanied by a letter expanding on his attribution. He unquestionably overpraised pictures in whose acquisition he had a stake;[29] and the extent to which his involvement with the trade affected his judgments of works of art has since become subject to much debate. In addition, it is unfortunate for his reputation as a disinterested scholar that he lived on into a world in which another major type of connoisseur arose. By the late twentieth century, with art history a well-established academic discipline and works of art now mostly in museums, connoisseurs have become university-trained curators. The present curatorial type of connoisseur displays the traditional concerns of her/his forerunners, but she does so more clearly for the institution by which she is employed and without personal monetary gain beyond a fixed salary.

As a young man, Erwin Panofsky published a series of papers – the first in 1915 – dealing with the problem of method in art history. In Podro's *The Critical Historians of Art*, he features as the last of those German intellectuals working between 1827 and 1927 whose concerns and procedures were responses to Hegel's philosophy of art. Podro argues that Panofsky revived the Hegelian project of constructing an absolute viewpoint from which to regard the art of the past, a viewpoint from which the inner structure of all works of art could be made clear; and that in this project, he was following Wölfflin and Riegl, though he rejected their assumptions that there were certain innate principles of the mind which could guide our interpretation of works of art. Podro discusses Panofsky's attempt to construct a systematic art historical method which links the subjectivity of the interpreter – and of the artist – with the objectivity of the object of study, centrally focusing on the notion of the coherence of the art work. Panofsky set himself the task, in other words, of constructing an *a priori* system of interpretation which would locate a particular mind–world relation within any particular work. This mind–world relation was seen both as the source of the work's internal

27 William Ivins, in his influential *Prints and Visual Communication* (1953), claimed that until the invention of photography, there had been no way of making pictures of objects that could serve as a basis for connoisseurship, but that photographs were true reproductions, and could therefore fulfil that function.

28 The Courtauld Institute's Witt Library and Survey of Pictures in British Country Houses, which are collections of (predominantly) black and white photographs of art works used mainly for teaching purposes, indicate the still current connoisseurial approach to art history.

29 Brown, op. cit.: 25.

coordination and also as unifying it with surrounding culture. It is characterised in the introduction to *Studies in Iconology* (1939) as an essential tendency of the human mind.

However, in mid-career Panofsky's life and thought were subjected to profound change. In 1933, he was ousted from his professorship at Hamburg by the Nazis, and he emigrated to the United States. He took up lectureships at Princeton and New York Universities, and continued writing and publishing for another twenty years. From then onwards, the English language was to be his vehicle of communication. In 1955, Doubleday Anchor published *Meaning in the Visual Arts*, a paperback selection of his articles; thus making them widely available to an English-speaking public. These papers span thirty years of his scholarship; and some were completely rewritten by Panofsky for this publication while others were revised and brought up to date. The introduction, which has greatly influenced English-speaking art historians, is entitled 'The History of Art as a Humanistic Discipline'; and at times it gives the impression of a quite different author from the one that Podro discusses. So does the epilogue, 'Art History in the United States', for in it Panofsky expresses a dislike of German thought and language: 'The German language unfortunately permits a fairly trivial thought to declaim from behind a woolen curtain of apparent profundity and, conversely, a multitude of meanings to lurk behind one term' (Panofsky 1955: 329). He goes on to suggest that for the German immigrant scholar, it has been a blessing to come into contact and occasionally into conflict with an Anglo-Saxon positivism which is 'in principle, distrustful of abstract speculation' (Panofsky 1955: 329). These views are more strongly expressed and their implications further developed in the writings of his younger fellow-compatriot, Ernst Gombrich (see below).

In 'The History of Art as a Humanistic Discipline', the relationship between art history and connoisseurship is discussed. Panofsky claims that the difference between them is a matter of emphasis: 'The connoisseur might be defined as a laconic art historian, and the art historian as a loquacious connoisseur' (Panofsky 1955: 20). One wonders what Podro's German critical art historians would have made of this statement. Certainly it represents the kernel of what the 'new' critical art historians (discussed in section 4 of this chapter) set out to demolish; they argue that the art historian, in this sense, is merely a lackey of the capitalist system. Even the ideas which Panofsky had previously expressed in German, as part of the Hegelian project, now seem to take on a different meaning in this English text. Associating himself with humanism, he emphasises that this system of thought classically differentiates the arts from the sciences, and concerns itself with the former. He explains that the humanist rejects authority, and instead tolerates – indeed respects – the individual, his thought and actions. And in addition, the humanist respects tradition because it is real and objective, and can be studied, and if necessary, reinstated. Thus, the humanist historian of art has a key role to play as the theorist of cultural records which have come down to us in the form of works of art. Art history 'must describe the stylistic peculiarities, neither as measurable or otherwise determinable data, nor as stimuli of subjective reactions, but as that which bears witness to artistic "intentions"' Panofsky 1955: 20). However, 'The artist has alternatives. . . . Thus it appears that the terms used by the art historian interpret the stylistic peculiarities of the work as specific solutions of generic "artistic problems"' (Panofsky 1955: 21). Here, we can see the influence of Wölfflin's emphasis that the art historian should empathise with the artist whose work he is studying; and in the generalised art-historical project which Panofsky outlines in this essay, there are similar traces of an attempt to produce a 'totalising theory'. However, the humanist art historian, as Panofsky describes him, often sounds more like an Anglo-Saxon empiricist; while the privileging of the artist's intentions has been criticised by later Marxist art historians on the grounds that it represents a romantic ideology which is associated with capitalist connoisseurship.

In 'Art History as a Humanistic Discipline', Panofsky explains that what differentiates works of art from the natural phenomena with which scientists deal is that the former demand to be experienced aesthetically. And it is the unity of materialised form, idea (subject matter in the case of the visual art work) and content which is realised in the intuitive aesthetic experience. Obviously the naive beholder has a different experience from that of the humanist art historian, who is not only conscious of the constituents of the aesthetic experience, but also 'primes' his intuition by acquiring as much factual information about the art work as possible in advance. Thus the art historian combines intuitive aesthetic recreation and archaeological (empirical) research: 'Archaeological research is blind and empty without aesthetic recreation, and aesthetic recreation is irrational and often misguided without archaeological research. But "leaning against one another", these two can support the system that makes sense' (Panofsky 1955: 19), that is, a historical synopsis.

These two, 'leaning against one another', are probably descendants of the 'mind–world relation' which featured in Panofsky's early Hegelian project to construct an *a priori* system of interpretation which would locate a particular mind–world relation within any particular work, expressing both the nature of the work's internal coherence and its relationship with surrounding culture. Yet in another way, Panofsky's text can be read as a kind of practical guide for the would-be empirical Anglo-Saxon art historian.

John Tagg (1975) is deeply critical of Panofsky's art-historical approach, and emphasises the extent to which Panofsky's writings have influenced British art history. For example, he argues that Panofsky's work reinforces the English attitude to the visual arts which sees them as furnishing decoration, distraction, delight for the senses but never the mind; and where the art historian's job amounts to cataloguing. He contrasts this approach with the German art historical tradition:

which developed in a very different social and intellectual context and in which we find studies of art based on a philosophical aesthetic, drawing on general philosophy, sociology and psychology, and seeking to unify them in a synthetic art historical method.

(Tagg 1975: 3)

At the time he wrote this, Tagg presumably did not know the 'early' Panofsky, whose largely untranslated German texts Podro had yet to analyse and publish (in *The Critical Historians of Art*, 1982). As a result of undertaking that later analysis, Podro was to claim that in no writer was the conception of art as like knowledge so elaborately developed as by Panofsky.

Some conclusions of a more general nature can be drawn from this brief examination of Panofsky's history – or histories – of art. First, his work tends to disturb the generally held view that European 'Geist philosophy' and British and American empiricism are incompatible. But second, and on another level, what Panofsky 'stands for' presents a very interesting socio-logical study, since his publications indicated very clearly the influence of social context on the formation of theory and ideas. In the context of Hegelian scholarship in Germany, he attempted to produce an absolutist theoretical stance in relation to art. But after emigrating to the United States, the very fact of writing in English – and in an intellectual context of empiricism and positivism – changed his approach considerably. When the commentaries upon his work are considered in conjunction with his own publications, we find a veritable tangle of intellectual positions. It is only when all these texts are taken cumulatively, in the *contexts* of changing historical, geographical, political and intellectual circumstances, that it becomes possible to start to understand the contradictory theoretical approaches that have been associated with the name of Erwin Panofsky; and in the process, to glimpse something of the complexity of intellectual thought in relation to visual art in the West over the past seventy years.

John Tagg associated Panofsky with a specifically English type of art history. English art history was synonymous, for more than thirty years, with the prestigious Courtauld Institute of Art in London, whose influence in Britain and elsewhere has been huge. I now turn to a discussion of it; and this discussion relates for the most part to the period of its greatest influence, 1950–70.[30] A department of the University of London, the Courtauld Institute was founded in 1931, and until the 1960s it was the only place in Britain offering an undergraduate course in art history – although Cambridge, and later Oxford, offered components of art history in a general history degree course. A large part of Samuel Courtauld's unparalleled collection of French late nineteenth-century paintings was displayed on the premises at 20 Portman

---

30 This section is, to a certain extent, based on the memories of Stephen Chaplin who was an undergraduate student at the Courtauld Institute from 1955 to 1958, and a deputy librarian from 1958 to 1960; and on my own experience as a secretary at the Institute from 1959 to 1961.

Square, London (until the collection was removed in 1960 to a purpose-built gallery); and this gave the Institute – itself one of the finest examples of the work of the brothers Adam in London – an extraordinarily 'authentic' quality. In the post-war years 'the Courtauld', as it was known, was an elite establishment whose approach to art history was widely accepted.

It has been closely allied with the Warburg Institute, whose library was evacuated from Germany shortly before the Second World War and came almost by chance to England rather than to the United States. The Warburg was originally founded by Aby Warburg in Hamburg in the early 1920s for the study of antique thought in the post-antique world. The story of its evacuation, and that of its German refugee staff and their philosophical outlook (the ethos of *Geistesgeschichte*), suggests certain parallels with the history of the Frankfurt Institute. Distinguished Warburg professors – Rudolph Wittkower, Leopold Ettlinger and Ernst Gombrich (see below) – all lectured at the Courtauld Institute in the 1950–60s.

Anthony Blunt started teaching at the Courtauld in 1934, and became its third director in 1947. He was appointed Surveyor of the King's Pictures in 1945, a post he held until 1972. In the 1930s his writings on art showed a definite Marxist tendency; yet by the 1950s the Courtauld, very much under his influence,[31] was associated with an art history which was formalist and 'value-free', while it adopted a generally humanist attitude towards artists and their production. With hindsight, this stance is perhaps unsurprising, given the Cold War climate of the 1950s and early 1960s; but it also helped to provide a cover for Blunt's espionage activities, which were publicly exposed in 1979. Certainly, the training which students received was not political in an overt sense. The relationship of art to politics was never explicitly made. For example, Johannes Wilde,[32] who as a refugee from Germany had been accused during his internment on the Isle of Man of 'signalling to submarines', would show students Rubens' drawings of hands in order to impress on them the quality of 'good' art. On the other hand, the subject matter of certain of Blunt's lectures, Picasso's *Guernica* and Rouault's *Miserere*, for example, indicates concern with human hardship.

But 'good' art was the order of the day; particularly the art of the Italian Renaissance, and British art from 1530 to the present. The emphasis on Italian Renaissance art stemmed from the legacy of Vasari, Wölfflin, Berenson and many other scholars: quite simply, this was the area in which most art-historical research had been undertaken, and most value judgments made. Italian Renaissance art was seen as the very foundation of excellence in Western art. British art was another matter. From its inception, one of the Institute's 'special aims had been to develop research on British Art'

31 Stephen Rees-Jones, the Courtauld's scientific expert said: 'After he [Blunt] became Director of the Courtauld in 1947 he ruled it like a medieval court. He was the prince and we were the court' (Penrose and Freeman 1986: 295).
32 For ten years Deputy Director of the Courtauld Institute.

(Courtauld Institute of Art Prospectus 1950), and its library and collections of reproductions 'had been planned with that purpose in view' (op. cit.). Students were expected to become curators of British provincial art galleries and museums; and consequently the study of British art and of Italian Renaissance art were compulsory. Optional courses on 'Special Periods' were also offered; for example, 'European art c. 1700–90' and 'European art c. 1790–1880'.

Indeed, periodisation was a crucial feature of the Courtauld's conception of art history. Western art (with a pronounced emphasis on European painting) was divided up into historical periods, which were seen to develop one out of another. In the 'photograph paper' of the final examination, students followed a set procedure: date the work in terms of century, then place according to country, then school, then town, then family, then work-shop, then particular artist, then precise date. The job was done if and when you could say, for example: Leonardo, 1505. In detail, this entailed analysing the specific work in terms of its iconography – and students without a knowledge of the Bible were disadvantaged. It also involved an analysis of the work's morphology, and a knowledge of changes in form over time. This was taught in lectures, following Wölfflin, via the comparative method using two slide screens.

'Good' art was evaluated with reference to the perceived skill of the artist, and the resultant beauty of the object in terms of its formal attributes and quality of drawing. Scholars tended to identify with the creativity of the artist on a personal basis. Getting inside the mind of the artist, one was thought to be in a position to understand and appreciate his aims; then looking at the work, one could assess the manner in which – and the degree to which – these aims had been accomplished.

Thus, European art history was conceptualised and taught as a series of landmarks. A number of outstanding, authenticated works – arranged according to periodised stylistic groups relating to specific countries – was seen as contributing to the continuity of development of Western art, century by century, up to the present day. An artist's œuvre, consisting of a chronological list of first authenticated then unauthenticated works, was drawn together as part of the process of charting this 'art history'; and the monograph was a standard publication. Any information about the social context of the artist and his work was given as an introductory or background supplement; its purpose was solely to enhance the Courtauld conception of art history. Patronage, particularly by Italian Renaissance popes, received some attention; but in an hour's lecture on, for example, Leonardo, one-twelfth of the time – a brief introduction – would be spent on so-called background. Arnold Hauser's *Social History of Art* – in the library but not on any reading list – proved an eye-opener to students who came across this alternative account.

Subsequent accusations that the 'Courtauld method' was only concerned with the 'pure visibility phenomenon', and that its political stance was concealed, are to a large extent justified – indeed in the case of Anthony Blunt, the relationship of art to politics turned out to be spectacularly Byzantine. But some small rejoinders should be made. First, Wilde and several other academic staff were determined to try to teach art history from sources; for example, to read Vasari on the Italian Renaissance. Second, the courses on British art did have more social content, perhaps because of the centrality of such figures as Hogarth and Blake. But, by and large, this prestigious establishment continued for many years to turn out art historians who, as Mark Roskill says (1974), knew that their profession was concerned with style, attributions, dating, authenticity, rarity, reconstruction, the detection of forgery, the rediscovery of forgotten artists and the meaning of pictures.

Ernst Gombrich was director of the Warburg Institute from 1959 to 1976. He provides a different kind of account of the development of visual representation – one which 'is based on the psychology of recognition and how the skills of invoking it are learned' (Podro 1982: 215). This has introduced a new set of concerns into the analysis of painting. A starting point for Gombrich is that: 'If art were only a matter of personal vision there could be no history of art. . . . The art historian's trade rests on the conviction once formulated by Wölfflin, that "not everything is possible in every period"' (Gombrich 1960: 4). Gombrich claims that we can communicate with a fair degree of assurance what we mean by 'baroque' (organ loft) or 'impressionist' (painting), but he objects to the idea that Wölfflin's categories, if applied to an art work, would produce an objective or even a sufficient analysis of the work. In *Norm and Form* (1966) he warns that

> the labels we use must of necessity differ from those which our colleagues who work in the field of entomology fix on their beetles or butterflies. In the discussion of works of art, description can never be completely divorced from criticism. The perplexities which art historians have encountered in their debates about styles and periods are due to this lack of distinction between form and norm . . . [They] must never forget that language is a man-made thing, inherently capable of adjustment, and that *aesthetic categories* are not *natural classes.*
> (Gombrich 1966: 81)

However, Gombrich appears to believe that in nature there *are* 'natural classes'; in other words, that science is neutral and objective, and that the scientist's job is to discover these classes. This positivistic notion of science, and the method of proposing a tentative hypothesis and modifying that hypothesis in the light of experimentation are inherited from his philosophical mentor, Karl Popper. Working within this positivist ethos, Gombrich's aim has been to apply the idea of a 'scientific' measure – in the sense of a psychological theory of perception and optics – to art works. He sees the artist as inheriting certain visual skills and conventions, and learning (by trial and error) to develop others, by which to invoke a plausible illusion of the reality he seeks to represent. And the art writer's job is to discuss the artist's problems of representing reality in a language that makes sense to both of them and also to the science-based student of perception. Proof of the relative success of this project lies in the fact that *Illusion in Nature and Art* (jointly edited by Gombrich and the psychologist R. L. Gregory, 1973) is often classified in university libraries under psychology.

Gombrich's work has been widely admired, but *because* of its popularity and consequent effect on attitudes towards art, it has also attracted the kind of criticism that Read made of Wölfflin's categories ; namely, the idea that the artist develops plausible illusions of the reality he seeks to represent which cannot be straightforwardly applied to abstract art – though this is actually to oversimplify the richness and complexity of Gombrich's œuvre, another strand of which contains the argument that the contemporary general public is to blame for just expecting 'new Art', and for not giving present day artists specific tasks to perform. Nevertheless, some abstract artists practising today consider that Gombrich is partly responsible for the unpopularity of abstract art in Britain.[33] His work has also been heavily criticised by social art historians, who object to the idea of a neutral science and deplore the political implications of his humanist psychology. They argue that a capitalist metatheory is inherent in an approach which focuses on the individual's acquisition of skills and visual conventions, and that this is unacceptable because it ignores what they see as the crucial role played by ideology in the construction of subject positions and therefore of the subject. However, Rees and Borzello, in their introduction to *The New Art History* (1986) note that radical scholars abroad tend to value Gombrich's writings alongside those of Jacques Derrida. In Britain, where Gombrich is currently seen as tradition personified among radical art historians, this comparison would seem to be unimaginable. His belief that Popper's account of the way science works is eminently applicable to the story of visual discoveries in art is what distinguishes his often complex and subtle work from that of the critical historians discussed by Podro (1982), and also from that of the social historians of art discussed in the next section.

4 CRITICAL WRITINGS ABOUT VISUAL ART: CLASS ANALYSES II

Principal works discussed:

T. H. Clark, *The Absolute Bourgeois; Artists and Politics in France 1848–1851*, 1973a
  Image of the People; Gustave Courbet and the 1848 Revolution, 1973b
  'The Conditions of Artistic Creation', *Times Literary Supplement*, 24 May 1974
Nicos Hadjinicolaou, *Art History and Class Struggle*, 1978
Janet Wolff, *The Social Production of Art*, 1981
Fred Orton and Griselda Pollock, 'Les Données Bretonnantes: La Prairie de la

---

33 I am grateful to Tam Giles for this observation.

Representation', in *Modern Art and Modernism*, 1982
Paul Wood, 'Art and Politics in a Workers' State', in *Art History*, 8, 1, 1985
John Tagg, 'Art History and Difference', in *The New Art History*, 1986

During the 1960s, capitalism in Britain was yielding a comfortable surplus. Such events are often associated with a loosening of the financial belt and a tendency for the political regime to move leftwards. In 1964, the Labour Party was returned to power for six years. During this time, it revised and expanded the education system. For example, it introduced a two-tier system of higher education by establishing the new polytechnics. There was subsequently a heightened political awareness among British students, which was fuelled by the Paris riots of 1968. Although the wave of student revolts in the wake of those riots eventually died down, and a Conservative government was returned to power in Britain in 1970, the previous political upheavals had the effect of producing more lasting intellectual changes. For example, the *New Left Review*, founded in 1960, became increasingly influential; and in the late 1960s Birmingham University set up its Centre for Contemporary Cultural Studies, which began to translate and publish French theoretical texts on semiotics, and to give a broader social and political meaning to the concept of culture. By the beginning of the 1970s, the women's liberation movement was gathering momentum; and in the field of visual art, women's sense of themselves as artists began to alter. Previously conceiving of themselves simply as women artists, they now began consciously to develop new forms of practice with a political and moral purpose; and that purpose was to expose and destroy patriarchy. At roughly the same time, the film and media journal *Screen* began to have a widespread impact on the intellectual vanguard. Reacting against what it saw as the political failure of the libertarian 1960s, *Screen* adopted the structural Marxism of Louis Althusser. This envisages theorising as intellectual labour; and thus the door was opened for Marxists, until then excluded from British academic life, which had hitherto been affected by the Cold War climate, to come in and start revitalising the arid intellectual ground on the Left. *Screen* promoted the little-known ideas of the Russian Formalists and the Brecht–Benjamin circle; it introduced semiotics from Saussure to Barthes; and it presented the post-Freudian psychoanalysis of Jacques Lacan.

This leftwards-shifting intellectual climate produced a new socio-political approach to art history.[34] In 1973, T. H. Clark – who had received his postgraduate training at the Courtauld Institute – published two books: *The Absolute Bourgeois; Artists and Politics in France 1848–1851* (1973a), and *Image of the People; Gustave Courbet and the 1848 Revolution* (1973b). The titles alone give a clear enough indication that Clark's interest in art was politically rooted. However, it was his article in the *Times Literary Supplement* the

---

34 This is discussed by the contributors to *The New Art History* (Rees and Borzello 1986).

following year, 'The Conditions of Artistic Creation' (1974), which unambiguously called for a new approach to art history. The article is deeply critical of Courtauld-taught, connoisseurial art history, which Clark argued had become manservant of the art market; checking dates for the dealers and providing pedigrees for rich collectors. He further suggested that iconography had deteriorated from examining the conditions in which an artist met an ideology into desultory theme chasing. Clark wanted to go back to a period before the 'pure visibility phenomenon' had taken hold; to re-examine the work of nineteenth-century European art historians who saw visual art as part of the wider social spectrum.

In the article, Clark argued that the kinds of problems addressed by Georg Lukács, and certain other European critical historians of art,[35] should be reconsidered. What are the conditions of artistic creation? What are the artist's resources? What do we mean when we talk of an artist's materials? Do some 'materials' determine the use of others? Clark noted that questions like these had subsequently been turned by art historians into a concern with 'methods', formal analysis, 'iconography'. He aimed to develop a new social history of art which re-addresssed those problems and re-established the dialectical thinking of the earlier art historians; arguing that a revival of such questions in the light of new insights from contemporary cultural theory would allow art historians to situate visual art more firmly within a much wider theoretical context.

In 1974, Clark was appointed Professor of the History of Art at the University of Leeds. He subsequently formed a department of staff who had been thinking along similar lines,[36] and in 1975 Leeds University initiated an MA course in the social history of art. Around this time, several of the polytechnics (subsequently styled universities) were also becoming established as centres for the 'new art history'; and in 1979, Middlesex Polytechnic published the first issue of *Block*, which quickly became a forum for debate about cultural theory and the social history of art. In the words of John Tagg, the new social art historians set out

> to undertake an analytical description of a concrete historical moment and the specific nexus of conditions which are, at once, those under which the artist's consciousness is formed and the artist's work created, and those within which the artist's work has public meaning. This nexus is itself sited within a specific ideological field and informed by a general social conflict.
>
> (Tagg 1975: 5)

The first of the two books that Clark published in 1973, *The Absolute Bourgeois; Artists and Politics in France 1848–1851*, is a study of the years following the 1848 Revolution, and in particular of four artists who tried to cope with the unfamiliar situation in which art and politics could not escape

---

35 He mentions Heinrich Wölfflin, Max Dvorak, Erwin Panofsky, Aby Warburg, Fritz Saxl and Julius von Schlosser.
36 Its members included Terry Atkinson, Fred Orton, Griselda Pollock and John Tagg.

each other. It centres on the painting and politics of Daumier, Millet and Delacroix, and the writings of Baudelaire. Clark shows that in their attitudes to revolution, these four artists had little in common, and that the intentions of the first three were not to produce revolutionary art; though he demonstrates that their work is often more closely tied into the context of politics than might be apparent at first sight. Underlying the study are questions about when art becomes political, and how it becomes politically effective. How can an artist use the conditions of artistic production without being defined by them? How can he produce an art work which does not stay in the studio or end up on a drawing-room wall? How to bypass the art market? How to destroy the conventional art public and invent a new one? How to make art 'popular'? How to exploit one's privacy, and the insights it allowed, and yet escape from it? Clark indicates that in a second book he will discuss the work of Courbet who, for a short while, almost achieved the impossible by finding answers to these questions. But he stresses that art's effectiveness, in political terms, is limited to the realm of ideology. And although a political struggle always involves competing ideologies, it is only occasionally that within a political struggle ideologies take on exceptional importance. When that happens, works of art can attack.

Which leads us to *Image of the People: Gustave Courbet and the 1848 Revolution*, Clark's second publication in 1973. To call this a companion volume to *Image of the People* is to conventionalise the fascinating relationship between the two works, and to dispel the invitation to explore that relationship dialectically. By producing two books almost concurrently, which focus on the same short period of time in France, Clark is demonstrating his method of situating works of art in a highly complex, fluctuating socio-political structure, and showing how the history of art cannot be seen apart from history as a whole.

Chapter 1, 'On the Social History of Art', sets out his theoretical position. He argues that a social-historical analysis of Courbet's painting between the years 1848 and 1851 must involve explanation of the connecting links between artistic form, the available systems of visual representation, the current theories of art, other ideologies, social classes, and more general historical structures and processes. But importantly, concrete transactions are involved, which means that the study must also be historically specific. For it is the artist himself who makes the encounter with history and its specific determinations. Thus Clark's social history of art sets out to discover the general nature of the structures that the artist encounters; but it also seeks to locate the specific conditions of one such meeting in the making of an art work at a particular place and at a precise historical juncture. Clark argues that this process of situating the specific in the light of wider social and political processes entails working with a multiplicity of perspectives. It also entails dialectical writing – the method of his European mentors.

Within this conceptual framework involving interaction between structure and agency, the making of a work of art becomes a series of actions in but also *on* history. Such a work may become intelligible only within the context of given and imposed structures of meaning; but Clark argues that in its turn, it can alter and at times disrupt these structures. A work of art may have ideology (those ideas, images, and values which are generally accepted) as its material, but it works that material; it gives it a new form, and at certain moments that new form is in itself a subversion of ideology. Clark believes – and convincingly demonstrates – that something approaching this dual process was achieved in the context of the public's response to Courbet's painting, *Burial at Ornans* (1849–50), exhibited at the Paris Salon of 1851.

Clark's treatment of *Burial at Ornans*[37] entails detailed historical analysis of contemporary responses to the work itself and to the wider social situation of political and economic upheaval in France after the 1848 revolution. This painting emerges not as an illustration of 'revolution', but as the depiction of a specific occasion at which the artist and members of his family were present. Yet the political overlaps with the personal in this work. Contemporary records show that Courbet's family was new bourgeois – peasant stock recently made good. They lived at Ornans in the valley of the Doubs, and Courbet, who had left to try to establish himself as a painter in Paris, paid fairly frequent visits home. His parents experienced an ambivalence which stemmed from their social position between peasant and bourgeois classes, while he himself alternated between country life and Parisian society with its Salon-buying public. Clark argues that this picture shows Courbet's home community in an ambiguous way, for some of the mourners depicted in this burial scene sport dress-coats, whilst others who are less directly involved wear their working smocks. However, the audience for the work – the buying public – was in Paris. Clark explains that for those who had recently emigrated to Paris from the countryside and were struggling to achieve urban bourgeois status, it was important to maintain the myth of order in the countryside, of rural unity, of a one-class society in which peasant and master work in harmony; for by enforcing distinctions and eliminating ambiguities, the bourgeois category was strengthened. He argues that Courbet exploded that myth by muddying the boundaries between town and country: *Burial at Ornans* shows the Parisian bourgeois institution of a grand formal burial in conjunction with identifiable members of a specific country community whose peasants had recently suffered terrible deprivations.

But Clark argues that the responses made to this work when it was hung at the 1851 Paris Salon tell us more: the writings of contemporary art critics indicate that they did not know what to make of the work; they evidently found it disturbing but were unable to pin this feeling down in words. It was not the romantic rural scene wanted by the right; it was not the picture of peasant suffering and hardship which would have satisfied the left. It had a

---

37 Other paintings are also considered, but *Burial at Ornans* is given the most extended analytical treatment.

lack of open declared significance. However, contemporary sources also show that *Burial at Ornans* spoke to the wider Parisian society, who appear to have greeted it with a mixture of outrage and enthusiasm. And far from being a cohesive, rich, sophisticated bourgeoisie, this society appears to have consisted of a disparate, ill-assorted group of people to whom the work meant different things. Clark suggests that in this work, Courbet challenged the contemporary aesthetic ideologies by suggesting a new relationship to popular art. He did not use popular art in order to further the development of high art, but the opposite – he exploited high art in order to revive popular art; this picture was for the people, and they responded. It was not for connoisseurs.

In the end *Burial at Ornans* was assimilated into the art milieu, but for a time it had troubled that public which it excluded. One contemporary writer sarcastically called it 'socialist painting', 'an engine of revolution'. However, Clark argues that for a short while, it was precisely that. Courbet, an inarticulate, naive, instinctive painter, was able to cut through the complexities entailed in radical writing. Embedded so deep in the matter it describes, so accurately in its sense of what disturbs its public, the painting effectively questioned and stirred up social boundaries when, in the perceptions of its viewers, to keep these clear meant the difference between peace and war. Clark argues that Courbet put his finger on the shifting political situation of the moment and disturbed it.

There have been criticisms of Clark's writings. Some have asked just how new his approach really is; claiming, for example, that a social history of Dutch art has always been practised in Holland; and arguing that a thin red line of social art historians can be traced right through the years when the Courtauld method predominated.[38] One might also ask why Clark invokes past art historians such as Wölfflin, Dvorak and Panofsky rather than Adorno and Raphael whose approaches were so much more sociological, and indeed dialectical. In addition, Paul Overy (1986) suggests that Clark's more recent publication, *The Painting of Modern Life: Paris in the Art of Manet and his Followers* (1985), is in many ways curiously conventional and unchallenging, for there the author attends to exactly the same artists that concern other texts on later French nineteenth-century painting: Manet, Seurat, the Impressionists, Degas – to the exclusion, for example, of Gustave Caillebotte, who was both artist and patron, and therefore of great interest to a social art historian. Indeed, Overy suggests that the American art theorist Clement Greenberg still appears to be the touchstone of the new art history,[39] as he is of modernism – that bastion of the pure visibility approach; and that if art history is genuinely to renew itself, it will have to look elsewhere.

However, it is clear that Clark's ideas spoke to many in the 1970–80s; and

---

38 A. Hauser; F. Antal; F. Klingender; M. Baxendall.
39 On the evidence of Greenberg's contribution to the television programmes associated with the Open University course, *Modern Art and Modernism*, A315; and his interview with T. H. Clark in *Art Monthly* (Greenberg 1984a, 1984b, 1984c).

that an art history which persists in ignoring the missing dimension of lived social relations is no longer as dominant as it was. I shall show that others have since developed his theoretical position, and that the context in which the artist and viewer are seen as class-related producers of meaning has been broadened to encompass consideration of other types of social stratification. In addition, the conventional category of 'art' has been scrutinised; and the implications of the new art history's theoretical stance for its own practice within the wider political scene have also been explored.

In 1973 (the year that 'The Conditions of Artistic Creation' appeared in the *Times Literary Supplement*) *Art History and Class Struggle* by Nicos Hadjinicolaou was published in France. It was available in English translation in 1978, and quickly became important to critical sociologists of art, for it was one of the very few contemporary works which examined systematically the implications of a Marxist approach to the production of visual art at a time when the new social approach to art history had yet to make an impact on adjacent disciplines.

Hadjinicolaou's is a historical materialist approach, and he takes as the starting point of his analysis Marx's statement that 'the history of all hitherto existing society is the history of class struggles' (Marx 1968: 35). The production of visual art works is therefore a class practice; it is an aspect of class struggle. Hadjinicolaou argues that the subject matter of the science (i.e. the historical materialist treatment) of art history is the history of the production of pictures in the context of class struggle. The concept of ideology is central to his subsequent analysis. Following Althusser (1984), ideology is taken to signify the imaginary relation between men and their conditions of existence. It is a system of representations (images, myths, ideas or concepts) through which men and women live their relation to their conditions of existence. So ideology is at once an allusion to the real world and an illusion of it. Hadjinicolaou distinguishes between those positive, dominant ideologies which support and reinforce the status quo, and critical ideologies which are more or less openly opposed to particular class practices or class ideologies.

It follows that pictures cannot be produced in an ideological vacuum; and Hadjinicolaou is particularly concerned with the ideological sphere relating to the production of pictures. He notes that traditionally 'art' and 'style' have been very closely linked. Indeed, he argues that style is considered as a kind of kernel which contains the essence of art, and in this sense, style would seem to be the subject matter of art history. Whilst most bourgeois art historians have an a-social conception of style, a minority do treat style as the outcome of society's ideas, expressed through the medium of the artist. Frederic Antal, indeed, argues that style always belongs to a class or a section of a class.[40] Hadjinicolaou accepts this notion of style, and then sustitutes the term 'visual ideology', which he defines as

40 In *Florentine Painting and its Social Background* (1948: 4).

A specific combination of the formal and thematic elements of a picture through which people express the way they relate their lives to the conditions of their existence, a combination which constitutes a particular form of the overall ideology of a social class.

(Hadjinicolaou 1978: 95–6)

'Visual ideology' is the central concept in *Art History and Class Struggle*, and Hadjinicolaou now proceeds to put it to work in his 'scientific' approach to art history. He argues that each class or layer or section of a class ought to have at each historical moment its own visual ideology, given the particular vision each has of itself, of other classes and of society in general. However, since the ideology of the ruling class has always been so powerful, he concludes that its visual ideologies have strongly permeated the visual ideologies of the dominated classes, and the latter may in practice have been greatly distorted. Indeed, he suspects that in certain periods, the dominated class never had a developed visual ideology of its own, and consequently did not produce visual art works at all. He suggests that if we speak of class struggle as the struggle of competing styles in the production of visual art works:

It must be recognised that *this 'struggle' takes place more often between the visual ideologies of layers or sections of the same class or of the ruling classes than between the visual ideologies of the ruling classes and the dominated classes.* [Author's emphases]

(Hadjinicolaou 1978: 102)

He thinks it is fair to suggest that the history of the production of pictures up to our own times is the history of ruling-class visual ideologies. Roger Taylor, in *Art, An Enemy of the People* (1978), also argues that art has largely been the concern of the ruling class, and while he concludes that the working class would consequently be well advised to have nothing to do with it, Hadjinicolaou, in the tradition of critical theorists, argues that certain visual art works do contain the potential to bring about political change.

This argument is based on his view of the relationship of visual ideology to knowledge. He claims that visual ideology, with its double aspect of comprehension–misapprehension and illusion–allusion to reality, can bear no relation to the scientific knowledge (i.e. the historical materialist analysis) of reality. Visual ideology and scientific knowledge are two distinct realities which do not coincide. However, in the sense that there are both positive and critical ideologies, there are also positive and critical visual ideologies. Whilst all collective visual ideologies are positive and apply to most visual art works, an individual picture which belongs to a collective positive visual ideology may at the same time manifest a critical visual ideology. Hadjinicolaou shows, for example in an analysis of Rembrandt's *Rape of Ganymede* (1635) and Hogarth's *Marriage à la Mode: I. Signing the Contract* (1745), that these are both paintings which, either by choice of subject matter or treatment of it, criticise contemporary ruling-class ideas and have disturbed bourgeois art historians, while at the same time each belongs to a collective positive visual ideology. He argues that by presenting both a dominant and a critical ideology on the same canvas, works such as these help viewers to glimpse the dominant ideology of the period in which they were painted, and to give us an understanding of the class struggles that were taking place at the time (cf. Clark's analysis of Courbet's *Burial at Ornans*). And our understanding – this experience – *does* constitute a kind of felt knowledge, but it requires the art historian's intervention to transform it into scientific knowledge.

Finally, Hadjinicolaou turns to the question of the relationship between visual ideology and aesthetic effect. He denies the existence of any 'independent' aesthetic effect, claiming that there is a correlation between the pleasure felt by the spectator on viewing a picture, and the picture's visual ideology: aesthetic effect is the pleasure felt by the observer when he recognises himself in a picture's visual ideology. And since that picture may contain different values, it may appeal to one person and not to another. Yet aesthetic judgments which evaluate works of art differently and which pronounce on their 'aesthetic effect' or 'beauty' always derive from the aesthetic ideologies of social groups. Aesthetics, *per se*, is doomed because it is a discipline without subject matter: '"What is beauty?" or "Why is this work beautiful?" must be replaced by the materialist question "By whom, when and for what reasons was this work thought beautiful?"' (Hadjinicolaou 1978: 183).

Clark would agree, yet at the same time, his dialectical approach seems by comparison to place less of a theoretical straitjacket on visual art works. This is because empirical analysis is an integral part of Clark's method: it reveals precisely how the production of a specific work of art, in all its various and surprising detail, becomes a series of actions in and also on history. By contrast, Hadjinicolaou's approach is deductive; the concept of 'ideology' entails that of 'visual ideology', and 'visual ideology' entails analysis of the formal and thematic elements of a picture. In this theorisation of visual art within an historical materialist framework, the art works themselves seem to recede as the strong theoretical framework is projected on to them.[41] And in fact, overall, the relationship of 'visual ideology' to 'style' does not seem to be very clear.[42] In addition, Hadjinicolaou's development of historical

41 One might argue that most texts which start out from a heavily theorised viewpoint tend to produce less compelling and vivid critical insights about visual art in society than those *based* in critical art practice or critical art history, because the latter are usually concerned with specific art works: and when close attention is not paid to the visual work, any sense of its potential *visual* power tends to recede.

42 This is perhaps because in analyses of individual pictures, Hadjinicolaou uses the term 'visual ideology' to refer variously to visual form (including colour), choice of subject matter, and the manner in which the artist treats the subject matter; and as a result, the sense of a clear link between visual ideology and what is generally understood by the style of a picture, even a socially rooted notion of style, becomes rather tenuous.

materialism does not adequately theorise the artist as active producer; even the producer of a painting which contains a critical visual ideology is virtually a socio-political construct. By comparison, the dialectical approaches of both Raphael and Adorno provide a fuller theoretical account of the critical artist's potential role, in which he struggles to distance himself from society and to produce art which is critical of it.

We should also consider the status of Hadjinicolaou's 'scientific' stance, which he is careful to differentiate from 'critical ideology'. Fairly recent developments in the sociology of scientific knowledge have shown that science, however this is defined, is not epistemologically privileged.[43] And historical materialism, whether associated with science or not, can no longer be regarded as guaranteeing the 'truth' about anything, even though it may be systematic in its approach. In the preface to the English edition of *Art History and Class Struggle* (1978), Hadjinicolaou notes that the book had already reached the printers when it was pointed out to him that he had used the male gender throughout. He comments that he was astonished to find this was correct:

> The fact that I have used instinctively the male gender when speaking of a profession where probably the majority of the people exercising it are women; the fact that I did this contrary to my conscious opinions; the fact that no one has noticed it up to now among those responsible for the publishing of the book in other languages, as well as this English edition, proves to what extent even so-called progressive people are victims of some very old and reactionary attitudes.
>
> (Hadjinicolaou 1978: 2)

However, he does not explore the implications of his comments. The fact that he now sees he has been a victim of 'some very old and reactionary attitudes' is tantamount to an admission that his theoretical stance is, after all, a type of ideological stance – though different in kind from those analysed in his book; and thus from the start his epistemological claims have been relativised. We are led to speculate that a class analysis of visual art, though important, might not constitute a sufficient critical treatment of the subject.

Three years after Hadjinicolaou's *Art History and Class Struggle* appeared in English translation, Janet Wolff published *The Social Production of Art* (1981).[44] In her introduction she says that she agrees with most of Hadjinicolaou's account of the history of art and of the ideological nature of

---

43 See, for example, Mulkay (1979).
44 She has now produced a second edition. This leaves the original text unaltered save for a ten-page Afterword, which reviews and restates the main issues raised in the book in the light of developments which have occurred since the publication of the first edition. In the Afterword to the second edition, Wolff states that she has not changed her mind on any of the main claims she originally made, and believes the book may still be useful as a review of some of the most important ways in which art is a social product. For this reason, I have not felt it necessary to modify my *own* discussion of *The Social Production of Art* which was prepared prior to the publication of the second edition. However, those interested in pursuing Wolff's arguments, as a result of reading my account, should, of course, turn to the second edition of her book.

painting, and will advance many of his arguments herself. In her opinion, historical materialism offers the best currently available (i.e. 1981) analysis of society, despite its omission of the analysis of sexual divisions and the oppression of women.[45]

However, Wolff's sociological treatment of art is rather different from Hadjinicolaou's. To start with, he is concerned specifically with the history of visual art, whereas she addresses the wider field of all the arts. And while Hadjinicolaou's work does not cite many other critical texts on the arts, Wolff's does the opposite: there is a large number of references and footnotes to other authors' theoretical contributions throughout the book. He works more or less deductively from basic Marxist premises while she tends to eclecticism. It is impressive to find such a wide grasp of the current theoretical state of play – especially in the areas of critical sociology and social philosophy. It is very useful to have hermeneutic theory, semiotics and the phenomenology of perception all compared on a particular issue, such as the active role of the cultural consumer. And although Wolff says that the book is not intended as a textbook, sociology of art students have found it useful. This is because various theories that they have assimilated elsewhere are here synthesised and assessed in relation to the arts. By the same token, because of the very number of theoretical strands that are woven into the basic framework, it would be quite impossible to give an overview of the book's contents which did justice to it. Peter Dormer, reviewing it in *Art Monthly*, says:

> The presentation of [her] views as an inevitable conclusion to a closely argued sociology of art is chimerical. . . . The sociology of art, as represented in this book, is little more than a bundle of conjectures that are interesting but unproven and tied together by footnotes and references.
>
> (Dormer 1982: 33–4)

This seems harsh, but her project does come over as an attempt to make a coherent job of weaving the various theoretical strands into an overall historical materialist framework; and consequently we seem to be viewing the arts through a long theoretical telescope, in which the specific features of *visual* art works, at any rate, seem distant (rather as they did in Hadjinicolaou's model), occluded by the mechanism of the telescope itself. I will briefly refer to the topics in the order in which she deals with them.

First, she argues that the notion of 'artistic creativity' as some kind of divine gift is a myth created by the Romantic movement, one of the consequences of the prominence that capitalism gives to the notion of individualism. Wolff emphasises that artists are not a special case. They are products of society just like everyone else, and should be seen in terms of the economic, social and cultural factors which direct individuals and determine their work. Indeed, 'any concept of "artistic creativity" which denies

---

45 Wolff has since written a good deal on women and the arts. For example, see her essay 'Postmodern Theory and Feminist Art Practice' (1990: 187–208).

this is metaphysical and cannot be sustained' (Wolff 1981: 9). Here she is arguing the classic sociological case against what sociologists believe is the taken-for-granted view of artists. But Dormer (see above) objects that no contemporary visual art practitioners and critics he knows believe in divine inspiration, and that she has set up a 'straw-stuffed artist person' in order to knock it down and make her case appear stronger. Sociology students may feel on familiar ground but art personnel evidently don't.

Wolff's second topic is the social production of art. Just as there is no justification for allowing the artist a special status, she argues that neither can we condone philosophies which maintain the autonomy and universal quality of works of art. She applauds 'recent critics' like Clark, who emphasise that the relation of art to ideology must be a central part of any analysis of works of art. A focus on social divisions and their economic bases has rendered the origin and reception of art works more comprehensible. But the corollary of this emphasis, she notes, is a curious lack of interest in institutional factors involved in the production of art, and in the actual processes through which art – and its ideology – are constructed. She refers specifically to such factors as the development of technology, patronage, recruitment and training of artists, and wider economic influences like the impact by multi-national capital on production and its costs. Critical art writers may have ignored institutional influences on the production of art, but this is not true of 'empirical' sociologists, for example Becker (1982). However, Wolff has grave reservations about such empiricist studies for she argues that, unlike historical materialist analyses, their political stance is not made explicit; it is naturalised, suppressed.

Wolff's third chapter is called 'Art as Ideology'. Her definition of ideology is 'deliberately agnostic', as opposed to the Althusserian inflection that Hadjinicolaou accords the term. For her, ideology consists of the ideas and beliefs people have, which are systematically related to their actual and material conditions of existence. She rejects the simplistic notion that an art work's 'ideology' reflects the economic base of the society in which it is produced. She is also dissatisfied with Lukács' and Goldmann's more so-phisticated versions of this idea: that there is a complex interrelationship between economic base and superstructure which includes the spheres of ideologies and aesthetics, but that, ultimately, the economic base determines the superstructure. This model is still uni-directional and therefore ultimately denies the possibility of any autonomy to the aesthetic sphere. Instead, and drawing on semiotic theory, Wolff focuses on the idea that aesthetic codes operate as mediating influences between ideology and particular works of art by interposing themselves as sets of rules and conventions which shape cultural products and which must be used by artists and cultural producers. So the novel or painting re-works current ideology in aesthetic form, in accordance with the rules and conventions of contemporary artistic pro-duction. This means that the ideological nature of art is mediated in two ways: through the material and social conditions in which works of art are produced, and through the existing aesthetic codes and conventions in which they are constructed. Drawing on recent research in this area, Wolff argues that the relationship of art to ideology has proved to be very complex; and she criticises John Berger's *Ways of Seeing* (1972) for putting forth a crude and oversimplified argument to the effect that painting is not innocent of political and economic considerations. However, she notes that 'This book's intervention into the discipline of art history has proved to be extremely critical and influential, and it has stimulated a good deal of more detailed analysis' (Wolff 1981: 56). This raises an important point. One of the reasons why Berger's book has proved so influential is because his writing is very sensitive to the specific art works which he allows to *inform* and *enrich* his theoretical position. In other words, his analysis does not 'pin down' art theoretically, as Wolff's sometimes seems to do: instead, art work and theory are dialectically linked. His own experience as a producer of visual art – one might almost say his artist's eye – helps him to analyse Gainsborough's *Mr and Mrs Andrews*, and to give a vivid, critical account of the ideological nature of this oil painting. As Panofsky remarked, quoting Flaubert: 'le bon Dieu est dans le détail' (Panofsky 1955: 1).

Pursuing further her discussion of the relationship of ideology to art, Wolff now focuses on the question of aesthetic autonomy and cultural politics. Although semiotic theory shows that art reworks ideology, using aesthetic codes and conventions, the question arises as to how these codes and conventions have come about. For example, are they independent of the economic base, and if so, how? She notes that in several ways the arts are susceptible to cross-cultural influences and not just to those from the economic sphere. And importantly, as we have seen, there has been a persistent belief on the part of certain artists, critics – and censors – in the transformative power of art. How does this belief in the autonomy of art square with the base/superstructure relationship, which is, after all, a crucial aspect of historical materialism? Wolff argues that if we regard the radical potential of art itself as being historically determined, then there is no contradiction between the view that art is socially and ideologically constructed, and the idea that artistic and cultural intervention in politics is a possibility. In order to theorise this position, she draws on Althusser's notion that the superstructure is relatively autonomous and has its own specific effectivity. Following Althusser, we can see that cultural production – as art on the level of ideology and of the superstructure – is relatively autonomous; that is, its codes and conventions can be more or less independent of economic determination, and in some cases can also be historically effective and a force for change. Wolff notes that certain cultural theorists, especially Adorno, Marcuse and Brecht, have emphasised that it is through the development of new artistic *forms* – rather than in the content of art works – that relative autonomy and thus the potential to transform society is attained. But she rightly emphasises that ultimately the debates about political content, or radical form, or subversion of codes, all centre on the question of audiences. How will they be affected, and who are they? The techniques and styles of cultural intervention are therefore closely related to the context and conditions of its occurrence. And the possibility for the reception of radical culture is itself determined by the economic base, and by the extent and type of autonomy accorded to general and aesthetic ideology by the stage of development of that society. Wolff argues for a populist rather than an elitist view of arts' relationship to its audience, for: 'It is "popular consciousness" which is essential to the stability of our present society, and which is also vital to any ideological change, from the recognition and rejection of sexism to the understanding of the class nature of society' (Wolff 1981: 92–3).

This leads her to a consideration of the *interpretations* that cultural consumers make, and to emphasise that they are actively involved in the construction of the work of art, in the sense of complementing and completing it. She stresses that we cannot think of the 'text' as having a fixed and objective meaning. But if this is so, and a 'correct', 'objective' interpretation is out of the question, is the author's interpretation in any way privileged? While deploring a psychologistic emphasis on the author as individual, and any project which attempts to recover a work's 'original meaning', Wolff argues that authorial meaning does indeed have some sort of priority over other readings because it historically informs the present reading of the text. However, she maintains that we need to go beyond interpretation; and that critical social science does this because it *explains* meanings and ideologies by examining them in the context of the specific historical socio-economic structure in which they occur. At the same time, she argues, critical sociology is reflexive, in the sense that it makes explicit its own assumptions and their social location, rather than hiding behind a false notion of value-freedom. As a result, there arises the possibility of a new kind of objectivity. I agree that the social analyst's standpoint should be reflexively sound and available for inspection, but whether historical materialism is superior to other perspectives in these respects is a matter for debate. However, Wolff is right to add that there is a general sense in which we can never get outside our own social position because we cannot get outside language. And she emphasises that there is always a dynamic interrelationship between writer, reader and text. But the polysemic nature of texts that this implies, along with the importance of the role of the reader, sits uneasily with the Marxist conception of the materialist basis of aesthetics, with its emphasis on production rather than reception. Wolff claims that the sociology of art cannot assume the priority of production over consumption, or vice versa: 'As Marx makes clear . . . production and consumption produce and determine each other in a number of ways' (Wolff 1981: 114–15).

Her final chapter, 'The Death of the Author' examines a series of theoretical positions in which the artist, or author, is increasingly marginalised.

Foucault, for example, shows that there is a problem in deciding exactly what, or who, an author is:

> Just as we have ways of determining which of an author's productions to include in his or her œuvre (drafts, marginalia, letters, or notes concerning domestic matters), so we also have ways of deciding which attributes or facts of the person's life to take as relevant to that person as author. In both cases, these practices are prescribed by the discourse of literary history.
>
> (Wolff 1981: 122)

Whilst Wolff cannot agree with Barthes that the author should be theorised out, she argues that the sociology of art must include a theory of the artist/subject where, *pace* Foucault, the subject is stripped of its creative role and analysed as a complex and variable function of discourse. In order to construct and clarify such a theory of the subject, she calls upon the more general approaches of Althusser and Lacan. Althusser claims that the idea that man has a subjective essence is a bourgeois myth. He argues that even before its birth a child is always already a subject; it is appointed as a subject in and by the specific familial ideological configuration in which it is 'expected', once it has been conceived. But by what mechanism is Althusser's 'subject' constituted by ideology? Here Wolff invokes Lacan's development of psychoanalytic theory: subjects are constituted in ideology via the child's subjection to language. Furthermore, because psychoanalysis divides the conscious from the unconscious, it can indicate how the erratic and devious presence of the unconscious insists on heterogeneity and contradictions within the (speaking) subject itself. Despite dissatisfaction with the reified status that Lacan accords to language and sign systems (how were they themselves constituted?), Wolff argues that his work, together with that of Althusser, begins to indicate how a satisfactory theory of the subject might be built up. And she maintains that a theory of the subject as agent must be an integral aspect of any sociology, including a sociology of art. For here, the author as constituted in language, ideology and social relations retain a central relevance.

The Social Production of Art is in many ways a theoretical *tour de force*. But to those, like Peter Dormer, who inhabit the world of art rather than the world of sociology, the book has a conception of art which does not seem very relevant. This entails some serious problems, one of which is Wolff's treatment of aesthetics. In both her introduction and conclusion, she admits that she does not know the answer to the problem of 'beauty' or of 'artistic merit', but does not believe they are reducible to social and political factors – as certain critical sociologies would have us believe. However, she argues that 'greatness', when perceived sociologically, becomes more analysable: 'The accredited judges of art and arbiters of taste are themselves socially defined and constituted, and bring to bear in their judgements specific ideological and positional values' (Wolff 1981: 139). Although this is true,

I would contend that it is no longer possible to say in general terms that art *is* about 'beauty' or 'artistic merit'. Nor would I assume that the task of constructing a satisfactory critical account should be presumed to lie solely with verbalisers (e.g. sociologists). The work of the verbal theorists examined in this chapter amounts to a strong case for the idea that visual artists can themselves produce critical work. (And although the art work's potential to transform society may itself be historically situated, by the same token, so is Wolff's own account.) Visual art is not a static and cordoned-off entity whose artefacts await either 'appreciation' or critical analysis by verbalisers like sociologists. Some of the most interesting visual art work today constitutes an 'internal' critique of the concept of aesthetic beauty. It may, for example, satirise 'bourgeois' art styles by parodying them.[46] In so doing, such works critique capitalist aesthetics, and thereby contribute to a wider critique of bourgeois society. But they also demand to be judged *as* art works because in subverting bourgeois aesthetic codes, they are at the same time *using* and *developing* alternative codes. Critical art practice therefore forces a different kind of relationship between itself and verbally based disciplines such as sociology; one in which the two are, in a broad sense, working together on a common project of critical analysis. (And in this context, I would agree with Lyotard (1984: 30) that the verbal theorist has a lot to learn from the visual artist.) This means that it is rather misleading to say, as Wolff does in her conclusion, that the relative value of different works is determined within the discourse of art and aesthetics, and is not amenable to appropriation by a different discourse (sociology). The two spheres are not entirely separate: much critical art practice is now informed by sociology, among other disciplines, just as sociologists are themselves experimenting with 'new literary forms'.[47] The very term 'cultural production', which Wolff favours, helps us to conceptualise this merging process. And in any case, recent work in the sociology of scientific knowledge which shows that sociology – among other things – influences the content of scientific knowledge, makes it seem implausible that 'aesthetic value', whatever that is taken to mean, should still remain a special case.

'Les Données Bretonnantes: La Prairie de la Representation' by Fred Orton and Griselda Pollock (1982: 285–304) demonstrates the type of alternative art-historical approach demanded by Clark in 'The Conditions of Artistic Creation'. But whereas in the latter, Clark's criticism was levelled in a general sense at Courtauld-type 'bourgeois' art history, Orton and Pollock clearly state that *modernist* art history is the object of their critique. 'Les Données Bretonnantes', then, sets out to oppose a more precisely defined body of theory. However, in the introduction to *Modern Art and Modernism:*

---

46 For example, the work of Terry Atkinson shown in the exhibition, *Approaches to Realism* (1990).
47 See Chapter 6.

A Critical Anthology (1982) – in which this article is published – its editors say:

> One issue which does seem to distinguish Modernist theories from those critical texts and methods which we have grouped under the heading of 'Art and Society' is that the issue of the class character of culture is seen as crucial in the latter, while it is generally not raised at all in the former.
>
> (Frascina and Harrison 1982: 2)

This suggests, then, that in common to both 'The Conditions of Artistic Creation' and 'Les Données Bretonnantes' is a concern with the class character of culture, and an opposition to depoliticised art history.

In their article, Orton and Pollock claim that the modernist art history espoused by the art establishment in the early 1980s offered a developmental, unilinear progression, an illusion of continuity. The article is in part a scathing attack on this ideology and in part a demonstration of the authors' alternative approach to art history; and these two aspects are intertwined in a fairly aggressive and at times emotionally charged piece of scholarship. The authors are deeply critical of the establishment's continued use of the term 'Post-Impressionism' to characterise the work of the artists Van Gogh, Gauguin, Seurat and Cézanne. They note that the term was originally coined by Roger Fry in 1910, was revived by John Rewald in the 1950s, and is pressed into service again by Alan Bowness in his introductory catalogue essay for the exhibition of *Post-Impressionism: Cross-Currents in European Painting* (1979–80). They say that initially the term 'Post-Impressionism', as used in modernist art-historical discourse, indicated 'a reaction against that which preceded it, a reaction which instantly fragmented into various competing and disparate alternatives' (Orton and Pollock 1982: 285). The authors ask why the term 'Post-Impressionism' is still used in this sense when it is admitted by those who use it to be both vague as a label and useless as a categorising device. They claim that deploying the term has enabled modernist art historians to evade the 'intricate network of visual and textual discourses and representations in specifiable and changing historical conditions' (Orton and Pollock, 1982: 287). Instead, a movement has been conjured up – an art-historically coherent entity – in which the works of these four artists are presented in terms of 'mythologies of magical creativity and mythic genius' (Orton and Pollock, 1982: 287).

In the first section of 'Les Données Bretonnantes', then, the authors accuse the Royal Academy exhibition organisers in general terms of grossly simplifying and distorting historical complexities in their treatment of the paintings of Van Gogh, Gauguin, Seurat and Cézanne. Orton and Pollock then seek to empirically reconstruct that complexity in order to justify those accusations. They take as their starting point a reference in the Royal Academy Exhibition Guide to what its organisers term 'an interlude in the exhibition' (Orton and Pollock 1982: 288) where paintings on the theme of 'the French province of Brittany' (Orton and Pollock 1982: 288) are shown. Orton and Pollock set themselves the task of revealing just how much this bland categorisation of the 'Brittany paintings' conceals. Following Clark, they begin by asking the kinds of questions entailed by a *social* history of art. What were the works made for? Whom were they made for? To do what kind of job? What do they mean? Do they achieve meaning? How were they understood by their producers, their first viewers, their first public? Asking these questions leads them to explore the ways in which the land-use and therefore the landscape of Brittany altered during the nineteenth century, in the context of the changing economic and social geography in France and beyond. They show how these changes affected the various perceptions of Brittany which were held by its natives, by city dwellers, by urban tourists, by each of the artists and in relation to their knowledge of each other's work, and by the audiences for whom the works were probably intended. In this way, they painstakingly reconstruct the subject matter of each of the paintings they discuss in the light of the complex set of alternative meanings which those works must have attracted when they were first shown. Like Clark, in his analysis of Courbet's *Burial at Ornans*, Orton and Pollock draw on a wide range of contemporary documents. And in a broader sense, they also work dialectically; alternating between a detailed empirical study of the local situation and an examination of the wider structural changes taking place at the time, allowing each of these dimensions to inform and modify the other with regard to their specific art historical problem. This method enables them to *demonstrate* that 'in the "Literature of Art" these complex social realities are absented, and modernist art history is built upon and structured by that evasion' (Orton and Pollock 1982: 302).

'Les Données Bretonnantes' is polemically charged. Its militaristic vocabulary and dense, concept-crowded prose themselves constitute an effective strategy in its authors' assault upon the simplifications and the distortions which modernist art history is shown to produce. Indeed, the belief that this tradition has promoted a whole series of devious intellectual exercises permeates the article.

An art movement or style which is associated with revolution by 'the people' against political authority holds a very particular kind of fascination for the critical art writer. 'Art and Politics in a Workers' State' by Paul Wood (1985: 105–24) is a review of Christina Lodder's (1983) *Russian Constructivism*; and Wood's evident fascination with the period of the Russian Revolution helps to fuel this powerful text. It is reminiscent, in some ways, of Clark's treatment of art and revolution in mid-nineteenth-century France; but 'Art and Politics in a Workers' State' has its own distinctive contribution to make to the growing corpus of critical art-historical texts. I shall show that Wood's general methodology brings 'the new art history' closer to the approach, if not the interests, of some of the empirical sociologists whose work is discussed in the second half of this book.

While applauding Lodder's very extensive researches, Wood argues that in one important sense her account does not differ from previous art historical accounts of Russian Constructivism, all of which were intent on prising Constructivist art away from its political context in order to annexe it for American or Western modernism. He argues, like Wolff, that to treat the political as contingent upon a primary and inviolate 'art' will not do. For 'bricks cannot be made without straw and art cannot be made without social relations' (Wood 1985: 109). However, the broadly socio-philosophical metatheory underpinning Wolff's text does not allow her to extend her sociological critique into the realms of aesthetic experience and aesthetic evaluation. But Wood's text, which is underpinned by a Marxist *historical* approach, argues that the most satisfactory account of Russian Constructivism is achieved by drawing on the most recent and informed accounts of the economic and political context in which Constructivist art was produced and received; and this approach consequently may entail a critique of bourgeois aesthetics. However, for Wood such an approach does not deny a *relatively autonomous* status for art. He points out that the quality and meaning of an art object are not fixed by the political context in which it is produced: if a political regime fails, as happened in Russia in the early 1920s, for example, or if artists fail to understand the philosophy of the regime, it does not follow that the objects they produce are useless or meaningless. What is important is that they were made under the philosphical, social, political, economic demands of that regime. And since any given ideological position will generate projects ranging from the exceptional to the ordinary, discussions about form, and formal analysis, become crucial. What is important to the social art historian is that such discussions will have originally taken place within a cultural discourse in which the works refer to, or perhaps, by extension, 'represent' that discourse.

Like Orton and Pollock, Wood engages in the critical analysis of *texts*; in this case, previous art-historical accounts of Russian Constructivism. However, what is notable about his approach is that it shows that bourgeois accounts of Russian Constructivism, by the very way they are textually constructed, are ideologically permeated so that they tend to appear inevitable, natural, self-evidently right. As a result, they may avoid having to *argue* a case, and thus avoid having their arguments refuted. Sentence construction is vital, for key terms can be situated in verbal contexts that naturalise them and render them static. Choice of terminology is crucial: terms such as 'the masses', 'sensibility', 'regime', 'avant-garde', 'artists', even 'art historians' already have taken-for-granted meanings which can be utilised to reinforce a modernist account of Constructivism; while others – 'artistic climate', for example – have their own built-in suggestion of naturalism. Wood argues that the ultimate purpose of these textual strategies which service bourgeois art-historical accounts is to put Constructivism 'at point X on the curve of modern art' (Wood 1985: 106).

Empirical sociologists of scientific knowledge (SSK) analyse formal scientific research reports in order to reveal the textual devices which authors routinely use to convince readers of the objective status of their scientific 'findings'. But empirical sociology is *relativist*, in the sense that it seeks to show how textual devices shape the meaning of *any* scientific text.[48] Wood's approach is historical and critically selective; his target is more precise. He wants to show how the textual *strategies* (rather than devices) deployed in 'bourgeois' art-historical accounts generate an *incorrect* account of the art in question. He cites an article by John Bowlt (1984) which refers to a multiplicity of art styles in Russia during the 1920s. Wood argues that Bowlt's use of the plurality thesis (many art styles during one political regime) is a strategy which makes the relationship between politics and art seem contingent; and that this therefore has the effect of strengthening and generally reinforcing the bourgeois notion of artistic autonomy. It seems that for Wood there can be a *true* account (and certain histories of the period such as Nigel Harris's 'Mao and Marx' (1976) are accorded special status); whereas for empirical sociologists there is no true or right account, but rather a plurality of socially constructed accounts.

These two approaches are also concerned with the problem of whether a body of knowledge has an *internal*, immanent development or whether, on the other hand, it is inevitably influenced by and bound up with *external*, contingent factors. Wood is uneasy with Lodder's tendency to perpetuate the division between the internal development of Constructivism and the external (political and economic) influences on it; and he seeks to show that external influences have a fundamental effect on the social production of the art work itself. For, as he argues: 'The fact that social relations of production are transformed in Russia in the revolution means that "the meaning" of practices and products is changed too' (Wood 1985: 109). Nevertheless, he retains these two categories; for example, he does not criticise Lodder's remark that Rodchenko's work, by 1920, had produced *within the logic of formal investigation* an ideological standpoint which became central to utilitarian Constructivist work. Rather than reject a differentiation between internal and external determinants, Wood posits a dialectic between them: 'Politics doubtless cannot explain art, but then neither can art explain itself alone' (Wood 1985: 109). By so doing, that is by the use of a strategy of his own, he can retain the notion of 'internal development', and consequently the relative autonomy of art. SSKers, who seek to deny any special *epistemological* status for scientific knowledge, have abolished the distinction between internal development and external influence because case studies have convinced them that it is quite untenable.[49]

However, their methodology also shares Wood's concern with 'the facts'. Wood applauds Lodder for unearthing so many new ones. The old-style

48 See, for example, Gilbert and Mulkay (1984: 39–62 and 63–89).
49 See Holton (1988), and Mulkay (op. cit.).

positivist social scientists collected facts; indeed, one reason why they never used the term ideology (which is centrally important to Wood) was because they argued that scientific objectivity obtained at all times and in all places: it was outside history. Ideology is still irrelevant to the post-positivist sociologist who continues to operate within an a-historical framework, yet s/he would now argue that the 'facts' themselves are socially contingent and impregnated with theory: at the very least, they have to be noticed from a mass of other 'facts', selected by the researcher as worthy of note, and then extracted and strung together by way of textual devices, or strategies. This problematises the empirical status of the fact. SSKers would not support Wood's apparent belief that facts have a clear existence apart from the context in which they are textually deployed.

The parallels and divergences between Wood's approach and that of SSKers are intriguing to map out. However, we should treat Wood's text first and foremost as a demonstration of the fact that built into bourgeois histories of Constructivist art are textual strategies which convey the impression that art is autonomous and that Constructivist art forms part of the immanent development of modernism. While his historical researches enable him to show that Constructivist art cannot be separated from the complex political and economic context in which it was produced, and that what previous accounts have left out demands investigation and explanation, his deconstructions of bourgeois accounts of Constructivism indicate that the latter have distorted the political context in which that art was produced. This suggests that one purpose of *all* historical accounts including Wood's – is to get 'the story' told in such a way that it serves specific ideological ends; and that this is routinely achieved by the use of textual strategies.

Wood's own text operates on several levels. First, it offers a general method for critical art historians: textual analysis will reveal the strategies by which previous bourgeois art-historical accounts have annexed art for an autonomous 'aesthetic' realm. A critical history of art, on the other hand, will be informed by critical histories of the political and economic contexts in which art is produced. It will show how these overlapping contexts determine what art is produced but do not dictate its value as art. On a second level Wood is sketching out the history of Russian Constructivism. He is trying to find out, in as much detail as possible, what the period of political and economic transition from capitalism to socialism in Russia in the 1920s was like – in all its muddle and complexity, experimentation and revision. He wants to examine the different and changing relationships of the individual Constructivist artists to the turmoil of events which took place during that period, and to understand how these affected their lives and work. But at the same time, Wood's own Marxist political stance shapes his task of critiquing bourgeois textual strategies, and directs the construction of the 'right' history of Russian Constructivism: 'It is not possible to understand what happened to these artists without understanding what happened to their revolution; and neither a watered-down stalinism nor an academic liberalism provides the equipment for that' (Wood 1985: 118). He ends by noting that Rodchenko wrote home from Paris: 'One is either a capitalist or a communist. There is no third way' (Wood 1985: 122). Wood asserts – in 1985 – that this is still true. Now it is important, as Wolff has argued, that the analyst reveal his/her own political stance, for this provides the basis on which arguments – available for inspection by others – can be built. However, the demise of socialism in Eastern Europe makes a rethinking of this particular 'either/or' stance imperative.

In 'Art History and Difference', John Tagg (1986) casts a critical eye over the ways in which the new social art history has changed and developed during its first ten years. He observes that in 1974, Clark's was a central unified project. This intervention into the discipline of art history was informed by a conjunction of Marxism and art history. But Tagg argues that it has since become clear that a single methodological solution to all art history's ills does not follow from this. For class analysis has been developed to include (indeed in some cases it has been replaced by) analyses reflecting the interests of other oppressed groups of people, notably women. Opening up the field in this way has shown how complex it is, and in Tagg's opinion there is a danger of underestimating the problem of categorising different critical analyses together.

He also considers the object of study of the new art history. He comments that many social art historians are conservative in that they still tend to think that their object of study consists of discrete artefacts, whereas it is, in fact, the *relations* between particular cultural products, particular meanings and particular conditions of existence. It follows that we should not be asking what an object expresses: instead, we should be investigating its effect, in terms of these relations.

Tagg's main argument is that the new art history cannot really become effective as critique until it has wrought a radical change in its *own* relationship to the existing system of education, and to the wider political structure of British society. He observes that it has remained almost entirely within the university campus, and has made no effective links with other cultural bodies such as the National Trust, leisure services and school teaching; with the result that when financial cuts were made in the universities, new art historians were axed, leaving just fewer of them in place: a so-called radical movement has simply grafted itself on to an existing network, and when times are lean it pays the price. Tagg argues that if this movement is to be politically effective, it must know 'how it is touched by and touches in turn this dispersed structure of governance' (Tagg 1986: 171) so that it can effect new relations and thereby attempt to establish a firmer hold. Political critique does not end at the lecture-room door: the problem of where to practice is as pressing as the problem of methodology.

This historical survey of accounts which offer critical analyses in relation to visual art, and of 'conventional' art-historical approaches, constitutes the first part of the story of 'sociology and visual representation' from within the critical paradigm. The accounts I have discussed are all distinguished by the fact that analysis is *verbal*, and the object of that analysis, either directly or indirectly, is visual *art*. The critical accounts are *class* analyses. In Chapter 2, I show how photography (and critical accounts relating to it), semiotic theory and feminism have each played a part in altering the relationship between sociological understanding and visual representation.

Chapter 2

From written, class analyses of visual art to the use of visual representation in critique

Principal works discussed:

John Tagg, *The Burden of Representation: Essays on Photographies and Histories*, 1988
(Contributions to semiotic theory.)
Griselda Pollock, *Vision and Difference: Femininity, Feminism and the Histories of Art*, 1988
Victor Burgin, *Between*, 1986a

INTRODUCTION

Before 1970 very few critical analyses of visual representations were made outside the realm of visual art. But that situation subsequently began to change. Photography and film have played a major part both in broadening the visual field available for analysis and in shaping recent critical approaches to visual representation. For nearly a hundred years the relationship of photography to visual art was hotly debated, and while photography has now become accepted as a flexible medium which acquires a different cultural status according to the context in which it is shown, the effect of this shifting cultural status has been that photographers partake of several worlds, whilst those who write about photographs and photography are also well placed to cross cultural boundaries. So photography tends to disturb the distinction between 'visual art' and other social categories of visual representation; but so does the politicised concept of culture itself, for this treats both 'photography as reportage' and 'fine art photography', for example, as cultural production. Semiotic theory also tends to blur the boundary between art and 'non-art', since it focuses on communication as a social process, and treats visual art as one form of communication. Rather than rehearsing old debates about what visual representations count as art, semiotic theory explores how communication works at the visual level.

While 'non-art' visual representations, particularly media images, are now subjected to critical analysis,[1] and the boundary between visual art and 'non-art' visual representation is sometimes blurred, the concept of critical analysis has itself undergone changes. Critical analysis used to be virtually synonymous with written, class analysis. But class analysis of visual art has largely been superseded by an analysis based on gender inequalities, and on the relations of gender divisions to other forms of social inequality, including class. And the situation in which the verbal analysed the visual is shifting too. While Raphael and Hadjinicolaou, for example, do identify specific critical visual art works, these works appear to have been few and far between. However, some visual artists now produce work which is informed by the class analyses of Gramsci, Althusser, Adorno and Raphael,[2] but more have been influenced by the politicising of the term 'culture'; for the concept of cultural struggle implies that there are many dimensions of social inequality, and that power relations are not necessarily synonymous with class relations. It also implies that no area of cultural production, whether verbal or visual, is innocent of the play of power relations. An understanding of this situation has encouraged feminist artists – or feminist cultural producers as some prefer to be called – to expose the patriarchal ideology which permeates much of our visual imagery by creating works which subject examples of such imagery to feminist visual critique. And here we have a situation where 'critique' involves neither written analysis nor class analysis; nor does it necessarily entail a distinct category of visual art. In addition, the semiotic perspective indicates that many effective communications have both visual and verbal components (advertisements, for example), that these components interlace, and that the *manner* in which they do so is crucially important to the meaning of a communication, and therefore to its effect. This suggests that there is considerable scope for a scripto-visual critical practice.[3]

In sum, 'critical works' no longer necessarily address class inequality; and they may include a visual component, or be entirely visual, thereby abolishing the distinction between the verbal as critique and the visual as object critiqued. Where those critical works involve photographs, they may also position themselves in a critical relationship to the concept of art. This chapter examines the contributions that have been made by photography and writing about photography, semiotic theory, and feminist art theory and practice to this situation in which critical analysis of visual representation can no longer be taken to mean written class analysis of visual art works. The chapter ends with an examination of Victor Burgin's *Between* (1986a), whose critical statements often combine visual and verbal representation. Throughout,

---

1 Judith Williamson's class analysis, *Decoding Advertisements: Ideology and Meaning in Advertising* (1978) was a pioneering work in this respect. It has been widely influential.
2 Including several British Systematic Constructive artists.
3 John Heartfield's photomontage is an early example of critical work which incorporates and juxtaposes visual and verbal representation; see Evans and Gohl (1986: 39–69).

I speculate upon the implications for critical sociology of the developments which are described above and are investigated in more detail below.

The Burden of Representation: Essays on Photographies and Histories is a collection of essays by John Tagg (1988), written between 1979 and 1988. Tagg taught the social history of art at Leeds University from 1979 until 1984, but these essays are concerned with the medium of photography rather than with the cultural institution of art; and Tagg notes that the essays were originally presented in spaces pointedly 'outside' the discipline of art history. Yet at the same time they are a response to it, and especially to Clark's innovatory attempt to synthesise historical analyses with his readings of French Marxism, semiotics and psychoanalysis. Indeed, Tagg shares with Clark

> the central belief that the problems of art history were at root *methodological* and that what the subject needed was 'theory', something which could only be imagined as coming from outside – outside the discipline and even, in Britain at least, outside what was thought to compose the national intellectual culture.
>
> (Tagg 1988: 22)

In Chapter 1, I examined some of the contributions that Orton, Pollock and Wood have made to the critique of bourgeois art-historical accounts and to the methodology of the new art history. In a sense, Tagg continues this project in *The Burden of Representation*, but he does so from outside the boundary surrounding the cultural institution of art. He is an insider-turned-outsider, as it were, and this enables him to discard what he claims both bourgeois and social art historians still hang on to, which is a reductive, expressive model of art history, in which a focus on the development of a history of art, as such, is usually taken for granted. While this model is scrutinised in Paul Wood's 'Art and Politics in a Workers' State', it is not discarded, for Wood's central concern is still the history of Constructivist art. Tagg is not interested in a history *of* photography-as-art, nor indeed in a history of the medium of photography. Instead, he theorises photography as a function of the history of power relations. And *this* history, as he says, is not a smooth one, although it is a continuous history.

So a central issue for Tagg is unequal relations of power: the struggle for power between oppositional social groupings within a general cultural context. From this viewpoint, certain forms and relations of power are brought to bear on practices of representation, or constitute their conditions of existence. And, in turn, these representational practices also come to engender power effects, producing an interlacing of power fields, patterns of interference. In this sense, Tagg treats cultural representations, such as photographs, as the manifestation of knowledge which is the outcome of power; and thus photographs cannot be regarded as windows on the world, or as records of something 'out there'. Indeed, Tagg argues that the existence of the photograph is no guarantee of a corresponding pre-photographic existent:

At every stage, chance effects, purposeful interventions, choices and variations produce meaning, whatever skill is applied and whatever division of labour the process is subject to. . . . The photograph is not a magical 'emanation' but a material product of a material apparatus set to work in specific contexts, by specific forces, for more or less defined purposes. It requires, therefore, a history, outside which the existential essence of photography is empty. We work with the material reality, the print, paper.

(Tagg 1988: 3)

Yet the image that the material product bears is part of the discursive system that makes the material product meaningful, and this discursive system is also real. Thus it is that we need to ask what practices and institutions give photographs meaning, exercise an effect on them, and cause them in turn to contribute – as the manifestation of knowledge – to the formation of subsequent events. For example, how is it that via a social semiotic process photographs have come to stand as evidence in court?

Tagg addresses this particular question in his fourth essay, 'A Legal Reality: The Photograph as Property in Law'. He argues that we must turn to the history of the development of systems of control, and scrutinise court procedure and legal processes in Britain compared with those in France during the late nineteenth century. For the very idea of what constitutes evidence has a history. It is a history which implies definite techniques and procedures, concrete institutions, and specific social relations – that is, relations of power. And it is into this more extensive field that we must insert the history of photographic evidence. During the course of the nineteenth and early twentieth centuries in Britain, bureaucracy, record-keeping, law-making and professionalisation were increasingly used by a small minority to impose control on the vast mass of the rest; and Tagg shows that the development of photography and of these new forms of power and the new knowledges they yielded could not, on a profound level, be separated. Instrumental photography was caught up with the more general and dispersed transformations in society, and therefore with ways of thinking about it, representing it, and seeking to act on it. The negotiation of the photograph's status as evidence and record, and the development and establishment of that status, were bound up with a shift in the regime of power and the regime of sense. Each of the essays in *The Burden of Representation* focuses on a time and a context in which photography and photographs played a crucial part in the development of systems of control, and shows that at certain conjunctures, and as part of a complex historical process, photographs came to exercise real effects of power. And throughout, Tagg stresses that the ideal of a 'history of photography', or more specifically, of a continuous 'documentary tradition', which takes the status of photographic evidence as neutral and given, virtually obliterates this fact.

Because his analyses problematise the apparent naturalness of predefined categories such as 'the history of photography' and 'documentary photography', and cut relentlessly yet meticulously across the grain of what is taken for granted, we have much to learn from their contribution to sociology. To these analyses Tagg also brings a trained art historian's sensitivity, as it were, to visual images: for his written analyses of photographs are penetrating and enlightening.[4] This is particularly evident in his sixth essay, 'The Currency of the Photograph: New Deal Reformism', where he discusses two photographs: *Union Point, Georgia*, 1941, by Jack Delano, and *Hidalgo County, Texas*, 1939, by Russell Lee. The approach in this, the earliest of the essays, is strongly reminiscent of the dialectical method of Max Raphael, whose work Tagg has done so much to expound and promote. First, he invites us to examine the two images. Then he describes them. Each depicts a man and woman sitting together looking at books in their living room: 'representations of two interiors, two groups of people, two collections of furniture and ornaments' (Tagg 1988: 158). He notes differences between the images, but argues that in common to them are the concepts of *family* and *home*. At this point, he switches to the level of ideology and a discussion of how ideology works to convince us of the naturalness of photographs, of the possibility of 'straight photography'. He observes the 'double movement' within ideological discourse: ideology leads us to see the image as 'family', while our acceptance of this ideological conception leads us to see these 'families' as participating in universal truths. But this is the *effect* of ideology: its contradictions are concealed. When we look again at the photographic images, in the light of this understanding of the effect of ideology, we search for *differences* between these 'families', and find that one image indicates a 'comfortable room' and the other shows a 'sparsely furnished room'. In other words, there appears to be a difference of class; and we can now see that our original view of the sparsely equipped family had been formed through the hegemonic influence of the other image. Back at the global level now, photographs are evidently objects of manipulation; and Tagg notes that they exert a power to colonise new experiences and capture subjects across a range never envisaged in painting. Taking these ideas back to the two photographic images, Tagg then notes how the difference of eye-level between the two photographs changes our relation to the subjects and alters the meaning of the apparently identical images. He says that to make an analysis at this level is exactly to observe what Foucault calls the 'capillary form' of the existence of power.

> What I am trying to stress here is the absolute continuity of the photographs' ideological existence with their existence as material objects whose 'currency' and 'value' arise in certain distinct and historically specific social practices and are ultimately a function of the state.
>
> (Tagg 1988: 165)

And his analysis continues dialectically on towards its conclusion.

---

4 Rather in the same way that Berger's detailed analyses of visual images in *Ways of Seeing* (1972) are so compelling.

We have seen that Tagg operates outside the social history of art; and although, like the social historians, he undertakes detailed empirical studies of visual representations, these studies focus on the historical conjunctures where photography and power relations meet, since he theorises photography as a function of the history of power relations. The more recent of the essays included in *The Burden of Representation* demonstrate another major difference from the work of Clark, Orton, Pollock, and Wood that I examined in Chapter 1. For here, Tagg discards grand narratives, overarching theories. While emphasising the centrality of power relations, he rejects such theories because he thinks that, by their very nature, they cannot encompass and represent the extraordinary subtlety, unexpectedness and uniqueness of power relations as they operate and are experienced in real-life situations: grand theories simplify and ultimately distort these essentially unique situations and the complex yet specific sets of power relations entailed in each one. Indeed, he argues that the critical historian who uses such a theory is actually trapped within its presuppositional framework, and, ironically, cannot escape from its grip to act freely, to make an effective critique. And to put critical knowledge to *work* is Tagg's ultimate aim. So from this perspective there are no pre-set 'problems of aesthetics', for example, because there is no grand narrative framework to pose such 'problems' in advance for the empirical investigator. Lastly, Tagg criticises grand theories for being reflexively unsound: for being unable to explain satisfactorily their own privileged standpoint in relation to those ideologies which they critique.

Tagg's own empirical analyses which correspond with this theoretical stance are constantly informed by discussion of the wider political spectrum, but now he does not make global generalisations from his localised conclusions. However, he argues that where and when he does locate the operation of power resulting from the use of the knowledge that photography brings to those who control it, such an analysis will be highly specific and accurate; and this therefore constitutes a sound basis from which to attempt to reverse the flow of power which the analysis has uncovered. This process of reversal, which is entailed in the act of analysis, involves active intellectual labour on a broad front; for Tagg claims (as he did in 'Art History and Difference', 1986) that it is the task of today's intellectuals to disperse rather than to shelter in a university department, with its sanctioning of one grand theory or another. Intellectuals should not take for granted that they will operate from positions within the existing structure of academe. He argues that the importance of working in areas of tourism and leisure consumption, for example, should not be underestimated; for it is in such areas that the dominant art history tends to be encountered and absorbed. Thus, the critical analyst should consciously aim to situate him or herself in one or other of those paid employment posts which promote 'our culture'. From an implicated internal position, she or he should set about uncovering and charting those minute processes in which relations of power gradually and unobtrusively change, and should act to reverse the flow of cultural power, in the knowledge that his or her activities are linked to those of others who also share an interest in analysing and reversing dominant power relations in our culture.

We have seen how the photograph can be used to reinforce the power that officials wield over a political minority group; for example, a 'mugshot' identifies and thus contributes towards the conviction and subsequent control of a prisoner. If photographs can affect power relations in this way and be affected by them, we should ask how the knowledge of these processes that we have now gained from reading Tagg's account of them can be used in the construction of critique. Tagg seems to suggest that critique involves verbal analysis and 'action in the field'. But can the power of photographs themselves be harnessed to work for intellectuals/critics in the field? Advertisers routinely use a *combination* of visual image (usually photographic) and verbal text to persuade us to consume what is produced in capitalist society. Can we not turn the tables and put a reverse strategy into operation, in which image and words are combined in a critical analysis *of* capitalism?[5] This might make for a more effective critique than one which used words alone, since – following Tagg's analysis of the two images above – the photograph is so successful at covert persuasion. And although the ideology that presents photographs as windows on the world or as records of something 'out there' may be pervasive, Tagg has shown that, like other forms of visual image such as drawings and paintings, photographs are cultural *representations*. While 'representation' implies that images and texts refashion their sources, articulating pictorial or textual codes and the social practices and forces which underlie them, it also implies communication. It is to the theory of the communication of visual and verbal representation that I now turn.

SEMIOTICS AND DISCOURSE

In this section I use the theoretical framework provided by semiotics to explore and compare the ways in which sociology texts and visual art works communicate both visually and verbally. This is followed by a consideration of the political implications of literary and of pictorial communication. And finally, I outline a concept of critique which, informed by those two dis-

---

5 In an article in the *Guardian*, 16 March 1992, entitled 'The Medium is the Massage', Hugo Young quotes Robert Worcester of *Mori Poll* as saying: 'The main message that TV news gets across in an election is visual. The things that stick in people's minds are what they saw and not what they heard.'

Later in the same article, Young notes that words alone, the stuff of rational arguments, are not so devastatingly neglected in TV coverage of British election campaigns as they are on US television. He quotes a Harvard University study as saying that, in the USA, words are on course for terminal disappearance from the news.

cussions, brings the discourses of sociology and visual art close together.[6]
The content of this section links in one way or another with the topics of
previous and subsequent sections: with the medium of photography which
concerns both discourses since its codes are predominantly pictorial and it
forms part of the history of power relations; with feminist art theory/practice,
much of which is informed by semiotic theory, and where a combination of
image and text is routinely used; and finally with the work of Victor Burgin
in *Between* (1986a), which most closely corresponds with the concept of
critique that I shall shortly outline. But the order in which the sections in this
chapter are placed is not meant to suggest a progression or even a linear
sequence. Rather, the central topics of each are like a series of overlapping
snapshots: they represent linked facets of a larger project whose aims are to
identify and further encourage a trend towards the use of visual representation in critical practice/sociological understanding; a trend rooted in
cultural theory.

John A. Walker (1979) argues that the discourse of visual art has developed in two fundamentally different directions. Certain painters and
critics, following Clement Greenberg (1986), have sought to establish
painting's specificity as a medium by emphasising its unique characteristics
at the expense of those that it shares with other media. This emphasis implies
that a painting's meaning is generated by its formal elements, and is therefore
contained and is entirely locatable 'within' the work. Hence, the respondent,
or viewer, is reduced to a pair of eyes, and the work's meaning is divorced
from social processes. However, Walker notes that a quite different stance is
taken by cultural theorists who use semiotic theory to stress the iconic,
representational character of a 'picture', rather than the process and material
basis of the art of painting. From this second position, which has very
different social implications from the first, the viewer interprets the picture
by means of the semiotic principles which inform all our acts of communication; and the work forms part of the total signifying system of society, and
thus contributes to broader cultural patterns. It is clear that a sociology text
can also be viewed as a representation of reality which communicates to its
readers via semiotic codes, and contributes to society's cultural patterns. In
this sense, both sociology and visual art are cultural discourses. Nevertheless, there are seemingly obvious differences between the two areas. For
one thing, visual art is visual – and Walker refers to the iconic character of a
picture – whereas sociology is predominantly verbal. Second, visual art is an
art, whereas sociology is not. I will explore these similarities and differences
with the ultimate aim of constructing a critique which draws these two
discourses together.

---

6 By 'discourse' is meant an array of related statements, produced under definite social and
historical conditions, which define a field of knowledge, e.g. psychiatry, art criticism,
theoretical physics. It is used in the Foucauldian sense in which ideas never form or function
in isolation from institutions and relations of *power*.

First, let us look at the idea that visual art is 'visual' and sociology is 'verbal'. Although a sociological text is in substance verbal, its layout and typography draw on a *visual* repertoire. In other words, the text is visually coded; indeed, arguably, it is pictorially coded in the sense that letter shapes are originally drawn or depicted.[7] However, the layout and typography of sociological texts have become so conventionalised that we tend to take them for granted and to ignore the operation of their visual codes; our attention is concentrated almost exclusively on the textual codes.[8] Nevertheless, in order to interpret a sociological text, we need an understanding of the visual codes used in its layout and typography. In addition, Victor Burgin (1986b) argues that there is a clear sense in which visual art representations do not operate in a purely visual medium. Even the uncaptioned art photograph, framed and isolated on the gallery wall, is invaded by language in the very moment it is looked at: in memory, in association, snatches of words and images continually intermingle and are exchanged one with the other.[9] It is misleading, then, to think that a sociological (or any) text communicates as a purely verbal text (though it is a moot point as to whether its visual codes can be called pictorial), and to regard a visual art work as operating in a purely visual medium. Each of these cultural discourses relies on both visual and verbal forms of communication.

Charles Peirce's semiotic theory (Peirce 1955) draws visual art and sociology, as forms of communication, even closer together. I will briefly outline his typology of signs. In this, the *iconic* sign proposes a 'fitness' of resemblance to the object it signifies, as a portrait represents the sitter. The *indexical* sign has a concrete, actual relationship to the signifier – usually of a sequential, causal kind – in the sense that smoke is an index of fire. The *symbolic* sign signifies by virtue of a contract or rule – the equivalent of Saussure's arbitrary linguistic sign (Saussure 1974). It therefore requires the active presence of the interpretant to make the signifying connection. In this triad, the iconic, indexical and the symbolic signs are not mutually exclusive. Rather, they are three modes of a relationship between signifier and object or signifier and signified which co-exist in the form of a hierarchy in which one of them will inevitably have dominance over the other two. And each of these signs bears a different relation to the interpretant as well as to the

---

7 Chinese 'characters' are more clearly pictorially coded: they are sometimes referred to as pictograms.
8 As social analysts we should not do so, for ideologies operate in the visual crevices of a verbal text. Foucault (Gutting 1989) has pointed out, for example, that written reports contain large margins for comments by superiors.
9 Burgin comments, further:

> The ideological resistance, in the name of the 'purity' of the Image, to the consideration of linguistic matter within and across the photograph is no more or less well founded than that which met the coming of sound in the cinema.
>
> (Burgin 1986b: 69)

object. In the following paragraphs, I shall be concerned primarily with the iconic and symbolic signs.

Analysis of figurative paintings clearly shows how images may signal both iconically and symbolically. While an image of a table may propose a 'fitness' of resemblance to the table it signifies (iconic signal), this is not the only message that the image gives off. It may symbolise upper-class affluence and dinner parties (a large, well-polished, ornately carved table) or it may symbolise poverty and toil in the kitchen (a small, plain, rickety, scratched table). Colour often signifies symbolically: thus the black of the witch's robe and hat symbolise evil, while the faces in posters for the Black Power Movement in America symbolise black-is-beautiful. However, Margaret Iverson (1979) argues that there is an area of common ground between pictorial and linguistic signs. She uses Peirce's model to argue that while visual images signal symbolically, linguistic signs also exhibit iconic characteristics. She points out, following Roman Jacobson, that the way certain sentence structures are designed is according to a rationale; that is, such patterned structures are not arbitrary and do not signify symbolically. Thus, when we say 'the President and Secretary of State attended a meeting', we always give precedence to the President in the linguistic chain. There is a rationale here, as in the iconic communication of visual images.

Iverson's work suggests, therefore, that how visual art works and sociology texts communicate can be even more closely identified than was suggested in the initial comparison. To summarise so far: while both forms of discourse contribute to society's cultural patterns, visual art works cannot be purely visual, and sociological texts cannot be purely verbal even when they contain no images. And while in visual art works iconic communication may predominate, whereas in sociological texts symbolic communication is stronger, both texts and images exhibit iconic and symbolic characteristics in different hierarchical combinations.

Visual art works and sociological texts may have this much in common, but what about the fact that visual art is an *art*, whereas sociology is held not to be? Terence Hawkes (1977) claims that works of art, both visual and verbal, do not signify 'in the normal way'. He argues that they consist in part of signs that are auto-referential – that is, they signify themselves. Respondents are thereby initiated into a 'special language' peculiar to the work of art, which induces a sense of 'cosmicity' – that is, of endlessly moving beyond each established level of meaning the moment it is established. Thus, though visual art works and sociological texts may both use hierarchical combinations of iconic and symbolic signs, the former may differ from the latter through their use of some signs that are auto-referential.

Hawkes goes on to ask why literacy and writing – as opposed to imagery – are predominant in our society; and this question serves to introduce my discussion of the political implications of literary and of pictorial communication. He argues that mass literacy and an education system firmly based on it have tended to establish and reinforce an equation between literature and life in twentieth-century Europe and America that would have astonished any preceding age. He notes that our education system, and the political system that both authenticates it and is reinforced by it, continue to promote a 'literary' version of the world as 'real'; they give it a dominant, formative status, and require all other possible versions of the world to accommodate themselves to its shape. As a result, we tend to 'literarise' all our experiences; to reduce them to a kind of 'book'. And literacy, which is, in substance, verbal, and whose mode of signification is predominantly symbolic, facilitates and encourages a divorce between meaning and symbol, and thus leads to the form/content, objective/subjective dichotomies which are so central to Western thought and which serve to distance people from others and from their environment.

Hawkes argues that for a society which has imposed and institutionalised the written form of language as an overall dominating feature of its way of life, all writing is political writing. And in this same context Philippe Sollers has remarked that: 'Writing is the continuation of politics by other means' (Sollers 1968: 78). From this point of view, it seems to be incumbent on the intellectual, of whom Tagg speaks, to use the visual image instead to communicate his or her critique of society. Yet we have seen that to communicate in a 'purely' visual form or in a 'purely' verbal form is likely to prove impossible, and that the visual image does, in any case, communicate via the symbolic code, through which it transmits social conventions, i.e. knowledge, ideology. Hence, we can hardly regard the visual image as ideologically/politically innocent. But it still represents a less ideologically grounded alternative to the dominant, verbal form of communication; and, furthermore, if works of art consist in part of signs that are auto-referential, and initiate the audience into a 'special language', then *visual art* would appear to be a relatively satisfactory medium for the communication of critique. For it offers the possibility of transforming our perceptions of the world into a new form ('visual art understanding'), and communicating this via the less contaminated of the two channels. It is more or less in this context that Lyotard's (1984) claim that visual art has a crucial role to play as critique of society can be understood.

Yet to talk about visual *art, per se,* as the preferred mode of critical communication leads to confusion, because the institution of visual art is itself host to competing ideologies, as Walker's analysis at the start of this section makes clear. Taking the case of the modernist ideology, he argues that this reduces the respondent to a pair of eyes, so that 'critique' merely entails apprehending the work's formal relations as a totality. Thus the critical task in modernism is shortcircuited and there is no sense in which it is a *social* critique; it is merely parasitical. However, if we maintain with an increasing number of visual artists, including Burgin (1986b), that critique is social and that it cannot be separated from the practice of art itself, this suggests the notion of a socially grounded *critical* visual art practice under-pinned by a theory of communication informed by principles of semiotics. It is a critical practice which understands the positive political implications of communicating via visual art whilst acknowledging that a *social* critique must nevertheless involve the verbal dimension. At this point, however, it must be clear that we have by now shifted away from our earlier focus on semiotic theory, and are working instead with the *sociologically* grounded concept of discourse. Discourse analysis is a tool of institutional, ideological investigation, in a way that a Peircian typology, which is based on the rules of logic, cannot be. While semiotic theory *expresses* the meanings of a pre-existent social order, discourse *constructs* those meanings and that order.

Burgin (1986b) urges a critical art practice which forms part of a wider critical discourse, or more accurately, a discursive formation.[10] This practice acknowledges that both visual and verbal media are implicated; and its work may include both pictorial and textual elements. The pictorial element addresses topics shared by other contributors to the discursive formation, rather than consisting of modernist abstract 'painterly' marks which only refer back to themselves and to the modernist rationale. The verbal element may include text – and is, therefore, not simply to be understood in the sense that a visual work is invaded by language during the course of interpreting it. And since we have seen that the verbal permeates the artwork anyway, there is no good reason to ban its formal presence on or alongside the image, so long as it remains in a tempered relationship with the image, such that that relationship enhances the total critique.

Bearing in mind the semiotic principles which operate in both visual art work and sociological text, and the fact that both visual art and sociology are discursive formations, such a critical practice can at the same time be seen as a form of sociological practice: a practice which makes conscious use of the symbolic code in visual imagery to emphasise social conventions and a conscious knowledge of the image's iconic properties. And it surely con-stitutes a particularly apposite form of sociological practice if, following Hawkes, we want to attempt to minimise the ideological content of critique by disrupting the solely literary form in which it is conventionally couched. Furthermore, an 'injection' of visual art into sociology offers the possibility of transforming our perceptions of the world into a new form; and this can be made to enhance, give a new kind of meaning to, the textual component of the critique with which it interacts. It therefore behoves critical sociologists to study with care the scripto-visual critical *art* practice of those who, in recent years, have been prepared to transgress the hallowed division

---

10 Following McCabe, he prefers to substitute the notion of discursive formation for discourse, because this emphasises that there can be no simple one-to-one homology between institution and discourse. The notion of discursive formation focuses on the systematic interconnections between an array of related statements which define a field of knowledge, its possibilities and its occlusions.

between visual and verbal in the institutionalised system of representational practices. They have met very few critical writers (for example, sociologists) coming in the opposite direction. Few art critics make art; and few sociologists incorporate visual images into their texts.[11] One of the purposes of this section has been to suggest that a sociological understanding which moves closer to the position of critical visual art practice, and which consciously deploys both visual and verbal channels to produce critique, builds on a sounder base than one which merely offers verbal text. In the last section of this chapter, I examine the critical practice of Victor Burgin in *Between* (1986a), which originates in the discipline of visual art and corresponds with this concept of critique that I have begun to indicate. In Chapter 5, I look at the work of several photographers and social scientists whose exhibition and book, *Exploring Society Photographically* (Becker 1981), represents a fairly similar project, but originating in the discipline of social science.

FEMINIST ART THEORY/PRACTICE

Griselda Pollock's *Vision and Difference*

In *The Burden of Representation*, Tagg (1988) argues for an analysis of power relations; an analysis which is critical, empirical and operates at the local level. This approach is adopted by many feminists, whose specific emphasis, however, is that class analysis ignores the social position of women. Tagg distances his analysis from the institution of visual art, but there are feminists who have chosen to work within the area; and this section focuses on feminist approaches to visual art and art history. However, there are many feminist art theories and practices, and this reflects a situation in which there is a plurality of feminisms and no central dogma. One strand of feminist art theory/practice, sometimes refered to as 'scripto-visual', is close to the semiotically informed critical practice outlined in the last section: that is, a cultural, or sociological, critique which incorporates both visual art images and text.[12] Below, I examine Griselda Pollock's influential *Vision and Difference: Femininity, Feminism and the Histories of Art* (1988). This work is also informed by the notion of cultural practice, and by a semiotic explanation of how cultural products communicate.[13]

There was a massive expansion of feminist studies in the late 1960s in almost all academic disciplines. This changed the politics of knowledge, and conse-

---

11 There are notable exceptions, for example, the contributors to *Exploring Society Photographically* (Becker 1981).

12 'In Defence of the Indefensible' by Katy Deepwell (*Feminist Art News*, undated, 9–12) situates 'scripto-visual' feminist art practice in a critical context.

13 In this section, I have used several of the phrases, including descriptions of theoretical positions and processes, which Pollock herself uses. Her phraseology cannot be bettered; and indeed there seems little point, and possibly some danger, in altering it.

quently the discipline of art history. In *Vision and Difference*, Pollock argues that the object of feminist studies is to question the apparently coherent *social* identity of women, by analysing the social construction of gender difference.[14] While *sexual* differences between men and women are more or less biologically pre-determined, *gender* differences are socially negotiated, which means that the inequality which obtains between masculine and feminine-gendered identities could be otherwise. Tagg observes that where there is oppression there is always a countervailing force; and feminists seek to expose this social imbalance, and to reconstruct gender relations so that the balance of power is much more favourable towards women. Pollock argues that the feminist problematic is shaped by the terrain on which it has chosen to operate – in the present case, visual art representations and the practices which produce them – but that it is ultimately defined within the women's movement. It is here that her base is.

But we need to ask what visual art and art history have to do with the struggle for the liberation of women. Are they not an irrelevant side-line? Pollock insists that they are not: visual art is a growing aspect of big business, it is a major component of the leisure industry, and it has become the site of corporate investment. In other words, 'art' is an integral part of economic and social life – a life which is dominated by men's decision-making and men's actions. She argues that it is important for feminists to analyse critically this phenomenon and the scholarship that authenticates its works, both of which influence bourgeois ideology.

However, a growing number of scholars, feminists among them, reject the term 'art history', and argue that the theoretical and methodological debates of Marxist historiography have produced a paradigm for the study of what it is proper to rename cultural production. Tagg (1985) notes that the notion of cultural production has shifted what was previously a focus on the art object to an analysis of the totality of social relations which form the conditions of the production and consumption of objects designated in that process as art. Pollock claims that there is a communication breakdown between art historians who still work within the normative discipline of art history and those who are contesting the paradigm. Consequently it is misleading to talk of a 'feminist art history'; rather, there are feminist interventions (since there are many types) in the histories of art.

Pollock's feminist intervention uses and develops the terrain around the Marxist-informed notion of cultural practice. She argues that cultural practices, such as visual art, contribute towards the articulation of meanings about the world, the negotiation of social conflicts and the production of social subjects. Cultural practices are thus signifying systems; and as such, they represent reality. They use specific cultural conventions to present to an

---

14 In this, she follows the line of argument taken by the Cambridge Women's Studies Group (1981).

audience a particular ideological view of reality. Like Burgin (1986b), she argues that when semiotic theory, which explains how images or languages produce meanings and positions for the consumption of meanings, is approached through developments in theories of ideology and is informed by analyses of the production and sexing of subjectivity in psychoanalysis, this can explain the role of cultural activities in the making of meanings and social subject positions. Pollock also uses the concept of discursive formation to deal with the systematic interconnections between an array of related statements which define a field of knowledge, its possibilities and its occlusions. Thus, she argues, on the agenda for analysis is not just the history of art, i.e. the art of the past, but also art history, the discursive formation which invented that entity to study it.

However, Pollock also argues that even when art history is itself informed by cultural theory, it is a masculinist discourse; for structured into it is a sexism which has contributed actively to the production and perpetuation of a gender hierarchy, which focuses attention on male artists and their work, while systematically excluding women from the production of art and from a history of the production of art. Nevertheless, she concedes that Marxism's *general* method and critical insights are very important. Her position therefore is that there is a difficult but necessary relation between feminist theory and Marxist theory: while it is important to challenge the paternal authority of Marxism and the way that it allows gender differences to remain unanalysed, it is equally important to take advantage of the theoretical and historiographical revolution which the Marxist tradition represents, and to build on this. Women, art and ideology have to be studied as a set of varying, and unpredictable, relationships.

In *Vision and Difference*, each successive empirical study contributes a theoretical dimension to Pollock's total analytical framework. The first of these studies, 'Modernity and the spaces of femininity' (Pollock 1988: 50–90), shows how class and gender analyses can be used together. A subsequent study, 'Woman as sign in Pre-Raphaelite literature' (91–114), introduces semiotic theory to explain how a Victorian painting of a middle-class female face signifies male desire; and this analysis is reinforced in a subsequent 'photo-essay'. In a later essay, 'Woman as sign: psychoanalytic readings' (120–54), Pollock shows how semiotic analysis approached through developments in theories of ideology and informed by psychoanalytic analyses of the production and sexing of subjectivity can contribute much to feminist readings of Pre-Raphaelite paintings. Finally, in 'Screening the seventies: sexuality and representation' (155–99), she demonstrates how some recent feminist art works use psychoanalysis and class analysis to produce meanings for their viewers.

'Modernity and the spaces of femininity' discusses Impressionist pictures which show the new bourgeois life of Paris in the second half of the nineteenth century. This life centred on the phenomenon of modernity, which was concerned with the novel activities of leisure and pleasure, consumption and money, suburban weekends, and the fluidity of class in the popular spaces of entertainment. Yet Pollock notes that the bourgeois revolution was in many ways a historic defeat for women, and that the freedom associated with modernity was not a freedom which women enjoyed. But she also argues that modernism's theoretical approach[15] to paintings of modernity takes entirely for granted that there is one modernity, and that its artists are male. Furthermore, she observes that modernism's masculinist myths are widespread and structure the discourse of many counter-modernists – including social historians of art, whose Marxist class analysis leaves intact the bourgeois and modernist assumption that the male is the creator of art whereas woman have babies.[16] So Pollock's first essay is a feminist critique of both modernist *and* social art historians' accounts of Impressionist pictures showing the new bourgeois life of Paris in the second half of the nineteenth century. However, she *uses* the Marxist analysis of the operations of bourgeois society and bourgeois ideologies to identify the specific configurations of bourgeois femininity, and thus to show that class relations and gender relations cannot be separated; that they are historical simultaneities and mutually inflecting. In this, she demonstrates the necessary relationship between Marxist and feminist theory.

Her analysis of Impressionist paintings reveals that artists who are men depict two distinct classes of women. There is the respectable middle-class wife and mother who is banished to her private suburban domestic space, while the husband works in the public world of the city. But his modern life in these more anonymous spaces includes 'recreation' in the bars and brothels where quite a different kind of woman is needed, and depicted: the fallen woman, whore, who is generalised to the working-class woman. Pollock argues that very often canonical works like Manet's *Bar at the Folies Bergères* show the marginal spaces where the fields of the masculine and feminine intersect and structure sexuality within a classed order (in *Bar at the Folies Bergères*, a middle-class man is served at the bar by a working-class girl); and furthermore that such paintings became the very *site* for the construction of sexual difference.

She shows that Impressionist paintings by women, on the other hand, depict the private domestic spaces around which their lives were structured by the bourgeois, masculine regime. These works demonstrate a sound knowledge of the daily routine and rituals which constituted the spaces of femininity, whereas men's paintings showed these spaces from a totally different perspective: men entered them on commission to celebrate a special occasion. However, Pollock comments that the painter Mary Cassat

---

15 Referred to in the previous section of this chapter.
16 For example, Clark (1984) offers a class analysis of modernity; and Pollock notes that, like the Impressionist paintings themselves, the analysis assumes a masculine viewer; while many of these works focus precisely on sexuality as a form of commercial exchange.

was using class power when she asked her maid to model half-dressed for scenes of women washing; but she argues that the maid was not subject to a voyeuristic gaze, and that her body is pictured as classed but not subject to sexual commodification.

She further argues that the sexual politics of looking function around a regime which divides into several binary positions: voyeur/exhibitionist, activity/passivity, looking/being seen, subject/object. The use of this series of bipolarities is subsequently explored in 'Woman as sign in Pre-Raphaelite literature: the representation of Elizabeth Siddall'; a study of the reciprocal positioning of masculine creator and passive feminine object in art-historical texts. In this essay, Pollock argues that in Victorian metropolitan England, as in Paris of the 1850s, the bourgeois lady's 'a-sexuality' was in the process of being defined against the sexuality imputed to working-class women in general (whore), and that Pre-Raphaelite works of the 1850s also functioned as sites for the renegotiation and redefinition of femininity and sexuality within a dominant bourgeois regime.

Elizabeth Siddall was a member of the Pre-Raphaelite circle, and produced a considerable corpus of work. However, Pollock notes that her work is seen and defined only in relation to that of Dante Gabriel Rossetti,[17] and asks why this should be so. Furthermore, she notes that in Rossetti's paintings of her, and in his writings, Elizabeth Siddall's name was altered to the term 'Siddal'. Pollock argues that this does not signify her as a person, but rather communicated a consumptive, melancholic, beautiful enigma: woman as passive object, whose mirror-image was masculine creativity. So 'Siddal' signals the simultaneous bipolar establishment of masculine dominance/ feminine subordination. Yet Pollock points out that in patriarchal ideologies of art, the role ascribed to the feminine position is not only as art's object, the model, but as art's muse by virtue of a romantic affiliation with an artist. And for this affiliation, a bourgeois woman with all the bourgeois feminine virtues was essential – a working-class 'fallen' woman would not fit the bill. Pollock argues that Elizabeth Siddall, one of several working-class women desired for their difference, was drawn into this select circle of basically bourgeois artists, and re-formed with the qualities required; namely silence, a pleasant appearance, deferential manners, self-sacrifice. 'Siddal' is thus repositioned as the epitome of the feminine virtues of purity, gentility, refinement – and this functions as a sign for masculine creativity.

So images of 'Siddal' helped to negotiate the differences between the sexualities of Victorian men and women. And as visual representations, Pollock argues, they signify in the ideological process of a redefinition of woman *as image*, and as *visibly* different. 'Siddal' images stand for a certain type of physical appearance. Pollock suggests that the lack of emphasis on facial bone structure lends an ethereal quality to Rossetti drawings of the

17 See, for example, *The Pre-Raphaelites* (1984), London: the Tate Gallery.

faces of several female models; and that rather than representing individual women, these drawings of faces all display a remoteness which signals a type – beautiful, passsive, sexualised, woman as mirror image and function of masculine pleasure and masculine creation. Her subsequent four-page 'photo-essay' (116–19) develops and strengthens this point, and is consistent with her overall *structural* approach. The fact that the facial features in each image are so similar that attribution becomes 'necessarily tentative' reinforces her argument that those images collectively signify a visual type rather than separately representing individual women. But in any case, the information given by the captions indicates that Pollock is not attempting categorically to identify individual sitters; nor is she interested in grouping portraits of the same sitter together, nor in placing them in chronological order as might be expected in a catalogue raisonnée. She juxtaposes portraits of 'different' women in order to show near-identical hairstyles, face profiles, positions of the head and facial expressions. The second two pages of her photo-essay are set out in a similar fashion. The captions identify a similar type of remote female face, this time produced by the twentieth-century social institutions of advertising and film. These six images demonstrate that the ideology of women's sexuality as visibly defined and visibly typecast in mid-nineteenth-century representations of woman is still powerful. Now it could be argued that artists were depicting this type of female face with a lack of facial bone structure long before the Pre-Raphaelite period; the type is evident, for example, in Lely's *Windsor Beauties* (1660s) and Kneller's *Hampton Court Beauties* (c. 1700). But the main point I want to make is that Pollock's overall analysis *includes* a photo-essay. Its presence suggests that the notion of cultural production, informed by a semiotic explanation of how images operate, has the effect of blurring both disciplinary and visual/verbal boundaries and of encouraging work which crosses over these boundaries. Furthermore, Pollock's photo-essay shows how precisely worded captions in relation to a set of images can further and strengthen a structural analysis; and this serves to reinforce my contention that image-and-text presentations can make an important contribution to critique.

In her next essay, 'Woman as sign: psychoanalytic readings', Pollock notes that the development of theories of ideology within Marxism has involved recognition of the *unconscious* level of its operations in producing us as subjects for specific regimes of meaning; and has also led to an acknowledgement of the unconscious as a site of social inscription of gender/class formations operative through social institutions, particularly the family. She argues that a historicised use of psychoanalysis can alert us to the historical and social structures which function at the level of the unconscious: it places the bourgeois family as both social institution and discursive formation for the production of masculine and feminine subjects. A historicised use of psychoanalysis leads us to treat the bourgeois family as the locus of sexualisation; the site of the initial installation of sexual difference. She

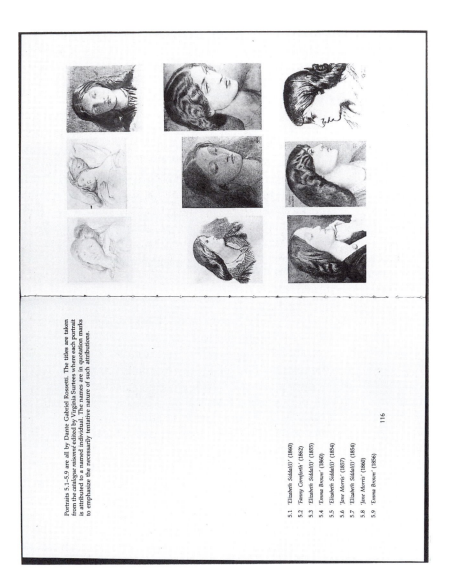

Portraits 5.1–5.9 are all by Dante Gabriel Rossetti. The titles are taken from the *catalogue raisonné* edited by Virginia Surtees where each portrait is attributed to a named individual. The names are in quotation marks to emphasize the necessarily tentative nature of such attributions.

5.1 *'Elizabeth Siddal(l)'* (1860)

5.2 *'Fanny Cornforth'* (1862)

5.3 *'Elizabeth Siddal(l)'* (1855)

5.4 *'Emma Brown'* (1860)

5.5 *'Elizabeth Siddal(l)'* (1854)

5.6 *'Jane Morris'* (1857)

5.7 *'Elizabeth Siddal(l)'* (1854)

5.8 *'Jane Morris'* (1860)

5.9 *'Emma Brown'* (1856)

116

5.10 (a–d) Advertisements for cosmetic products

5.11 The faces of Greta Garbo and Marlene Dietrich

118

Figure 3 Griselda Pollock. *A photo-essay: Signs of Femininity; Vision and Difference* (1988)

argues that the work collectively labelled 'Rossetti' is an especially significant trace of these psychosexual formations. Pollock reminds us that the new category of 'woman' which was negotiated in the mid-nineteenth century is represented in Rossetti works by an abstracted (idealised) face. This face, and sometimes parts of a body, are often severed from the whole. Contemporary accounts of the 1859 Rossetti portrait, *Bocca Bacciata*, suggest that the way such works signal the difference between man and woman induces a sense of anxiety in the male viewer, and that their message is apparently deeply ambiguous. While *Bocca Bacciata* is seen as erotic, it is also interpreted as high art, which suggests that it ought to have a moral function. Pollock argues that such works have a fetishistic quality, signifying not what is there, but what isn't – dangerous – dominant yet desired. She shows that Lacan's psychoanalytic theory of the real, imaginary and symbolic stages of development of the human speaking subject can explain the fetishistic, anxiety-provoking quality of these representations of woman in the context of the ideological construction of masculine and feminine sexualities within the bourgeois family. She focuses on Lacan's account of the potential slippage between the two orders of meaning – the imaginary and the symbolic – which he claims are constitutive of our making as subjects. He argues that although the completion of the formation of the ego is synonymous with accession to the symbolic order, there is always the possibility of regression in man to the imaginary mode, with its hankering after the super-real permanent object, its image of the perfect caretaker/mother to whom the infant is attached in the first stage. When this regression occurs, there is a withdrawal from open exchange of truth in human discourse. Pollock argues that the Rossetti type of petrified, unreal representations of woman serve as scopophilic fetishises for the hallucinatory satisfaction of primal desire. Lacan thus introduces a function for the image: it is a means of regaining visual access to the lost object.

Pollock argues that Rossetti and his circle effected an ideological form of representation which negotiated the accommodation of masculine sexuality on behalf of the class they served; and that works of this period functioned as a screen on which masculine fantasies of knowledge, power and possession could be enjoyed by those who acquired them. We might say, then, that Lacanian readings of the works enable us to study the process of the image: what is being done with it and what it is doing for its users.

Pollock concludes by claiming that one Rossetti work, *Astarte Syriaca*, in its scale, active posture and empowered glance, is an image which transcends the stalemated, fetishistic quality of so many of the others. (Its facial type is derived from the features of Jane Burden Morris.) Pollock argues that in this one case, the dominant ideological structures within which the fetishistic regime of representation is founded are exposed: 'the image depicts a figure before which the masculine viewer can comfortably stand subjected' (Pollock 1988: 153). I do not wish to go into the detail of her justification for this reading. I would simply point to the fact that it constitutes a positive feminist reading; and that this in itself serves to shift attention towards a problem which faces feminists who want to *make* visual work, rather than 'simply' to critique patriarchal images; for they are confronted by the problem of how to create the kind of visual pleasure that other women can share.

It seems reasonable that, from their base in the women's movement, feminists should treat interventions into *histories* of art and *current* feminist art practice as part of the same critical project on behalf of women (in a certain sense, bringing the textual and the pictorial closer together). In her last essay, 'Screening the seventies: sexuality and representation in feminist practice – a Brechtian perspective', Pollock crosses the conventional divide between art of the past and current art practice. She pays particular attention to those feminist art practices which address the relationship between feminism and modernism, which deploy a Lacanian understanding of how infants' sexuality is initially constructed in the family,[18] and which pursue the problem of women's visual pleasure. Mary Kelly's corpus of visual art work has addressed all these areas, and Pollock devotes a considerable part of her essay to an analysis of it.

She explains that while the major but not exclusive theoretical framework of Kelly's *Post Partum Document* (1973) embodies a revision of the psychoanalytic schemata of Lacan, the representational strategies are informed by the Brechtian uses of montage, text, objects in a sequence of sections which actively invent the spectator as someone who will engage, remember, reflect and reconstitute the traces of the relationship between mother and child which is the document's material. Pollock claims that the end-product is a new understanding of the passage of the mother and the child through the reciprocal process of socialisation as feminine and, in this case, masculine subjects. However, this represents only a small part of her analysis of the *Post Partum Document* and its strategies; her complete explanation of it is extensive. With her help – and after several years of studying visual art and feminist theory – I think I can understand the work's intention; but how many women could achieve an active, positive and 'informed' reading without outside help? The theoretical sophistication of this work assumes a very considerable degree of learning on the part of the spectator, and indeed suggests to me that the viewpoint of the spectator is becoming lost at the expense of a heavy concentration on the artist's theoretical position. Towards the end of the essay, Pollock seems partly to concede this, for she notes that the economic, political and cultural climate of the mid-1980s in

---

18 Pollock notes that the emphasis on psychic rather than social levels of socially constructed subjects has been criticised by other feminist theorists; but explains that during the 1970s close historical links were developed between the journal *Screen*, where significant developments in psychoanalytic theory were taking place, and a psychoanalytically inclined feminist art theory/practice, which it clearly influenced.

which she writes is dramatically different from that of the 1970s when the *Post Partum Document* was produced; and she advises that artists must constantly adjust their strategies to the conjunctures within which they intervene.

Yet she proceeds to examine in detail a more recent feminist art work by Mary Kelly, *Interim 1984–*, which is also theoretically sophisticated, but which draws on psychoanalytic theory with the purpose of making the work pleasurable to other women. Pollock argues that this work is not caught up in the ideology of patriarchal imagery, yet neither does it return the feminine to a domain of the pre-linguistic utterance: it deploys a system of imaged discourse in what is, in effect, a new feminist language. It is addressed to a social spectator – a woman, a feminist, aged roughly 45, who is invited to share in the process of constructing meanings. Yet the paradox is, as Pollock admits, that whereas such feminist art is made for and addressed primarily to women, it cannot speak to women in 'easily consumed terms'. Why it cannot do so, she argues, is because women must reject those structures of viewing with which we are familiar since they are rooted in oppressive regimes. The argument is that only when these patriarchal structures have been critically deconstructed can the foundations be laid for a new language – and a new regime of meaning. The new language will, by definition, be unfamiliar.

This insistence on the necessity of a new language has been much criticised by other feminist theorists and art practitioners.[19] I do not wish to enter into this debate; and would, instead, make a simple point which is implied in Wolff's *The Social Production of Art*.[20] That is that work whose acknowledged base is in the women's movement must be sensitive to the responses of other women. I am not refering to *the artist's conception of*, or theoretical construction of audience, but the real responses of real women. A few years ago, I was in Barnsley, a solidly working-class town in South Yorkshire, looking at the feminist exhibition, *Along the Lines of Resistance: An Exhibition of Contemporary Feminist Art* (1988). A woman was cleaning the gallery, running her duster round the skirting board. I asked her what she thought of the art, and she seemed surprised, even put out, to be asked a question at all, let alone one about the art. To her this was a room to be dusted and, to judge by her stuttering reply, she had not even begun to think of looking actively at the art – it belonged to someone else, to 'them', to another class, another group . . . it was nothing to do with her. The art on exhibition was, in my opinion, much more accessible than Kelly's. If this is in any way a typical woman's response to feminist art theory/practice, then something seems to be wrong. Of course, all feminist art cannot reach all women, there are different 'levels' of production and reception and, furthermore, the task of feminist art is to change women, rather than merely

---

19 See, for example, Partington (1987).
20 By her preference for a populist rather than an elitist approach to art.

to satisfy popular taste. Yet whatever new ground the highly sophisticated work of Kelly and others has broken at the levels of art and feminist theory, it is surely worrying that most women will not understand it, either as 'art' or as having anything to do with women. In my opinion, Pollock's structural feminist interventions into histories of art are highly instructive and illuminating for their acknowledged audience of feminist intellectuals. But one of the chief merits of the *contemporary* feminist art works which she analyses seems to be that they constitute a coherent extension of her theoretical analyses of the art of the past. The worry is that these works are short-circuiting, and appeal only to the feminists who share Pollock's theoretical approach. One might hope that feminist art work would reach out to a broader audience than that commanded by feminist interventions into art history, because it overlaps more discourses (leisure, commerce, etc.).

However, there are many feminist art practices – as Parker and Pollock (1987) have shown; and feminist art theory/practice can perhaps best be seen as a constellation which operates on different levels simultaneously, each level appealing to a different type of woman. For my own part, while I think the idea of feminist critique which combines image and text is important, I also think that the authors of such work should at least aim to reach an audience which is not restricted to highly educated intellectuals; and this would seem to call for a certain amount of audience research before embarking on work to be exhibited. However, this is a very difficult area, and there are no clear solutions, only a number of options. One of them is to examine critically the category of *art* itself. For Pollock's analyses indicate that the social institution of art has been and still is a thoroughly unworking-class concern, besides being patriarchal. All art work, including feminist art practice, inevitably responds to previous work in the tradition of art, and that factor alone makes it relatively inaccessible to many women.

Pollock does note that *Vision and Difference* omits to address the struggles of black women artists, and that she would want to see this remedied in subsequent documentations and analyses of feminist interventions into the histories of art. And indeed, recent editions of *Feminist Art News* (and other publications) have begun to rectify this. An early edition of *FAN* (undated, 2, 4) contained four theoretically weighted articles by white women, and one section devoted to white women's visual art works and their accompanying written texts. By comparison, Part 1 of the 1992 edition (4, 1) is devoted to 'Black women in the arts: 1992'. This consists of thirty-one different pieces, all by black women, all relatively short and 'untheoretical', exploring their families' migration to Britain through image and/or text. Part 2 is about black women artists in Europe, and as such, continues the process of documenting 'Black women's herstory and the arts'.

So far, this chapter has offered an account of how the relationship of critical writing to visual art practice has been altered by Tagg's treatment of the

medium of photography, by developments in semiotic theory, and by feminist interventions in the fields of art history and current art practice. I have
noted a tendency for critical theory and visual art practice to converge in
certain types of critical work; and in the next chapter – following Tagg's
treatment of the medium of photography, and consequent upon criticisms of
Pollock's promotion of a particular type of feminist art theory/practice – I
shall examine cases where the *art* component, the artness, of critical visual
works has itself become less prominent. However, this chapter ends with a
discussion of Victor Burgin's book, *Between* (1986a), which represents a
point at which critical theory and visual art practice merge.

VICTOR BURGIN'S *BETWEEN*

Burgin trained as an artist, and much of his visual work is still produced
within an art context.[21] *Between* (Burgin 1986a) is normally to be found in
the art section of bookshops, though it might well be categorised as 'cultural
studies', 'politics' or even 'sociology' – see Figure 4.

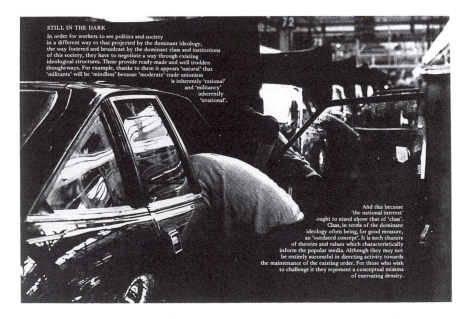

Figure 4 Victor Burgin. *Still in the Dark, Between* (1986a)

Note: Figures 4–8 are reduced in size compared with the originals in *Between*.

21 Since the publication of *Between*, Burgin's work has increasingly taken account, and
   advantage, of developments in modern technology. In 'Realising the Reverie' (*Ten 8*, 1991, 2:
   2), he discusses how he takes stills from moving pictures, digitalises them on a computer, and
   then shifts the elements around on the computer screen.

The title of the book itself suggests the blurring of categories, and – consistent with his approach – this blurring also operates visually. The colour of the front cover is 'between' light blue and mauve; the black and white photographic image in the centre of the cover is a negative printed as a positive; and the figure depicted is a woman with a mask which partly conceals her face.

Between consists of photographic image-and-text pieces, which are interspersed with separate verbal texts.[22] Both forms are used to convey cultural critique. The earlier pieces are class analyses, and the later ones which contain a strong psychoanalytic emphasis are feminist and sometimes anti-racist in orientation, as in Figure 5. Some of the image-and-text critiques are single presentations; others consist of a *narrative* sequence of image-and-text pieces, in which the dimension of time is thereby added. Devices such as montage, mirrored figures, figures reflected in car windows, figures juxtaposed with statues and with other figures on television programmes convey a sense of social interaction, and serve to reinforce the socio-political dimension of Burgin's work, as in Figure 6.

Figure 5 Victor Burgin. *St Laurent Demands a Whole New Lifestyle, Between* (1986a)

---

22 These verbal pieces consist of short essays, the author's commentaries on the image-and-text pieces, and interviews previously conducted with the author.

Figure 6 Victor Burgin. *Police-of-mind; Between* (1986a)

Despite being book reproductions, the image-and-text critiques have a positive, artefactual quality, which is generally lacking in verbal texts. This quality is clearly related to the fact that both the structure of each image and the spatial relationship of image to text are very deliberately calculated and constructed, thus giving a degree of artistic autonomy and a physical presence to each image-and-text piece. While the work's quality as visual art initially stimulates our imagination, and the intellectual content of the verbal text engages us at a cerebral level, we encounter the piece as a *whole*; and rather than reading off 'direct' correpondences between image and text, Burgin hopes that we will allow irrational processes, such as those found in dreams, to help form an association between the two. In particular, the later works in *Between* appeal 'to a "dream-logic" rather than common-sense' (Burgin 1986a: 135). Clearly, these image-and-text pieces are of a different order from Pollock's photo-essays. For one thing, they are perhaps visually more complex than Pollock's, since the text is positioned in an exact relationship to the image on the page, and does not constitute a 'caption'. In Figure 7, 'Life demands a little give and take. You give. We'll take', the text obliterates a man's head and part of a white woman's hair, while the first sentence in block capitals extends towards a black woman, the centre of the composition, who is visually untouched by the text. In 'St Laurent demands a whole new lifestyle', the text traces the outline of the Asian woman's head, whilst at the same time suggesting the silhouette of the kind of woman who

Figure 7 Victor Burgin. *Life demands a little give and take. You Give. We'll take; Between* (1986a)

would wear the haute couture clothes described in the text. This text physically hovers between the Asian woman worker and her work. In both pieces, the juxtaposition of image and text opens up a gulf between ideologies, making inequalities of class, race and gender difficult for the reader/viewer to ignore. Here, Burgin is using the method advocated by Pollock and other feminists, in which structural determinations are excavated and exposed via the use of an unconventional context. Critical analyses of capitalist advertisements and of patriarchal images in Hollywood-type narrative films have shown how both text and image – and the relationship between them – are subject to ideological manipulation at both psychic and conscious levels.[23] In some of the pieces in *Between*, Burgin uses the knowledge gained from such analyses to *his* own political advantage, and reverses the flow, so that the relationships between image and text that he constructs become critically provocative. For example, in an early work, 'Possession' (Figure 8), the verbal text superficially relates to the image in the manner of a classic advertisement. Thus we approach the piece as though it *were* an advertisement – but this state of mind is shattered when we read the text and relate its meaning to that conveyed by the image.

Looked at another way, Burgin's image-and-text pieces disrupt the

---

23 For fuller discussion of this topic, see Mulvey (1975), and Williamson (op. cit.).

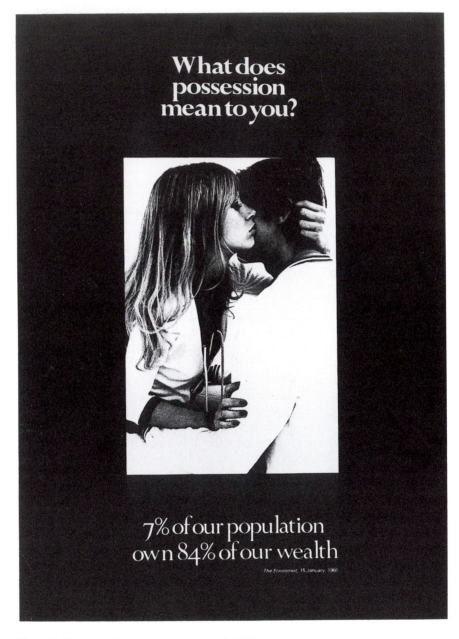

Figure 8 Victor Burgin. *Possession; Between* (1986a)

conventional practices of *captioning* the image and *illustrating* a text, with all the connotations that these conventions carry. The text, in its unconventional spatial relationship to the image, discourages any stereotypical interpretation of that image, and instead suggests alternative ways of interpreting both it and the whole piece – of which the text forms an integral part. At the same time, the meaning of the text is sharpened and given emotional force by its close and unconventional relationship to the imagery and to the visual presentation as a whole. And since visual images are, on the whole, open to a wider range of interpretations than verbal text – because their symbolically coded messages are less overtly signalled than those of texts and because they tend to stimulate the emotions and the imagination in non-linear, non-rational ways – Burgin's critical image-and-text pieces invite a range or constellation of readings around a theme, rather than a specific reading. The piece as a whole demands dialectical work – backwards and forwards between image and text – on the part of the reader, who engages in what amounts to speculation within fairly precisely defined conceptual limits. And the work's artefactualness gives the critique a positive quality; a sense that as an object, it can be put to *practical* use. 'Possession' was put to work on an advertisement hoarding in the streets of Newcastle.

Art demands judgement, and feminism is for women. My criticism of the feminist art theory/practice promoted by Pollock was simply that it is in-accessible to many women, and this leads them to judge it negatively, if, indeed, it comes to their attention at all. One reason why I consider *Between* to be important is because it appears more accessible, and yet there is no sense of compromise at the theoretical level – which, moreover, appears to be close to Pollock's approach in *Vision and Difference*. However, when *Possession* was displayed as a poster on the streets of Newcastle, an interviewer found that very few passers-by (in what is admitted to be an undersized sample) were able to 'make sense of it' on anything like the level at which it was presented. This is a stark reminder, if any were needed, of the problems facing those cultural producers who would reach a wide audience. In one of the verbal texts in *Between*, Burgin remarks that the question of audience is under-theorised: that it isn't a personal question as is usually assumed, but a political one. It is about 'a politics of discourses in conflict on a given institutional site' (Burgin 1986a: 87). This political ques-tion of audience will be addressed in Chapter 3, in my discussion of the Pavilion women's photography project at Leeds.

Sociologists could, I think, learn from the critical approach taken in *Between*. Nearly all now reject the idea that they can produce a value-neutral, philosophically neutral account of the social world. After all, they use a verbal language, not a mathematical one, and verbal language can never be objective; indeed, it enables them to discuss the meanings of social events and social actions; and this they regard as a very clear advantage. However, in this post-positivist era, no single account of the meanings of social events and social actions can be claimed to be definitive; producer and respondent become more nearly joint participants in the construction of accounts and meanings.[24] But in such a situation, an image-and-text format surely encourages joint participation even more. For the visual image's symbolic communication is less precise than that of the text, and introduces non-linear, even non-rational elements into the whole presentation, such that this presentation cannot pretend to convey one precise message, one clear set of meanings. It offers participants a range of suggestions: it presents them with the opportunity of constructing a constellation of meanings around a topic which is artefactually presented.

Furthermore, the insistence in post-positivist philosophy that there is no 'right answer', no 'true account', but instead many versions, a range of interpretations, would appear to have specific implications for the production of *critical* work. Given that such work will be variously interpreted, we need to consider how the manner in which it is presented can benefit from the knowledge that this will occur. This is to say, we need to ask how producers can encourage yet at the same time broadly direct the range of interpretations desired. How can they stimulate the respondent to imaginatively recreate the utopian ideas embedded in their work? An image-and-text *art* practice, which is at the same time an artefactual critical analysis, invites participants to *share* positively and *imaginatively* in the *construction* of a utopian forcefield, the like of which a purely verbal critique with its rationalising tendencies and lack of artefactualness cannot offer. The special contribution to a shared, actively constructed critique that visual art artefacts can make is clearly spelled out by Burgin:

> We are a consumer-society, and it seems to me that art has become a passive 'spectator sport' to an extent unprecedented in history. I have always tried to work against this tendency by producing 'occasions for interpretation' rather than 'objects for consumption'. I believe that the ability to produce rather than consume meanings, and the ability to think *otherwise* – ways of thinking not encouraged by the imperative to commodity production, ways condemned as 'a waste of time' – is fundamental to the goal of a truly, rather than nominally, democratic society. I believe art is one of the few remaining areas of social activity where the attitude of critical engagement may still be encouraged – all the more reason then for art to engage with those issues which are critical.
>
> (Burgin 1986: 138)

In *Vision and Difference*, Pollock argues that, while feminists ought to challenge the paternal authority of Marxism, they should at the same time take advantage of the theoretical and historiographical revolution which the Marxist tradition represents. In the next chapter I examine some recent images and image-and-text pieces by women, in which the legacy of the Marxist tradition is evident, but where Marxist theory, *per se*, is vestigial or even absent. I am referring specifically to practices in a local rather than in a

---

24 This is clearly demonstrated in Ashmore, Mulkay and Pinch (1989), which is discussed in Chapter 6.

national or international context by women of colour, working-class women, women with disabilities, lesbian women – whose multiple 'disadvantage' is such that their work's relationship to the mainstream concept of art is often also rather remote. I examine these works in terms of their accessibility to other women, bearing in mind Burgin's idea that the question of audience is a political one. This is followed by a section which lays out various post-modernist theories, and shows how these highlight the significance of spatial relationships and the prevalence of visual communication in present-day Western culture. Our critical focus is thus broadening out from an initial concern with visual art and then with photography to one which encompasses visual representation and communication as an integral part of everyday life.

Chapter 3

Visual and verbal critique: feminism and postmodernism

Principal items or works discussed:

The Pavilion Women's Photography Centre, Leeds
Jean-François Lyotard, *Driftworks*, 1984
Jean Baudrillard, *The Mirror of Production*, 1975
    Simulations, 1983
Scott Lash, 'Discourse or Figure? Postmodernism as a "Regime of Signi-
fication"', *Theory, Culture and Society*, 5, 2–3, 1988
Fredric Jameson, *Postmodernism, or, the Cultural Logic of Late Capitalism*,
1991 (1991a)
    'Third Ear', BBC Radio 3, 9 January 1991 (1991b)
David Harvey, *The Condition of Postmodernity: An Enquiry into the Origins of
Cultural Change*, 1989

Other contributions to postmodern theory:

Mary Maynard, 'The Re-Shaping of Sociology? Trends in the Study of Gender',
Sociology, 24, 2, 1991

Other contributions to feminist theory:

John Roberts, 'Out of Our Heads', *Art Monthly*, 156, 1992

INTRODUCTION

Chapter 1 surveyed verbal class analyses of visual art works, while Chapter 2
described various theoretical developments which have brought about
change both within and between the two sides of that 'equation' during the
last twenty years: change in the relationships between image and text, theory
and practice, sociology and art, author and topic of analysis, 'art' and
'non-art' visual representation. We have reached a point in this story at which
critique relating to visual representation may draw on a pluralist, localised,
minority group-based yet generally Marxist-informed approach to cultural
representation; where image and text are no longer necessarily kept apart,
where socio-political theory and visual art practice may be seen as two sides
of the same coin, and so on. There follows an account of The Pavilion at
Leeds, where some of the tendencies outlined in the previous chapter have
been further developed in a practical context.

The Pavilion at Leeds opened in 1983.[1] It remains unique in being the only women's photography centre in the country. In 1992, an exhibition and conference were held to mark its tenth anniversary – and this piece of writing is, in part, intended to mark that anniversary. However, from the viewpoint of current Pavilion workers and management committee members, this project is now quite different in character and organisation from when it started.[2] The Pavilion was founded by tutors from Leeds University Fine Art Department (including John Tagg), who converted a redundant park pavilion into a photographic darkroom and an exhibition area for the purpose of teaching students to produce photographs informed by feminist art theory.* In contrast with today's all-women collaborative organisation, the relationship between staff and students was hierarchical, and those involved in the project were not exclusively women, while they were overwhelmingly white, middle-class, and theory-oriented.

A second stage evolved with the day-to-day running of the Pavilion and with its general management. The women who took on these tasks wanted the Pavilion to operate more as a women's collective, with its darkroom facilities more accountable and accessible to women in the local community. Their aim was not so much to promote a photographic practice informed by feminist art theory as to provide a photographic resource for the women of Leeds to use. By 1985, workers who shared these ideas were being recruited, the darkroom was made available to women other than university fine art students, the emphasis on academic feminist theory faded, and the Pavilion began to run major educational projects, involving young women, girls and youth workers from all over the city.[3] Its aim by now was to encourage critical photography by women which was at the same time accessible to local women and addressed their immediate concerns. One of these projects was called *That's Action Women* (1988–9).[4] It focused on community issues and on the impact of recent housing legislation on local authority housing areas in Leeds. Let us look at this project in more detail, for it involved the Pavilion in outreach work, and represents a move away from an emphasis on art and 'academic' theory.

The 1988 Housing Act allows the government to select areas of local authority council housing and to turn them into Housing Action Trust areas. This means that the housing may be bought by private landlords and housing associations. Tenants may vote on the transfer but the voting procedure is such that anyone failing to vote is deemed to have voted in favour

1 Shirley Moreno, one of the project's originators, gives an account (1986) of how and why the Pavilion was set up.
2 My thanks to all those associated with the Pavilion who have helped in the preparation of this section.
3 The darkroom has remained accessible to all women, where the tuition of darkroom skills is available at affordable prices – the lowest in the country for this kind of service.
4 The other projects (1986–9) were: *A Dog Called Bronski*, *Dog II*, and *Package to Pluto*.
* In 1994 the Pavilion relocated to 2 Woodhouse Square, Leeds.

of the new landlord. This method of procedure has, in itself, been heavily criticised; and the Act has been widely opposed on the grounds that it would encourage higher rents and ruthlessness among landlords. It was also feared that it would lead to a decline of 'social housing' so that people were no longer housed according to need but according to whether or not they could afford the rent. Indeed, landlords and housing associations have no legal duty to house homeless people.

The housing estates of South Seacroft, Gipton and Halton Moor in Leeds were chosen to become Housing Action Trust areas, and a local pressure group called *That's Action* was formed to combat this political manoeuvre on the part of the government. Soon afterwards, a photographic workshop, *That's Action Women*, was organised. Its purpose was to encourage women residents from the three communities to make a photographic account which expressed their criticism of the Housing Act. *That's Action Women* involved collaboration between the campaigning organisation Shelter, tenants' groups from the three local authority housing estates, the Pavilion (who supplied cameras, support and coordination), and a community photographer who provided training for the women residents who agreed to take part in the project. The women learned how to make photographs and to process black and white film; and their work, which makes use of photomontage with text, was eventually put together as an exhibition. It records the campaign, locally and nationally, against the selection of Housing Action Trust areas, challenges stereotyped ideas about council housing estates and their communities, and raises general issues in connection with housing, such as privatisation, poverty and homelessness (see Figure 9). The exhibition was lent to other tenant groups to use in their own struggles against local authority housing authorities, and it has since been toured by the Impressions Gallery in York. As a public *exhibition*, the work inevitably has associations with art, but during the course of its *production*, its relationship to art was more tenuous.

At around this stage in the Pavilion's development, there was an increased emphasis on photography by Asian, African and Caribbean women and by lesbians. In addition a crèche was provided, when necessary, for women with young children. Women with physical disabilities were encouraged to participate; and the facilities – including the darkroom – were altered to accommodate wheelchairs. The services of a signer were also offered. The exhibition *5 Women* (1988–9), commissioned and curated at the Pavilion, is an example of the emphasis that was now being placed on the *diversity* of women's groups, and on the *different* issues to which women's photography could be directed. Five women were invited to produce separate sets of photographs which would become one exhibition. The women were given free supervised darkroom sessions, and general support. The resulting exhibition shows Nudrat Afza's photographs depicting the traditions and skills within her Asian community, Valerie Anderson's positive images of the African–Caribbean community, Isobel Baylis's collages about her local area

HOMELESSNESS

THE NEWLY APPOINTED HOUSING MINISTER, MIKE HOWARD, IN HIS PREVIOUS ROLE OF PREPARING THE "SELL-OFF" OF THE WATER AUTHORITIES, SPENT 22 MILLION POUNDS ON ADVERTISING THE EXISTENCE OF THE 10 WATER AUTHORITIES.

In 1986, 109 households were accepted as homeless by the council in Leeds.

Gipton, Halton Moor and Seacroft have always been areas where homeless households have been housed in Leeds. HATS WILL HAVE NO LEGAL DUTY TO HOUSE HOMELESS PEOPLE.

They only have a duty, as do housing associations, to co-operate with the council, who remain the only body legally obliged to house the homeless.

If Gipton is taken out of local authority control, where will these homeless people be housed and how will the local authority fulfill its legal obligation towards them?

Homelessness has more than doubled in the past ten years. Almost 130,000 households were accepted as homeless by local authorities in 1987. Twice that number presented themselves as homeless, but were not accepted for help with housing.

It is estimated that some two million single people are homeless who are not accepted as such under the current laws.

Over 150,000 young people are estimated to become homeless each year, many being forced to sleep rough or on friends' floors.

Figure 9 That's Action Women. *Homelessness* (1988). A photomontage frame which shows the Housing Minister washing away the Council's right to provide housing for the homeless

in Leeds, Sharon Campbell's images celebrating lesbian parenting and Lisa Williamson's work relating to disability rights. Lisa, who is hearing- and speech-impaired, produced photographic images of stereotypical representations of the disabled; but she presented these images in various ways which challenge the stereotype. For example, in Figure 10, the edges of photographs are torn, and the fragments are heaped together, producing a striking overall image which critiques and rejects the stereotype.

The Pavilion arranged with Leeds City Council for *5 Women* to be toured to Dortmund, as part of the twinning celebrations between the two towns. One Pavilion worker and a member of the *5 Women* group went over to Germany to present the show. This recognition by the local authority consolidated the Pavilion's public status. Another significant development was that by now several African–Caribbean women had appointments as workers and as management committee members at the Pavilion; and as a result, art was put back more firmly on its agenda. For while art may be a remote concept for white working-class women, many black women are actively involved in the arts. In 1986 there was collaboration with black women artists Lubaina Himid, Brenda Agard, Ingrid Pollard and Maud Sulter to produce the exhibition, *Testimony*. And in 1988 the Arts Council's Black Visual Arts Exhibitions Franchise funded a new three-year appointment at the Pavilion for the promotion and curating of exhibitions of black women's work – not just photography but a wide range of visual arts and crafts. *Looking for Sheba*, the Black Arts workers' first curated show, was an exhibition by two local African–Caribbean photographers, Paulette Stirling and Olinthia Fleming, celebrating women's contribution to the Leeds African–Caribbean carnival in 1990. The photographs show the different ways in which African–Caribbean women have been involved each year in the making and wearing of costumes in carnival (see Figure 11). The accompanying text states that

> At the heart of the Leeds Carnival are its Queens, the glamorous women who parade the street in their amazing costumes . . . (there is no Carnival King). But carnival is also a story of a number of unacknowledged queens, the women who work behind the scenes providing the powerhouse of energy and ideas to make it happen.
>
> (Hendrickson 1990: 2)

By 1992, the Pavilion entered yet another phase in its development: it could now look back on the solid achievements of the past ten years, although much was still needed, both in terms of finance and other factors, in order to be able to anticipate a reasonably secure future.[5] However, workers and management see the Pavilion as changing all the time, moving on, perhaps

5 These factors include adequate office space, more gallery space, an area for crèche facilities, security of funding, particularly from the local authority, funding to secure full-time posts instead of part-time, and adequate funding to support initiatives and developments within the organisation. As a women's organisation, the Pavilion is especially vulnerable to alterations in funding policies by local authorities and local arts authorities.

Figure 10   Lisa Williamson. Photomontage (1988); 32 × 21 ins

Figure 11 Paulette Stirling and Olinthia Fleming. *Carnival Queen.* Photograph. *Looking for Sheba* (1990)

more smoothly, certainly more professionally. In some ways, it has become an institution; and what the Pavilion stands for – its particular kind of critical approach to photography and black women's arts – is becoming more firmly established in the locality and further afield as a result of an accumulation of personal and formal contacts made over the years, and also because of national and local arts policy changes (towards which the Pavilion has itself contributed).

Recent exhibitions at the Pavilion have explored in detail issues which were treated at a more general level in the past. For example, Rachael Field's exhibition of paintings: *Real Lemon: Broadening Out* (1992) (see Figure 12) addresses not just lesbianism, but the issue of 'fat politics' among lesbians. It has been ecstatically received by the local women's community, to judge by the remarks made in the Pavilion gallery's comments book. Respondents indicate that Field's work has given them more confidence and an increased sense of independence. The Pavilion seems to have created an atmosphere in which certain minority groups can open themselves up and show images which speak of the complexity of their internal concerns.

Thus the Pavilion is becoming a barometer, as it were, which registers the feelings of some women's communities in Leeds: it balances the issues raised in the work exhibited against the ideas and opinions of respondents. But it clearly does more than just balance. It often leads, since some of its exhibitions introduce issues which are contentious, have to be talked through, and may turn out to attract much criticism. In one sense, then, some of the visual work is avant-garde. And through the process of negotiating issues

Figure 12 Rachael Field. *Whale* (1991). Oil on canvas. 108 × 72 ins. Photograph: Ann McGuiness

interactively in this way, the Pavilion is surely addressing the political question of audience which Burgin (1986a) raised.

However, the barometer does not indicate much interest in the complex issues of class: at the time of writing, there is little evidence of visual work in this area at the Pavilion. Is this because the category 'working-class woman' seems increasingly difficult to define, and therefore its target of criticism is unclear? And little attention has been paid to the category of 'older women'. Yet if few working-class and older women want to participate in Pavilion activities, this raises the problem of tokenism, which the Pavilion now wants to resist.[6] Indeed, official policy is that its exhibitions should represent a collective critical viewpoint. Individual artists with individualistic viewpoints are therefore discouraged because they only represent themselves and leave no corporate presence behind them when their exhibition finishes; whereas collective work represents shared interests, and thus lays solid foundations for a continuity of practice into the future.

So group exhibitions are promoted, and collective work in the darkroom is encouraged. In the case of exhibitions, it is also Pavilion policy to show positive images of women. A collective exhibition loaned from the Cambridge Darkroom, *Stolen Glances: Lesbians take photographs* (1991–3), explores the limits imposed by the notion of positive images. For example,

> Jacqui Duckworth's 'Coming Out Twice' creates a fictionalised account of her experience of 'coming out' for a second time as a disabled person. In an attempt to escape the limitations of 'positive' images of disability she draws upon the rhetoric of surrealism to explore a growing sense of physical dislocation.
>
> (Boffin and Fraser 1991: 18)

In the Pavilion darkroom, women are also encouraged to explore ways of making positive images of themselves. And any reference to racism, sexism, etc., whether overt or implicit, is banned. People who make racist or sexist remarks about works on show are asked to leave; and where it seems that discrimination is being expressed, workers always seek the photographer/ artist's advice on how to proceed. Indeed, consultation with the artist on all points is a Pavilion policy; in the long term this helps to create more sensitive and enlightened attitudes towards minority women's groups in Leeds, and further afield. And everyone who participates at the Pavilion, in whatever way, is regarded as a cultural worker.

There have been notable technological developments since the Pavilion was founded, but it is still concerned with photography, and has not become involved with video and computer art since there is provision for women's video work elsewhere in Leeds. However, workers and management believe

---

6 At present, Pavilion workers and management are inclined to look back on the 5 *Women* exhibition as being somewhat tokenistic. Yet at the time, this show marked an advance on the previously yearly held *Open Submissions* show of which far more serious criticisms could be made, since it gave an advantage to those who could afford expensive equipment, and tended to attract some voyeuristic work.

that photography remains an excellent medium for their specific purposes: not only is it good at representing social events (e.g. *Looking for Sheba*) and presenting issues (e.g. *That's Action Women*), but importantly, cameras are relatively cheap and accessible, and black and white film is not difficult to process. By means of photography, women can construct their own accounts of their lives, instead of having to accept alternative versions which may distort or ignore their own viewpoints. Furthermore, photography is at the heart of the Pavilion's education programme; and this is arguably the most radical aspect of its total project.

Moving now to the Pavilion's attitude towards theory: 'issues arise, develop, and are discussed'[7] around such events as the submission of work for exhibition and the anticipation of audience response. In this way, theory tends to be empirically grounded. Let us take a specific example of how this happens. Della Grace's *The Ceremony* (in *Stolen Glances*) celebrates lesbian eroticism and appropriates the visual language of pornography in order to hijack heterosexual sites and customs. It includes sado-masochistic relationships. This particular topic began to be debated at the Pavilion when some members expressed a desire to hire *Stolen Glances*. But it was recognised that more informed discussion was needed before the exhibition could be shown, and the *Feminist Art News* collective subsequently ran a workshop on lesbian sado-masochistic relationships at the Pavilion.[8] This provided information, examined pre-conceived ideas and provoked argument; thus ensuring that *Stolen Glances* would have an educated audience. When it was ultimately shown at the Pavilion, it was received more in an atmosphere of spirited debate than of judgment based on prejudice. In answer to the question, 'What is lesbian art: necessity or indulgence?' a new theoretical position was reached.

Yet all workers and management committee members have their own academic understanding of theory, in relation to feminism, lesbianism, black women's issues, etc.; and the collective understanding of these differing theories is realised in the organisation and accomplishment of the Pavilion's activities. However, its members are not interested in 'academic' feminist theory/art practice as such. Workers argue that that this tends to be associated with specific individuals (for example, Griselda Pollock and Mary Kelly), and that it is better to have a collectively based and accessible practice – whose theory reflects these criteria and is more directly grounded in empirical experience.

---

7 As one of the Pavilion workers put it in conversation with me during preparation for writing this section.

8 *Feminist Art News* (FAN) has its administrative base in Leeds, and has always maintained close links with the Pavilion. Its magazine has provided an invaluable forum and resource for feminists who work in and around the field of visual art. However, in 1993 the Arts Council of Great Britain which had funded the project abruptly withdrew all financial support. As a result, though the FAN collective continues to run workshops on various aspects of women's art, publication of the magazine has been suspended.

However, at a more general level, the Pavilion project connects with the whole tradition of critical thinking. It clearly has a certain amount in common with Tagg's theoretical approach, for example; while links can also be made between the Pavilion project and the critical theory of Adorno, who argues that the process enacted by every art work is 'a model for a kind of praxis wherein a collective subject is constituted' (Adorno 1984: 343). Put slightly differently, he sees the autonomous artwork, in conjunction with a constellation of related factors, as creating the possibility of an increased autonomy for a class or group of viewing subjects; while this whole process in itself could subsequently act as a blueprint for other potentially liberatory social situations outside the world of art. We might relate this set of ideas to the context in which Rachael Field's paintings were received at the Pavilion. In conjunction with a constellation of related factors (position of paintings on gallery wall, unique character of Pavilion, audience types, date of viewing, specific attributes of the city of Leeds, and so on), these paintings gave viewers an increased sense of personal and group autonomy – to which the writings in the Pavilion comments book bear witness. And it is to be hoped that this emancipatory situation may subsequently have helped to generate others like it in different areas of social life. In any case, we are provided with a superb example of Adorno's notion of the liberatory potential of the autonomous art work.

I remarked earlier that the Pavilion is becoming an institution. With the process of institutionalisation goes a tendency towards 'establishment' views. In the case of the Pavilion, this tendency is accentuated through the showing of exhibitions from other organisations like Camerawork and the Cambridge Darkroom. The Pavilion has always taken touring exhibitions, and these can introduce an element of sophistication and a certain type of intellectual advance[9] which move current debates on. But in my opinion, local outreach work and Pavilion-produced photographs must serve continually to counter-balance the tendency to become 'mainstream' – given that I use the terms 'mainstream', 'institution' and 'establishment' in a strictly relativist sense. Every truly radical collective faces the inescapable long-term dilemma of continually walking the tightrope between the establishment (with its funding ties) and collapse. In order to achieve the formidable task of staying on the tightrope, the Pavilion must perpetually resharpen its own unique critical edge by nurturing the social and political demands of local women's groups.[10] This means helping them to transform those demands into photographic image (-and-text) pieces whose critique is hard-hitting and effective.

---

9 For example, in *Stolen Glances* (1991), where Duckworth is said to draw on the rhetoric of surrealism in her attempt to escape the limitations of positive images of disability (Boffin and Fraser 1991).

10 Which is in itself fraught with complications. A project like *That's Action Women* assumes in the first place an issue to fight and, just as importantly, a group of women willing and active enough to learn photography in order to fight the issue. Politically active women may prefer far more direct action.

The Pavilion has pursued issues that were addressed by Tagg in *The Burden of Representation* (carrying out a locally based critical programme), by Pollock in *Framing Feminism* (the problematic for visual artists who are women) and by Burgin in *Between* (constructing photographic image-and-text critique). The notion of cultural critique is centrally relevant, but neither Marxist nor academic feminist theory is now prominent on the Pavilion's agenda; nor is Tagg's approach quite compatible with the Pavilion's emphasis on theory-grounded, *collective* projects by *women* which are *accessible* to local women's communities. However, while developments over the past ten years at the Pavilion indicate some of the directions in which visual cultural critique is being steered, today *theory-led* critique is virtually obliged to negotiate the concept of postmodernism. Whatever the position taken on the relationship of modernism to postmodernism (see, for example, Bauman 1992: 173–5), debates in this area have highlighted the spatial and visual dimensions of our lives,[11] and have made us aware that the most developed form of the commodity has become the image, rather than the concrete material product. The Situationists, a group of radical social critics writing in France during the 1960s, forecast that the image would replace the railway and the automobile as the driving force of the economy in the second half of the twentieth century. Since that prescient prediction was made, there have been various attempts to theorise the increased importance of visual images and visual communication in modern capitalist society. And in these theoretical developments we can see the focus on visual representation clearly broadening out from what was principally a concern with visual art images to an interest in a much wider range of visual representations. In what follows, I examine the ways in which accounts of postmodernism and postmodernity theorise visual representation. This analysis is then related to the Pavilion project and to the general themes of this section of the book. The first text I examine *is* concerned with art, however. It is included because it signals those debates which concern us: debates about critique, about visual communication and about postmodernism.

Jean-François Lyotard's belief in the radical potential of visual art was introduced in Chapter 2, and is the topic of *Driftworks* (Lyotard 1984). In this early work Lyotard claims that the age of 'imperial Reason' is coming to its end (later, he would characterise this as the beginning of the postmodern era), and that critique, which is verbal and based on reason, is increasingly ineffectual and pointless. He suggests that something more fundamental than critique is needed to confront our political system since critique just shifts ideological positions and still focuses on exchange-value in capitalism. He argues that deconstruction is an infinitely preferable tool, for instead of

11 For example, the British Sociological Association Bookclub, May 1992, advertises *Places on the Margin* (McCrone 1992) as follows: 'The debate on modernity and postmodernity has awakened interest in the importance of the spatial for cultural formations.'

changing an ideology, it dismantles it; instead of just shifting a position, it also shifts space. Rather than merely interpreting and critiquing a text's 'meaning', deconstruction investigates the structure of the text, challenges the status of bourgeois signifying practices as 'natural' or 'true', and exposes the illusion of a speaking position which is outside or above structures of representation. Therefore, deconstruction is a deeper process than critique. Lyotard suggests that it involves the imagination, the free play of ideas which surface from the unconscious, where 'the bastion of signification' (Lyotard 1984: 36) is dismantled. Deconstruction finally produces demystification; and for Lyotard 'demystification is the permanent revolution' (Lyotard 1984: 29).

He is fascinated by artists, because of the way some have reacted in their practice to the situation capitalism has created. He observes that these artists seem largely to ignore political theorists and politicians; and instead of continuing to produce 'unifying, reconciling forms' which are analogous to current political debates, their activity has become a deconstructive one which is necessarily critical. Instead of repressing their imaginings, as ordinary people (including social theorists) have done, they have dared to show them. In the visual arts, in music and in dance, these artists produce what Lyotard calls *figural forms*; that is, 'an order of figure' which can't be put into words nor transformed into practical experience. This suggests that these arts are ontologically located outside the political system, for they do not deal with the signifieds of things but with their plastic organisation, their signifying organisation. Indeed, they are outside 'reality', if reality is taken – following Freud – to be that which can be verbalised. Lyotard argues that figural forms are present in the gaps of reality precisely in places where the testing of reality through its transformation into verbal representation does not intervene. Art can thus be both an instrument allowing us to *see* through the gaps of dominant ideologies, and the source from which new methods could be drawn in the struggle against the system(s). While critique is negative, and a secondary process, art is a primary one: it allows glimpses of otherness, of elsewhere. According to Lyotard, this positive quality in the case of visual art has to do with its artefactualness, its autonomy, its uniqueness – as I also suggested in the discussion of Burgin's work in *Between* (1986a). However, Burgin himself would strongly refute any claim that visual art lies outside reality, and would argue instead that art is a *cultural* formation consisting of both visual and verbal discursive strands which interconnect with those of other cultural formations.

But how precisely are art, imagination and deconstruction linked in Lyotard's schema? He argues that deconstruction must involve desire – the body's energy charge, its libidinal intensity. According to Freud, desire is intolerable, and must be released. Lyotard argues that all cultures, including capitalism, use their power to dam it up and thereby to profit from it. Thus power prohibits the free rei(g)n of desire, forcing it to seek release in fantasy, in the contemplation of ideologically generated fetishes. Yet that release is only temporary, and desire is drawn back into the relations of capitalism (for example, into the buying of another pornographic magazine); it is caught in a continual loop-back process. Lyotard argues that the artist, and above all the visual artist, can free desire from fantasy, from this continual and futile feedback into fetishes, by channelling the motor of desire into the visual art work instead. Certain visual art works entice, indeed almost compel, the viewer's eye into wandering over its lines, shapes, forms and colours; and after a while, the viewer experiences a visual oscillation between the depicted object and the formal system of the work. To demonstrate this process, Lyotard refers to the diaries of Paul Klee (1964). Klee writes that he was in the habit of drawing from nature; but that having done so, he turned the drawing around. This enabled him to 'free' himself from the depicted object and to re-emphasise the formal plastic elements of the composition. Finally, he put the page the right way up again and attempted to reconcile the figurative image with the formal design. Lyotard maintains that this process of oscillation, back and forth between content and form, which is free from linguistic constraints, from ideology, from 'reality', produces an (in)sight into something quite other, a glimpse of elsewhere. He says: 'Art exasperates desire in people. Herein lies the possibility of the practical transformation of the reality of social relations' (Lyotard 1984: 77). However, he emphasises – like Adorno – that not all art contains this potential. Much of it is capitalist-led. And art which illustrates critique – so-called revolutionary art – cannot by definition be deconstructive, since it is subservient to discourse. Nor can art be deconstructive if it merely *expresses* fantasy. To be deconstructive, art – or anti-art as Lyotard calls it – must be *formally* innovative. Only new visual form is able to startle the eye, to free it from the alternative of fantasy.

While the viewer of deconstructive art is required to cultivate a type of alert receptivity, an active passivity, a similar kind of postmodern attitude is also demanded of the *deconstructionist* of other people's texts. S/he must allow his/her attention to float evenly over 'the errant one's discourse' (Lyotard 1984: 41) so that the cry or the slip or the silence coming from elsewhere may be heard. The stage must be free for the figural event.

The idea that the artist, unlike the philosopher, can produce a glimpse of an alternative future society has a history which goes back a very long way; and the demystifying power of imagination was recognised and discussed long before Lyotard wrote *Driftworks*. But this constellation of emphases on drifting rather than navigating, on active passivity rather than purposeful argument, on imagination rather than system, on figuration rather than discourse, on artefact rather than critique, is important for its suggestion of the postmodern attitude and the place of visual – or figural – representation in relation to it. Yet I do not agree that there is a world of difference between visual art and verbal discourse, and would maintain that although the image has unique properties which visual art transforms through its own meta-discourse, critique in the form of visual art cannot be and is not 'separate' from verbal critique in any metaphilosophical or even more 'fundamental' sense. Visual and verbal, image and text, contribute towards the representation of our reality, towards the construction of interlinked cultural formations such as art and social science, towards an understanding and a critique of society.

Lyotard's fundamental distinction between 'anti-art' and critique, and his scornful rejection of the latter, have implications for his own textual practice. Despite the title, *Driftworks* appears more formally organised, more sequential, less fragmented in form than some of Adorno's work (see, for example, Adorno 1984: Appendix I, p. 425) and is very carefully argued. Lyotard couldn't do without reason. Perhaps he would say that we have to use the method we know, and work from the paradigm or system in which we are based, in order to achieve a firm foothold on the bridge to elsewhere. But *Driftworks* demonstrates another attribute of the discursive form it rejects. Quite early on, Lyotard points to the association between men, reason and power; and while he attends to the relationship between reason and power, he does not deconstruct the concept of 'men'. I sense that this is a text about men's world, and a man's 'radical' alternative. I wonder whether any existing work by black and/or disabled women would be 'formally innovative' enough to produce visual oscillation, figural form for the viewer that Lyotard has in mind. Would it even be in there with a chance?

Lyotard's treatment of visual art – like that of many other critical theorists – raises the problem of elitism. Like Adorno, he insists that only *formal* innovation can have a radical potential. But formal innovation is a relative concept; what is formally innovative for some may appear visually banal to others. The kind of 'anti-art' works he has in mind are likely to engage those who are already attuned to the visual subculture of high art, and to baffle most people – who may, in any case, not even want or have access to art at all. And, ironically, while Lyotard suggests that Pop Art contains transformational qualities, there are many (artists in particular) who would want to argue that Pop Art is more closely linked to the capitalist regime than most other types of contemporary innovative art. However, though there is much to disagree with in *Driftworks*, it gives a fascinating early glimpse of the postmodern attitude, and of the increased importance that is accorded to the visual image in postmodernist theory. The paradox, then, is that this work constitutes an influential piece of critical writing, and critical writing is precisely what Lyotard claimed cannot make any political difference.

Jean Baudrillard believes, like Lyotard, that the authority of traditional metaphysical assumptions has disintegrated. But while the main thrust of Lyotard's *Driftworks* is to suggest that with the collapse of 'imperial Reason', the aesthetic may offer glimpses of an ideology-free and therefore truly radical alternative, Baudrillard insists on confronting why that collapse has occurred. He points to the fact that one of the most important and perplexing aspects of today's industrial society is the proliferation of communications through the media. He argues that it is because the new culture of the media is impervious to the old forms of resistance and is impenetrable by traditional theories that reason has lost its authority, and collapsed. The problem arises, therefore, as to how to characterise the structure of communication in today's world where the media increasingly dominate. Out of a closely argued critique of Marxism, Baudrillard has constructed an alternative theory: a historical theory of sign structures. It focuses on the effect of those images which increasingly intrude on our lives, and are to be found on street hoarding advertisements, in junk mail pushed through our letter-boxes, and above all on our television screens.

Marx maintained that underlying every social and economic system and forming its secret identity-principle is its 'mode of production'; which products get produced, by whom and how. Baudrillard originally wrote as a Marxist, but his position has changed over the years, and he has come to discard this Marxist emphasis on production; replacing it with a series of analyses of modern industrial society. In *The Mirror of Production* (1975) he shows each of Marx's major positions to be mirror-images of capitalist society, and consequently argues that Marxism does not get far enough away from capitalism to be its gravedigger. As Poster remarks: 'Marxism emerges in Baudrillard's pages not as a radical critique of capitalism but as its highest form of justification or ideology' (1988: 4). Baudrillard rejects the assumption of man the producer and the economic doctrine of *homo economicus*, which are shared by capitalism and Marxism alike. His critique also suggests that the sociological acceptance of individual action and taste, and a determinist concept of society, are again assumptions which do not stand up well against the test of contemporary empirical data from advertising and the media. He argues that the relationship of sign to commodity and to individual consumer is not a function of the stage of capitalism in which that historically specific relationship is located; instead, the stages of capitalism mirror the stages of development of the *sign system*. In terms of this theoretical reversal, and in the current stage of development of the sign system, consumer objects now constitute a system of signs that differentiate the population. This system of signs cannot become intelligible if each sign is related to each object, but only through the play of difference between the signs. For example, advertising codes products through symbols that differentiate them from other products, thereby fitting the object into a series. According to Baudrillard, the object has its effect when it is consumed by transferring its 'meaning' to the individual consumer. A potentially infinite play of signs is thus instituted which orders society while providing the individual with an illusory sense of freedom and self-determination.

In this theory about the autonomy of the sign system, 'representation' becomes an obsolete, misleading concept. Baudrillard argues that in today's commodity the relation of word, image or meaning and referent is broken and restructured so that its force is directed, not to the referent of use-value or utility, but to desire. The restructured sign does not 'represent' the object as something of use. Indeed, it does not represent anything but itself and, according to Baudrillard, is therefore more accurately characterised as a simulation: an object or discourse which has no firm origin, no referent, no ground or foundation, and is completely separated from its referent. It emits its own meanings, extracted from the social, but now deployed as its own 'floating signal'. For example, television advertisements constitute a new language form in which the code (the rationale or guiding force behind the transmissions, but never clearly explained by Baudrillard) transmits signifers to the population who are subject to this 'terroristic' mode of signification.

In *Simulations* (1983) Baudrillard presents a weird new world constructed out of models or simulacra which have no referent or ground in any 'reality' except their own. The distinctions between object and representation, thing and idea are no longer valid. A television soap opera, like 'the news', draws the outside world into its own media-reality. Figure 13 is of a picture-postcard. Its overall presentation is typical of many picture-postcard views of tourist 'beauty spots', and it may, at first glance, appear to represent a 'real' piece of English countryside. However, the stronger emphasis is on a television reality: the world of the BBC series, *Last of the Summer Wine.* 'Norah Batty's cottage', regularly featured in the programme, is shown in a prominent position, top-left, to establish this television reality. But the postcard, echoing the television series, introduces views of the real-physical Holmfirth and its surroundings (though Holmfirth is not mentioned by name) into its overall presentation of the television reality. The postcard is itself evidence of the strength of that television reality. *Last of the Summer Wine* has evidently become so real that it has generated a demand for this by-product, this physical commodity, which is, in a sense, a 'less real', or second-degree, version of the television reality.[12]

The emergence, in 1992, of Ross Perot as a popular potential US president also suggests a situation where object and representation, thing and idea may be increasingly hard to distinguish.

> He is proffering an increasingly appealing, some say dangerous, solution to the problems of politics and politicians-as-usual: turn them off, turn them out, take it back, and leave the programming details for later. In Mr Perot's real-unreal world, television is both medium and metaphor – and he promises a happy ending.
>
> (Tisdall 1992)

Baudrillard uses the term 'hyperreality' to refer to this 'real-unreal world' in which simulations abound, and where the very notion of 'simulation' renders that of 'reality' unclear, inappropriate. It presents the imaginary as real, and undermines any contrast to the real, absorbing the real within itself.

---

12 Holmfirth Tourist Office supplied me with the postcard, and I am told that it sells very well.

Figure 13 *The 'Last of the Summer Wine' Country.* Picture postcard. Balmforth and Co. Ltd Publishers, Holmfirth, Yorks

Seen thus, Ross Perot's policies and activities, his relationship to the American people and their enthusiasm for him, appear in a bewildering and frightening light rather than 'promising a happy ending'. Are we being drawn into a hyperreality where all the 'important decisions' will be made via our seemingly active participation, but where that participation consists of our being seduced into wanting their effects; where we are powerless to think about any alternatives to those which the media 'beam' into our minds, stimulating our desire?[13]

It can be seen that the general implications of this theory are depressing because the subject no longer has an effective vantage-point on reality. The privileged position is now occupied by the object, specifically the hyperreal object, the simulated object (is Ross Perot a simulated object?). 'Subjects' are more accurately seen as consumers, and hence the prey of objects. Which is to say that in place of a logic of the subject, Baudrillard proposes a logic of the object. He argues that the media generate a world of simulations which is immune to rationalist critique, whether Marxist or liberal; they present an excess of information in the form of a signal which precludes response by

13 Virtual reality presents the ultimate, to date, in 'hyperreal' confusion. There have been many television programmes and articles in the press about virtual reality; for example, 'Colonising Cyberspace', *BBC Horizon*, 22 April 1991, and Paul Fisher's 'Serious suits get lost in space', *Guardian*, 7 January 1993.

recipients. The only way out for the subject, according to Baudrillard, is death, or non-response. Death is not an attractive option. However, non-response is a possibility: the media cannot cope with non-response, since they feed on desire.

Yet how widespread is this condition of hyperreality? Critics point out that Baudrillard writes about particular experiences, mainly television images, as if nothing else in society mattered; and that he extrapolates a bleak view of the world from that limited base. In fact television also gives us information, on which we may act. In Romania in 1990, there was an extraordinarily rapid and violent transition of power from an enfeebled Ceaucescu to those controlling the television station and then the whole country. This dramatic series of events owed much to the influence of television images which had previously been beamed into certain border regions of Romania from other Eastern European countries; for these images showed the part played by ordinary citizens in bringing about the downfall of those countries' governments.[14] This suggests that Baudrillard ignores contradictory evidence. Yet his theory is very important in certain respects. Marxism produces uninteresting conclusions when applied to the production of many commodities today. Compact discs are a good example: production is largely automated and their 'object-value' is small. Instead, skill and money go into the sleeve design, for it is this that in large part attracts us to a particular disc; differentiating the category of person who acquires it from the category of person who acquires another. Baudrillard's theory engages with the peculiar contemporary condition in which images are powerful, and in some cases 'take off' into their own world, piercing subjects with their 'meanings'. By comparison, Marxist theory, and especially a theory of production, can seem like a nineteenth-century response to nineteenth-century Western industrial society.

Critical theorists cannot ignore Baudrillard's arguments. His theory may not be relevant to some aspects of modern industrial society: reason obviously informs certain actions, but Baudrillard has shown that it does not allow a general, historically informed grasp of the present. With Americans apparently watching upwards of seven hours' television each day (while their British counterparts put in nearly four hours), it isn't difficult to come up with instances where media images are influencing our thoughts and actions, particularly those of children; consequently confusing the line between the television images we see and other aspects of our daily lives. 'There's Lassie', cry the little voices when I walk our rough-haired collie. On a more intellectual note, Poster argues that: 'critical theory now faces the formidable task of unveiling structures of domination when no one is dominating, nothing is being dominated and no ground exists for a principle of liberation from domination' (Poster 1988: 6), indeed where reality itself

---

14 According to G. Baines in 'Beams fuel the flames: television has been one of the key catalysts to change in Eastern Europe, particularly Romania' (*Guardian*, 8 January, 1990).

has become a rather meaningless, fuzzy concept. If we add to this the proposition that liberal and Marxist meta-narratives have collapsed, thus depriving the rational subject of its privileged access to truth (a theme to be found in several postmodern texts), then critical theory would appear to be in disarray.

However, it is argued by other theorists of postmodernism that Baudrillard's model is highly irresponsible (Harvey 1989), that we ignore the continuing development of capitalism at our peril (Jameson 1991a and b). I shall eventually examine some of these alternative presentations of the postmodern condition and of postmodernity. But first, I would emphasise that Baudrillard's theory has helped to show how widespread and powerful visual images are in modern industrial society. Both his work and the world of advertisements and consumer goods on which he focuses indicate the extraordinary potency of the visual image. Perhaps it was Adorno's understanding of this potency that led him to dread late capitalism. It is probably why media communication is increasingly replacing words with visual images. McRobbie (1991: 183–4) shows that teenage magazines now contain less narrative than they used to. Their pages are primarily *visual* presentations and are divided into juxtaposed fragments consisting of advertisements, or quasi-advertisements, with their own mini-narratives, often in the form of strip cartoons. Young (1992) has noted that British election messages are now delivered predominantly in visual form; while political party rallies are turning into spectacles.[15] Media researchers prophesy that the American 'news' will soon be portrayed entirely in images (Young 1992). So, visual images can no longer remain the province of visual artists and theorists of high culture. Because of their widespread deployment in our everyday lives, they pose a challenge to cultural theory on a broader front.

There are theorists who understood this before Baudrillard's work became widely known. For example, Williamson (1978) has argued from a Marxist standpoint that advertisements provide us with an ideology, a structure in which we, and the goods they advertise, are interchangeable, and thus they are selling us ourselves. However, Baudrillard's ideas have been particularly influential – perhaps because they are so controversial – in focusing the attention of other social scientists on the power that media signals, particularly electronic media signals, can wield. His ideas are especially controversial for social science because if the cultural sphere is autonomous, as he maintains, and we now inhabit a world in which the various aspects of our lives have been 'hyperrealised' by cultural forces, then theory cannot any longer distance itself from its object: they are collapsed into one. Furthermore, if postmodernity is our current condition and post-modernist theory seeks to account for it, these are virtually impossible to distinguish one from another. Fredric Jameson (1991b) has remarked that

---

15 For example, the Labour Party pre-election rally at Sheffield in 1992.

one of the main problems about postmodernism is that we can't get enough critical distance from it.

There are several responses to Baudrillard's work which entail the possibility of a more visual sociology, and each of these scenarios is quite different. First, if we follow the 'logic' of his ideas, then a sociology which merges with, say, visual art is quite 'in order' – in the sense that they merge in hyperreality; although by the same token, sociology's scientific or theoretical status is annulled (not to mention art's status as art) by the fact that the social world it would address is also part of hyperreality. Second, the reflexive character of sociological understanding has recently become an issue for some social scientists, and Baudrillard's claim that social science and social life merge in hyperreality kindles the debates surrounding this issue. His work may consequently have had the effect of stimulating experiments, now underway, to find new literary forms for sociology that enable the construction of theory which is reflexively sound. This experimentation has drawn attention to the visual aspects of textual presentation, and some new literary forms involve the manipulation of typography and layout as part of the theoretical argument.[16] Third, sociologists who insist that they are *not* operating in a hyperreal world may nevertheless wish to assess the soundness of certain of Baudrillard's arguments and claims, for example, by examining the empirical effects of media messages on various sectors of society. This presumably entails working closely with and on visual imagery,[17] and could contribute to an increased awareness of the visual possibilities for sociology itself.[18] And when images are in the forefront of our minds, then the tendency may be to use them, particularly when they are shown to be so powerfully effective. In any case, it is well-nigh impossible to analyse a topic closely without incorporating elements of it into one's own analysis, as Baudrillard remarked about Marx's analysis of capitalism.

Scott Lash has argued that late twentieth-century industrialised societies signify more through images than through words:

> What we are perceiving, in TV, in video, in the spread of information technology, on the Walkman, on the audio-cassettes we listen to, in adverts, in popular magazines, are mostly images. We are living in a society in which our perception is directed almost as often to representations as it is to 'reality'. . . . And/or our perception of reality comes to be increasingly by means of these representations. Even much of our perception of representations comes via representations.
>
> (Lash 1990: 23–4)

---

16 These are discussed in Chapter 6.
17 For, as Featherstone remarks:

> We possess little systematic evidence about day-to-day [postmodern] practices, and we need information in terms of the stock sociological questions 'who? when? where? how many?' if we are to impress colleagues that postmodernism is more than a fad.
>
> (Featherstone 1988: 207)

18 Compare the fact that the form and content of some more recent advertisements indicate that their producers have probably read Williamson, op. cit.

As a self-proclaimed rationalist, Lash dismisses Baudrillard's 'uncritical and even irresponsible celebration' of postmodernism (Lash 1990: 2). However, he argues that the *cultural terrain* on which we operate today (as distinct from the total socio-economic system) is predominantly 'postmodernist'. He suggests that we would be unwise to ignore the significant cultural shift away from modernism and towards postmodernism; though he notes that many on the Marxist left continue to disregard it because they think modernism offers a more favourable arena in which to wage their cultural struggles. I now turn to his 'Discourse or Figure? Postmodernism as a "Regime of Signification"' (Lash 1988: 311–36). In this article, Lash acknowledges and builds upon the distinction between 'figural' and 'discursive' which Lyotard made in *Driftworks*. He also draws upon Sontag's (1967) insistence that the work of art must be a sensory experience (and is not to be 'interpreted' for a 'meaning'), and upon Benjamin's (1973) prediction that the cultural realm would become increasingly less auratic. However, Baudrillard's later texts surely have an indirect influence, for their controversial nature alone tends to lend an urgency to Lash's focus on postmodern culture, and to provide a point of departure into an alternative, and possibly sharper, theoretical appraisal of the contemporary cultural terrain.

For Lash has endeavoured to move to a more precise definition of postmodernism, in which *de-differentiation* and the *figural* are held to be central to postmodern regimes of signification in contemporary culture. Postmodernist de-differentiation is contrasted with modernist differentiation, and this distinction relates to the proposition that modernist signification is largely discursive, whereas postmodernism's mode of signification is 'importantly figural'. Let us first examine Lash's explanation of how modernist signification through discourse leads to differentiation. Discourse is a mode of signification where the word (and for Lash it is, above all, the word) *represents* the object it describes. There is the assumption that nature, or an object, can be described accurately (realism) – and that there is a clear separation between reality and what is representing it; a distinction between nature and ideas. This separation leads to a tendency for a discourse to become increasingly autonomous, concerned with its own 'inner logic', its immanent development. There is a predisposition for 'specialisms' to develop, in other words for *differentiation*. Post-foundationalist, modernist society has distinguished aesthetic, theoretical and moral discourses. It has made a distinction between the social and the cultural, between the secular and the religious. There has been a growth of self-legislating 'academic' disciplines such as sociology, which develop their own conventions and modes of valuation. However, as we have seen, Lash argues that in industrialised societies there has been a change from a predominantly modernist – *discursive* – cultural paradigm to a predominantly postmodernist – *figural* – cultural paradigm where signification is largely iconic and works through impact. Iconic signs are closely tied to the objects they show, or 'mirror'; that is to say, images resemble referents to a greater degree than words do. Lash maintains that as figural signification begins to take precedence, autonomous discursive 'disciplines' start to crumble (and we have already seen evidence of this in Chapter 2, and in the section on the Pavilion in this chapter). The 'cultural economy' becomes *de-differentiated*, so that author and text merge or the author disappears, critic and literature merge, commerce and culture come together, as in pop videos and teenage magazines. Our everyday life becomes pervaded with a reality which increasingly comprises representations in which the space of the signifier is invaded by the referent, and where the signifer invades the place of the referent. While modernism has the problem of how to represent reality, postmodernism injects a flimsiness and instability into our experience of reality, and thus poses the problem of what reality *is*.

Despite the distinction between differentiation and de-differentiation, Lash argues that the latter does not necessarily preclude the former; rather de-differentiation can create the space for differentiation. Maud Sulter's *Zabat: Poetics of a Family Tree*, an exhibition of photographs (1989) signifies in Lash's terms of de-differentiating postmodernism and, I think, demonstrates this point. The ornately framed photographs, which in a sense resemble oil paintings, are individual, life-sized 'portraits' of unconventionally but very deliberately dressed African–Caribbean women. The images appear realist while they also seem highly symbolic. Yet when the viewer attempts to *interpret* them in terms of either the discourse of realism or the discourse of symbolism, neither project can be successfully accomplished. This is apparently in part because each project is confounded or blocked by the other. But *any* interpretation of the work's meaning is also blocked by the enormous iconic impact which is effected by the juxtaposition of the visual works, one against another, and by the juxtaposition of irresolvable items within each work; for example, oil portrait against photograph, black woman friend against white Greek mythological figure; and these juxtapositions question the discourses of both realism and symbolism. In this way, the co-presence of the discursive and the figural are addressed. De-differentiation does not banish differentiation; it problematises it.

Lash observes that such a situation problematises not only the real and the symbolic, but also the subject. And this mobile – or 'nomadic' – subjectivity, which allows for the possibility of both discursive and figural, is in itself political as it offers space for alternative forms of identity construction as well as the toleration of 'difference' in identity construction. He argues that the idea of a nomadic subjectivity which allows for the construction of identities that may deviate from the social norm indicates a left pluralism, while it may also further the tolerance which difference and left pluralism require. However, he notes that postmodernism conceived as cultural de-differentiation also holds political implications of another sort. It is associated with the restabilisation of bourgeois identity; with the increasing interpenetration of culture and commodity.

One of the most crucial aspects of 'Discourse or Figure?' must surely be Lash's account of *why* the cultural paradigm of modernism has been superseded by that of postmodernism. He suggests that perhaps 'the key to this lies in the realm of culture itself' (Lash 1988: 333). He proposes that our socially constructed archive of knowledge comprises both 'natural' facts and 'cultural' facts. 'Natural' facts are information (representations) about nature, for example an image, or verbal description of an iceberg; whereas 'cultural' facts are information (representations) about representations, for example, an advertisement for a compact disc. The cultural history of the West clearly indicates that 'cultural' facts gradually became more numerous than 'natural' facts; so numerous, indeed, that their own objective status, their materiality could no longer be ignored (the onset of modernism). And later still, they became so pervasive that they challenged 'natural' facts for hegemony, and have become the norm (the onset of postmodernism). 'Cultural' facts are now not just representations with an acknowledged objective status; they are our reality. This, Lash argues, has led to a crisis in our perception of the character of reality itself: nature is evidently still 'real', yet representations of it, and representations of representations of it, are so pervasive as to convince us *they* are reality as well – or instead? . . .

There are various conceptions of postmodernism, and of modernism. The visual artist and cultural theorist Victor Burgin identifies with a conception of postmodernism which breaks with the aesthetic realm of modernism. However, Burgin's (1986b) postmodernism places emphasis on the concept of *cultural discourse*, which is understood to contain both visual and verbal strands interwoven in a complex fashion to produce a total message; while Lash (1988) talks about the verbal discourse of differentiated modernist culture as distinct from the figural, iconic images of de-differentiated postmodernist culture. Perhaps Burgin's work can be seen as more nearly compatible with Lash's if we stress that the latter conceives of modernism and postmodernism as ideal types, and thus they can be seen as representing tendencies. In this light, the work of Burgin (1986b) and Iverson (1979), discussed in Chapter 2, might indicate that Lash's 'de-differentiated postmodern culture' consists of communication in which figural signification predominates over discursive signification but where the latter is by no means absent (and by its presence renders communication complex); and where that figural signification consists of images whose iconic facet is more powerful, effective than their symbolic facet, while the iconic facet of discursive signification is also operational. This suggests that postmodern signification is predominantly figural, predominantly iconic, operating predominantly by impact; but that verbal discourse and images which signify symbolically still constitute an important part of our cultural process of communication.

In emphasising that our culture signifies increasingly through images, 'Discourse or Figure?' raises questions about the implications of this trend for *sociological* accounts of postmodern culture. For Lash's work indicates not only that it is crucial for sociology to *engage* with images, with visual representation, but that to keep the visual out of sociological *practice* may actually become quite difficult since communication is increasingly via images. This suggests that we should scrutinise images to learn how their symbolic signification can be put to sociological use, and that we should examine them in order to appreciate how their iconic impact can be used to force home a particular argument.[19] But in addition, we should remember that very often images do not stand alone; and we can learn from Burgin how image and text (including layout and typography) work *together*, how they can be combined advantageously to produce cultural critique.

Visual representation and communication play a key role in Fredric Jameson's model of postmodernism, as they do in the works of Lyotard, Baudrillard and Lash that I have examined. However, Jameson believes that 'only Marxism offers a philosophically coherent and ideologically compelling resolution . . . to the mystery of the cultural past' (Jameson 1981: 19). And he suggests that anyone who believes that the profit motive and the logic of capital accumulation are not the fundamental laws of this world lives in an alternative universe. His is thus a Marxist analysis of society; and his theory of postmodernism is the analytic outcome of his attempt 'to correlate the emergence of new formal features in culture with the emergence of a new type of social life and a new economic order' (Jameson 1985: 113).

Using the periodising structure of Ernest Mandel's *Late Capitalism* (1980) which sets out a three-stage theory of capitalism (market, monopoly, multi-national), he proposes that in the present multinational stage there has been a fundamental shift in global economic organisation, and that this has entailed an intensification of capitalism's forms and energies; a prodigious expansion of capital into hitherto uncommodified areas. Predictably – for those who have followed this chapter up to now – he identifies representation itself as the major new area of commodification which is being developed under multinational capitalism: cultural forms are no longer part of the ideological veil which prevents the real economic relations in a society from being seen. Instead, production, exchange, marketing and consumption of cultural forms have become the central focus and expression of economic activity. However, Jameson does not describe this situation as one in which culture has finally been swallowed up by the forces of commodity capitalism, since that would imply an outdated, modernist conception of culture; one where culture is initially envisaged as separate from the socio-economic realm. Rather, he argues that there has been an explosion of culture throughout the social realm; and that this characterises our post-modern society, in which everything from economic value and state power to practices and the very structure of the psyche itself has become 'cultural'.

---

19 Many of Hedges' photographs (Hedges and Benyon 1982) show the horrors of factory life and emotionally reinforce the power and value of Marx's theory.

A later formulation, which is in some ways reminiscent of Baudrillard and of Lash, seems to transform the economic into the linguistic or representational by recasting Mandel's three-stage history into a history of the sign. Jameson observes that throughout the history of capitalism, signs have gradually moved further and further away from their referents. Thus in early capitalism scientific language was able to control its referent, the forces of nature, from a distance. Later, language became more removed from its referent, though not entirely detached from it; and in that modernist phase the sign achieved a degree of autonomy, allowing for critique and utopian aspiration. Now, in the postmodernist stage, signs are entirely relieved of the function of referring to the world. This brings about the expansion of the power of capital into the realm of the sign, of culture and representation. Signs are now marketed for themselves, and we are left

> with that pure and random play of signifiers which we call postmodernism, and which no longer produces monumental works of the modernist type, but ceaselessly reshuffles the fragments of preexistent texts, the building blocks of older cultural and social production, in some new and heightened bricolage: metabooks which cannibalize other books, metatexts which collate bits of other texts.
>
> (Jameson 1987: 222)

Jameson argues that these characteristics of postmodernism can also be seen at the level of style. In place of the 'deep' expressive aesthetic of unique style characteristic of modernism, there is now schizoid pastiche, the 'flat' multiplication and collage of styles; and an art whose imagery appears depthless. This is paralleled by a repudiation of depth models in philosophy, for example, dialectic and Freudian models. There is also a retreat from the idea of the unified personality to the 'schizoid' experience of the loss of self in undifferentiated time, and a disappearance of models which emphasise the past, like hermeneutics; we have surface in time, a single present. And that is very significant because it means that history by itself recedes and gets harder to incorporate into people's lives. In addition, postmodernism entails a new experience of space which results in particular from the transformation of urban spaces.[20] According to Jameson, we live in a depthless present – a hyperspace – where for example, mirror glass buildings deny their volume. He claims that architecture has been the dominant art form of this new condition called hyperspace,[21] although video may be the postmodernist medium *par excellence*. And he points out that music is itself spatialised on television, which is a very powerful way of reconceptualising it. In fact, a glance at the contents page of the more recent and expanded version of *Postmodernism or, The Cultural Logic of Late Capitalism* (1991a) makes it clear that the visual and spatial dimensions of our culture occupy a prominent role in Jameson's account of postmodernism. Four of the chapters

20 This is the topic of Jameson's 'Cognitive Mapping' (in Nelson and Grossberg 1988).
21 Jameson (1991b) notes that although postmodernism in architecture is already passé, the underlying postmodernist philosophy is not.

concerned with specific fields or domains focus on the visual/spatial – video, architecture, space, film – whereas only two are about 'non-visual' topics – sentences and economics.

But at the same time, to describe the characteristics of postmodernism is also to talk about a *technological* transformation – and Jameson notes that every transformation of production is accompanied by technologies which herald the emergence of a new form of capitalism. It is the new electronic technologies that seem capable of mastering space, of eclipsing it, of re-ducing distance and creating simultaneities. Jameson agrees with those who emphasise the importance of the media culture and the dominance of communication information. He suggests, therefore, that the true theories of today are linguistics and semiotics – and this remark serves to reinforce the importance of Iverson's work (1979) investigating the symbolic and iconic properties of both words and images.

Jameson is also fascinated by the problem of how these new technologies are themselves to be represented and thinks that there are some very special problems in mimesis and in representing the postmodern. In Art Deco painting, the ocean liner and the aeroplane represented the modernist classical emblems of speed and energy. However, he argues (1991b) that although we now actually live in an image culture, we have as yet no images that can represent all the technology which projects these images in our lives. He suggests that these technologies are actually very difficult to represent visually (apart from in joke form – for example, Japanese buildings which are made to look like stacks of cassettes). Language, the predominant form of representation in modernism, can talk about itself. But can a photo-graphic image be self-conscious, reflexive? Is there a homeopathic medicine of the image whereby awareness of its properties allows one to change the situation one is in? He notes that a number of experimental video-makers are working on this problem – that is, they are attempting to combat the image by way of the image.[22] However, Jameson suggests that photography has been promoted to a very privileged position in postmodernism:

> It seems that in the modernist phase photography was always trying to work up its credentials for being a great art by mimicing the aesthetics of painting. Now I think it has shot off into some new areas of its own which have nothing to do with painting; and I think it's exciting.
>
> (Jameson 1991b)

Yet he observes that one is bound to ask whether this positive reaction is, in fact, an addiction to these very intense and often beguiling stimuli; to image

---

22 For example, Joan Braderman, an independent feminist film-maker and academic, intrudes herself into soap operas. *Joan Goes Dynasty* (1987: Edinburgh Film Festival, Workshop Event) is the result of recording and rescreening some thirteen hours of the serial *Dynasty*. Having identified clips that suited her purpose, she laid these down on tape, and reduced them to one-half of their original screen area. She filled the other half with a precisely timed tape of her own critical response, then retaped the combined performance, so that both were shown simultaneously.

bombardment. This remark will serve to introduce some problems which Jameson faces.

The first of these problems clearly arises from the fact that he evidently enjoys aspects of postmodern culture – in comparison with Baudrillard who at times appears to regard the mass of media messages beamed at us as loathsome and ultimately debilitating. So how can Jameson reconcile his enjoyment of postmodernist culture with his loathing of the industrial and social relations which produce it? Connor (1989) notes that Jameson is almost unique among leftist theoreticians in refusing to condemn the productions of postmodernist culture: 'Rather, he attempts to grasp post-modernist culture dialectically, in both its positive and negative aspects, just as Marx could perceive the progressive aspects in the bourgeois capitalism he condemned' (Connor 1989: 49). But Connor considers that the evidence of this dialectical reading that Jameson is able to offer is very thin. And surely the use of dialectics itself poses something of a problem since Jameson himself noted (above) that dialectics is a 'depth model', and as such, is inappropriate – perhaps even unavailable – in the postmodern situation. This suggests a deeper problem. Does the logic of Jameson's theoretical model in fact even allow him to extricate himself from the cultural explosion which is postmodernism, in order to critique it? Commentators have pointed out (e.g. Montag 1988) that this model makes no distinction between domin-ant and oppositional: even when dealing with modernist culture under the conditions of modernity, it attributes the same formative conditions both to social and economic life and to cultural forms; although in one sense these forms are understood to be separate from the society which produced them, they also mirror its most fundamental conditions. In the case of postmodernist culture, Jameson's model appears to provide no means of separating culture from everything else, and there is greatly reduced scope for claiming that within culture there may be ways of thwarting consumer capitalism's in-exorable rhythms of appropriation and alienation. So is the model implying that we are experiencing *capitalism* in its most vigorous all-encompassing phase – into which critique may yet be inserted – or does it suggest that capitalism's postmodern *cultural* products have themselves overwhelmed all else, including the possibility of critique? How can Jameson remain faithful to the analysis of postmodernity which he has produced, while yet preventing that which the analysis reveals from overwhelming the possibility of critique? How to go about analysing a situation which appears to resist analysis? This connects with another problem which Jameson himself poses. It concerns the character of postmodern cultural representation. He com-ments that this is an odd moment in human society because none before it has ever been so suffused with culture, and yet it is a standardised culture; one where images have been taken in charge by a corporate style and are based on stereotypes (1991b). He suggests that the basic ambiguity, the problem of postmodernism, consists in asking about the hyperreal character of these stereotypical cultural representations. In other words, what is their distance from the 'real' of capitalism?

Jameson insists (1991b) that in one sense his project is a utopian one. He thinks it is imperative to recapture the urgency of theorising our difficulties, to recapture our lost ability to imagine difference in a situation where we are being pushed back by the system, closed into it. He suggests that the deeper function of the utopias of the past (such as Thomas More's in the sixteenth century [More 1965] – the significance of which More himself could not imagine) was to reveal to later generations, by the very things they left out, what the human collectivity of that time was as yet unable to visualise in a utopian mode. Jameson hopes that his struggle and failure to conceive utopia in his project, in as much as he is trying to achieve this, will be politically and culturally effective in the sense that it may eventually contribute a glimpse of another – post-postmodern – era.

Some would argue that in any case – and although his writings are not always consistent with the implications of his own theoretical position – Jameson does provide the most suggestive account to date of the difficult and uneven relationship between postmodernist culture and socio-economic postmodernity.[23] Somehow, the very style of writing of *Postmodernism or, The Cultural Logic of Late Capitalism* evokes his predicament; and the impact that this makes on the reader is perhaps as memorable as the meaning of the words he writes. And on at least two counts his writings leave us in no doubt as to the importance of visual representation today. First, there is emphasis on the fact that the new technologies generate predominantly visual images; and second, for all the vaunted autonomy of modernist visual art works, postmodernist cultural representation is shown to be far more powerful in its effect. As Jameson says, postmodernists must now learn how to combat the visual with the visual.

The Condition of Postmodernity: An Enquiry into the Origins of Cultural Change, (1989), by David Harvey, broadens out and extends the discussion about the role of the visual in postmodernism. The author is a prominent advocate of Marxist analysis in geography and urban studies. Like Jameson, he is also concerned with the perceived collapse of time and space in late capitalist societies. However, in Harvey's Marxist analysis, time and geographical space are presented as key historical variables. His thesis is that since 1972 new dominant ways have emerged in which we experience time and space, and these are bound up with new economic, political and cultural – postmodernist – practices. He sets out to demonstrate that postmodernist culture constitutes 'shifts in surface appearance' (Harvey 1989: vii) but does not signal the emergence of a post-capitalist society; and that it is the financial reorganisation of capitalism which underlies the transition to postmodernity.

---

23 For example, Connor (1989: 49).

While Harvey argues that the relationship of geographical space to the process of capitalism is of central importance, he also accounts for the roles which postmodernist visual signification and aestheticisation play in present-day capitalist society. What follows is an attempt to show how visual and spacial dimensions figure in his model.

Harvey observes that in the past, theorists (for example, Marx and Weber) regarded the spatial dimension of capitalism as contingent to human action while they treated time as a fundamental aspect of it; and consequently time was incorporated into critical theory whereas space was not. However, he notes that by the 1980s, Berman (1982) was arguing that spatial categories dominated those of time for contemporary Western capitalism and its culture; and he suggests that in the present phase of capitalism, modernist faith in the temporal notion of 'becoming' has been replaced by a philosophy of 'being' (a search for permanence). He observes, however, that such philosophies are not a new phenomenon, and that in the past they have been associated with the search for a permanent location, and with nationalism; and that, furthermore, they have tended to engender an aestheticisation of politics. In Nazi Germany, for example, following a period of capitalist overaccumulation, aesthetic judgements were used as powerful criteria for political, social and economic action. So Harvey argues that there is evidence that aestheticisation signals a dangerous move to the right. However, since aesthetic judgement prioritises space/place over time, he notes that under certain circumstances spatial practices and concepts can become central to social action.

Yet he thinks there is much to be learned from aesthetic theory about how different forms of spatialisation inhibit or facilitate processes of social change – after all, architects and painters try to communicate certain values through the construction of spatial forms. And he suggests that, equally, there is much to be learned from social theory about the flux and change which aesthetic theory has to cope with. He proposes that playing these two currents of thought off against each other may help us better to understand the ways in which politico-economic change informs cultural practices. In addition, he draws attention to anthropological studies which show both that the symbolic orderings of space and time provide a framework for experience through which we learn who or what we are in society, and that spatial reorganisations signal a shift in social relations. He argues that because time is remembered in terms of a series of events rather than sequentially,[24] the spatial image (for example, the photograph) asserts an important power over history. And he also explores the idea that in money economies, particularly capitalist ones, the intersecting command of money, time and space forms a substantial nexus of social power that we cannot afford to ignore; and that capital and its fluctuating value dominate how space and time are organised.

---

24 This point was also made by Julia Kristeva during the course of a series of four lectures on the philosophy and writings of Marcel Proust, given at the University of Kent on 26–9 May 1992.

Having shown that neither geographical space nor the process of aestheticisation can be divorced from social, political and economic considerations, Harvey then starts to analyse what he identifies as the capitalist crisis of overaccumulation in the 1960s. He observes that pressure to accelerate the output of goods and services has forced an investigation of more efficient ways of managing time and of controlling particular spaces; and that this search for spatial and temporal resolutions has created an overwhelming sense of time–space compression, while the attempt to achieve an ever-increasing output has, of necessity, been paralleled by a drive to speed up exchange and consumption. Electronic banking and plastic money now enable and encourage mass fashion linked to a choice of lifestyles, while they also engender a greater consumption of leisure and other services. We are bombarded with stimuli, which promote not only goods but the virtues of instantaneity and disposibility. Harvey argues that the overall effect has been of overload and volatility; and that mastering or intervening actively in the production of volatility entails manipulation of taste and opinion, which in turn requires the construction of new sign systems and imagery.

Harvey is one of several theorists who emphasise that imagery is a key feature of postmodern culture. But while Baudrillard, for example, argues that postmodern society's concern with the production of signs, images and sign systems rather than with commodities indicates that, at the very least, Marx's analysis of commodity production is obsolete, Harvey contends that the 'rhetoric of postmodernism' is itself dangerous because it avoids confronting the realities of political economy and the circumstances of global power. He argues that

> Given the pressures to accelerate turnover time (and to overcome spatial barriers), the commodification of images of the most ephemeral sort would seem to be a godsend from the standpoint of capital accumulation, particularly when other paths to relieve overaccumulation seem blocked.
>
> (Harvey 1989: 288)

Harvey shows that there are several ways in which visual images promote and strengthen consumer capitalism, and have thus become a prominent feature of the postmodern scene. Because they can communicate instantaneously (cf. Sontag, Lash), advertisement images seduce us into buying what has been overaccumulated, and they persuade us to do so without delay. By comparison, words take time to assimilate and tend to create a situation where the purchaser can more easily reject the invitation to buy. And images are used increasingly as logos. These provide the impression of continuity and stability while stressing the adaptability, flexibility and dynamism of whoever or whatever is being imaged.[25] In addition, brand-

---

25 For example, British Telecom's logo, which depicts Mercury, the Roman messenger of the gods, is intended to achieve the dual purpose of providing a sense of continuity while giving the impression of speedy communication over distance. It is, however, curious that this logo more accurately represents British Telecom's principal rival, Mercury.

name recognition encourages an association with 'quality', 'respectability', 'reliability' and 'innovation': the image serves to establish an identity in the market place. Consequently, the production of such images has itself become an area of innovation; which leads to the notion of the 'simulacrum', and its much-discussed role in postmodernism.

Harvey describes the simulacrum, the fantasy image, as a reality which conceals its origins in labour processes and the social relations underlying them. Simulacra are often produced through television. Mass television ownership enables a huge number of people to experience a rush of images from different spaces almost simultaneously, collapsing the world's spaces into a series of images on a screen. Harvey argues that in turn, the very ephemerality of these images or simulacra, and their instantaneous communicability over space, become virtues to be explored and appropriated by capitalists for their own purposes. And he notes that capitalism has profited greatly from its exploitation of the power that the simulacrum holds over our imaginations; witness the development of industries which exploit our fascination with 'the past' – new 'antique' furniture, old-style paintings, and the replication of building components from previous architectural styles for use in the construction of postmodern buildings. But he suggests that images and visual objects also take on a compensatory role in this shifting world, this condition of postmodernity: they play a part in the search for more secure moorings and longer-lasting values. Photographs, inherited objects (a chair, a clock) become the focus of a contemplative memory, and hence generate a sense of self that lies outside the sensory overloading of consumerist culture and fashion: 'the home becomes a private museum to guard against the ravages of time-space compression' (Harvey 1989: 292). This is perhaps the nearest Harvey comes to considering that the postmodern condition might itself generate some form of countervailing, if not 'critical', visual product. However, this is not the kind of relationship between images, visual objects and the postmodern condition that he wishes to promote. Rather, he argues that simulacra such as Disneyland and television images conceal social relations by rehashing them – aestheticising them – as entertainment, as leisure. He argues that the ubiquity of these aestheticised products has the effect of removing inequality from the political agenda, and consequently results in a political move to the right – echoing the situation in Germany which suffered from capitalist overaccumulation in the 1930s. He suggests we have a 'casino economy' where images dominate over narrative, where aesthetics has triumphed over ethics, where confidence in the association between scientific and moral judgements has collapsed.

But what of the future? Is the reactionary politics of an aestheticised spatiality our only option, now that we have lost the modernist faith in 'becoming'? In answer, Harvey argues that only historical materialism enables us to understand postmodernism as an historical–geographical condition. From that critical basis it becomes possible to launch a counter-attack of narrative against the image, of ethics against aesthetics, of a project of becoming rather than being, and to search for unity within difference, albeit in a context where the power of the image and of aesthetics, the problems of time–space compression, and the significance of geopolitics and otherness are clearly understood.

Harvey's demonstration that geographical space is fundamentally implicated in social, political and economic action contributes an important dimension to any social analysis; and his Marxist critique of capitalism and of the ways in which capitalism deploys geographical space and generates postmodernist images and visual objects is very skilful,[26] while it also shows that one of the most patently obvious features of postmodernism is that it is rooted in daily life. However, his attitude to postmodernist culture is clearly quite different from that of Jameson. Harvey's model, rooted in Marxist urban geography, suggests that through the process of aestheticisation and in the guise of postmodernist culture, late capitalism seeks to conceal its own underlying social relations, and is therefore reactionary and dangerous. Whereas Jameson's approach, with its roots in Marxist literary criticism, suggests a theoretical *tension* between capitalist processes and postmodern culture: it upholds certain postmodernist cultural productions whilst at the same time seeking to critique the global capitalist explosion which has generated them. Jameson believes in the power and efficacy of cultural representations; he sees the possibility of a countervailing postmodern culture, whereas Harvey does not. Jameson argues that visual critique has a crucial role to play *because* it uses the dominant mode of communication; while Harvey wants to combat the visual with the verbal, the presumed tool of rationality. For him, visual images lead to aestheticisation; and aestheticisation means the annulment of competing moral and political values. Images are the enemy; words empower critique.

Linda McDowell, in her review of *The Condition of Postmodernity*, says:

> This is a fascinating *tour de force*, a masterly summary (and I choose my adjective with care) of contemporary debates but it leaves the reader feeling the package has been wrapped too well. Yet again the narrative of the white male establishment has been recentred.
>
> (McDowell 1990: 532)

She claims that the overwhelming significance of postmodernist thought is the space it opens up from which 'others' can emerge: women, homosexuals, lesbians, ethnic groupings, the disabled. There is very little about women and other political minority groups in Harvey's book – nor for that

---

26 This dimension has also been addressed by other Marxist geographers, for example, Massey (1984). However, Harvey's *The Condition of Postmodernity* has been influential in helping to generate a literature on the relationship between capitalism, postmodernism and geographical space (see Robins 1990).

matter in the other primary theoretical texts on postmodernism,[27] although early feminist thinking must surely have made some contribution to the subsequent postmodernist turn. This particular white, masculinist, rationalist, Marxist narrative barely allows for a discussion of feminism, just as it appears to preclude the possibility of contemporary critical visual practice, since images portend bad news: the aestheticisation of politics.

But imagery can also be used to convey alternative moral and political values, and new information and to critique social conventions. As we have seen, some members of minority groups – especially women – *are* taking advantage of the visual means of communication which modern technology makes available, and are producing their own visual critiques. They are addressing Jameson's problem of how to combat the visual by the visual. But their *problematic* is not exactly his, because they are not solely concerned to analyse capitalism. Indeed some of them argue that twentieth-century Marxism has used the generalising categories of production and class to delegitimise the demands of women, black people, gays, lesbians, and others whose oppression cannot be reduced to economics. Even though capitalism may be a part of what they seek to criticise, their critiques relate to their own positions on the margins of society. Furthermore, these critiques are not necessarily just a matter of combating the visual with the visual, as Jameson would seem to have it. Postmodern representation may be predominantly visual, but any 'visual' representation is permeated by verbal discourse which forms part of the cultural context in which the work is embedded and given meaning (see Chapter 2). Indeed, Burgin's *Between* (1986a) shows how the critical potential of images may be considerably enhanced when they are combined unconventionally with textual passages; and much feminist visual critique does in fact incorporate textual passages.

This is all very well, Harvey-like Marxists may reply, but how can a predominantly visual critique by members of a minority political group make any kind of a dent on a postmodern culture in which electronic banking and money markets shape people's lives on a global scale? Though such a project is inevitably modest in scale and locally-based, in the long-term it may be very effective. The work of postmodernist theorists emphasises that visual signification pervades everyday life to an extent unequalled since medieval times, when the majority of ordinary folk could not read, and – in the context of an oral tradition – learned Bible stories from stained glass windows in the churches. While visual literacy is again on the increase, Marxism has actually lost much of its credibility, and it is argued that people are beginning to invest in *culture* the idealism and radical aspirations they once reserved for 'politics' and 'ideology'.[28] And in addition theorists are now focusing

---

27 Norman Denzin, in the preface of *Images of Postmodern Society* (1991), corroborates this.
28 Two articles in the *Guardian* within the space of a fortnight make this point. These are: Wilson, 'Art at the cutting edge of politics' (30 July 1992), and Landesman, 'Pagans at the church of culture' (6 August 1992).

attention on local economies, local political groupings, local artistic and religious formations, in order to examine how the relative autonomy of these pieces in the global jigsaw puzzle is changing.[29] I would suggest, therefore, that the authors of strongly visual critiques (that is, critical cultural practices with a marked visual component) which tackle gender, disability, ethnic and class issues at the local level can count on an audience accustomed to visual communication, some of whom are increasingly attracted by the radical potential of culture; while these authors may use the new knowledge of how local factors influence and are influenced by the global situation, and can thus reasonably expect to be keying into global cultural processes. In this context, it is interesting to note that one of the Pavilion's priorities in 1992 was to prepare for an exchange with a similar women's group in Hamburg in 1993, which also had links with a group in Russia.

Norman Denzin, in *Images of Postmodern Society* (1991), says he aims to write a postmodernist theory of cultural resistance, and that 'this must be a feminist, post-colonial cultural studies theory of micro-politics which sees "networks of power-relations subsisting at every point in a society"' (Denzin 1991: xi). While the notion of a postmodernist theory of cultural resistance which is also a feminist theory appears to come close to the type of visual critique I have just outlined, and to resonate with McDowell's claim that the significance of postmodernist thought is the space it opens up for 'others' to emerge from, it should be emphasised that there are feminists who regard the relationship of feminism to postmodernism as highly problematic. Although some women acknowledge points of overlap between feminism and postmodernism, others wish to be dissociated from postmodernism entirely. We need to examine the debate about the relationship between feminism and postmodernism before we can be clear how a strongly visual feminist practice might position itself in relation to theories of postmodernism, and indeed to those theoretical approaches which represent the discipline of sociology.

In her introduction to *Feminism and Postmodernism* (1990), Linda J. Nicholson notes that both feminists and postmodernists have questioned the vision of true scholarship as a universalising tendency; that is, as an attempt to reveal general, all-encompassing principles which can lay bare the basic features of nature and social reality in the form of a grand narrative. Both feminists and postmodernists argue that such a vision conceals the embeddedness of scholars' own assumptions within a specific historic context – in particular the white, Western masculinist views of its creators – and that such knowledge expresses the perspectives of particular persons or groups. Indeed Nicholson points out that postmodernism is not only in this sense a natural ally for feminism, but also provides a basis for avoiding the tendency to construct theory that generalises from the experiences of Western, white, middle-class women.

---

29 See, for example, Robins, op. cit.: 196.

And some feminist visual practice does indeed seem to overlap feminism and postmodernism. Cindy Sherman photographs herself, always herself, but in many different (dis)guises: 'I am always the other,' she says (1991). This may suggest the postmodernist emphasis on fragmentation; specifically the fragmentation of the subject. She has produced a series of these images of herself called *Untitled Film Stills* (Sherman late 1970s and early 1980s); see Figure 14. Each photograph looks as though it is a moment captured from a narrative moving through time. Each 'shot' appears frozen, falsely isolated, giving off a sense of having just moved on and being on the way to somewhere else. Yet this visual effect is contrived. The 'still' is a formally composed photograph. This suggests conflated time, the past and future collapsed into the present. It treats the narrative as an aid to a postmodern statement about rhetoric. In addition, her photographs make us query their reality-status, in terms of the juxtapositions which they present. Are they records of 'real life' – are they self-portraits? Or are they fictional in the sense that she is dressed as someone else? Are they chemical photographs, or collaged segments of photographs, or are they digitalised video-film shots? Do they depict fleeting episodes from a narrative or are they composed scenes? But Sherman's self-portraits have also been claimed as feminist. Like other artists who are women, she uses herself as subject matter – a classic strategy for avoiding the problem of exploitation. She appears to be exploring her own body, her own identity, discovering how she wants to be, instead of conforming to the norm of producing a self-image which has been designed for the male gaze. If we use Lash's (1988) argument that post-modernist de-differentiation not only renders reality ambiguous and mobile, but also allows for the mobility (liberation) of subjectivity – which in this case is being manoeuvred partly for feminist purposes but also to achieve ambiguity for the subject and her work – then Sherman's figural 'self-portraits' can be read as addressing an area of overlap between post-modernism and feminism.[30]

While Sherman's photographs bridge feminism and postmodernism, the work of Maud Sulter – feminist artist/photographer and woman of colour – is perhaps more consciously addressed to the overlap between the two areas. Her exhibition *Zabat: Poetics of a Family Tree* (1989) was discussed in relation to Lash's model of de-differentiating postmodernism. Yet it is also a feminist work. Sulter's oil portrait-sized smooth, slightly vulgar-looking coloured photographs in expensive gold frames of women of colour dressed as Greek muses drain the aura of the work of art, and at the same time question the discourses of realism and symbolism through the figural impact of juxtapositions. These juxtapositions include oil portrait/photograph;

---

30 In an interview ('Third Ear', BBC Radio 3, 18 January, 1991) Sherman professed to have little interest in theory, but said she was always willing to consider the various constructions that other people put on her work. She said she was happy if her work appeared ambiguous, and that she aimed to inhabit a nether-world between photography and art.

a) *Untitled Film Still #21, 1978*. Photograph

b) *Untitled Film Still, 1979*. Photograph
Figure 14 Cindy Sherman.

black woman friend/white Greek mythological figure; large expensive elaborately framed photograph/preconceived notions of small cheap photo; academic textual style/modern idiomatic language. In problematising reality and symbolic signification, these figural juxtapositions also 'unfix' subjectivity. Sulter's work allows a mobile subjectivity for herself, her friends who are depicted, and for women of colour in general. It gives them the freedom not to be positioned by patriarchal verbal discourse. In terms of Showalter's (1981) feminist theory, it crucially enables the muted to speak for themselves, via the impact of these figural juxtapositions on the viewer.

Having examined some of the arguments for an alliance *between* feminism and postmodernism, and also two examples of visual critique which uphold such an alliance, I turn now to those feminists who are much more sceptical about the value of the postmodern turn for feminism. Di Stefano (1990) suggests that postmodernism might be a theory whose time has come for men but not for women. She argues that men have had their Enlightenment, so that they can afford a sense of a decentred self and a humble attitude towards the coherence and truth of their claims. But, she argues, for women to take on such a position is to weaken what is not yet strong; which indicates that a politics of alliance, suggested by postmodernism, would be necessarily unreliable. And, more fundamentally, she suggests that the adoption of postmodernism may in fact entail the destruction of feminism, since feminism depends on a relatively unified notion of the social subject 'woman', which is a notion postmodernism would attack.[31]

Indeed, there are many women who see postmodernism, theories of which are overwhelmingly constructed by men, as threatening to feminism. Postmodernism is seen as having a tendency to colonise and absorb feminism or to distort it and, either way, ultimately to weaken it. Some argue that the very currency of the terms '*post*modernism' and '*post*structuralism' may encourage the idea that the term 'feminism' is outmoded and should be replace by '*post*feminism'. And the idea of postfeminism, with its connotations of the 'New Man' is proving to be a dangerous one. For example, research undertaken at Lancaster University in 1992 by psychologist Jane Ussher showed that the emergence of the so-called New Man has dismally failed to change men's double standards about female sexuality (those of madonna/whore).[32] The feminist art historian, Katy Deepwell, argues that it is time to put feminism, *per se*, back on the critical agenda since 'Poststructuralists and other post-modernists seem happy to declare that feminism is no longer the principle site of struggle, even though the current recession has increased women's marginalisation in the market place' (Deepwell 1992: 6). She is also wary about the fact that the debates around feminism have

---

31 There are many other philosophical arguments relating to the debate about the relationship of postmodernism to feminism. I have given only a flavour of that debate, but enough, I hope, to indicate its complexity.

32 See also Mihill, 'New Man – still an old-style sexist' (*Guardian*, 11 July 1992).

become intellectually sophisticated and the theoretical terms of engagement have become difficult, which puts feminism at odds with its political ideal of inclusiveness:

> feminist theory cannot be confined to academia, nor to neutralised courses on gender studies where yet more space is given to men as subjects and teachers. Political praxis remains fundamental to feminists working at whatever level and in whatever medium/mode of work.

(Deepwell 1992: 6)

The feminist sociologist Mary Maynard, in 'The Re-Shaping of Sociology? Trends in the Study of Gender' (1990), also argues that feminist theory must not become remote from feminism's basic concern with the actual conditions of women, and she therefore emphasises the importance for feminist sociologists of *empirical* research into aspects of women's oppression. She observes that it is only by listening to and recording women's own descriptions and accounts of their lives that researchers can achieve a better understanding of how their world is organised, and of the extent to which this differs from the world of men. Research of this kind can in itself be seen as a form of political praxis, since it builds solid foundations on which projects for further change can be constructed. And, importantly, such research is based on the assumption that the researcher works with her research 'subjects' and not on them. I work *with* a group of artists who are women. We produce exhibitions to which we contribute as equals (for example, *Countervail*, 1992–3). Our joint catalogue essays represent our different personal and professional concerns about gender issues; although they also increasingly reflect a merging of viewpoints, which is the result of working together. And while the artists produce paintings and sculpture, my visual contribution consists of a photographic account of the event (see Chapter 5).

Maynard also argues that gender issues should not be regarded as a sub-area of sociology (just as certain feminist philosophers argue that feminism must not become annexed by postmodernism). This viewpoint, with its assumption of an empirical approach to feminist research, has its parallels in the visual critique of feminists who wish to avoid their work being colonised by art. Nina Edge, British-born woman of colour, states that she is a feminist communicator in images – not an artist.[33] Hers is a dialogue not with and in art, but with and in life. In this, she is fully in sympathy with the Pavilion project. She observes that the education that women of colour receive in Britain shatters their confidence in their own abilities. For example, women art students are often not allowed to work the way they want to, but must produce art which accords with how white men *see* the world, since full-time art school lecturers are nearly all male, and it is they who are authorised to give grades. Edge's visual research aims to restore that confidence. Her work often has the appearance of lower-status craft rather than fine art. This is

---

33 Here, I have drawn upon Edge's own account of her work, given in a talk on the occasion of the Pavilion's tenth anniversary celebrations on 6 June 1992.

because she incorporates materials associated with women's work such as fabric, buttons, batik and pots, and because she also constructs images of Indian women in an 'ethnic' style. However, these images, in conjunction with written inscriptions on and around the images, give off mixed messages which mock and challenge British stereotypical notions about Asian culture and Asian women (see Figure 15). When Edge's work is exhibited in British art galleries, remarks made in their comments books indicate that it succeeds in jarring against the norms of the higher-status male professional art world. This feminist project shows how differently Asian women see the world compared with white male art personnel; it contrives a confrontation between two competing accounts of social reality.

We have seen arguments that there are points of overlap between feminism and postmodernism; and in an analysis of the very different photographic projects of Cindy Sherman and Maud Sulter, I suggested that each of these projects demonstrates an account of this alliance. We have also seen that some feminists argue against the possibility of such an alliance while others are equally wary of an association with other male-dominated areas like art and sociology; and this viewpoint is represented in Nina Edge's visual communications. My own opinion is also that feminism must not be compromised either by an alliance with male-dominated 'disciplines', or by an overly theoretical approach. However, in 'The Re-Shaping of Sociology? Trends in the Study of Gender', Maynard takes the matter further. She proposes that the study of gender is an important means through which sociology itself is being re-shaped. This suggests a more constructive kind of relationship between feminism and other intellectual positions or disciplines areas; one in which feminism and gender research mould an already existing discipline into a less patriarchal, more gender-aware tool of critical inquiry. However, Maynard's remark is also important for the fact that it serves to bring sociology itself back into focus. It may seem that latterly, sociology has hovered on the edge of my analyses of theories of visual signification or representation, and sometimes on the edge of those theories themselves. But in fact an underlying sociological approach informs, if tacitly, each of the discussions of specific texts and topics in this book. Indeed, a sociological conception of inequality, for example, underlies the type of feminist empirical research advocated above by Maynard, carried out by myself in conjunction with the women Systematic Constructive artists, and shown in the visual work of Nina Edge. Thus it is important to stress that those feminist projects which are reshaping the discipline of sociology are themselves already informed by a sociological understanding. While refusing 'old-style' white, masculinist sociology the exclusive right to define the concept of inequality as it has done in the past – which leads to an emphasis on class inequality – there is nevertheless a broadly sociological approach underlying the feminist project. So what I am arguing for is the re-shaping of sociology through the visual and verbal critiques of feminists and other minority

Put on the Oriental-ists
Glasses, climb and slide
On the snakes and ladders
Child,
Spectacles
To buy or rent – what
They don't yet 'know'
They'll soon invent
All full of East and
Promise . . .

Figure 15 Nina Edge. *Snakes and Ladders* (1988). Batik on paper, ceramic and text
98 × 48 ins. Photography: Alan Moss.

groups whose approach is already broadly sociological. And it is at this point that we can reintroduce postmodernism and its relationship to feminism. Individual feminist visual critiques may take on the task of re-shaping one or other of the theories of postmodernism, while others wish to dissociate themselves from such theories, but *all* feminist and minority group critiques can learn and benefit from the emphasis that these theories put on visual communication in our present culture. For despite considerable differences between their perspectives, the more recent theories of postmodernism that I have examined identify the increase in visual representation and visual communication as a key characteristic of contemporary Western society. They show that visual communication reaches to the heart of popular culture and does not just involve elite groups like art personnel. This means, as I have observed, that feminist critique involving visual images has a potentially 'visually literate' audience, and that the means exist to make it widely available. It also implies that a visual critique which contributes to the feminist re-shaping of sociology will have analysed those visual idioms which current visual communication uses; its visual representation of reality will rework those idioms, and part of its long-term project will be to re-shape them.

While the work of Terry Atkinson and the other artists who exhibited in *Approaches to Realism* (1990) can teach us a good deal about the critical reworking of visual idiom,[34] certain books containing visual critique are also instructive, though in different ways. Both the photo-essays and image-and-text essays by John Berger and his colleagues in *Ways of Seeing* (1972) broke new ground in terms of the feminist perspective deployed in essays two (pp. 36–43) and three (pp. 45–64); while the even earlier *A Fortunate Man* (Berger and Mohr 1967) is remarkable for the way in which Jean Mohr's photographs and John Berger's text interact, suggesting how the country doctor visually perceives his surroundings and his patients, and how the patients see their world. Victor Burgin's *Between* (1986a) presents a trenchant critique of both capitalism and patriarchy (see Chapter 2), while the image-and-text analysis of British factory life in *Born to Work* by Nick Hedges and Huw Beynon (1982) conveys the horrors – and camaraderie – of factory work; and here the photographs evoke emotions which lend urgency and give new inflections to a Marxist analysis of capitalism.

However, there is a key issue which has yet to be discussed. Which visual medium is most appropriate for the proposed feminist critique? Theorists of postmodernism emphasise that it is the electronic media which have brought about the revolution in visual communication and are a quintessential part of postmodern culture; yet most of the visual work which I have referred to is photographic. Is chemically-based photography not retardataire, even

---

34 *Approaches to Realism* (1990) was curated by John Roberts. The participating artists were Rasheed Araeen, Art & Language, Sue Atkinson, Terry Atkinson, David Batchelor, Sonia Boyce, Dave Mabb.

outdated, in a culture flooded by electronic communication? While photography is still acknowledged to produce the highest-quality images, and research into photography is not declining, Kodak, for example, is now investing considerable resources in the field of electronic digital image processing.[35] The *Blue Skies* conference on 'Art and Technology' at the Newcastle Museum of Science and Technology (September 1991) explored the differences between these two techniques of visual communication, and the implications of the now widespread use of electronic digital-images. Some contributors to the conference argued that the crisis in prevailing forms of image-production, engendered by the serious challenge which the computer-simulated electronic image presents to the status of the chemically produced photograph, represents a fundamental cultural transformation: a qualitative *and* quantitative shift in forms of visual and textual reproduction and their transmission, similar to the transformation of Renaissance culture by typography, which radically transformed how knowledge was generated, systematised and stored. John Roberts, in his review of the conference 'Out of Our Heads' (1992), claims that the impact of these changes will be huge, leading to the ending of the domination of mathematics in science, and to a new process of scientific visualisation. And he observes that the technical supersession of the chemical photograph by the computer-simulated electronic image means that the dominant monocular pictorial tradition of representation in art is once and for all buried. He argues that this means, in addition, that documentary photography is fundamentally degraded, since the status of reality has been demoted by the new simulated images to the extent that an iconic or indexical representation of it no longer has any force. That is to say, the new imaging techniques engender the *cultural displacement* of the automatic link between 'truth' and the photograph's indexicality; and the chemical photograph is *relieved* of the burden of veracity which, however, leaves it open to the possibility of political rewriting and struggles relating to the issue of interpretation.

The use of the new technology has clearly shifted in the interests of conservative forces (crucially influencing Baudrillard's view of computer simulation); but Roberts believes that in a world of increasing media simulation where naturalistic-looking images are made rather than taken, there is every good reason to believe that photographers and artists will look to the indexical and iconic resources of photography as an empirical antidote to such effects. This is somewhat reminiscent of Harvey's suggestion that people attach importance to inherited objects and photographs as evidence of a past life when the pace was slower, values were longer-lasting and there was no sensory overload. So what Roberts is suggesting is that in a culture flooded by electronic images, chemically produced photographs may be valued for their 'access to empirical evidence', while – relieved of the burden

---

35 According to Kodak customer services and inquiries.

of veracity – they are likely to become the focus of increased political argument over interpretation.[36]

The indications are, then, that the advent of electronically simulated imagary does not necessarily forecast the death of chemical photography.[37] Indeed, James Hall in 'Art is the loser in a photo-finish' (1992) argues, in the year of the *Blue Skies* conference, that photography 'is now one of the most pictorially correct and nineties things to do'. He observes that even the Royal Academy of Arts, which previously had a shoot-to-kill policy over photography, staged a major retrospective, *The Art of Photography*, in 1989. And the official British artist for the 1992 Olympic Games, David Hiscock, was a photographer. But what are the implications of this evidence of photography's prominence, and of Roberts' arguments, for a visual practice which contributes to the feminist re-shaping sociology? In the short term, I think that the kind of policy associated with the Pavilion at Leeds is reinforced. Cameras are relatively cheap and easy to operate, and black and white film is not complicated to process. This is a very important consideration, since we are not primarily concerned with art (or indeed, with avant-garde art) but with the inclusiveness of feminism, and with community-based critique. And in the longer term, such work will be able to profit from the association of chemical photographs with empirical evidence. While simulated images are conjuring up a virtual world, photographs connote this one. And it is this world that concerns our feminist sociologists/cultural workers. But in addition – if Roberts is correct – they must expect to have to defend their own interpretations of their work against alternative ones; for while they will be operating in a situation where a more visually literate public attaches fresh empirical significance – and even emotional security – to photographs, they may also expect political debate about the interpretation of their images to be intense. And this is good because such a situation is challenging; it puts pressure on authors to sharpen the visual/political character of their work in order to prevent alternative interpretations of it from prevailing. This process should itself ensure that the work does not become merely an aestheticised object, with all the dangers of aestheticisation that Harvey spells out.

In this first section of the book, I have traced historically the strand of critique which relates to sociology and visual representation. This strand has shown a tendency, latterly, for various of its categories to become blurred: verbal/

36 Chemical photographs do still have a great deal of status as reportage, and as empirical evidence. For example, a couple of photographs of 'Fergie' with her foot in her financial advisor's mouth (22 August 1992) have had considerable consequences for Fergie and the other royals, and have contributed to growing public criticism of the British royal family and its relationship to the State, culminating in a public announcement by the Queen that she is working on arrangements to pay income tax. No one seems to have suggested that the photographs have been digitally manipulated.

37 In fact, digital imaging is now being used as 'electronic glue' to restore the missing parts in very old photographs of historic significance (Gerrard 1993).

visual, theory/practice, art/photography, subject/object of research. Building on the evidence of this tendency, what I am tentatively proposing here is a sociologically informed feminist or minority group critical practice which has a strong visual – probably photographic – component. It uses insights and evidence about modern technologies of communication which theories of postmodernism provide; and, indeed, it is associated with the theoretical and historiographical revolution which the Marxist tradition of art history represents, with developments in cultural studies, gender studies, semiotic researches, critical art practice, and with Tagg's programme for a network of linked local interventions (Tagg 1975). It is cognizant of the fact that people are beginning to invest in culture the idealism and radical aspirations they once reserved for 'politics and ideology'; and it would aim to draw on this strength to produce analytical yet accessible visual/verbal work in which many participate. Here is a whole constellation of related factors, with the sociologist deeply implicated, and the relationship to her/his research project changed in several ways. The kind of sociological practice I have attempted to outline seems to resonate with Denzin's eleventh feature of postmodern theory: 'Radical experiments with the writing of theory and interpretation, including poetry, performances and multi-media "mystories"' (Denzin 1991: 27).

There is, in fact, much to be learned about such radical experimentations from the *empirical paradigm*, where research into the analysis and reworking of visual idiom has also been undertaken. These and other developments will be examined in subsequent chapters; and it is to the empirical tradition that I now turn.

Part II

The Empirical Paradigm

Introduction to Part II

Clearly part of what one refrains from studying because the only approach is through verbal vagaries has a specific nature and is precisely perceived, the vagary being a characteristic of one's literary incapacity, not one's data.

(Erving Goffman, *Gender Advertisement*, 1979)

The critical paradigm focuses attention on the unequal relations between social strata, and analysis is informed by a vision of a more equitable society. Such an analysis is therefore also an argument for change; it is concerned with what *should* be. The empirical paradigm, on the other hand, has classically not been concerned with what should be; one of its tenets has been that social inequalities have first to be empirically established. Its proponents want to explore what human society is actually like in all its detail and complexity, here and now. While the critical paradigm takes our actions and the meanings we give to them to be historically situated and ideologically permeated, the empirical paradigm places emphasis on the fact that meanings and actions are *context-dependent*, and that therefore this context-dependency must be empirically demonstrated in individual case studies. After several such studies have been completed and compared, it may transpire that there are factors common to each which allow more general, theoretical statements to be made; and in this sense empirical theory is customarily *grounded* in fieldwork, while at the same time it modifies and builds upon previous empirical theory. Empirical sociology is often concerned with aspects of everyday life; for example, with common sense, which it treats as a resource, a form of knowledge. Ordinary people are seen as participants and informants in the research process; and research methods aim to elucidate people's existing knowledge about how to act, which includes their resources for representing the world visually – the visual idioms and visual clichés that are customarily used. As an extension of their interest in everyday life, empirical sociologists may focus on 'specialist' areas such as natural science. They may analyse scientists' textual discourse, aiming to reveal the interpretative resources which authors deploy; for texts also represent reality, and have the advantage that they can be subjected to very close scrutiny. The attention of empirical sociologists is now turning to visual representations in scientific and other texts; indeed, some are actively and 'creatively' incorporating visual material into their own textual presentations.

In this second part of the book, the focus is again on sociology's relationship to the visual; but again, it is not just a matter of a 'sociology *of* the visual'. Sociology has a more complex relationship with the visual domain than that phrase implies. One reason for this is that the new visual technologies not only generate data for sociologists to study; they are increasingly affecting the communication and the constitution of sociological knowledge itself. Chapter 4 looks at empirical sociological analyses *of* visual representation and topics which involve visual representation. Chapter 5 discusses the use that empirical sociologists and anthropologists *themselves* make of visual representation; and most of the 'texts' examined in the chapter contain a large percentage of visual material, which in some cases consists of the author's own photographs. Chapter 6 discusses the recent project to construct new literary forms for sociology. This project is based on the argument that sociological knowledge should be reflexively sound.[1] While unconventional sociological texts inevitably *look* different, authors may intentionally depart from current visual conventions in order to construct texts which are reflexively sound; with the result that the visual dimension is fundamentally and actively implicated in their methodology as well as in their argument. In this overall section, as in the last, the organisation of the material in a particular sequence of chapters indicates a coming-together of categories – of verbal and visual, and of participants – in the construction of sociological knowledge, or understanding.

---

1 This topic is very fully treated in Ashmore (1989).

Chapter 4

Sociological analyses of visual representation

Principal works discussed:

Charles Madge and Barbara Weinberger, *Art Students Observed*, 1973
Colin Painter, 'The Absent Public. A Report on a Pilot Survey of Objects hanging on Walls in Households in Newcastle-upon-Tyne', *Art Monthly*, 29, 1980
Howard Becker, *Art Worlds*, 1982
Gordon Fyfe and John Law, 'On the Invisibility of the Visual: Editors' Introduction', *Picturing Power*, 1988
Gordon Fyfe, 'Art and its Objects: William Ivins and the Reproduction of Art', *Picturing Power*, 1988
Geof Bowker, 'Pictures from the Subsoil, 1939', *Picturing Power*, 1988
G. Nigel Gilbert and Michael Mulkay, 'Working Conceptual Hallucinations', *Opening Pandora's Box*, 1984
Michael Lynch and Steve Woolgar, 'Introduction: Sociological orientations to representational practice in science', *Representation in Scientific Practice*, 1990
Bruno Latour, 'Drawing Things Together', *Representation in Scientific Practice*, 1990
Robert Dingwall, Hiroko Tanaka and Satoshi Minamikata, 'Images of parenthood in the UK and Japan', *Sociology*, 25, 3, August 1991

Until recently, empirical social science projects concerned with visual representation have tended to focus on the world of visual *art*. However, there have been relatively few such projects, which may be because the *critical* tradition had already established a fruitful relationship with the arts long before empirical social research got under way.[1] Yet such empirical studies as there are – of the routine, mundane, taken-for-granted social actions of visual art personnel – have done much to demystify the world of visual art, which had long been perceived as 'special' both by insiders and outsiders, including many critical sociologists. To show that the production and reception of visual art works are social processes, and that they cannot

---

1 Empirical social science in its early positivist phase was much more concerned with the natural sciences than with the arts. Claiming to *be* a science, it had apparently less to learn from an analysis of the arts, and less to emulate.

satisfactorily be explained by reference to internal aesthetic factors, is often the aim of empirical sociologists of art.

I start by discussing *Art Students Observed* by Charles Madge and Barbara Weinberger (1973). This is a case study of 'Midville' College of Art in the late 1960s, and in particular of its fine art students and their work.[2] The authors looked at the social world of these students from pre-college influences through four years of art school training to the start of post-college life. They paid particular attention to a small sample of fine art students, but they also made comparisons with a group from the graphic design department. Participant observation was the principal method employed during the first year of the project. In the following year, questionnaires were administered to the sample, individual statements were elicited, short interviews were undertaken with both staff and students, and staff comments on student work were noted. Meanwhile, informal conversations between sociologists and art school personnel took place throughout the two-year period in which the authors were resident at Midville College. While a critical sociology of art typically groups material according to a sequence of linked chapter headings which together are likely to indicate the key features of the author's theoretical framework,[3] the basic chapter sequence in *Art Students Observed* is temporal (pre-college, pre-Diploma, Diploma, post-Diploma). In each chapter, collated data are presented, some of which are displayed as statistical tables. The authors' interpretation of that data generates their sociological account and prompts occasional remarks of a more general nature. Unlike critical texts which are prescriptive, this empirical text tends to leave the reader to draw her or his own moral and political conclusions.

Before the report of the National Advisory Council on Art Education, British art schools were independent and issued their own diplomas. However, the Council advised that approved art school courses be linked on a national basis, with a central administration and a panel of external examiners. It recommended a three-year course of degree equivalence which would lead to a nationally recognised Diploma in Art and Design. In 1963 these recommendations were implemented for the first time in approved British art schools, of which Midville College was one. The sociological project started in 1967, and at that time the Midville College Principal, together with most of his staff, was firmly of the opinion that art cannot be taught. He had previously written that the Diploma course in Fine Art at Midville was aimed at those with special talent, but below genius level. It was intended to develop talent, teach skills, and promote a study of art, and it was seen as a means towards the 'irregular, unexpected or

2 'Midville' is probably Coventry. Evidence to suggest this can be found in Harrison and Orton (1982). Coventry Art School later became incorporated into Lanchester Polytechnic.

3 For example, in Wolff (1981) the chapter headings are entitled 'Social Structure and Artistic Creativity', 'The Social Production of Art', 'Art as Ideology', 'Aesthetic Autonomy and Cultural Politics', 'Interpretation as Re-creation', 'The Death of the Author', 'Cultural Producer and Cultural Product'.

revolutionary'.[4] The conviction that art cannot be taught does not fit well with the idea of a nationally administered degree-equivalent course in Fine Art. Furthermore, this conflict of aims has to be seen in the context of the late 1960s, a time of rapid change, of student revolts and underlying doubts about the viability of art in the modern world, leading to constant reformulations of the artist's role and of the products and activities that could be counted as art. In one of their few judgemental passages, Madge and Weinberger say that 'a student who had decided to go to an art college was entering a maelstrom' (Madge and Weinberger 1973: 17).

Evidence collected by the researchers indicated that the ideas which the Pre-Diploma students held about art were subjected to severe questioning as soon as they entered the college.[5] Madge and Weinberger concluded that the purpose of the Pre-Diploma course at Midville, to judge by the variety of approaches and shock tactics deployed by the staff, was to ensure the survival of the fittest. But this begs the questions: fittest for what? And what in what does fitness consist? Their subsequent study of the three-year Fine Art Diploma course students aimed to provide answers to these questions. They found that those who were accepted as Fine Art Diploma students at Midville were left to their own devices for much of their time on the course. However, long periods of solitary activity were interspersed with short projects set by the staff, who made very direct criticisms of their work. The data which the researchers collected suggest that students were being trained to shun the ordinary and the academic, to regard themselves as special, to cultivate their own personal sensitivities, to develop independence – and all this in order to achieve 'creativity'. At the same time they had to learn to give rational explanations of their work, and to develop a questioning attitude. Madge and Weinberger observe that learning to strike the right balance between freedom and explanation proved one of the major problems that students (and staff) had to try to solve. In another of their rare judgements, the authors say:

> The problem of the art student is . . . three-fold: he has opted out of the dominant occupational system; he is driven to behave as though he had access to a charisma which may not be his to command; and he has to justify this, to himself and to his peers and teachers, in intellectualized terms and under conditions of almost unbearable ambiguity.

(Madge and Weinberger 1973: 21)

The situation appeared to encourage martinet-type behaviour on the part of the staff (several of whom were internationally exhibited). They had the authority to discriminate between what they termed 'interesting' and 'mediocre'

---

4 Statement made by the Principal of Midville College in 1968 to the committee of the National Council for Diplomas in Art and Design, for their *Second Report* (issued in 1970).

5 Under the Coldstream dispensation, all potential art students were required to complete a Pre-Diploma Course in Art and Design at their nearest art school. They could then apply to a Dip. A.D. approved art school of their choosing to do the three-year course leading to the Diploma in Art and Design.

visual art work, but because 'art can't be taught' they did not have to justify their decisions according to any recognised academic precedent. Their tolerance of 'art' products of which they did not approve was strictly limited,[6] and it is apparent from the research data that their disapproval was frequently directed towards the work of women students. Yet even a student who won the tutors' approval during his [sic] first year at college could not be sure that his work would subsequently remain in favour. He had to learn how to go on making 'individual statements' in a currently acceptable way, while at the same time retaining something of his original motivation towards art.

Interviewed students appeared to show symptoms of the onset of anomie: they said they felt dissatisfied, disillusioned, lacking in confidence, cynical, and increasingly remote from the outside world. One remarked that 'individual development is encouraged in theory, but in practice I don't feel free'. In marked contrast graphic design students, who had been unenthusiastic about their course during the first year because it contained a large element of 'fine art', felt much more positively disposed towards it in the second and third years. The researchers discovered that the main values which fine art students came to espouse were those held by the staff; namely, a total commitment to their work, a belief that art can't be taught, and the consequent necessity to further their personal development and to develop a unique vision. Madge and Weinberger note that the only fine art student of their research sample to get a first class degree, Dave, maintained an inner reserve and a watchful eye on the college situation from his first day on the course, while he always managed to operate within the system, rather than feeling impelled to opt out.[7] Early in the course, he told the researchers privately that he did his serious work at home. What he did at college was just a front. However, towards the end of his third year, 'the two had come together', and he was able to show staff his serious art work. The researchers remark that in Dave's case the socialisation process at the college was, in a formal sense, successful.

Michael Baxendall (1972: 1) has observed that a fifteenth-century painting is the deposit of a social relationship. Madge and Weinberger regard the visual art works produced by Midville College students in a similar manner. These works are seen as representing the outcome of a series of overlapping social relationships, and in particular as evidence of conflicting demands made on students by staff. Those demands, relating to the kind of a person an artist should be, and the purposes that art and art education ought to serve, were given formal expression, and evaluated, at the end of the course, when the 'aesthetic' value of specific student works was rated according to a degree class. Dave's work (Figure 16a) represents his interest in 'chickeny

6 Expressionism in any form, for example, Abstract Expressionism, was frowned on. A cognitive approach to visual art was encouraged.
7 Dave went on to do a postgraduate Diploma at the Royal College of Art, and to be nationally exhibited.

things', but beyond this, it represents his determination to remain aloof from other students' concerns and from overt staff influence. In adopting this stance, he was demonstrating from the start his autonomy as an artist, and a self-reliance which stemmed from the belief that art is a matter of personal conviction. But in another sense, of course, he was conformist; his work represented a set of approved Midville values, and it gained him a first. Clive's work (Figure 16b), in the Pop Art manner of Jim Dine (which the sociologists observe was relatively acceptable at Midville) gained him a second, whilst Diana's 'old-fashioned landscape paintings' were pronounced a third. Her tutor described them as 'very neurotic' and 'defensive'. Overall, these visual art works represent a broader set of social relations; and these concern the political context of education and of art production and reception in the late 1960s.

This study was written before feminism had begun to re-shape the discipline of sociology. While the researchers (one male and one female, with two female assistants) sometimes distinguish between the attitudes and responses to tuition of male and female students, they don't pursue this very far, nor do they give information about the gender of staff members. One suspects that all the staff in the fine art department were male.[8] Today, feminists would produce a very different analysis of this material which appears to represent the patriarchal ideology of Romantic art in an acute form. Midville College students were, in effect, being brainwashed into becoming autonomous, educated into anomie; and some female students found themselves unable to complete the particular socialisation process which this male-defined art world demanded. Visual art work is also the expression of gender relations, and these can be traced in the student work. Whereas Dave's 'original' constructions found favour in a world of patriarchal aesthetics, Clive's sexist work depicts some of what that world took for granted. The women students had to learn to take on those values in their work or be branded as deviations from the norm (failed artists).

It is interesting to note that the student upheavals of 1968, in which Hornsey Art School students featured prominently, produced little response from Midville fine art students. This is perhaps because they were so subservient to the staff that they had difficulty in acting independently in a wider context. But this also raises an important methodological question for empirical sociology: while the context-dependency of meaning is beautifully (and ironically) demonstrated in this study, how typical in fact were 'Midville' students in the 1960s? To what extent would sociologists subsequently be justified in generalising from Madge and Weinberger's case study of a British art school, in which students were being educated into anomie?

In the critical paradigm, authors seek to persuade us about what ought to be, and the reader's judgement tends to be directed towards the quality of

---

8 This suspicion is reinforced in Harrison and Orton, op. cit.

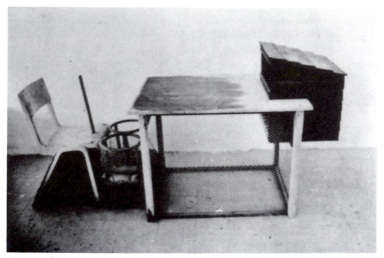

Figure 16a   Dave's work

Both photographs from *Art Students Observed* (Madge and Weinberger 1973).
Photograph: Barbara Weinberger

Figure 16b   Clive's work

the author's critical argument. However, in this study, in the near-absence of critique by the researchers, the reader's judgement tends to centre on the data presented. *Art Students Observed* elicits a powerful discriminatory response from the reader, and in this sense, demonstrates that the empirical paradigm possesses a highly effective technique – or strategy – of persuasion.

Critical writers such as Adorno, Raphael and Lyotard have put forward the argument that certain visual art works have a potential to transform capitalist society; they believe that in the long term such works may contribute towards producing a more equal balance between social strata. These authors are, in effect, suggesting that art is able to improve the conditions of oppressed peoples. Roger Taylor (1978) opposes this view. He argues that Marx's own treatment of art is methodologically unsound because his approach to the State and to religion is historical, while he treats art as a universal. Taylor argues that this is unjustified; he suggests that evidence points to the fact that art arose with bourgeois society, and that the values associated with art conspire to preserve that society. Art is, therefore, some-thing that 'the masses' should resist. He observes that art takes their money (for example, their taxes help finance the Royal Opera House in London). Art even invades their own culture (for example jazz); first killing its spon-teneity, then appropriating it. This controversy raises some very important questions for empirical social scientists. Do working-class people generally identify with the value of art? If so, what kind of art do they like? Do they identify with the art in museums which is collected and curated by the middle classes? A poll conducted on behalf of the *Daily Mirror* in 1992 goes a little way towards answering these questions. Readers were invited to name a famous artist. Fifty-six per cent named Rolf Harris.[9] Twenty per cent named Rembrandt. Virtually no other visual artists were mentioned.[10]

In 'Offical Art and the Tate Gallery', Brighton (1977) also discusses the relationship between the values of the fine art establishment and the wider community. He argues that the Tate Gallery and other contemporary art galleries are quite remote from the world of popular art, and that the prevailing historical account of modern British art has largely been estab-lished through State institutions of art, and can therefore be called an official orthodoxy. This orthodoxy sees art as a 'self-generating culture' which transcends social life, and has become the shaping and evaluating rationale of our national collection of modern art, the Tate Gallery, and of those institutions which dispense Government funding for the visual arts. He argues that the apparent coherence of the orthodoxy is achieved by exclud-ing certain kinds of art; for example, art which is popular in reproduction. He had previously proposed (1973) that there should be more discussion about the exclusion of popular art from the official orthodoxy since it is a

9 An Australian television personality who draws and sings, mainly on children's programmes.
10 Research in this area has also been undertaken by Lole and Willats (1975).

matter which concerns public money and the taste of the wider British population, not just a small sector of it. Whereas Brighton, like Taylor, appears to resent the appropriation of working-class money by the ortho- dox, bourgeois art establishment, the two authors clearly have different ideas about how working-class culture should itself be preserved and publicly presented.

These studies, and my discussion of them, may give the impression of a simple bifurcation between high art and popular culture. An empirical survey undertaken by Colin Painter suggests that the situation is a little more complex. In 'The Absent Public. A Report on a Pilot Survey of Objects Hanging on Walls in Households in Newcastle-upon-Tyne' (1980), Painter addresses the kinds of questions about 'class' and 'art' that I raised on the previous page:

> The intentions were to discover what kinds of images people hang on their walls, how objects were introduced into the house, why they are liked, how long ago they were acquired and at what cost. In addition a central concern was to explore the concepts of art existing in relation to the works discovered.
>
> (Painter 1980: 9)

Painter focused on four 'socio-economic urban areas', and visited several households in each of these categories. Area One consisted of pre-1919, traditional, terraced, working-class accommodation, while Area Two was a newly developed working-class council estate. Area Three consisted of private houses valued at the time at £15,000 – £25/30,000, and Area Four was composed of private houses valued at over £35,000. Some of the material from this project is now out of date (for example, house prices); and in fact, the samples of households visited in each area were probably too small to yield data of statistical significance. Nevertheless this is a very rare and valuable survey of its type.

Painter found that in Area One, only 32 per cent of objects hanging on the walls were pictures. The rest were mirrors, clocks, calendars and other objects which were either functional or alluded to a function. In Area Two, 44 per cent of the objects were pictures. In both areas, objects were very often gifts brought by friends and relatives who had been on holiday. So householders did not necessarily like these objects; rather, they felt obliged to display them. On the rare occasions, in Areas One and Two, where a *picture* had been bought *by* a householder, it tended to be chosen either because it matched the decoration of a room, or for its novelty value (for example, a picture of a dog wearing a false nose and pointed hat). In Areas One and Two, men had little to do with the acquisition and display of the objects, and what paintings were in evidence were not, on the whole, considered as 'art'. There appeared to be an acceptance that art consists of the works of 'indisputably' great artists.

In Area Three, 64 per cent of the objects were pictures; while in Area Four,

77 per cent were pictures, of which 70 per cent were originals. In both these areas landscapes predominated (compared with Areas One and Two, where pictures tended to contain animals and people). In Area Three, people sometimes bought a picture because they liked the artist, and men were involved in making such purchases. In Area Four, knowledge sometimes extended to making collections of particular kinds of works, and 23 per cent of the pictures were inherited. None had been inherited in Areas One, Two and Three. In Area Four, there was the greatest concern for objects as art; for the instrinsic qualities of art objects.

In this abridged but, I hope, representative account of Painter's pilot survey can be seen a corroboration of the suggestion, made in different ways by both Taylor and Brighton, that fine art and its associated values are the active concern of a particular social sector of the population. However, this empirical study suggests that rather than a bifurcation between high – or fine – art and popular culture, there is something more like a continuum: the higher a person's position on the socio-economic scale, the more likely she or he is to be interested in the concept of fine art and its associated values. Art as an emancipatory force seems a rather remote, even hollow, idea in the light of this survey. The notion that avant-garde art, produced by art-school trained, mainly middle-class artists, can bring change in the long term begins to seem like an excuse for artists to carry on working as they always have done, but in an acceptable political guise.

Howard Becker's *Art Worlds* (1982) is a major sociological study in the empirical paradigm. Its perspective on art is quite opposed to that of the Midville College staff and students, for it argues that an appearance of artistic autonomy is superficial, and that the Romantic conception of the artist – which suggests that people with 'a gift for art' cannot be subjected to the social constraints which affect other members of society – is a myth indeed. *Art Worlds* treats art as the work that some people do, and its ground-line is that all art requires the cooperation of a network of participants in order for it to appear as it finally does. Becker proposes that an understanding of the extensive division of labour entailed in most types of art production could serve as a model for an empirical investigation of *other* forms of work, and that his study can be used on an even more general level as a framework for studying 'the basic unit of sociological investigation': collective actions and the events they produce.

Any activity which has more – or less – successfully competed for the honorific title of art becomes the focus of Becker's attention. This means that visual art (and craft) are treated alongside music, literature, theatre, cinema, dance, and so on. The author was for a while a professional jazz pianist, and is now a serious photographer. These strands in his own career may have pointed him towards a sociological study of the arts and are the source of much fascinating empirical material. However, the only theoretical connection made between sociology and art in *Art Worlds* is that *doing* sociology involves patterns of cooperation and other kinds of social processes which are also necessarily involved in the production of artworks. Unlike critical texts, *Art Worlds* keeps the *content* of art and the *content* of sociology quite separate. And Becker (like Madge and Weinberger) discusses the specific features of a visual work only when he wants to show that they represent the evidence or outcome of a particular social relationship.[11]

Becker argues that his empirical sociological stance allows a much more complex notion of an art world than philosophers normally use. This, he maintains, is because philosophers often argue from hypothetical examples which have no empirical meat on their bones. These examples tend to lead back into the philosophical 'problems' they are attempting to clarify, making them seem all the more intractable; whereas when a problem is placed in a specific empirical context, this gives it real substance, and thereby enables analytical progress. Becker's empirical approach is particularly illuminating in his treatment of aesthetics. While Wolff's critical sociological analysis (1981) finally (perhaps regretfully and certainly respectfully) leaves aesthetics alone – leaves it to art world personnel like aestheticians[12] – Becker regards the making of aesthetic judgements and the construction of aesthetic rationales and systems as a necessary part of the cooperative enterprise which gets the product or performance finished and defined as art. By means of empirical instances, he shows that aesthetic rationales are constructed – either by professional aestheticians, artists or others – because if they were not, the ongoing process of art production would be impossible since every aesthetic judgement would have to be argued out from scratch. Becker argues that aesthetic rationales, whether they take the form of manifestos or agreed but unspoken rules for making judgements arrived at through workaday choices of materials and forms, are essential because they provide normative guidance; indeed, they bind art-work personnel into a routine cooperative work pattern. In this sense, an aesthetic represents consensus. And he points out that art personnel want to be linked via an aesthetic because having work named as art brings advantages: if you can argue that your work justifies serious consideration on aesthetic grounds, then you can compete for grants and awards. This is why writers on aesthetics strike a

---

11 For example, Becker discusses and illustrates Robert Arneson's *Sinking Brick Plates* (Becker 1982: 280), a series of five ceramic plates in each successive one of which a three-dimensional brick appears to sink further into some liquid. Arneson's plates are intentionally non-functional, and its visual features show the artist deliberately differentiating himself from potter craftsmen who make plates to eat off.

12 She says:

> I do not know the answer to the problem of 'beauty' or of 'artistic merit', and will only state that I do not believe this is reducible to political and social factors; nor do I believe it consists in some transcendent, non-contingent quality. I hope that this agnosticism does not impair the arguments of this book . . .
>
> (Wolff 1981: 7)

moralistic tone. He argues that an aesthetic continuously adapts the premises of a theory to the works artists actually produce, while such a consensus also enables art historians to discover value in previously unstudied painters, and allows dealers to look for such works to sell. Here the difference between Becker's approach and that of critical writers is very clear; for Becker focuses on the shared activity of producing an aesthetic rather than adopting an evaluative stance in relation to the content of one. In this way he completely sidesteps the problem of theorising the political component of value judgements about visual art. To Becker, writers on aesthetics 'strike a moralistic tone', but critical sociologists must decide how *they* are implicated in those morals and, in the light of this, how they want art works and other art world personnel to be judged.

Becker shows that an aesthetic constitutes one of the interlinked *conventions* which binds an art world together, enabling it to function smoothly over a period of time. Sharing knowledge of conventions makes cooperation possible, and ensures minimum waste and effort. For example, in an efficient patronage system artists and patrons are able to work together to the same end, the patrons providing support and direction, the artists creativity and execution. When conventions are not shared, chaos may ensue. At a BBC Promenade concert in August 1992, the piano was tuned to a 'standard' frequency for middle C, but the Russian orchestra accompanying the solo pianist had prepared their instruments according to a different frequency. The result was an excruciating experience for 'art world personnel'. This phrase, 'art world personnel', includes the audience; and Becker argues that the fact that audience members are often not regarded as contributing to the accomplishment of an art work is again a matter of convention. From a critical sociological perspective such as Wolff's, the popular conception of the audience is held to be an effect of the dominant (Romantic individualist) ideology. However, it is worth noting that both critical and empirical approaches are concerned, in their different ways, to decentre the artist: the former wishes to denaturalise the dominant ideology and the latter to demonstrate what is convention and could be different. And Wolff's last chapter in *The Social Production of Art*, 'The Death of the Author', parallels Becker's last chapter, 'Reputation', in the sense that both, finally and in their different ways, argue for 'the social construction of the artist'.

In the visual arts, some social conventions are represented visually. Robert Arneson's *Sinking Brick Plates* consist of a series of ceramic plates, into each successive one of which a ceramic 'brick' sinks deeper into some ceramic 'water'. These plates are manifestly non-functional, and thus provide visual evidence of the distinction that artists customarily draw between themselves and craftspeople who make plates to eat off. The other side of this coin is that such visual conventions are used to manipulate viewers' expectations. They also enable artists to render familiar objects in a shorthand that knowledgeable viewers can read; and by the same token, there are books on the market, aimed at amateurs, which teach drawing and painting as the acquisition of particular conventions and formulas.[13] However, Becker argues that serious professional painters aim to criticise and change visual conventions, while at the same time achieving a correspondingly altered aesthetic consensus among art world cognoscenti. This consensus can then become a new routine base from which to make further developments. Berger's *Ways of Seeing* (1972) is, in one sense, about showing the visual conventions that artists have used. However, it is written from a critical perspective, and therefore puts emphasis instead on how a dominant group has been able to naturalise a particular ideological *view*point. Berger gets us to look critically. We learn to understand that Gainsborough's oil painting of *Mr and Mrs Andrews* naturalises the property owners' outlook for viewers. Becker's empirical perspective, on the other hand, would argue that this is painting according to a set of visual conventions; and that these visual conventions enable the cooperative work that has to be accomplished in order for an art product to be realised and labelled as art.

Becker shows that conventions, including visual conventions, change over time. For example, engravers used a visual syntax which developed over several hundred years (see Figure 17), but this development came to a halt and engraving eventually died out when photography became widely available (see pages 177–9). Fifteenth-century Italian artists sometimes depicted their subjects in large, strangely shaped hats, but this convention dwindled when the skill of gauging the volume of barrels among merchant patrons was no longer commonly practised.[14] In fact, conventions can never remain completely the same, because a group of people acting cooperatively never do quite the same things each time; each context being slightly different from the last. However, Becker notes that when one particular set of visual art conventions becomes all-important for a considerable period of time, the result is academic art. In this case, how you do it, rather than what you do, becomes the most important issue.

In view of the difference between critical and empirical writings about visual representation, Becker's chapter entitled 'Art and the State' is especially interesting. In his review of *Art Worlds*, Toni del Renzio notes that Becker's approach 'does little to question capitalism's deep effect upon the social formation and its cultural constructs and . . . studiously avoids the problematics of ideology' (Renzio 1983: 27). Renzio is convinced that *Art Worlds* would have been greatly improved if its author had been aware of Marxist studies in this area. Yet Becker is probably referring to this body of work in his first chapter, when he says:

> So many writers on what is ordinarily described as the sociology of art treat art as relatively autonomous, free from the kinds of organizational constraints that surround other forms of collective activity. I have not considered those theories

13 For example, Battershill (1990).
14 Baxendall, op. cit.: 86–7.

here because they deal essentially with philosophical questions quite different from the mundane social organizational problems with which I have concerned myself. Insofar as what I have to say questions the assumption of freedom from economic, political, and organizational constraint, it necessarily implies a criticism of analytic styles based on it.

(Becker 1982: 39)

Even if Becker is not referring specifically to the body of work that Renzio recommends, it seems clear that grand-scale Marxist analyses would not have helped in the writing of *Art Worlds*, given the author's approach. His sociological stance is objective, or at any rate set apart from the aesthetics and ideologies of the art worlds that he analyses. And this is sociological analysis which *starts* from the small-scale: it focuses on the minutiae of how collective action is achieved in a specific context, and then generates sociological theory from a variety of such instances. And the smaller-scale the focus, the less directly a sociological analysis confronts broad political issues. However, in adopting an empirical approach which is *critical* of theory that gives the artist relative autonomy and treats art as a special case, Becker has taken a political decision of sorts; and one of its consequence is that thereafter he makes no judgements about art whatsoever. The title of Renzio's article is, perhaps, a comment on this: 'Works of Art are Produced by Committees'.

Yet Becker emphasises that all art has a political dimension, because all artists must respond to the particular requirements of the State in which they operate, and their work reflects and embodies that dependence. While Adorno identifies with the truly radical artist who fights the constraints imposed by the capitalist State through his use of innovatory artistic forms, Becker remarks that, in order to get art produced *at all*, artists need sufficient political and economic freedom to achieve this, and not all societies provide it. And because he is concerned with the cooperation that the production of art involves, Becker tends to stress the *opportunities* that a State can furnish in its role as art-world participant. It seems that those analysts who themselves identify with art and its values tend to envisage artists continuously struggling against social constraints, while analysts who observe art worlds and their social processes are more likely to see those constraints as enabling.

Renzio comments that Becker's writing is particularly good on the way art worlds change (and I have already discussed his treatment of change in relation to social conventions). Empirical sociology examines how the meanings of social actions alter with each context in which they occur; and, consequently, empirical analysis is fundamentally concerned with social change. Becker shows that change is endemic to art worlds. His concern is to examine how changes find an organisational basis and thus last; for lasting is the major criterion by which people recognize great art. Art history deals with winners; that is, with innovators who won organisational victories by managing to persuade other participants to engage in a changed form of cooperation which sustained and furthered their ideas. While art practices cannot stand still and minute changes happen all the time, there are also innovations which are consciously introduced; even revolutionary changes. Becker argues that the success and permanence of conscious innovations rest on organisation, not on their intrinsic worth; and that we cannot distinguish continuous from revolutionary change on the basis of the change itself. What is important to understand, he argues, is the process (that is, the different types of networks of relationships which get formed) by which participants ignore, absorb, or fight change; for those responses define the seriousness and extent of the change, making it a revolution or something less dramatic. Generalising from Becker's model, there appears to be no good reason why the production of sociological knowledge in future should not involve more use of visual representation (unconventional typography, page layout and depictions), given the potential of new technologies like desk-top publishing. Just how new and how significant that visually more informed sociology is perceived to be would depend on the nature of the organisational processes by which participants on the one hand promote and deploy it, and on the other, ignore, absorb and fight it.

In the introduction to this section I observed that sociologists are now turning their attention to visual representation in areas other than visual art, and that plates and diagrams in scientific and other texts are being subjected to analysis. Five out of the nine essays in *Picturing Power: Visual Depictions and Social Relations* (Fyfe and Law 1988) are concerned with the use of depictions outside the domain of visual art, and are thus evidence of this change. In their editors' introduction, 'On the invisibility of the visual', Fyfe and Law suggest that sociologists in the past have been wrong to ignore visual material in subject matters that are not necessarily at first sight explicitly visual. They argue that social change is at once a change in the regime of re-presentation. We can therefore learn much about changing social conventions, customs and ideologies from analysing a historical sequence of visual depictions – for example, medical textbook drawings of the human anatomy, and from comparing the different depictive conventions used in each. From such a comparison, we learn how visual languages and depictive conventions have allowed readers to envisage and conceptualise the human body; and thus how these have contributed towards shaping readers' *views* of the world, and consequently their overall interpretation of it. Although the messages that these images impart are partially shaped by captions and by text, the images in turn promote a particular reading of the text, and therefore form part of the overall textual argument. Fyfe and Law emphasise that depictions in texts are never merely illustrations.

Many sociologists, including Fyfe and Law, have noted that their discipline is actually built around a set of visual metaphors such as 'structure', 'network' and 'model'. Indeed language, including that of social scientists, is permeated with visual metaphors. We talk about the 'insights' that a model may give us, about being 'blind' to new ideas, about 'seeing' the light, or 'seeing eye to eye'; we 'focus' our attention here and 'see' a new 'perspective' there.[15] However, sociologies have rarely used depictions, and Fyfe and Law suggest several reasons why this is so. One of these is that:

> The centre of gravity of sociology, lying close, as it does, to the expression and articulation of general philosophical differences, neither lends itself well, nor allocates much priority to differences that might be resolved by recourse to visual depictions of its subject-matter.
>
> (Fyfe and Law 1988: 6)

A. J. Swinburne's *A Picture Logic* (1896) may be something of a rarity, but its existence – and devotees – bear witness to the fact that reasoning does not have to be verbal. And although in Western society the dominant form of comunication has long been verbal, this has not always been the case (Hawkes 1977; Alpers 1983), and may well not be in future. For the new technologies of communication have produced a revolution in visual representation. John Roberts (1992: 11–17) argues that as tools for making 'imperceptible phenomena visible', the new generation of computers allows vision and touch to be the new driving forces in scientific analysis and evaluation, and that a new process of scientific visualisation is under way. It may only be a matter of time before 'general philosophical differences' – and indeed the double hermeneutic character of sociological argument – also begin to find visual expression.

Fyfe and Law suggest that a more important reason for the lack of visualisation in sociology is to do with the theoretical fragmentation of the discipline, for

> Sociology does not have and has never possessed a generally agreed set of methods for identifying, discriminating and counting what it takes to be significant objects of study, and it may be that the meaning and lack of significance assigned to the visual reflect paradigmatic struggle within the discipline.
>
> (Fyfe and Law 1988: 4)

It may be that the more a discipline becomes subject to internal (methodological) debate, the more the dominant mode of communication is used because at least *its* status is not in doubt. Kuhn (1962) and Ravetz (1971) have shown that when a natural science specialism is not plagued by internal controversy about its basic assumptions, scientists can relax and 'get on'. With the philosophical and methodological foundations of their work reasonably secure, they can work in their specialist areas with imagination and

---

15 The visual is often invoked in the titles of sociological publications. The list of new books from Sage, Autumn/Winter 1992 (taken at random), includes: *Sociological Snapshots: Seeing Social Structure and Change in Everyday Life* ('designed as an accessible introduction to sociology') by Jack Levin. Also: *Indigenous Vision: Peoples of India, Attitudes to the Environment* ('this volume examines the environmental practices of the indigenous people of India'), ed. G. Sen.

daring. In the social sciences, the critical paradigm has now virtually rejected grand theory and the empirical paradigm has rejected large-scale generalising and the pursuit of 'laws', resulting in both cases in a focus on small-scale projects at a local level. This may indicate that sociologists are now entering a period when they do not need to spend so much time re-examining their own basic assumptions, and will be able to pursue their specialist work with increased confidence, imagination and daring. If this is so, then it is in just such an atmosphere that the visual dimension of their projects could provide an opportunity to produce innovative analyses.

Finally, Fyfe and Law suggest that the disappearance of the body from mainstream classic social theory may explain why sociologies have not used depictions. They argue that in order to distance their perspective from those of biology and psychology, sociologists have, over the years, produced a corpus of anti-reductionist theory; and that Foucault's reintroduction of an interest in the body has helped to draw our attention to this state of affairs. They point out that when the body was deleted from social theory, so was the eye, which meant that the analysis of perception and representation disappeared into psychology, biology, art history and anthropology. In Chapter 5, I show how anthropology, with its different intellectual concerns, has made use of visual depictions, particularly photographs; and that this has recently influenced the work of certain sociologists.

However, Fyfe and Law state that they cannot, and neither do they wish to, 'reform' sociology so that it uses the technologies of visual depiction more centrally in its *own* projects. It is important to note here that they refer to visual *depiction* rather than to visual representation or signification. This distinction has the effect of separating what is pictured from what is said or written. It suggests a *verbal* sociological approach to *visual* depiction. On the other hand, the phrase 'visual representation' embraces the typography of the text, the page layout, the colour contrasts between paper and text, the paper quality and size, as well as visual depictions themselves. Now, although I would agree with Fyfe and Law that a 'picture sociology' is not necessarily desirable, a sociological text in which the visual dimension has been put to active use surely is. By the use of unconventional layout and typography, for example, a text can show that the functions of such visual conventions are normally taken for granted in sociological texts, and that they can be made to make a more active contribution to an analysis, just as depictions can. Examples of such texts will be discussed in Chapters 5 and 6. In sum, the concept of visual representation, unlike that of depiction, allows an awareness of the ways in which a text is already visually conceived and could be further enhanced; and while it is important for social analysts to take other people's depictions seriously, they should not forget the visual aspects of texts, including their own.

I now turn to two of the essays in *Picturing Power* which deal with depictive convention. The first, 'Art and its Objects: William Ivins and the Reproduction of Art' (65–98) by Gordon Fyfe, is a critical analysis of William Ivins' classic *Prints and Visual Communication* (1953). It pays particular attention to Ivins' argument that there is a fundamental difference in status between the engraved print as reproduction of an original art work and the photographic reproduction. The second essay, Geof Bowker's 'Pictures from the Subsoil, 1939' (221–54), focuses on scientific visual depictions, and shows that visual conventions in a depiction can be made to mean different things to different people.

In *Prints and Visual Communication* (1953), Ivins emphasised that our culture was transformed by the invention of printing, which enabled the production of exactly repeatable pictorial statements. He argued that, since the Renaissance, printed images have crucially contributed to the formation of scientific and other knowledges and thus to the modernisation of the world. Yet the production of prints was not without its problems. In a medium in which only black lines on a white background were possible, engravers had to produce tonal differences (chiaroscuro) and to distribute objects in a rational space (perspective) in order for the engraved print to achieve a satisfactory resemblance to its subject matter. From the sixteenth century to the nineteenth century, there was considerable demand for engraved reproductions of original paintings, and engravers evolved depictive conventions that represented the world evoked by the conventions of painting. In *PVC*, Ivins used the term *visual syntax* to refer to the micro-level depictive conventions – the particular configuration of dots, flicks and dashes – which engravers used to build up an image. This term is valuable because it succinctly conveys the sense that visual depictions have their own grammar, and are therefore of a different order from verbal accounts.[16] Figure 17a shows the visual syntax used to construct the features of a face in a seventeenth-century engraving, and Figure 17b, taken from Fyfe's own essay, shows this visual grammar still more or less in use in a nineteenth-century engraving. Ivins noted that this visual syntax engendered its own aesthetic: 'The things that counted in public estimation were the brilliant moire of the damask of the engraved lines' (Ivins 1953: 172). This being so, engravers 'chose the pictures they were to make or reproduce not for their merits but as vehicles for the exhibition of their particular skills' (Ivins 1953: 69). Although engravers continuously adapted their visual syntax to match the style of painting currently in vogue (and Fyfe shows that by the 1880s there were engravers who could deliver an Impressionist brush-stroke), after the invention of photography, the terrain of reproduction was increasingly defined by a photographic way of seeing.

Ivins argued that the visual syntax of the print – the lines, flicks and dots

---

16 Fyfe comments that '*printed* images . . . are marked by syntactical forms which realize the scientific or the aesthetic character we assign to scientific reports and art criticism' (Fyfe 1988: 75).

Figure 17a Detail of an engraved portrait by Robert Nanteuil after Vincent Voiture by Philippe de Champaigne, taken from *Les Oeuvres de Monsieur de Voiture* (a collection of his own works), Paris, 1650

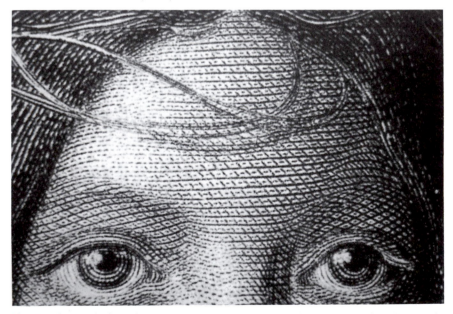

Figure 17b Detail of a mid-nineteenth-century steel engraving by H. Bourne after *The Last of England* by Ford Madox Brown. Reproduced in 'Art and its Objects: William Ivins and the Reproduction of Art' by G. Fyfe (in G. Fyfe and J. Law, eds, *Picturing Power*, 1988)

– spoke about that print itself, and about its difference and distance from the original painting which it copied. This visual syntax therefore obscured the possibility of an exact reproduction of the original. However, he believed that the photograph allowed communication *without* cultural syntax, and that this enabled the transmission of the image as a work of art, and allowed an immediate understanding of its unique properties. In other words, he believed that the mechanically produced photograph, unlike the engraving, gives an objective, scientific reproduction of the original, and that the photographic way of seeing is thus fundamentally different from that engendered by an engraved print. Although he admitted that at first the camera had to meet the visual anomie of those who experienced photographic distortion of the original art work, he observed that this was soon overcome, and viewers learned to appreciate from the photograph what the engraving could not show, which was the artist's personal manner of wielding paintbrush or chisel.

In 'Art and its Objects', Fyfe points out that Ivins was clearly influenced by the prevailing positivist philosophy. And he argues that not only is an 'exact' objective reproduction of an original an impossibility, but photography actually played a part in promoting the modernist, Romantic notion of the artist as unique, creative genius (the model for aspiring artists at Midville Art School). Fyfe notes that, broadly speaking, the paintings that were the subject of early engravings were neo-classical. A masterpiece of this genre was *like* other paintings in that it emphasised the same neo-classical qualities, but it *differed* from them in that its treatment of these qualities outclassed all other similar treatments. The meaning of the word 'original' in this context is simply to do with distinguishing the painting from the later engraved version of it. Fyfe argues that the aesthetic engendered by the photographic way of seeing hastened the replacement of the neo-classical 'masterpiece' with a modernist version. For photography, far more than engraving, showed how *different* one painting was from others of the same genre. Photography brought out the uniqueness of the artist's qualities, rather than a bundle of qualities which other painters also possessed. It thereby encouraged judgement according to a different criterion, that of uniqueness; and the word 'original' now came to mean novel, inventive, creative, even other-worldly. Fyfe comments that, according to this ideology, 'where art is, the social is not' (Fyfe 1988: 95). That would have made a good motto for Midville Art School in the 1960s.

The invention of photography soon made engravings redundant because it allowed practitioners to produce tonal differences and perspective with greater subtlety and ease. It rendered the visual syntax of engravings more opaque. People no longer used that syntax to see with; they began to look increasingly at it. Yet photography introduced a new way of seeing which had to be learned before it was rendered invisible. And photography, which involves mechanical and chemical operations, as opposed to the more 'primitive' hand processes, seemed to fulfil the requirement for a truly scientific method of recording. To Ivins, and to Bernard Berenson (see Chapter 1), photographs appeared to be untainted by aesthetic, social and ideological influences; they were scientific copies which enabled the *examination* of such factors in the originals. But Fyfe argues that the ideology of the photographic way of seeing was so convincing and influential that far from providing exact, objective reproduction, photography helped in the construction of the individualistic ideology of modernism. In this sense, then, the photographic way of seeing was poised between the 'neutral objectivity' of science and the 'subjective individualism' of art, and contributed to both these ideologies. However, in recent years, the debate about the relationship between 'original' and 'reproduction' has been taken further. Paul Winstanley's paintings (*Paintings*, 1992) are 'copies' of photographs, and play on this relationship. They tend to position Fyfe's *own* sociological account in the context of postmodern theory which proposes that original and reproduction are now increasingly hard to disentangle.

'Pictures from the Subsoil, 1939', by Geof Bowker, also in *Picturing Power*, is concerned with the proceedings of a pre-war court trial between two geophysical companies, Schlumberger and Halliburton. These companies were in the business of selling information to client firms about the likelihood of finding oil at specific locations deep under the surface of the earth. On the basis of exploratory bores, they produced graphs known as electrical logs which indicated whether oil (and on occasions, gas, or water) was present in sufficient quantities to be worth mining. Figure 18, which Bowker entitles 'Example of commercial resistivity and porosity curves', shows an electrical log produced by one of these companies. Schlumberger's geological research and technical expertise had (and still have) the highest reputation for accuracy. Bowker notes that in the 1930s, the firm accounted for 95 per cent of trade in this specialist area. However, when Schlumberger drilled an exploratory well for a client, the information registered on the electrical log had to serve several sets of interests. It had to give the client firm sufficient information to allow a decision to be made about whether or not to drill for oil, but it also had to conceal from that firm how such reliable information had been gained. For if *that* information were made available, the firm might be able to dispense with Schlumberger's services on future occasions. The information yielded by the exploratory bore also had to advance Schlumberger's own researches, so that it could keep ahead of its competitors, of which Halliburton was one. In 'Pictures from the Subsoil, 1939', Bowker examines the transcript of a court trial, in which Schlumberger brought a suit against Halliburton for the infringement of the two patents used in their electrical well-logging activities, in order to show how Schlumberger's electrical logs were able to represent the subsoil in such a way as to meet the requirements of this competing set of interests.

The transcript reveals that Schlumberger's representative in court was

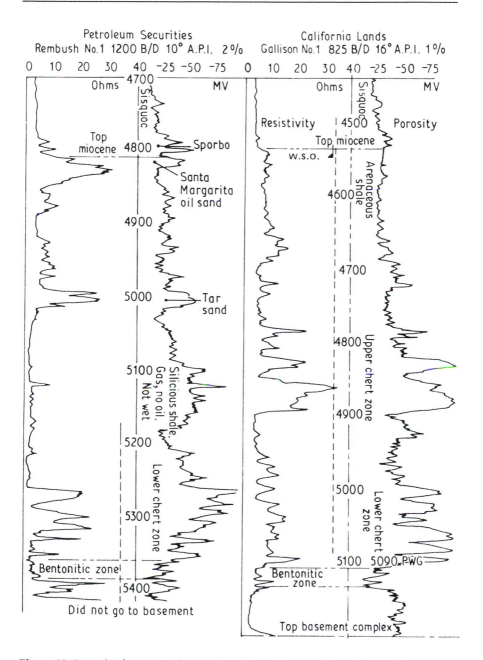

Figure 18 Example of commercial resistivity and porosity curves. Reproduced in 'Pictures from the Subsoil, 1939' by G. Bowker (in G. Fyfe and J. Law, eds, *Picturing Power*, 1988)

asked to explain why some of the numbers and scales on the electrical logs which were sold to client firms appeared to be redundant. The representative explained that the firm's policy was to keep the format of the log basically the same over the years because regular clients felt more secure if they knew what to expect. He argued that if Schlumberger kept changing the mode of graphic presentation in order to keep up with scientific developments in the field, this would make the curves very confusing to read. Indeed, he noted that one client was on record as saying that he became suspicious if the curve was too detailed and the information too complex, because such fine-tuning between the representation and the reality was surely impossible, and consequently it looked as though the purpose of the complexity was to dress up basic information, making it seem more accurate than it really was. And Bowker comments that from the clients' point of view the matter was, indeed, basically simple: an oil-bearing layer was defined by the fact that it gave a kick to the characteristically saw-toothed curve (see Figure 18 above); and if there was no kick, then as far as drillers, and thus the annals of human history, were concerned, there was no oil. However, Bowker argues that the 'non-essential' numbers and curves depicted on the log did serve various strategic purposes. They signalled to clients that the curves were a scientific production and not some French person's artistic impressions. And since each graph was different, the numbers and curves contributed to its originality, serving as a signature, while the fact that data were presented in the same way each time satisfied clients' desire for consistency and ease of reading.

Since the court proceedings had established that all the numbers and curves on the logs did not straightforwardly translate into client information, Schlumberger's representative was asked by counsel about the real meaning of the information given in the logs. The representative explained that a curve only took on meaning in the particular geographical context to which it referred, with the help of additional local knowledge. Any attempt to tie down the meaning of a curve in the courtroom was doomed to failure because the local knowledge necessary to interpret the curve was unavailable. And, he argued, since the log had to be interpreted in the light of local information, *the* meaning of a specific log was impossible to establish. And if a log cannot be said to have a definitive meaning, the court could not decree what the curve should look like.

However, the situation was more complex than Schlumberger's representative let on. The information on an electrical log related to one specific geographical site, but that site itself constituted more than one social site: it was both the site of Schlumberger's private researches for commercial purposes, *and* the site of its client's potential oilfield. Bowker observes that the trial threw into sharp relief the fact that Schlumberger deliberately produced graphs which were open to multiple interpretation. The court proceedings indicated that the company domesticated its clients, training them to expect information portrayed in a certain graphic form; and this habit, once acquired, served to deflect attention from other more sensitive and opaquely coded data which were intended for internal consumption only. Bowker argues that only by operating in this manner could Schlumberger create a space in which it could function successfully in the long term. Far from 'holding a mirror to nature', Schlumberger's logs were consciously constructed in a manner calculated to foster a situation that was stable yet ambiguous.

Latour (1987) suggests that the 'harder' a scientific fact, the more social it is. Bowker's sociological analysis involving scientific depictions is important because it dispels two myths at the same time; namely, the 'purity' of scientific facts, and the derivative character of visual material in subject matters that are not at first sight explicitly visual. He shows that because a scientific depiction can be made to mean different things to different people, it cannot be said to mirror *nature*, and it cannot be said *merely* to reflect what it depicts. He shows that Schlumberger's electrical logs were the *means* by which a complex set of competing social interests were held at bay and indeed served. We might conjecture, then, that one of the social purposes which depictive representations may be made to serve is that of achieving a situation of sustained ambiguity.

However, any attempt to generalise from the findings of sociological analyses of scientific depictions is fraught with complexities. This becomes clear when we begin to compare Bowker's analysis with another sociological study, 'Working Conceptual Hallucinations' by Gilbert and Mulkay (1984). These authors, like Bowker, examined what promised to be a sociologically interesting scientific controversy. They aimed to penetrate the formal side of science in order to show the social processes that were going on 'underneath'. Bowker's visual data consist of a series of unique geographical and geophysical depictive statements, produced for commercial purposes. However, Gilbert and Mulkay's 'pictures',[17] which relate to the discourse of bioenergetics, represent more general theoretical propositions; and these depictive representations were not intended, in any straightforward sense, to form part of a commercial transaction: they were produced by bio-energeticists who wanted to communicate various aspects of their subject to

---

17 The title of Bowker's essay refers to '*Pictures* from the Subsoil, 1939' (my emphasis), while the term 'figure' is used to denote each visual representation illustrated. On the other hand, Gilbert and Mulkay use the term 'picture' throughout their essay, in both the text and the captions. In fact, authors use a variety of terms, and I have found that the question of terminology in this area is complex and fraught with difficulties, because of the slightly different meaning of each term and the huge implications which follow from the use of one particular term rather than another. I have tried, throughout this book, to select the most appropriate term (visual representation, depiction, depictive representation, figure, illustration, etc.) for each context in which it is used. But this has not been easy, precisely because when one focuses on a particular area, the available terms associated with it can no longer be taken for granted, and the meaning of each term takes on a heightened significance and importance that it would not do in a text where the focus of interest was elsewhere.

fellow scientists who might have a less specialised knowledge of it. A further difference between the two sociological projects is that Gilbert and Mulkay *introduced* the topic of 'pictures' into their interviews with bioenergeticists, whereas Bowker's anaylsis drew upon historical data. Thus the two sets of scientific depictions and the social contexts in which they operate and are interpreted (including the contexts of the two sociological projects) differ in many respects. All this indicates the difficulties of drawing general conclusions from analyses of scientific depictions. For, as Fyfe and Law (1988) point out, while visual art works constitute the core material of the domain of visual art, thus lending coherence to the notion of a sociology of visual art, scientists represent nature in many different ways, and depiction is only one of them. We cannot, therefore, talk of a 'sociology of scientific depictions', nor draw firm conclusions from close comparisons between sociological studies of scientific depictions. However, what we might expect these two sociological studies to have in common is a basic argument that the depictions that are analysed are socially constructed arguments about the natural world.

Another complexity involves the fact that there are markedly different types of scientific depiction. Bowker's data consist of schematic depictions (graphs), whereas 'Working Conceptual Hallucinations' focuses on more freely drawn scientific depictions in addition to schematic depictions or diagrams. Now, different types of depiction are used to convey different orders of information, and they are produced for – and promote – different kinds of social situation. Indeed, Schlumberger's were able to use the reputation for scientific precision which graphs give off to shade the fact that its electrical logs were *each* capable of yielding more than one 'precise' reading, and thus met the requirements of at least two social situations. Bioenergeticists also use schematic depictions to convey precise information as in Figure 19a; while Figure 19b shows a depiction which is more realistic and freely drawn. However, Gilbert and Mulkay point out that in fact Figure 19b combines realistic depiction *and* standard scientific symbols, and thus a 'pictorial tension' is in evidence. It seems that the parts of the theory the author is sure about are represented schematically. (This is why, on Gilbert and Mulkay's evidence, colleagues are happiest when a depictive representation *is* schematic.) But in the parts of the theory that the author is less sure about, scientific visual conventions are abandoned; and attempts are made to portray realistically an analogy with something that *is* known, as in the drawing of the flagellum which suggests a great rotating cogwheel. So the resultant depiction is a hybrid: schematic depiction of theory combined with 'realistic' depiction of analogy. Gilbert and Mulkay suggest that the introduction of formal schematic conventions and numbers into more visually exploratory passages may give the impression to non-specialists that it 'really looks like that', and may indeed account for the fact that such depictions are sometimes interpreted too literally, thus posing communication problems between specialists and non-specialists. While the idea that science purveys certainty was used to advantange in Schlumberger's dealings with its clients, it proved a stumbling-block in the case of Figure 19b whose author wanted to convey the idea that theory in his field was, in some respects, unsettled.

However, a key argument in 'Working Conceptual Hallucinations' is that this potential confusion may be avoided when a 'joke picture' is used. In an analysis of one such depiction, entitled 'Proton-translocating respiratory chain', Gilbert and Mulkay note the startling effect which is produced by the combination of depictive conventions from two quite separate areas of discourse, those of bioenergetics and comic-book cartoon characters. The depiction immediately signals to the reader that it should not be taken too seriously, while the contrasting depictive conventions lend different degrees of realism to various of its components, thus suggesting that some areas of the theory are taken as certain while other scientific questions remain un-answered. This form of pictorial presentation stops the reader in her tracks, preventing her from interpreting what she sees as scientific truth. In fact, as Gilbert and Mulkay point out, the depiction has introduced visual reflexivity:

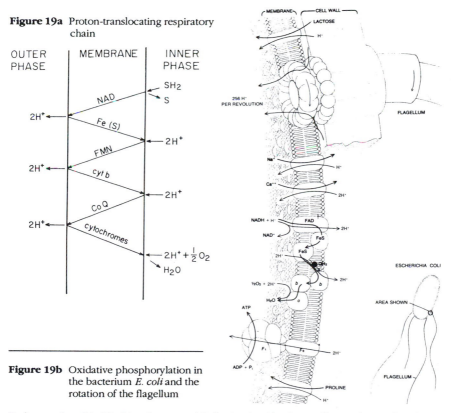

Figure 19a Proton-translocating respiratory chain

Figure 19b Oxidative phosphorylation in the bacterium *E. coli* and the rotation of the flagellum

Both reproduced in 'Working Conceptual Hallucinations' by G. N. Gilbert and M. Mulkay (in *Opening Pandora's Box*, 1984)

it visually reflects on the fact that the field is as yet unsettled. However, they note that the vast majority of depictions appear to be non-reflexive: '[Visual languages] seem to point rigidly beyond themselves towards the objects and process in the natural world which they represent' (Gilbert and Mulkay 1984: 148). Here Gilbert and Mulkay are close to the problem posed by Jameson when he suggested that postmodernism is predominantly a visual phenomenon, and that in postmodern society critical communications will have to learn how to combat the image by way of the image. In the present case, the purpose of the 'joke picture' is to persuade the reader to reflect upon the fact that the field contains uncertainties, and to prevent him or her from 'taking it as gospel'. Gilbert and Mulkay suggest that joke pictures thus fulfil an important function, and that this may explain why they are sometimes to be found as endpieces to chapters in student textbooks. The pictures are saying: 'Don't think that just because this is science, what you've learned in this chapter is fixed and true: in this area at least there is a state of uncertainty, and things are changing all the time.' I would suggest that such an important message is, perhaps, better signalled visually than verbally, since a verbal message could not capture and *sustain* this kind of reflection about uncertainty. It would, by definition, have to *spell* the situation out, which might then lead to further debate and criticism which reflected unfavourably on the status of scientific knowledge. This high status is in part a legacy of positivism, and although a positivistic attitude to science is precisely what bioenergeticists, in this instance, wish to dislodge from the minds of their readers/viewers, they would not want science itself to lose the status that has previously been accorded to it.

Depictions themselves do not constitute the core of the discipline of science, so each empirical study has to be considered separately, and integrated into the sociological study of the research area under investigation. However, both this and the previous study show that some scientific depictions are constructed in such a way as to fit the author's perception of the readers' requirements. And while Gilbert and Mulkay have shown that there are depictions by scientists that are capable of sending multiple messages to their readers, it is worth noting that in a very different sense, Schlumberger's electrical logs did the same. It seems that a feature of depictions is that they may be made to give off a plurality of messages and to create a situation of ambiguity, which is given stability through its distinctive visual format and a certain resistance to being 'pinned down'. Since our dominant form of communication is verbal, pinning down is usually done with words in textual discourse. The ability of depictive representations to create and sustain a situation of ambiguity appears to have been used to advantage by scientists in different ways.

Depictions, like all representations, are thought which has been externalised. By contrast, *visualising* is part of the subjective process of thinking, problem-solving, theorising. There is plenty of evidence that scientists' problem-solving involves visualising. For example, in geometry visualising is inseparable from the conceptual concerns of the geometer. Mathematicians also describe how they solve problems visually. For example, writing to a colleague, Albert Einstein said:

> The words or the language, as they are written or spoken, do not seem to play any role in my mechanism of thought. The psychical entities which seem to serve as elements in thought are certain signs and more or less clear images which can be 'voluntarily' reproduced and combined. There is, of course, a certain connection between those elements and relevant logical concepts. . . . Conventional words or other signs have to be sought for laboriously only in a secondary stage.
> (Hadamard 1949: 142)

For Crick and Watson, visualising the shape of the double helix was tantamount to 'the breakthrough' (Watson 1974). In all these cases, visualising, still a social process, is crucial to scientific problem-solving *before* the stage of making depictions arises. It seems that visualising helps scientists think. And, since they now tend to work with ever-increasingly sophisticated visual computer displays, it is likely that in future their thinking will become more visual. Sociology can probably not remain free of this trend – and indeed the current front cover of the journal *Sociology* (first used in vol. 24, 1990) seems to imply the double hermeneutic character of sociological theory in the way that the tonal gradation of the sequence of letters in the word 'sociology' interrelates systematically with the tonal gradation of the background cover, while the emphasis round the edge of the letters remains the same throughout, suggesting the enduring and persistent character of sociological theory (Figure 20). At a different level, some sociologists make their own depictions – usually photographs – which form an integral part of their analyses. This topic is discussed in Chapter 5.

The question of how sociologists make use of other people's visual representations is discussed in *Representation in Scientific Practice*, a collection of essays edited by Michael Lynch and Steve Woolgar (1990).[18] The word 'representation' in the title suggests that the book's concerns may be close to my own in this volume. But this term has recently gained considerable prominence in social science texts, and its precise meaning is shaped by the particular theoretical context in which it is used.[19] It features

---

18 In this context, 'visual representation' is a more appropriate term than 'depiction'.

19 The *Fontana Dictionary of Modern Thought* has no entry under 'representation' in its early editions. The term features for the first time in the 1988 edition, where the author of the entry remarks that it is only relatively recently that representations of reality have become a focus for interdisciplinary research, involving literary critics, social anthropologists, art historians and intellectual historians; and that this study has been encouraged and influenced by structuralism, with its presentation of cultures as systems of signs. The term 'representation' does not occur in the index of Lynch (1985). It is reasonable to suppose, however, that in this work the use of the term would have been appropriate had it been currently available. Meanwhile, the Open University's latest, and widely used, social science foundation course, *Society and Social Science* (1991), features 'Representation and Reality' as a course theme.

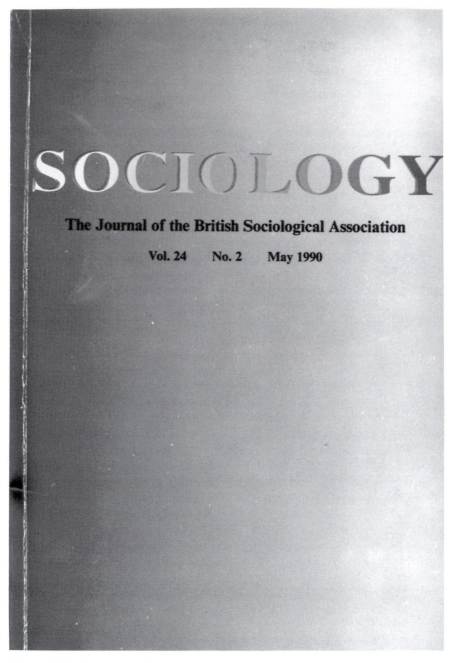

Figure 20 The front cover of *Sociology*

in Baudrillard's writings, for example, where he argues that in Western society the distinction between representation and reality is often impossible to maintain. For the contributors to *RSP*, however, 'representation' is a key theoretical concept: many of the essays, informed by constructivist and ethnomethodological themes, are studies of the modes of representation which scientists themselves devise in order to accomplish their particular scientific projects. Thus graphs, diagrams, models, photographs, instrumental displays, written reports, etc. are subjected to sociological scrutiny – within the context of the scientific settings in which they feature. However, in *RSP*, no formal distinction is made between visual and verbal representation, as it is in this book. In their 'Introduction: Sociological orientations to representational practice in science' (1–18), the editors argue that this distinction is of the sociologist's own making, and that it consequently pre-categorises data, and obscures a view of the context in which scientists themselves represent nature. However, the way in which 'representation' is used in *RSP* has itself got certain theoretical consequences. For example, it enables the editors to link science with art at a general level: 'Representation is an explicit issue in science (as in selected other activities like art) – it is addressed in and as the activity' (Lynch and Woolgar 1990: 10).

This link cannot be made by sociologists who use the term 'depiction' (Fyfe and Law 1988) and 'picture' (Gilbert and Mulkay 1984), because here the *product* of an activity tends to be stressed rather than the *doing* of it. In such studies there is a distinction to be drawn between a sociology of visual art, which is coherent though 'marginal to most sociological concerns' (Fyfe and Law 1988: 2), and a sociology of depiction – which is incoherent, 'an artificial creation' (Fyfe and Law 1988: 1), because each depiction is merely *part* of an area of activity, such as science, rather than what centrally constitutes it. *RSP*'s index does not list 'depiction'. And despite the editors' insistence that to focus on representations which are in one way or another visual is to assign undue privilege to a particular representational form, the majority of contributors to *RSP are* concerned with visual representations, because this enables them to question the privilege traditionally assigned to the verbal statement or 'proposition'. Ashmore, in his review of *RSP*, calls the essays 'a focused set of analyses of how scientists (and quasi-scientists) go about the business of "visualising" the world' (Ashmore 1992: 155–6).

The ethnomethodological approach emphasises that all meanings are context-dependent. The editors of *RSP* argue that when a scientist represents nature, that representation's distinctive format constitutes part of the scientific context. It provides the material with which theorising is visibly constructed, and thus clearly contributes to the meaning which the representation conveys. This emphasis on the *modes* of representation which scientists use is clearly incompatible with the widespread notion that representations are transparent images of objects and ideas. Indeed, it suggests that *how* representations come to appear transparent should be investigated; and this, in turn, indicates that the textual arrangements and discursive practices that produce and reproduce 'the mundane conditions of representational transparency' (Lynch and Woolgar 1990: ix) should be subject to close scrutiny. The editors of *RSP* argue that when extraordinary attention is paid to how representations are inscribed in contexts in the course of specific inquiries, it becomes evident that the process of assembling and interpreting accounts of research practices is *improvisatory* in character. This is demonstrated by amateur bird-watchers Law and Lynch (1990: 155–6). They show that each of the three most highly regarded manuals on the identification of bird species provides a different basic approach to the subject. This means that the choice of manual affects the process of identification, which itself involves distinguishing a male from a female, a mature from an immature specimen, perhaps glimpsed only for an instant and in an untypical pose and setting. There is also the problem of juggling a heavy manual, fieldglasses, pencil and paper in two hands while standing out in the open. All these practical difficulties oblige the bird-watcher to make *ad hoc* identifications based on similar past experiences; for any attempt to 'do it by the book' in a systematic, rule-informed manner turns out to be impossible.

Indeed, the editors of *RSP* argue that any project involves unanticipated contingencies, which means that bricolage is necessarily at the heart of sustaining a plan and remedying its provisions. They note that this point is entirely missed if attention is merely focused *on* representations; and consequently they advise that an improvisory manner is perhaps best adopted in the reading of such textual materials. They also recommend that serial and 'directional' relations between representations should be read as though these were movements along an assembly line; and that differences between abstracted and naturalistic parts of representations should be read in the same way. This is, in fact, more or less how the authors of 'Working Conceptual Hallucinations' read the pictorial tension produced by the combination of schematic and realistic conventions in Figure 19b. In short, these essays, with their emphasis on the crucial role played by *ad hoc*cery and bricolage in the construction and interpretation of scientific representations, show that specific instances of these processes cannot be reduced to a generalised formulation about scientific procedure. And although the editors refer to recent critical literature (a rare event in empirical sociology), likening their approach to that aspect of postmodernist theory which rejects the universal in favour of the specific and local, they emphatically reject any idea of a *criticism* of the fit between a representation and its 'reality', which is at the heart of a critical enterprise and distinguishes critical from empirical sociology.

At the start of this section, I noted that Lynch and Woolgar discuss sociologists' *own* use of representations. They observe that contributors to *RSP* deploy, as well as analyse, representations. That is to say, representative documents and excerpted passages attributed to 'scientists' are selected and reproduced as objects or evidence for 'sociological' claims. However, 'Not much is said about this in the [sociologists' own] papers as they mainly deal with how the features of such representations are reflexive to *other* textual uses and contexts of inquiry. What can we make of this?' (Lynch and Woolgar 1990: 12). It might suggest that sociologists do not wish their own work to be subjected to the kind of analysis that they make of other people's. Another sociological task is therefore indicated; that of analysing sociologists' use of scientists' documents in order to reveal the devices which effect a plausible link between the document selected and the sociological claim, or 'argument', made about it. But such 'second-level' sociological analyses are also representations, which require analysis in order to reveal the devices used . . . and so on . . . *ad infinitum*. While this is surely an important task, because to deny it would be to give sociology an unjustifiably special status, at the same time the regressive nature of the task apparently makes it impossible to complete. However, the editors of *RSP* maintain that even more crippling is the perspective of the critical paradigm (which in turn renders this ethnomethological project futile). A critical approach indicates that a fit between representation and reality is capable of improvement; but Lynch and Woolgar note that such a critique can be turned inwards on itself, thereby exposing it to the criticism it makes of other representations, and debilitating it. On the other hand, how convincing are the *RSP* contributors' own pretentions to critical neutrality? Although Lynch and Woolgar admit that there are problems here, since they are critical of the normal conventions of written academic discourse which 'seem to require the frequent use of a distinction between representation and object' (Lynch and Woolgar 1990: 13), they do not discuss the fact that their own approach can be situated within the wider political context. Critical writers would insist that political neutrality is impossible to maintain; that no discourse exists in an ideological vacuum.

Let us look again at Lynch and Woolgar's remark that there is a lack of comment made by sociologists on their own use of excerpts of scientific representations. Let us pursue the idea that an analysis of the uses sociologists make of such excerpts in their own work might reveal the devices they have used to make the scientific representations and the 'sociological' claims made for them appear to fit plausibly together. What might such a secondary analysis look like? What form should it take? Although Lynch and Woolgar claim that the essays in *RSP* demonstrate a questioning of the privilege traditionally assigned to the verbal statement or 'proposition', they appear to assume – in this volume at least – that sociological analysis proceeds according to the rules of conventional academic discourse; that the basic ethnomethodological tool is verbal language; that an analysis of sociologists' own strategies – of how they have made a fit between their chosen excerpts of scientists' representations and 'theoretical argument' – would be verbal and take the form of conventional academic discourse. But sociologists' use of excerpts of scientific representations would have to be treated to the basic policy of 'anthropological strangeness' (just as Law and Lynch submitted identifying-birds-with-the-help-of-a-manual to the experience of a novice birdwatcher), so that taken-for-granted aspects of it could be examined 'from a distance'. One taken-for-granted aspect would be its use of conventional academic discourse. In order to view this from a distance, the secondary analysis would presumably need to depart from this convention. Although Lynch and Woolgar say that it is not yet clear to what extent it may be possible to escape the constraints of conventional academic discourse, Greg Myers' contribution to *RSP*, 'Every picture tells a story: Illustrations in E. O. Wilson's *Sociobiology*' (Myers 1990) contains some detailed analyses of the relationship of photographs to caption and to text which begin to indicate how conventional academic discourse might be subjected to an image-and-text analysis. And in Chapter 5, I will examine some examples of sociological analysis which do make considerable use of image and text in order to achieve an 'anthropological strangeness', though the purpose of the majority of these studies is not to distance themselves from conventional academic discourse in order to analyse it, but to examine the social world in ways which words alone do not allow. Chapter 6, however, examines social science texts which use new literary forms *in order* to escape the constraints of conventional academic discourse; and while these all draw attention to the visual aspects of the printed page, some make active use of unconventional page layout and typescript. Although an unconventional text could not *analyse* the strategies sociologists deploy in their use of excerpts from scientists' representations – in the sense in which we understand the term 'analysis' – it could, through the manner in which the visual and verbal components of its own textual presentation relate to one another, provide an alternative which, by comparison, would unsettle the implicit claims of the conventional text.

Although most of the essays in *RSP* analyse specific, localised 'scientific' projects (like the attempt to identify birds from a spotter's manual), the second contribution is different. Bruno Latour's extraordinary materialist essay, 'Drawing Things Together' (1990) operates at a very basic and general level in its treatment of the concept of *inscription*. Latour describes this as the various processes through which 'data' are transformed into representations of data, and are at least temporarily fixed. He argues that when an inscription is both *immutable* and *mobile*, it becomes a potentially powerful instrument in the hands of the person who holds it. For an immutable inscription does not degenerate or alter when it is duplicated; and this means that many people can share the same information. And a mobile inscription will travel: it allows information about something to be brought back from 'there' to 'here' for the benefit of those who were not able to make the journey to see it for themselves. An immutable mobile inscription transforms three-dimensional data into two-dimensional information-on-paper, and this piece of paper can mightily assist its owner to win arguments. For a two-dimensional inscription which deploys perspective can be merged with geometry: measured lines extend from 'out there' on to the paper, and a diagram results (for example, Lynch (1990: 174) shows how the neuron of a rat is 'transmuted' into a photograph, then a graph, and finally into a punched IBM computer card). And diagrams establish rapid links between unrelated problems, thus allowing complex pieces of information to be held in the possession of one person. Indeed Latour argues that abstractions and formal propositions, far from originating in the mind or brain of a 'clever' person, are the result of an ever more rapid condensing of one set of figues or inscriptions into another set – held in the hands of an ordinary person.

Furthermore, he notes that files of inscriptions can be organised into cascades which are sequential and cumulative, giving even more information in one place. 'Centres of calculation' where files of inscriptions about the world are kept are thus crucially important, for they allow operators to reshuffle papers and hence to alter basic priorities. The bureaucrat has power. And anyone who disputes the bureaucrat's argument must mount a case which takes that argument into account and goes one further. This must be done from a similar 'bureau' but of slightly larger proportions. However, Latour emphasises that the power of the bureaucrat, or paper shuffler, does not simply consist in the accumulation of cascades of inscriptions; for their bulk would swamp her. One of the crucial properties of immutable mobiles is that they allow the merging and condensing of complex inscriptions into simpler ones. And Latour notes that not only do we privilege inscriptions about empirical data over that data itself, but we also have a 'peculiar tendency' to believe the last inscription in the series most, and contrary to any other evidence.

An indication of the soundness of his generalisations is that the other contributors to *RSP* use them in the theorisation of their own empirical data. In this sense, Latour's work does actually 'draw things together'. Yet his own basic arguments are not merely pitched at a general level. They are consistently backed by a wide array of empirical examples. I will try to show a little of this richness by examining one section of his essay in more detail, where visualisation, visual cultures and inscription are discussed. Latour observes that Chinese pictograms do not synthesise as well as written and diagramatic documents, because they do not allow for the condensing of information, the superimposition of different types of knowledge one on another. However, both Italian perspective and the Dutch 'distance point' method for drawing pictures do have these qualities. Consequently, 'what people knew' in fifteenth-century Italy was much influenced by artists who used Italian perspective with 'its logical recognition of internal invariances through all the transformations produced by changes in spatial location' (Ivins (1973) in Latour 1990: 27). Armed with perspective, you could go out of your way and come back 'with all the places you passed'. In addition, perspective allowed you to alter the scale, and reassemble the work differently, combining it with other elements if necessary. You could present a view of a coast line in its absence to others, who would then know what to expect. They would know how to negotiate it when they did sail up to it. Latour also draws upon the work of Alpers (1983), who shows how a visual culture changes over time. She discusses the many optical instruments which were developed and put to use in seventeenth-century Holland (among these were camera obscura, microscope, telescope, other types of lense, and various mapping devices). What all of them did was to enable space to be inscribed with optical consistency, thus allowing for the possibility of going from one type of visual trace to another. And these traces could be drawn together, inscriptions could be merged; and hence visual knowledge could be established and advanced in the sciences, arts and other areas. This state of affairs, in turn, focused the minds of ordinary seventeenth-century Dutch people on *looking*; and it helped to establish visual conventions which involved making progressively finer and sharper visual discriminations. It thus shaped *how* the seventeenth-century Dutch looked, and what it was possible for them to see. A society was drawn together by its commonly shared visual culture. Latour argues that 'a little lowland country becomes powerful by making a few crucial inventions which allow people to accelerate the mobility and to enhance the immutability of inscriptions: the world is thus gathered up in this tiny country' (Latour 1990: 31). In seventeenth-century Holland, sociological thought – or the nearest thing to it – would have been literally a *view*point, a predominantly visual knowledge of society. And it seems that a visual culture served Holland well.

The constructivist–ethnomethodological approach of *RSP* is a far cry from the viewpoint of conventional art history where the (inscribed) art work is taken as 'given', and an aesthetic response to it is somehow bolted to a historical account of it. However, Tagg's insistence that the object of knowledge of a *social* art history is the relation between particular cultural products, particular meanings and particular conditions of existence (Tagg 1986: 167), and Burgin's stress on the futility of distinguishing between 'purely' visual and 'purely' verbal discourses (Burgin 1977: 127) both correspond with certain crucial features of the *RSP* approach. But a detailed *empirical* study of the process by which an art work is produced 'in the studio' has not been attempted, so far as I am aware; although Painter's pilot study (1980), discussed earlier in this chapter, does begin to examine the various situations in which such a work is relocated and interpreted. Of course, there are obvious differences between representation in visual art practice and representation in scientific practice; for example, a visual art work is not, in itself, intended to be immutable. Nevertheless, a sociological analysis *of* representation in visual art practice has much to learn from the essays in *RSP*, for as Lynch and Woolgar remark, 'representation is an explicit issue in science (as it is in selected other activities like art)' (Lynch and Woolgar 1990: 10) The first step would seem to be to switch attention from the finished product to the processes of inscription and representation.

The last piece discussed in this chapter is 'Images of Parenthood in the United Kingdom and Japan' by Dingwall, Tanaka and Minamikata (1991). It contains four large black and white pictures; and is perhaps an indication that sociologists are starting to attend to visual representation in areas other than art and science – a tendency which is also noted by the current editors of *Sociology* (Stanley and Morgan 1993: 2). However, 'Images of Parenthood in the UK and Japan' is very different from the contributions to *RSP*, for its authors focus *on* the images – as in conventional art history – rather than on the contextualised process of representation. They analyse three images from Japanese parenthood literature and one from an equivalent British publication for what these reveal about the differences between the ideals of British and Japanese cultures. Two of the images – one Japanese and one British – are photographs, whilst the other two Japanese images are types of cartoon drawing. The authors argue that a comparison of images can be an effective general indicator of cultural differences, because images show a wealth of detail about the social situation they depict, while presenting it in a direct and immediate manner in a way that words do not. Thus a comparison between an image of 'parents with their new baby' in a British parentcraft handbook and an image of the same subject in the equivalent Japanese literature immediately draws attention to the different modes of visual communication used – the British image is a photograph, while the Japanese one is a cartoon – and this leads to broader cultural comparisons. The authors note that the adult cartoon book is a major element of Japanese popular literature – whereas this is not the case in Britain – and that in a culture which plays down individual differences, the cartoon can function as a statement of universals.

They make a *systematic* analysis of the images according to predetermined sociological categories, as Wölfflin did in his analyses of visual art works according to a set of art-historical categories (Wölfflin 1932 and 1953). The sociological categories, adapted from Millum (1975) via Graham (1977), are *the nucleus*, which refers to the nature of the shot (distance or close-up, composition, cropping, viewer's angle), *the mood* (largely created by focus and lighting), *the setting* (location, props) and *the actors* (age, gender, race, height, marital or social status, etc.). Analysis of the four images, roughly guided by this classification, and in conjunction with other information, is used to argue that current British parentcraft manuals use photographs – and hence realism – to present parenthood as the joint responsibility of choice-making adults, and birth as an event in which culture has interfered minimally with nature, even given the hospital setting. In this sense, the British parent is presented as an active consumer, not a passive recipient of instructions. By comparison, the cultural messages given off by the Japanese cartoons and 'posed' photograph indicate that in Japan women would appear to be marginalised, and subordinate to medical authority. The Japanese images suggest that parentcraft is largely for mothers – with fathers on the fringe – but that it is fraught with difficulties which require the knowledge of experts, and an unemotional, medicalised approach.

Just how powerful the impact of a photographic image can be in British culture is indicated by the fact that the editorial board of *Sociology* refused to allow the inclusion of a fifth picture in the article 'on the grounds that some readers might consider that pictures of this kind portrayed women at a private and vulnerable moment in an objectifying and offensive manner' (Dingwall *et al.* 1991: 443). This photograph, which had the consent of the original publishers and is widely available in British popular guides and health education material,[20] is integral to the authors' argument (see last paragraph). Consequently, they have had to resort to verbal description. They say that the image depicts the moment of birth in a clear and naturalistic fashion, with the father closely involved. So what is acceptable when characterised verbally may be unacceptable when depicted photographically. This incident nicely demonstrates the force and accuracy with which a photograph is perceived to communicate in our culture. Anthropologists have long known this, and I shall shortly examine their use of photographs.

This chapter has discussed some empirical sociological analyses of visual representation in art, science and parentcraft literature, and has suggested that sociologists' interest in visual data may be gathering pace. However, the discussion of 'Images of Parenthood in the United Kingdom and Japan' also clearly indicates that, in practical terms, the line between a sociology *of* visual representation and a sociology which *uses* visual representation is difficult to draw. This should serve to remind us that in general terms the distinction is impossible to maintain since visual represensions are not transparent windows on the world but social constructs, and in the sociologist's hands they are inevitably subject to reconstruction: framed, captioned and interacting with a carefully crafted verbal text, they become part of the sociological argument. However, a distinction can be made between the empirical accounts discussed up to this point and those examined in the next chapter, where authors have introduced large amounts of visual material into their textual presentation with the intention that this should in some way constitute a major integral part of the overall argument. In these cases, the sociological analysis shifts towards a situation in which visual understanding is imparted. Of course, this is not comparable with the extent to which a visual culture dominated seventeenth-century Holland; but Latour's discussion of that phenomenon is relevant to the point I am making here.

---

20 The authors say that it is reproduced in M. Stoppard's *Pregnancy and Birth Book* (1985).

Chapter 5

The use of visual representation in anthropology and sociology

Principal works discussed:

David Livingstone, *Missionary Travels and Researches in South Africa*, 1857
Clarence Stasz, 'The Early History of Visual Sociology', *Images of Information*, 1979
Gregory Bateson and Margaret Mead, *Balinese Character: A Photographic Analysis*, 1942
Erving Goffman, *Gender Advertisements*, 1979
Howard Becker (ed.), *Exploring Society Photographically*, 1981
Douglas Harper, 'Meaning and Work: A Study in Photo Elicitation', *Current Sociology*, 34, 3, 1986
Helen Stummer, 'Photo-essay', *International Journal of Visual Sociology*, 2, 1985
Elizabeth Chaplin, *Visual Diary*, 1988–91
Sarah Graham-Brown, *Images of Women. The Portrayal of Women in Photography of the Middle East 1860–1950*, 1988
Malcolm Ashmore, Michael Mulkay and Trevor Pinch, '"Fury over Prof's Kidney Call": Health Economists in the Media', *Health and Efficiency*, 1989

Today, mainstream sociology is caught in a Gutenberg syndrome: words and figures count, visual images are suspect.
(Leonard Henny 'Trend Report: Theory and Practice of Visual Sociology', *Current Sociology*, 1986)

So words still dominate. But yes, visual images, successive images, play an enormous part in our lives today, larger than ever before. Those images can show the same insecure inventiveness as do our manipulations of words.
(Richard Hoggart, *Life and Times, vol. 1: A Local Habitation 1918–40*, 1988)

When you talk about the aesthetic it's as though arrows are pointing inwards into the photograph you are discussing. When you talk about the documentary, the descriptive, the arrows are going outwards into the social world.
(Malcolm Hughes in conversation with Elizabeth Chaplin 1993)

It has often been remarked that what we remember of our dreams consists largely of visual images. And Berger proclaims on the front cover of *Ways of Seeing* that 'Seeing comes before words. The child looks and recognizes before it can speak' (Berger 1972). Even those who do not place such an emphasis on the primacy of vision would agree that there is a close inter-active relationship between what we see and how we represent the world. More specifically, the making of the twentieth-century Western world, which constitutes sociology's subject matter and at the same time gave birth to the discipline, has had a distinctively visual aspect. Indeed, photography and sociology date almost from the same year: in 1839, as Comte was finishing his *Cours de philosophie positive* (1936), Daguerre made public his method for fixing an image on a metal plate. And, in fact, the beginnings of social science in the United States are associated with some hard-hitting social photography. For example, Jacob A. Riis, a reporter, photographed the appalling slum conditions of New York in the 1890s; and Lewis W. Hine, a trained sociologist, who enlisted in the struggle against child labour in the years 1907 to 1918, produced photographs which are said to have helped bring about the passage of new labour legislation laws.

But from early on in the twentieth century until very recently, the visual has been marginalised in sociology. Fyfe and Law (1988) note the anti-reductionist stance taken by early mainstream sociologists which deleted the body – and thus the eye – from classical social theory; and they also suggest other reasons for sociology's marginalisation of the visual, which were discussed in Chapter 4. However, Stasz (1979) introduces another dimen-sion. Her researches reveal that thirty-one articles in the early volumes (1896–1916) of the *American Journal of Sociology* used photographs as illustration and evidence – and that these were associated with an approach which pressed for 'social amelioration', since photographs 'force a con-frontation with reality' (Stasz 1979: 134). Bringing the viewer face to face with the struggles and atrocious housing conditions of the poor helped put the case for change. However, Stasz notes that when the positivist sociologist, Albion Small, took over the editorship of the journal in 1914, photographs were banished from its pages in favour of 'causal analysis, high-level generalisations and statistical reports' (Stasz 1979: 133). For Small believed that the presence of photographs in a sociological text threatened the theoretical status and purpose of sociology itself. He claimed that al-though photographs might be an invaluable tool in the hands of those who argued for social change, the relationship of such a project to pure sociology was analogous to the relationship between public hygiene and biology.[1] The

1 Small was anxious for the *AJS* to be on a par with natural scientific journals. D. Jacobi and B. Schiele allow us to glimpse something of the attitude taken to photographs in such journals, although in the following excerpt they are concerned only with photographic portraits of natural scientists:

> . . . it is out of the question to publish photographic portraits of scientists in scientific journals because science is enunciated without reference to the enunciator. The author disappears behind an object that seems to speak for itself, or write itself out independently . . . . If science is universal, if it attempts to construct a truth that is unanimously and collectively ack-nowledged, individuals who formulate a small fragment of it are an anonymous element. Their personalities and – more significant – their faces, are not in the least important.
> (Jacobi and Schiele 1989: 750)

belief that photographs should be kept out of sociological discourse pervaded the *AJS* for a long time. Indeed, the extent of this ideological grip is perhaps indicated by the fact that when Shanas reviewed the first fifty years of the *AJS* (Shanas 1945), she made no reference to the presence of photographs in the journal.[2]

Whilst a combination of anti-reductionism and positivism has no doubt contributed to the marginalisation of the visual in sociology, Stasz's analysis further reveals that in the first twenty-one volumes of the *AJS* an average of 12 per cent of the authors were women, but that this was true for fully 50 per cent of the visually oriented group. She suggests that 'perhaps an association between females and photography contaminated the editors' view of the technique, causing it to be devalued or seen as frivolous' (Stasz 1979: 133). It is intriguing to speculate on the idea of an association between writing – our dominant form of formal communication – and the political dominance of men, and linked to this, an association between image-making – a less dominant form – and the political subordination of women. I shall return to the subject in Chapter 6. At any rate, it is clear, overall, that sociologists' attitudes to the use of visual material – more particularly photographs – in their work has varied over the years, and that these attitudes have been shaped by events outside the discipline, and by broader ideological currents and debates.

Although most sociologists in the past may have shunned the use of photographs, other social scientists, particularly anthropologists, have regarded photographs as sound objective evidence, and have built their work around a reliance on the accuracy with which a camera records. More recently, however, post-positivists have emphasised that photographic evidence cannot be objective, and that, far from being a technically effected window on the world, a photograph is socially – indeed politically – constructed like any other cultural representation (see, for example, Tagg 1988). While the idea that photographs provide sound objective evidence suggests that they are *taken*, the post-positivist emphasis indicates that photographs are *made*. However, there is no reason why the social scientist should not take account of the fact that photographs are socially constructed, whilst acknowledging that they can also provide detailed information about a culture of which s/he may previously have known little or nothing.[3] Indeed s/he can take *advantage* of this dual situation. Thus, in the case where the

---

2 It should be noted, however, that positivism and photography are not mutually exclusive. Ervin Zube's 'Pedestrians and Wind' (1979) is a positivist presentation (in the third person passive, accompanied by graphs and tables of figures) of a positivist study undertaken to document some of the effects of high-speed winds on pedestrian activity and to provide information that could ultimately influence urban design policy decisions regarding the location and design of structures in urban areas. Time-lapse photography was used for recording pedestrian behaviour, and examples of these are also included in the presentation.

3 The best description that I know of the photographic process – in terms of its combination of objective physical properties *and* the subjective input of the photographer – is by Euan Duff. He says:

social scientist is the photographer, s/he *takes* a photograph, or photographs, in order to preserve the detail of a particular culture – or micro-culture. Added to which, the photograph helps him/her to distance him/herself from that culture (s/he is here, but it is there in the photograph); the photograph allows her/him to see it as anthropologically strange. Yet at the same time, s/he *selects* the subject matter, *chooses* the type of shot (angle, lighting, exposure, etc.) and *processes* the film; in other words, s/he *constructs* the image in the manner that best suits her/his purpose. In the case where the social scientist is the *recipient* and *analyst* of the photograph, s/he is also presented with new information about a culture, while at the same time s/he has the task of analysing the reasons for the photographer's choice of subject matter, type of shot, and general presentation. In fact, s/he is presented with a situation in which one set of social processes has been imposed on another, and through her/his analysis s/he will impose a third. But it is likely that the photograph with which the analyst is presented will be captioned and accompanied by a written text; and here again, it is important to hold on to the idea that photographs are both taken and made. For while s/he gains information about a social world, and is presented with the challenge of trying to work out the particular decisions carried during the processes of photography and film-processing, s/he must *also* analyse the way in which the author has engineered the particular reciprocal relationship between photograph, caption and text in order to create the argument with which the reader is presented.

In this chapter I look at certain sociological and anthropological works whose authors have incorporated quantities of visual representations (sometimes their own photographs) into their textual presentations. In such cases, the visual material is intended to make a substantial contribution to the overall piece; and in consequence, the sociological or anthropological understanding which is imparted has a decidedly visual aspect to it. A few of these works are *themselves* social analyses of other people's image-and-text

---

Photographs are only straightforward optical representations of the external world, and the accuracy of the process provides the medium with a fundamental paradox that its realism, its root characteristic, is also the source of the widespread and false belief that photographs cannot 'lie', that they only verify what actually exists and that the role of the photographer is therefore quite minimal.

However, the mechanical nature of the medium does limit the range of techniques and visual effects available to photographers, and although the content of a photograph is obviously determined by the choice and treatment of subject matter, the basic design of the range of photographic tones or colors within the image is largely determined by the process, and is a direct consequence of the exact physical/optical relationship between image and object, between the camera and the subject.

. . . Photography, then, is a mechanical process crucially dependent on a single human decision. The process produces single images which are, again, crucially dependent on the context in which they are seen. Photographs might appear to be self-evident but they are more often open, incomplete and ambiguous, and to make sense of them they need to be seen with words or with other images.

(Duff 1981: 75)

pieces. These 'second-degree' texts, by their very inclusion of other people's visual material, also impart knowledge which is part-visual; while they allow us to examine how social scientists have viewed and theorised the use of visual material in other authors' work.

David Livingstone's *Missionary Travels and Researches in South Africa* (1857) was published before photography became widely available, and is copiously illustrated with engravings. The work is therefore interesting for the fact that the author makes no claims about the scientific accuracy and the objectivity of the depictions, as he probably would have done if the book had been illustrated with photographs; though there is a tacit assumption that the engravings do give a reasonably accurate impression of the subject matter they depict. Livingstone says he brought home from Africa 'a few rough diagram-sketches, from one of which the view of the Falls of the Zambesi has been prepared by a more experienced artist' (Livingstone 1857: vi). It is not clear whether this artist – whom Livingstone does not name – produced the forty-six drawings which were engraved for the book. The portraits of African people give the impression that the artist was not very familiar with his subject matter, and was influenced by the current British vogue for Pre-Raphaelitism (see Figure 21a). A few reproductions of line drawings after ancient Egyptian depictions are also featured (see Figure 21b). Of course, one of Livingstone's aims may have been to convey the exotic character of African culture; and the book's illustrations serve this purpose well. On the other hand, he would also have wanted to present readers with evidence that he had actually been in these foreign parts; and this aim would have been far better served by photographic reproductions, as would his desire to convey accurate ethnographic information about the Africans he encountered. Photographs were able to enhance the scientific status of such information, and the camera became a very important tool of trade for later explorers and anthropologists. Despite the obvious staging of early anthropological photographs, as in Figure 21c, this example – though not of an African – does at least show a more accurate, objective rendition of a person of colour from non-European stock than Livingstone's illustrations could supply.

'The Early History of Visual Sociology' by Clarence Stasz (1979) is itself a social analysis of the early use of visual material by social scientists.[4] Her essay (referred to at the start of this chapter) discusses the use of photography in articles published during the first fifty years of the *AJS*. Stasz informs us that Blackmar's (1897) case study of two impoverished families in Kansas, dubbed 'The Smoky Pilgrims', was the first *AJS* article to use

4 'Visual anthropology' and 'visual sociology' are established terms in American empirical social science. They register an approach which differs from verbal analysis, but are somewhat misleading in their implication that only the visual is involved, and that sociological meaning is somehow given off by the images alone. This is not, of course, the case.

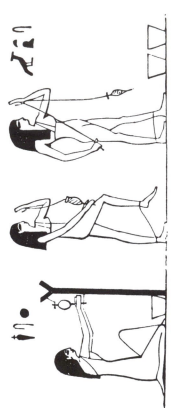

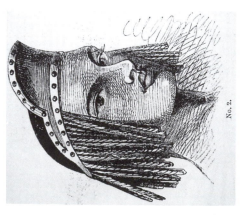

a)

b)

Figure 21a and b Illustrations from *Missionary Travels and Researches in South Africa* (D. Livingstone, 1857)

Figure 21c Aborigine, New South Wales. Photograph: Royal Anthropological Institute

photographs, and that in it Blackmar argued that the ills of the city were not limited to urban environments. To support his claim, he included nine photographs. Stasz describes two of these as portraying family groups before their cabins, and seven as presenting closer views of individual subjects. She remarks that none of the subjects smile; and that, while most look away from the camera, others stare or glare into it (see Figure 22). This 'staring' or 'glaring', as she terms it, surely relates to the fact that at this early date film had to be exposed for several minutes, during which time the subject was obliged to keep completely still in front of the camera, with a fixed expression, in order that an image might be obtained which was not blurred. But in any case, Stasz does not discuss Blackmar's own verbal contextualisation of his photographs. Would I have seen the subjects 'staring' or 'glaring' into the camera had I seen Blackmar's own verbal commentary and not just Stasz's discussion of it?

Stasz also argues that Blackmar manipulated the image in order to exaggerate the sense of isolation and depressed state of the people, and to this end, he obliterated the background in the photograph: 'hence, they are suspended, unsituated in space or time' (Stasz 1979: 121–2). But the background may have been obliterated because something moved during the long exposure, thus blurring the picture. More than one interpretation of Figure 22 can be made, even without access to Blackmar's written text. However, Stasz's analysis of his photographs is important *because* it indicates that photographs cannot be taken as objective evidence, and therefore they do not merely substantiate a textual argument. Rather, they are constructed and presented in conjunction with textual material in such a way that this *seems* to be the case. At the same time, an examination of Stasz's *own* account, into which some of Blackmar's photographs are incorporated, also shows the crafting of an interactive relationship between image and text.

She goes on to analyse subsequent essays-with-photographs by early American documentary sociologists, and reproduces a total of eleven photographs from these essays. She uses five of the photographs to show that their authors, like Blackmar, staged and selected their subjects, and deployed various devices such as the 'before-and-after' presentation to increase the plausibility of their claims. She argues that some of the authors used photographs 'in a . . . banal and frivolous manner' (Stasz 1979: 124) and that some photographs are 'not technically competent' (Stasz 1979: 124). She suggests that two-thirds of the articles employed photographs in a way that contemporary visual sociologists would question. Manipulated prints, iconographic poses, inconsistent before-and-after pictures, portraits out of context, and images based on clumsy technique 'fall well below today's research reporting standards' (Stasz 1979: 128). Finally she remarks that 'they would be good illustrations for that as yet unwritten book every social science student would be required to read before graduating, *How to Lie with Photographs*

Figure 22 Photograph from F. W. Blackmar, 'The Smoky Pilgrims',
American Journal of Sociology, 1897. Reproduced in 'The
Early History of Visual Sociology' by C. Stasz (in J. Wagner,
ed., *Images of Information* 1979)

(Stasz 1979: 128). She suggests that what constitutes a *good* photograph is a matter of 'contemporary preferences' – although she cites the quality of 'ethnographicness', following Heider (1976), as being crucially important. She finds this quality in Charles Bushnell's series of articles on the social aspects of the Chicago stockyards (1901a, 1901b, 1902):

> The photographs provide a sense of the work environment in a glance that written descriptions and tables fail to convey. Indeed, I think Bushnell knew this, because by including such pictures he did not have to discuss certain features of the situations.
>
> (Stasz 1979: 127)

In addition, 'he shows unposed youngsters as active and vital' (Stasz 1979: 127). In summary, Stasz argues that when photographs work well with the text and yet give information which words and tables cannot convey so adequately, when they are produced with minimum distortions of behaviour as a result of camera presence, and when they show basic technical competence and frame activities within a definable context, then 'these images retain their scientific value today' (Stasz 1979: 131).

Photographs made according to these criteria would certainly give us valuable information about strange cultures. Yet to leave it at that is sociologically naive. Stasz's conception of a 'bad' photograph gives us information as well, but it is of a different kind. We learn quite a lot from Figure 21c and from Figure 22. We learn that early sociologists and anthropologists 'cooked the books'; and this is important social scientific information. But even Bushnell's photographs – of which she approves – are constructed arguments, which use devices in order to convince. There is no photograph, nor category of photograph, that can escape this treatment when used by a social scientist or any other kind of author. Stasz appears to recognise neither this nor – by the same token – the problematic status of her own analysis. Any account whether it involves photographs or not, is *constructed* – using concealed devices in order to persuade readers that it is privileged over previous accounts; and of course my *own* account is no exception. But at the same time (and I agree with Stasz here), *some* photographs – in conjunction with captions and written text – *do* give a less fictitious, a more empirically informative account than others. And the information we obtain from such images and accounts increases our existing knowledge and understanding of the world in a relatively straightforward manner. It thereby helps to provide a more solid basis from which we may wish to critique the status quo and argue for social and political change.

However, Stasz and her fellow contributors to *Images of Information* are not so much concerned with political critique as with the question of *how* photographs can make a sound empirical contribution to social science. While they are convinced that photography has a crucial role to play, they seem to agree that the relationship between photographs, information and empirical social science is particularly hard to state, and is fraught with pitfalls. This may reflect the fact that the kind of empirical social science they have in mind is not in itself entirely unproblematic. But these authors' problems are compounded by the fact that at present our dominant mode of communication in the social sciences is verbal. Our conventions about what counts as social science relate overwhelmingly to verbal discourse. In social science, therefore, a photograph depends on caption and textual contextualisation to give it authentic and precise social scientific meaning. In this way, it loses its autonomy as a photograph, and thus any claim to make a contribution 'in its own right'. In social science, as in most other discipline areas, images need words, while words do not necessarily need images. Yet this situation puzzles and irks those social scientists who feel that depictions are somehow capable of making a more significant contribution to social science. I think they are right, and that on occasions, depictions do acquire more autonomy. In fact, when they are shown together in large numbers, without being intrusively punctuated by verbal discourse, this enables *sequences* of images, and *juxtapositions* of images to acquire a visual autonomy which the reader cannot ignore and must take on board, with the result that the social scientific understanding which is imparted by the overall account *does* include a significant visual component; and thus the status of the depictions is heightened in relation to the overall account.

This happens in *Balinese Character: A Photographic Analysis*, by Gregory Bateson and Margaret Mead (1942). The work is a remarkable collaboration between the two authors, whose aim is to capture and convey the ethos of Balinese culture. An 'Ethnographic Note on Bali', which is jointly authored, is followed by an essay on 'Balinese Character', written by Mead. This essay divides the culture into eight basic categories constructed around the themes of child-rearing practices and parent–child and sibling relationships, since these themes were taken to be indicative of the Balinese ethos. Mead's essay is followed by the core section of the work, which is by Bateson. It is divided into the same eight categories, and consists of 100 pages of plates – each of which contains between six and eleven individual photographic depictions grouped in sequences across and down the page – and 100 pages of captions to the photographs. These captions, which are often quite extended, include quotations from Mead's notes which were made at the same time as the photographs. A page of photographs faces a corresponding page of captions (see Figure 23). Each part of the account informs the other parts, but none dominates; every section retains a considerable degree of autonomy. This autonomy in the case of the photographic section is a very subtle thing. While Bateson and Mead stress that the photographs would be virtually meaningless without a verbal explanation, there are nevertheless enough of them grouped together in specific sequences – and separated from the captions on the opposite page – to constitute a visual micro-world which draws the reader/viewer into the Balinese ethos (see Figure 23). In Stasz's

Figure 23 *Trance and Beroek I:* Plate 18 from *Balinese Character* (Bateson and Mead 1942).
Photograph: Gregory Bateson

Plate 18

TRANCE AND *BEROEK* I

The word *beroek* is used by the Balinese to describe a corpse which is falling to pieces with decay. It is here used to epitomize the fantasy of the body as made of separate independent parts. This fantasy takes many forms, among others the notion that the body is like a puppet, just pinned together at the joints, and, as already noted (Pl. 17, figs. 8 and 9), the same fantasy is closely linked with phenomena of ecstasy and trance.

This and the following plate show various stages in the trance performance of the *sangiang* dancers (cf. Pl. 10, fig. 3; Pl. 38, figs. 1, 3 and 4). These are a pair of little girls who go into trance possessed by gods, and who dance in the trance state. They are sacred, and though the performance is given chiefly for entertainment, the *sangiang* dancers may also give special holy water, which is used for medicinal purposes. They must not dance after menarche.

1. The puppets on a string. The performance begins with a dance by the gods, who are represented by two dolls. They are threaded on a string which is tied at the ends to the tops of two sticks (*patokan*) to which bells are attached. Each stick is held by a man whose arm is slightly flexed at the elbow. After a few minutes, trembling or changes in tension of the string set up clonic contractions in the arms of the two men, and the dolls begin to "dance." They are said to be "possessed" (*kerawoehan*) by the gods. While waiting for the clonus, the man who holds the stick pays very little attention and often looks away, as in this picture. The native introspective account is that the man does not make the dolls dance — "they dance of themselves and the men cannot stop them."

Rhythmic clonic contraction is an example of a part of the body taking on its own independent integration. (Among the Iatmul of New Guinea, trance is preceded by ankle clonus.)

I Lasia holding the *patokan*.
Bajoeng Gede. May 26, 1937. 9 M 38.

2. The stick (*patokan*) and back view of the puppet. The puppet is weighted with bells at the lower end, so that it will stay in a more or less upright position while dancing.
Bajoeng Gede. Aug. 18, 1937. 13 U 19.

3. When the puppets are dancing and the sticks moving with sufficient violence, the two little girls, I Renoe and I Misi, come and sit beside the men with the sticks. They hold the lower end of the sticks tightly with both hands and are thus shaken by the movements of the sticks. Each child sits in the lap of an older girl who is ready to catch her when she falls into trance.

I Lasia holding left-hand stick; I Renoe holding the base of this stick and sitting in lap of I Wadi; Nang Ngetis holding the right-hand stick; I Misi holding its base and sitting in the lap of I Rinjin; Nang Karma, the priest of the club, in the right foreground.
Bajoeng Gede. May 26, 1937. 9 N 28.

4 and 5. I Misi falls into trance. The people sing while the little girls hold the sticks, and the girls begin to sway sideways. This swaying becomes more and more violent but later diminishes, and the girls begin to beat with the sticks on the supporting stands. They impose the rhythm of the song on the sticks which are moving with the clonic rhythms of the two men. Finally I Misi gives a stronger beat with the stick to coincide with a final beat of the song, and collapses limp in the lap of the woman who holds her (cf. Pl. 68 for discussion of falling backward and sleep as forms of regression toward the father).

I Misi in trance, in lap of I Rinjin; Nang Karma, in foreground; I Gati (daughter of Nang Karma) holding the baby, I Kenjoen.
Bajoeng Gede. May 26, 1937. 9 N 30, 32.

6. I Renoe not yet in trance. She is still holding the base of the stick and beating in time to the song.

The man who holds the stick has closed his eyes and appears to be on the verge of trance. He is not known to have gone into trance on this occasion, but there was one boy (I Malih, Pl. 21, fig. 1) in Bajoeng Gede, who several times went into trance while holding the stick. Such trance was discouraged, and he was finally told that he could not hold the stick any more unless he gave up going into trance. He was able to give it up.

Same people as in fig. 3 above.
Bajoeng Gede. May 26, 1937. 9 N 33.

opinion, 'their historic monograph, *Balinese Character*, has never been matched for its subtle blend of photographs within a tightly organized conceptual framework' (Stasz 1979: 119).

The precise nature of the partnership between the authors was surely crucial to the work's success. Bateson and Mead were used to working together (they were married). Close cooperation between two people (two pairs of eyes and four hands), both of whom were highly experienced field anthropologists with complementary skills, was essential in order to produce so many meticulously documented and precisely directed photographs.[5] However, the visual anthropologist John Collier (1979) notes that though teams of observers have worked over those images, and were primarily enthusiastic, Mead never developed a 'formal language' with which to research their imagery. I would argue that she probably never had any intention of forcing the images into a verbal social scientific straitjacket. Had she done so, that elusive quality of Balinese ethos might have been hopelessly distorted by the imposition on it of a Western rational abstract grid. For as the authors remark, 'The words which one culture has invested with meaning are by the very accuracy of their cultural fit, singularly inappropriate as vehicles for precise comment upon another culture' (Bateson and Mead 1942: xi). Therefore,

> In this monograph we are attempting a new method of stating the *intangible* relationships among different types of culturally standardised behavior by placing side by side mutually relevant photographs. Pieces of behavior, spatially and contextually separated – a trance dancer being carried in procession, a man looking up at an aeroplane, a servant greeting his master in play, the painting of a dream – may all be relevant to a single discussion; the same emotional thread may run through them. To present them in words, it is necessary either to resort to devices which are inevitably literary, or to dissect the living scenes so that only desiccated items remain. By the use of photographs, the *wholeness* of each piece of behavior can be preserved, while the special cross-referencing desired can be obtained by placing the series of photographs on the same page [my emphases].
>
> (Bateson and Mead 1942: xii)

As the authors so eloquently and persuasively argue, images which are grouped together in a precise manner can convey much that words cannot. In addition, because images do not constitute our dominant mode of communication, they are normally not so finely honed as words, and tend not to give off such culturally specific messages. And images which are insulated from words by being surrounded by other images are freer from the constraints imposed by Western ways of thought. Indeed, Bateson and Mead remark that aspects of culture never successfully recorded by the scientist are often caught by the artist. Lyotard (1984) would agree (see Chapter 3).

---

5 Bateson was an experienced photographer, and Mead had developed a technique of writing in a notebook while hardly looking at what she was doing, so that she could at the same time focus on what was going on in the field in order to select and direct Bateson's next shot.

Perhaps the main contribution that Livingstone's engraved drawings make is of this order.

Let us sample just one of the categories which Bateson and Mead use to organise their data: 'Integration and Disintegration of the Body'. This seems at first to be oddly titled, but the reader/viewer is gradually transported into a very strange world of death, decay, isolated body parts, hands 'in trance', puppets, puppet string sticks, and boys who are told they cannot hold the stick unless they give up going into trances (see Figure 23). It is difficult to even think about this world at first, yet its values become more familiar as we pore over the sequences and juxtapositions of images, backed up by verbal explanations. I sense that words alone could not have steeped me in the minutiae of routine Balinese behaviour, like the finger-bending, and the constant searching of the skin for irregularities, which form part of the Balinese ethos. And to write about it here, if indeed that were at all possible, would be to kill it off. Yet a type of social understanding has been imparted visually, and this can be *used*. Readers/viewers can relate this visual understanding to their knowledge of other cultures including our own, with the result that their knowledge of those cultures is made more subtle. As the authors comment: '[the photographs] represent a brief interlude in which verbal conventions and knowledge are suppressed in favour of visually conveyed strangeness' (Bateson and Mead 1942: xii).

In his notes on the photographs and captions, Bateson explains that he tried to shoot what happened normally and spontaneously, rather than get the Balinese to enact certain normative behaviour sequences in suitable lighting conditions. So from the start, he let the pictures 'speak'; he did not aim primarily to illustrate theory.[6] The 25,000 pictures generated the categories, and then those photographs were whittled down to 6,000 and finally to the 759 which were used to make the plates. He also shot 22,000 feet of moving film, none of which is included in the book. (It is worth noting that while still photographs can be displayed in book form, the moving image cannot – unless it is represented by stills.) In a specific example of the way that photographic information can contribute to anthropology, Bateson observes from one sequence of photographs (not illustrated here) that the left-hand fingers of the Balinese appear to be far more separated than the right-hand fingers, and that the sensory function of the finger-tips seems to be more accentuated in the left hand. As with many other cultures, the Balinese make a very profound distinction between left and right: 'the left hand is used for unclean things – the genitals, faeces, etc. – while the right hand should be used for eating and for giving or receiving gifts' (Bateson and Mead 1942: 100). Bateson wonders if the apparent emphasis on the sensory or perhaps exploratory function of the left hand may be connected with this

---

6 Somewhat similarly, Victor Burgin told fine art photography students to 'shoot first and theorise later: let desire come first', in a lecture at the Slade School of Fine Art, London University, in November 1992.

differentiation. But since he was not able to make this observation until the photographs had been printed, and were assembled together back in America, the matter could be taken no further. However, this demonstrates that when viewed *en masse*, photographs enable the social scientist to pick out recurrent features, micro-patterns of behaviour; a point which is developed by Erving Goffman (1979) in *Gender Advertisements* (see below).

The groups of images in *Balinese Character* acquire more social scientific autonomy and force than a single photograph does when it is surrounded, penetrated and moderated by verbal text. However, it is possible for depictions to acquire even more autonomy. This happens in *A Fortunate Man* (Berger and Mohr 1967), which also consists of photographic images and written text. Here, images are grouped together in sequences throughout the book. Yet because no passage in the text points *specifically* to any image or group of images, visual and verbal accounts run separately side by side, each telling its own story. It is up to the reader to integrate the two elements, and decide how the whole should be interpreted.

Photographs and film acquire even greater autonomy when the camera is handed over to 'the natives'. John and Malcolm Collier in *Visual Anthropology* (1986) recount an experiment by Adair and Worth (1966) in which seven Navajo men and women were invited to make their own films. This allowed the participants to produce a Navajo perception of their world, rather than a Western one. The film displayed cognition patterns, narrative style, and an ordering of time and pace markedly different from ours (Worth and Adair 1972). Yet it is significant that experiments like this one are rarely repeated. When showing 'his' film, Adair commented that it is traditional not to let the subject play any other role than to be observed. And John and Malcolm Collier suggest that 'only in theory are "we" willing to let the "natives" have authoritative judgment!' (Collier and Collier 1986: 157). In *Gender Advertisements*, Goffman observes that photographs taken by 'the natives' would avoid the tendency, inevitable among ethnographers, to record only the differences from one's own world and the unexpected similarities. Although Bateson and Mead's overall representation of the Balinese ethos is, of course, a Western one, the photographic section of *Balinese Character* does manage to escape much of the distortion which a verbal social scientific account would have produced. The massed images, in sequence and in juxtaposition, create a micro-world whose visual coherence is such that we acquire an understanding of that society and its ethos which is not straightforwardly a function of verbal conventions, and verbal social science.

Gender Advertisements by Erving Goffman (1979) also contains a great many visual depictions. These are all reproductions of advertisements, and the author uses them as visual data. He is concerned with the ways in which gender relations are depicted in advertisement photographs; and in this sense, he focuses on 'what a particular photograph is *of*' (Goffman 1979: 12).[7]

The commercial aspect of the advertisements is not a primary concern. There is no question, for example, of showing how advertisements are ideologically constructed by capitalists in order to persuade the consumer to buy, as there is for critical theorists like Williamson in *Decoding Advertisements* (1978).[8] By the same token, his analysis contains no theoretical critique of the inequality which characterises gender relations. Rather, Goffman's is an empirical micro-sociological approach in which he literally regards displays of gender inequality as a structural feature of individual experience. He sets out to argue that there are strong similarities between what can be seen depicted in visual advertisements and what can be observed in 'actual life', and that displays in depictions iconically reflect fundamental features of the social structure.

Two verbal essays, one called 'Gender Display' and the other 'Picture Frames', prepare the theoretical ground for the third predominantly visual section, 'Gender Commercials'. In the first essay, Goffman argues that gender displays grow out of the parent–child complex, and are possibly more pervasive than other forms of social inequality: any scene, even the most intimate, can, it seems, be defined as an occasion for the depiction of gender difference, and in any scene a resource can always be found for effecting a display of such inequality. In the second essay, 'Picture Frames', he makes a useful broad distinction between photographs intended for public as opposed to private viewing, and also between those which are 'arranged' rather than 'caught'. He observes that commercial advertisements feature public photographs which are usually arranged; and those reproduced in *Gender Advertisements* are of this type. Drawing on his previous work in which the theatre and drama provided productive analogies for social interaction, he suggests that advertisements can aptly be compared with what the stage presents. They represent scenes: we take it something is happening in time, a stream of events. He further argues that advertisements work by drawing upon and exploiting a particular combination of social conventions:

> The magical ability of the advertiser to use a few models and props to evoke a life-like scene of his own choosing is not primarily due to the art and technology of commercial photography; it is due primarily to those institutionalised arrangements in social life which allow strangers to glimpse the lives of persons they pass, and to the readiness of all of us to switch at any moment from dealing with the real world to participating in make-believe ones.
>
> (Goffman 1979: 23)

---

7 This being so, he disregards the writing which appears on some of the advertisements. And, indeed, since the reproductions in his text are in black and white, the original colours used in the advertisements are not discussed.

8 Like the vast majority of studies in the empirical paradigm, Goffman's text does not feature the words 'capitalism' and 'ideology'; although he does eventually claim that: 'Even those concerned to oppose commercial versions of the world must pictorialize their arguments through images which are selected according to much the same principles as those employed by the enemy' (Goffman 1979: 27).

Goffman argues that the ritual displays that individuals manage to inject into social situations are what advertisers try to inject into the scenes they compose around the product and then photograph. He therefore proposes to examine 'stereotypes' in advertisements for what they might tell us about the gender patterns which are prevalent in our society at large. He suggests that among the various social contexts depicted, it is possible to pick out recurring ritual idioms such as 'the feminine touch' (cf. Bateson's photographic analysis of the Balinese, which suggested the particular functions of the left hand) or 'the family'; behind a multitude of surface differences, there are a small number of structural forms which organise such idioms.

The third section, 'Gender Commercials', resembles Bateson's 'Plates and Captions' in the sense that it consists of quantities of photographs, and a smaller proportion of verbal text. There are over 500 advertisements pictured in this section. However, Bateson's presentation of ethnographic photographs with their captions and text show the 'strange' child-rearing practices and parent–child and sibling relationships of the Balinese, while Goffman's advertisements are from the Western world and are ordered so as to show the various ways in which taken-for-granted displays of gender inequality are enacted in our own society. And there are further differences. Bateson made his own photographs while Goffman's are second-order data, and Bateson's verbal captions are rather less theory-laden than Goffman's. Yet the group displays of advertisements also acquire a degree of autonomy as social science knowledge. This is again because the sheer quantity, massing and arrangement of depictions in sequences, juxtapositions and groupings breaks relatively free from the verbal text, temporarily converting the reader into a viewer, drawing him or her into a predominantly visual situation. Here, perceptions are visually made, the construction of categories is visually informed and, consequently, understanding has a strong visual element to it. But Goffman suggests that the contribution which his massed depictions make can be more precisely stated. He notes that when different pictorial examples of a theme, such as 'function ranking' are massed together, bringing different contextual backgrounds into the same array, the plate does the job of highlighting 'untold disparities'. Now, Figure 24 is a *schematic* representation of two of the five pages in *Gender Advertisements* which are devoted to function ranking. The drawings and bracketed captions represent, and are a substitute for, the advertisement photographs which feature in Goffman's book but which cannot be reproduced here. While Figure 24 indicates the overall layout of the two pages, and the captioned drawings show the assymetrical relationship between male and female collaborators which appears to be widely represented in advertisement photographs, the drawings – as schematic depictions of the photographs they represent – can only hint at the wealth of background detail displayed in the photographs themselves, and therefore at the job done by the plates in highlighting contextual differences. It has been necessary to make this point, since I wish to focus on Goffman's suggestion that

> It is the depth and breadth of these contextual differences which somehow provide a sense of structure, a sense of a single organization underlying mere surface differences, which sense is not generated simply by reference to the numerical size of the set relative to the size of the sample.
>
> (Goffman 1979: 25)

This enables us to be more clear about one of the contributions to social science made by Bateson's 'Plates and Captions'. For although the casting together of contextual differences is not primarily what Bateson's presentation is about, the photographs of Balinese society also give off a sense of structure, a sense of a single organisation. And again, this is gained from the sheer depth and breadth of contextual detail and differences within which recurring idioms, or behaviour patterns, occur; idioms such as the separatedness of the left-hand fingers, observed by Bateson in many of the photographs. Goffman further points out that the eye is very competent at social interpretation, and that viewers sustain an impressive consensus. The implication of these remarks is that not only is the individual viewer *adept* at gaining an appreciation of the social structure of the societies given off by the sheer detail within which recurring behaviour patterns are displayed in arrays of photographs, but that viewers of the photographs will collectively *share* this appreciation. And the fact that it is shared makes it a candidate for consideration as social science. For an essential characteristic of social science is that it consists of shared knowledge, shared understanding.

In his conclusion, Goffman reiterates that neither the various expressions of gender difference in 'real life' nor their expression in advertisements are natural. Both are 'artful poses'. He argues that, on the whole, advertisers do not create the ritualised expressions they exploit; they seem to draw upon the same resources as all participants in social situations, who want their 'glimpsed action' to be read. But he argues that advertisements depict hyper-ritualised poses, where gender differences are standardised, exaggerated and simplified to an greater degree than in real life. This is an answer to the question of how gender differences expressed in advertisements and in 'actual life' are related. Another way of putting it is that in advertisements all the bits of life which are not ideal have been edited out: 'So both in adverts and life we are interested in colorful poses, in externalization; but in life we are, in addition, stuck with a considerable amount of dull footage' (Goffman 1979: 84).

In sum, Goffman shows that verbally glossed photographs can direct the reader's eye to data which our literary skills may not be sufficient to enable us fully to describe. An array of photographs may, moreover, offer evidence of the structure of a society and, following analysis of the photographs, lead to a social scientific understanding that would not otherwise have been possible. In addition, the sheer detail which is brought to the viewer's attention by the arrays in *Balinese Character* and *Gender Advertisements*

FUNCTION   RANKING

When a man and a woman co-
operate closely in an undertaking, it seems that in our
society, at least, there is a
hierarchy of functions such
that the man is likely to perform
the executive role, so long as
one can be devised.   This
hierarchy appears to feature
widely in advertisements (see
1 - 20 which depict the
arrangement within an occupational
frame), since it assists the
viewer to make an immediate
interpretation.

3 [Cowboy, foreground, turns and
addresses cowgirl who follows behind]

7 [Doctor (m) shows records to
nurses (f) in ward.   Another
nurse 'gets on' (f) in background]

4 [Doctor (m) examines document; nurses (f) on either
side look on admiringly.   Document rack to left]

8 [Doctor (m) addresses three
attentive nurses (f)]

1 [Doctor (m) shines torch on
patient in bed with rails round
it;   nurse (f) looks on]

5 [Doctor (m) with stethoscope examines
child in bed; nurse (f) assists]

2 [Tennis coach (m)
shows player (f) how
to hold racket]

6 [Doctor (m) examines patient's leg; nurse (f) looks
on.   Locker with patient's possessions in background]

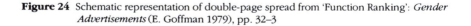

Figure 24   Schematic representation of double-page spread from 'Function Ranking': *Gender
Advertisements* (E. Goffman 1979), pp. 32–3

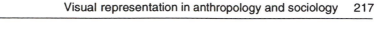

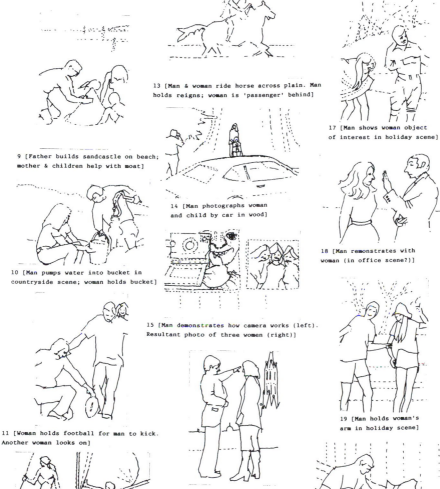

9 [Father builds sandcastle on beach; mother & children help with moat]

10 [Man pumps water into bucket in countryside scene; woman holds bucket]

11 [Woman holds football for man to kick. Another woman looks on]

12 [Man adjusts yacht sail; woman in bikini stands decoratively by him on deck]

13 [Man & woman ride horse across plain. Man holds reigns; woman is 'passenger' behind]

14 [Man photographs woman and child by car in wood]

15 [Man demonstrates how camera works (left). Resultant photo of three women (right)]

16 [Man points out building of interest to woman]

17 [Man shows woman object of interest in holiday scene]

18 [Man remonstrates with woman (in office scene?)]

19 [Man holds woman's arm in holiday scene]

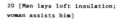

20 [Man lays loft insulation; woman assists him]

forces home the truth of the statement that this world is 'complex', and indicates that the tendencies to subject data to a numerical categorisation, to generalise and to construct grand narratives have produced a type of social science which leaves a great deal to be desired.

Exploring Society Photographically, edited by Howard S. Becker (1981), was originally produced to accompany an art exhibition of the same title which was held in 1981 at the Mary and Leigh Block Gallery, Northwestern University, USA. In his introductory essay, Becker notes that the division which is customarily maintained between art and science, and the contradictions embedded in the science–art relationship, are social conventions. This means that that division and those contradictions are not necessarily and finally fixed. In *Balinese Character*, the authors do not discuss the aesthetic quality of Bateson's photographs, and this is perhaps because they do not wish to detract from the scientific character of their work. But Becker suggests we would do better to think of the aesthetic quality of the image as *complementing* rather than detracting from its documentary contribution; and he re-presents Plate 83 from *Balinese Character*, inviting us to re-experience it in the light of this suggestion. The authors whose work is presented in *Exploring Society Photographically* are, like Bateson, photographers who are professionally involved in researching social life. They believe that the aesthetic quality of their images complements the contribution which those images make as social documents, and indeed may well enhance it. Their work thus enables us to broaden our exploration of what photographic images – with accompanying textual material – can tell us about the social world that words alone cannot; and this is a concern which those authors also share. Their work allows us to explore the contribution to social science understanding which may be made by the aesthetic quality of documentary photographic images.

Exploring Society Photographically is made up of twelve different image-and-text pieces, each of which constructs the relationship between visual and verbal material in a different way. For example, Euan Duff's text, which is largely about the act of photography – about what is involved in taking and making photographs – contains the claim that his photographs would be diminished by any kind of verbal explanation and speak for themselves – a claim frequently made by artists to emphasise the autonomous status of their work; while at the other extreme Douglas Harper explains that his uncaptioned photographs and continuous text are intended as 'an indivisible whole'. Some of the authors, like Duff and Harper, *discuss* the relationship between the different components of their accounts (i.e. photographs, captions, text) whereas others just *present* an image-and-text account of social life. Several comment upon and even celebrate the aesthetic quality of their images. These are indeed very striking, and seem to demand judgement. The reader/viewer finds her/himself choosing favourites. Yet does the aesthetic quality of the photographs in *Exploring Society Photographically* contribute to social science understanding? All of them tell us a good deal we did not already know about a particular society, but is this information merely complemented by the aesthetic quality of the images, or can it be enhanced by this quality? Trying to answer these questions is extremely hard without having *Exploring Society Photographically* reproduced alongside my text; and it is also difficult to convey precisely in words. However, given these severe limitations, I will attempt to do so.

Euan Duff notes that he selects a particular moment in time and a particular viewpoint in space from which to photograph his subjects, and that this inevitably produces an interpretation of human experience rather than an illustration of it. The resultant images are, in my view, ideologically arresting. One of them shows a bleak modern British factory interior with women at their 'work stations', and another shows a depressed-looking woman shopper resignedly surveying the frozen food section of a supermarket. The viewer is faced, in both cases, with some of the constraints which our paternalistic, capitalist society imposes on its members. This *confrontation* (for that is what it is) is achieved through the immediacy with which the subject matter is conveyed by the images, and by the overall quality of bleakness which pervades the visual detail; and all this without the aid of an accompanying verbal text.

Frank Cancian's line-up of Zinacanteco judges in Mexico is also an arresting image, and this is partly because the visual disposition of the figures in their extraordinary legal robes is so striking. But Cancian also writes a verbal account of the legal niceties of Zinacantecos culture, and the photograph makes this account vivid and memorable; while the text in turn elucidates the scene depicted in the photograph, thereby increasing its documentary reach.

Bill Aron uses one of photography's great assets, which is its ability to assist cultural comparisons by offering a primary exposure to cultural contrasts. He compares two very different worlds, one old and one young, which exist separately in the same vicinity of Venice, California. A short verbal account is followed by a sequence of multiple images, each of which consists of a pair of overlapped photographs, one from each of the two cultures. In one pair, the image of a young woman's hand on her knee is superimposed on the image of an old woman's hand on her knee; in another, the body of a young person roller-skating overlaps the body of an old lady walking with a stick – perhaps down the same boulevard. Aron's visual work achieves its aesthetic quality largely as a result of the size and disposition of each image in relation to its pair, by the manner in which the images are juxtaposed in each overlap, and by the sequence in which the pairs are placed. And the aesthetic effect of this sequence of overlapping pairs of images strengthens the overall account. It does this by rendering poignant and therefore memorable the contrasted detail of the two very different social worlds which are described in the verbal text.

Figure 25 Douglas Harper. Photograph from 'Selections from the Road' (in H. Becker, ed.,
Exploring Society Photographically, 1981). Photograph: Douglas Harper

Many of the photographs in this project seem to *gain* in aesthetic quality
once we have been informed by the text what they portray. Harper's photograph in Figure 25 is in itself a visually striking yet ambiguous image. The
men seem to be gazing at something – possibly this has to do with a religious
experience. Harper suggests that the general significance of the photograph
is heightened when we cannot be sure that our interpretation of it is correct.
However, when we read the verbal account, we find that these men are tramps
hitching a lift in a boxcar (British – waggon), that the boxcar is moving, that it
does so for long periods of time, and that the tramps are sitting, looking out at
the countryside as it passes before their eyes. This information then begins to
generate a dialectical relationship between our original interpretation of
the photograph and our new understanding of its documentary content.
Consequently, our original aesthetic appreciation of the photograph becomes
incorporated into our new understanding of what is going on, and is, if
anything, increased. This gives the new interpretation of the photograph
breadth and imaginative substance, and thereby makes it more memorable.

The Harvard University Film Center present photographs of the Dani,
who live in the mountains of New Guinea. These images are remarkable for
their combination of documentary richness and stunning visual quality
which produces delicate contrasts between light and shade. Yet the aesthetic
effect of these photographs also seems to become more remarkable once the

captions and accompanying text have been read, because we are then able to give so much more meaning to the detail of the beautiful shapes with which we are presented, to appreciate them for what they document as well as for their visual appearance. And, again, the verbal text gains from the aesthetic effect of the photographs because the verbal description of the culture becomes infused with vivid detail, and consequently becomes richer and more memorable.

While Mark Rosenberg's contribution to the project does not seem to involve the aesthetic dimension of images directly, it indicates another way in which photographs with text can expand social science analysis. Rosenberg's photographs of a young patient and his partner are technically fairly unexceptional, and their subject matter is not exotic nor in other ways particularly striking, yet when 'read' in conjunction with the text, they become riveting. This is partly because the text makes sense of the narrative sequence in which the photographs are placed, but it is principally because the text introduces us to real named individuals, Joel Bruinooge and Meg Crissara, and we become involved in the detail of their private lives as they confront a crisis and eventually resolve it. Mark Rosenberg's piece brings the personal to prominence, rather as a biography or a novel does. We are all interested in knowledge about the personal, as well as in more non-specific information; and yet social science writing tends to produce the latter by generalising out the former. Rosenberg presents a case history in which real people are portrayed with an immediacy which only photographs can provide. Yet, as Goffman has observed, the detail in the photographs provides a sense of the social structure of these people's lives; while the photographs, taken in *conjunction* with the written text, allow us to relate that structure to the actions of the real-life subjects described in the narrative.

All the participants in *Exploring Society Photographically* make photographs because they think that social science writing on its own is incapable of expressing important things that they want to say. Eduardo B. Viveiros de Castro, a Brazilian anthropologist, for example, feels that it 'leaves out the aesthetic, the personal and the pleasurable, and that these are dimensions that photographs can fill' (Becker 1981: 54). However, I would argue that the aesthetic quality of an image can enhance social science understanding, and I hope to have given some sense of the ways in which this occurs. But the matter is complex because the image has both aesthetic effect and documentary reach, and these aspects interrelate while they also interact with the information and ideas presented in the written text. The aesthetic and documentary aspects of the image enhance the meaning of the text, and the text itself can also enhance both the documentary and aesthetic facets of the image. Becker is surely right to insist that the customary way of seeing the 'contradictory' relationship between art and science is better seen as complementary; and the contributions to *Exploring Society Photographically* indicate that when experienced social scientists who are also skilled photographers aim to produce images which have *both* documentary reach and aesthetic quality, these can – in combination with verbal text – generate a type of social science understanding which is very rich.

The principal organisational base of visual sociology has been the International Visual Sociology Association. Established in 1981, it initially produced the *International Journal of Visual Sociology* (five issues) edited by Leonard M. Henny, who also compiled a special edition of *Current Sociology* (1986) entitled 'Trend Report: Theory and Practice of Visual Sociology'. Some of the articles in these publications help to extend the range of ways in which photographs can assist social scientists in their work. Two of these are Harper's 'Meaning and Work: A Study in Photo Elicitation' (Harper 1986) and Stummer's 'Photo-essay' (Stummer 1985). Harper draws on Bateson and Mead's (1949) use of photographs to provide a 'visual inventory' and on John Collier's (1967) description of how photographs can be integrated into the interview process. Over an extended period of time, Harper photographed the owner of a small mechanical and welding shop, Willie, as he worked on his premises. He then conducted a series of interviews with Willie, in which the photographs were used to elicit information about what was 'going on' in them. With the aid of the photographs, Willie explained to Harper the subtleties of a particular type of mechanical skill, and made connections between specific machines in the shop. The photographs also enabled him to explain how he acquired the machines, to describe how they had changed in design since he was young, and to say how this change had resulted in different ways of working. Harper comments that while the images opened up specific yet complex areas for discussion, they allowed the interviews to be sustained almost effortlessly over a period of time, and in depth. As a result of using 'photo-elicitation', he was able to 'narrow the gap between our mental worlds' (Harper 1986: 29).

By contrast, Stummer deploys photographs to effect political change in her study of the residents of a ghetto in Newark, New Jersey. She compiled a dossier of photographs of their harrowing lives, to which she attached brief autobiographical accounts which some of the inhabitants had supplied; then she delivered this combined document to the city authorities. She hoped that the immediacy with which it presented the appalling housing conditions of the poor might make it impossible for those authorities to disregard the situation any longer. She hoped that the images would serve to lessen the gap between those with power and those with none, and help force the City Council to take action to alleviate poverty and bad housing conditions. She gained full cooperation from the residents once they understood that she wanted to help them; and the sense of political urgency which permeates the photo-essay is increased by the fact that the residents appear to present their own case with the minimum of intervention on the part of the sociologist, whereas she has in fact skilfully constructed it. Stummer, like Euan Duff, uses the immediacy with which photographs depict their subject matter to political effect. But her work, in common with Harper's, also uses photographs to bridge very different worlds – in this case the world of the powerless and the world of the powerful. Both Harper and Stummer, like Rosenberg, show how photographs can be used to present the personal in the context of a wider social and political framework.

However, some of the articles in these journals devoted to visual sociology have a tendency to introspect. They bemoan sociologists' lack of interest in the visual dimension compared with the situation at the turn of the century, while they also rehearse the problems of combining sociology and photography. The strength of Becker's work, that of his fellow participants and the essays discussed above, lies in the innovative quality of their empirical researches, which extend the range of ways in which photographs can assist social scientists in their work, and thereby push back the limitations of 'visual sociology' which others have regarded as so problematic.

In 1986, the IVSA began a newsletter which evolved into the journal *Visual Sociology*. By 1994, this was in its ninth volume (published semi-annually and edited by Harper from the University of South Florida). Beautifully designed and illustrated, many of its articles focus on current sociological debates, for example in relation to postmodernism and the commercial mass production of cultural imagery; while others provide ethnographic data, through their visual and verbal documentation of community change in urban and rural areas. The IVSA and *Visual Sociology* enable 'visually driven thinkers' (to use Harper's phrase) – many of whom may formally have experienced a sense of isolation working within communities of verbally driven thinkers – to know each other's work and thereby gain the courage and enthusiasm to continue working, but now as members of a scholarly community devoted to the development and furtherance of visual sociology. At the same time, the fact that contributions to the journal (which has a steady, growing membership) are made by American, European and South African sociologists, would appear to indicate a fairly solidly based and spreading concern with the relationship of sociology to visual representation.

The photographic social science projects which have so far been featured and discussed in this chapter are presented to the reader as completed, formally organised, published pieces of research. Yet the process of transforming research notes and informal jottings into a formal account involves the author in reformulating, disguising or suppressing awkward and ill-fitting elements (see, for example, Wynne 1988: 101–22). I now give an account of my own ongoing project (Chaplin, *Visual Diary*), which I have chosen to present in a fairly informal fashion. This allows me to leave many of those awkward, ill-fitting elements exposed – although, inevitably, some will have been almost unconsciously 'smoothed out', and others will have remained unnoticed and/or unmentioned. In this way I hope to bring into the open several of the problems involved in undertaking research – especially 'visual research' – which are ordinarily hidden from view. An informal mode of presentation also allows me to reflect critically on the first three years of an ongoing project as it developed and was altered by circumstances and ideas that influenced it along the way.

In our interviews with British Systematic Constructive artists (referred to in the Introduction) my research partner and I used a type of photo-elicitation. We asked each artist to select one of his or her own works to discuss during the interview. This proved an excellent way of generating in-depth dialogue about the artist's way of thinking and working. But I sensed that if I was to understand their intense preoccupation with the visual dimension, I would have to start producing visual work myself. This is, perhaps, analogous to the situation where the anthropologist feels the need to learn the language in order to communicate with the 'natives'. Photography seemed the obvious medium to choose, for it is more easily learned than the traditional methods used by fine artists, and it produces quicker results. Moreover, I didn't aim to become an artist. Rather, I wanted somehow to incorporate photography into a sociological research project.

A remark by Goffman in *Gender Advertisements* set me off: he points out that routine behaviour and action cannot be shown in a photograph.

> . . . [W]hen one establishes that a picture of something really is of the subject it portrays, it is very hard to avoid thinking that one has established something beyond this, namely, something about the event's currency, typicality, commonness, distribution, and so forth. The paradox is that 'small behaviours' are what can be very fully instantiated by a single photograph, but one such picture can only establish the feasibility of actual occurrence.
>
> (Goffman 1979: 20)

While my visual project was originally driven by a desire to learn the language in order to communicate better with the artists, I decided to explore whether photographic images could, in fact, make a contribution to existing sociological theory on routine.

However, I knew from Bateson and Mead (1949), and Berger (1972), that a sequence of photographs can convey a more complex set of ideas than it is possible to generate from within a single photograph. And I had learnt from Burgin (1986b) that to attempt to produce work which is *solely* visual is to create an artifical situation; for in social science, as in social life, there can be no fundamental categorical separation between words and images. So I conceived the idea of a 'visual diary', which would (more accurately) consist of a daily photograph accompanied by a short descriptive verbal passage. This meant that already my attention was shifting away from the idea of a single photographic image – the object of Goffman's remarks in relation to routine – and on to a sequence of images with textual accompaniments. However, I hoped that via a daily diary photograph in conjunction with its 'caption', I might build up a whole sequence of images which, on examination, would reveal visual traces of routine in my life.

From *You Press the Button, We Do the Rest* (Ford and Steinorth 1988) I learned about popular photography, and consequently decided to use coloured film with an ordinary automatic camera and to have the results processed at a high street store. But unlike the sociologist Christopher Musello (1979), who treats popular photographs as artefacts to be analysed, I would be producing the artefacts, and my photographs might not fit into the conventional categories of popular family photographs, such as weddings, christenings and holidays. I was also aware of the distinction between 'taking' and 'making' photographs. Mine started off as taken photographs. I tried to capture moments of what might turn out, on looking back, to have been routine. Later, however, my photographs were to become more contrived.

The project started on 6 February 1988, and in the first months of the first year I took a photograph each day which I captioned; although I soon felt the need to add a more 'theorised' verbal monthly entry (and eventually did so). However, the activity soon seemed problematic because it showed that there are so many moments in the day which could be photographed, and so many alternative captions which could be attached to each photograph. So I made the daily rule more exact. During August 1988, I took a photograph each day between 11 a.m. and 12 noon, making as straightforwardly descriptive a caption as I possibly could of each shot. At the end of the month, with the all the photographs laid out in front of me, it emerged that five of these were of my computer screen, which suggested the routine of work. In September, I tightened the rule up still further, and took my daily photograph on the dot of 12 noon every day, wherever I was. Six of these turned out to be images of the computer and five others of related desk work (see Figure 26). However, the activity served to indicate that there were yet more variables to control. For example, there are countless alternative directions in which to point the camera at any one particular moment. And even in the case of the computer images, shots had varied from close-up to longer-distance. Significance might be derived from even this small variation; which leads to having to decide what counts as a separate item of 'small behaviour' (to use Goffman's phrase).

At the time when the second sub-rule was in operation, I was offered an exhibition of the year's work at Leeds University Art Gallery during the following February. I accepted it and, as a consequence, the original orientation of my project was altered. I now began to envisage the whole year's diary displayed at once, with one month set against the next on the gallery wall, instead of conceiving of it as a social science project formally presented over a sequence of pages in the form of a book or journal. At this point I decided to let the work of the current month (produced according to its particular sub-rule) generate a different (more useful?) sub-rule for the

Figure 26 Elizabeth Chaplin. *August 1988, September 1988, Visual Diary.* Photographs mounted on boards; each board 24 × 33 ins

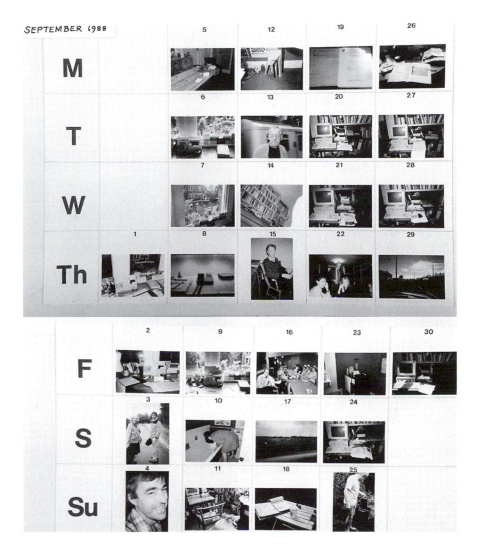

SEPTEMBER 1988

subsequent month; so that routine would in future be investigated along a series of different dimensions, each one generated by the previous month's work. But part of the reason for modifying the rules was that I imagined this might produce a 'more interesting exhibition' of twelve contrasting monthly blocks of photographs. By now, I faced what Becker (1981) describes as the personal dilemma experienced by photographers when the obligations that their work has by virtue of its status as social science come into conflict with a different set of obligations, those of art.

The monthly sub-rules forced a denser theoretical mesh on to my daily visual data, and at the same time demanded more technical expertise. Technical successes became a delight, and the visual quality of the image became much more important. I learned that my work was beginning to resemble those conceptual art projects where a time, place or chance dimension replaces a simple aesthetic one, as in Gabriela Muller's 'The Everyday Creative Process' (1987), Chris Drury's 'Nature Wheel' (1986) and David Perlov's 'Film Diary' (1972–82).[9]

The first year's visual diary was also exhibited at the annual conference of the Association of Social Anthropologists in 1989, where it took on a different, 'ethnographic', meaning. And in 1991 it was shown alongside an artist's visual diary of the same year in an exhibition at Dewsbury Museum.[10] This in turn produced a focus on the contrast between the medium of drawing and the medium of photography, besides drawing attention to a comparison of two different daily lives in 1988–9. While demonstrating that the context in which the work is seen has a crucial bearing on how it is perceived, this series of exhibitions gave the visual diary an independent character; it became a self-contained entity.

In the second year (6 February 1989–5 February 1990) I abandoned my investigation of routine according to different monthly sub-rules. Events along the way had caused me to modify my original aim, and almost to lose sight of the idea of a contribution to sociology in the form of an article or book; and besides, a new year seemed to demand new resolutions. But I wanted to hold on to the idea of producing a long-term visual diary. In any case, by now it was difficult to stop. I began to think of my daily photographic exercise as a continuing yet relatively flexible activity which could be used to explore social life photographically. This is more or less how I still

---

9 Chris Drury's 'Nature Wheel' is composed of 365 natural objects (sticks, pine cones, berries, leaves, etc.). In a given year, the artist picked up one item each day from a prescribed area of countryside. These are grouped together in weekly and monthly segments which together form the shape of the wheel, which is mounted on the wall. There is also a framed verbal 'key' which identifies each item in the total structure.

In Gabriela Muller's 'The Everyday Creative Process', the camera was positioned in Muller's kitchen, and programmed to operate on automatic release at regular intervals. Examples of this work are illustrated in her article 'Washing the Linen' (Muller 1987).

David Perlov's 'Film Diary' was broadcast on Channel 4, 29 October 1988, and on consecutive nights through the following week.

10 *A Diary for Dewsbury* (1991), with Stephen Chaplin, at Dewsbury Museum.

think of it. But in that second year, as a result of having the previous year's work produced as art and as ethnography, I decided to focus on the distinction between the discourse of photography as art and the discourse of photography as information. Here, I was influenced by 'On the Invention of Photographic Meaning' (Sekula 1982). For the first eight months, I took two daily photographs of a wall – any wall that caught my attention during the course of my day. The first shot was a close-up of the texture of the bricks (the 'art' image), and the second was a contextual longer-distance shot of the wall (the 'documentary' image). The art photograph of the wall was partly suggested by the formal, abstract, systematic nature of the work of the artists who were my research subjects. However, it was subsequently pointed out to me that the 'art' shots could be pages from a brick salesman's catalogue; and I learned what I was later to rediscover from *Exploring Society Photographically*, namely, that the aesthetic and the documentary facets of a photograph are virtually impossible to separate; and that, in any case, high-quality examples of both in which the aesthetic and documentary complement each other usually result from very prolonged periods of immersion in a topic, and are also a function of the format in which the work is ultimately presented. Besides, I eventually became bored by the subject matter of walls.

The Berlin wall was pulled down during this period. Newspaper photographs of this event brought home the fact that I had ignored the huge question of political symbolism. I was currently serving on the management committee of the Pavilion at Leeds (see Chapter 2), and increasingly regretted the lack of feminist input into my work. I decided to replace the close-up 'art' photograph of a wall with one which had feminist implications, and to leave the contextual one as a male counterpoint to it (having discovered daily that the long-distance view was almost always man-made). But a feminist – or any critical – photograph is problematic, for, as Craig Owens (1983: 57–82) has argued in a discussion of Martha Rosler's pair of images entitled 'The Bowery in Two Inadequate Descriptive Systems', 1974–5 (Figure 27), photographs do not represent others in the way that they themselves would wish to be represented. By refusing to photograph the inhabitants of Skid Row, and by denying the caption/text its conventional function of supplying the image with something it lacks, Rosler addresses the problems of 'victim photography' and of the stolen image. While I was influenced by Rosler's work, I found that the *dailiness* of diary photography presented a further complication; for I had to find legitimate subject matter on a daily basis. I decided *I* would have to stand for other women, to represent them. I therefore began to photograph myself.

The camera's self-timer function now became vitally important (I had barely registered its existence before), and I learned that the technical functions and limitations of the camera and film play a crucial part in producing the theoretical viewpoint which an image imparts. But besides making timed shots of myself, I photographed *evidence* of myself: my

Figure 27 Martha Rosler. *The Bowery in Two Inadequate Descriptive Systems*, 1974–5.
Reproduced in 'The Discourse of Others: Feminists and Postmodernists' by
C. Owens (in H. Foster, ed., *Postmodern Culture*, 1983)

reflection (in mirrors, puddles, shiny surfaces, TV screens), my shadow
(against various objects), my belongings of that moment (e.g. handbag,
camera case), my footprints (in snow, dew, sand), marks made by my hand
(writing with pen on paper, chalk on blackboard) – and now I understood
more fully why Burgin had made much use of statues and mirrors in *Between*
(see Figure 6). Although the results tended to look narcissistic, which
heightened the importance of the accompanying daily verbal entries that
attempted to counteract this tendency, once again the contriving of the shot
generated an interest in the visual composition of the print; and I was
encouraged by finding accomplished and beautiful examples of the same
kind of work at an exhibition of work by Asian photographers called *Fabled
Territories: New Asian Photography in Britain* (1989–90). Pulomi Desai's
photographs of herself gave me more pleasure than anything in an exhibition had ever done before; and, unexpectedly, I realised that my original
attempt to learn to speak the language of the natives might be beginning to
pay off.

So in the latter part of Year Two, I was making two photographs each day,
a feminist one and a longer-distance view of the man-made setting which
contextualised it, together with a daily verbal entry. The idea was that the
two daily photographs should be juxtaposed to bring out their constrasting
viewpoints, and that visual and verbal daily entries should be read against

```
        plastered        stuccoed

        rosined      shellacked

            vulcanized

        inebriated

        polluted
```

each other. And the project in its current phase again depended on being exhibited. This way, the temporal sequence would be compressed into one spatial area, and a sequence of monthly blocks could be viewed all together, and at once.

Excerpts from the two completed years and first few months of the third year of my visual diary were displayed on a wall at the 1990 annual British Sociological Association conference. I mounted this display next to a critical account of the development of the project up to that point. But at roughly this time I acquired a new camera which enables the date to be printed on the photograph. This meant that the diaristic element of the project was now partly taken into the image, whereas before the date had been written alongside the print after the shot had been made, and the film developed and printed. The implications of this technical facility for subsequent develop-ments of the project (including theorising and display) are considerable. I also began to develop and print my own black and white film, in order to gain greater control over the process. However, the daily requirement of two photographs began to generate more developing and printing work than I could cope with in the time available. I decided to produce two sheets of contact prints per month (which allow one pair of photographs per day) and to experiment with the idea of enlarging only those which seemed to have particular critical and aesthetic merit. I kept up this regime until the start of the fourth year (6 February 1992) . . . where this informal account of an ongoing project ends.

Key points in any summary of the work thus far would have to include the influence on the project of fixed and changing technological factors with respect to camera, film and film-processing, and also the effect of often unanticipated 'outside' events together with my responses to them. While my main criticism of the project is that I probably allowed outside events to exert far too much influence, these points at least give some sense of the difficulties involved in formulating a long-term photographic research project in advance, and sticking to it. But many formal accounts of empirical projects give the impression that a simple procedure is followed in empirical research in which a problem is postulated, then addressed and finally 'solved'. Rather than present readers with visual and verbal material which is more or less coherently arranged in relation to some key arguments, I hope to have indicated that the meaning of a photographic image for social scientists is rarely straightforward, yet that this complex matter is an important one to explore since photographs are able to capture and convey aspects of society which words cannot – and therefore are clearly capable of altering or adding to our social scientific understanding of it. Some sociologists of knowledge argue that empirical researchers should deliberately and systematically inject uncertainty into their accounts of their projects, for example Woolgar (1988). The manner in which I have constructed my account almost certainly does not correspond with what they have in mind. However, in some cases where uncertainty *is* deliberately and systematically injected into an account, the textual form of the account is fundamentally affected, and this includes its visual presentation. Such cases are examined in Chapter 6.

Images of Women: The Portrayal of Women in Photography of the Middle East 1860–1950 (1988), by Sarah Graham-Brown, is also concerned with the ambiguous character of photographic images. However, the layout of the text (pages 106–7 shown in Figure 28 are more or less typical of that layout) suggests a different kind of project from many of those previously discussed. In *Balinese Character* and *Gender Advertisements*, for example, the photographs are treated mainly as ethnographic evidence and are arrayed in a series of blocks or plates according to social scientific categories. However, *Images of Women* is not *primarily* concerned with ethnographic evidence nor with social categorisation, and although it ranges across the field of cultural studies, this is first and foremost a social history told in words and images. Graham-Brown offers a history of the portrayal in photographs of women of the Middle East from the earliest days of photography up to 1950. Her account includes a history of the Middle East and of women in relation to it, a discussion of orientalism, a consideration of the changing social geography of the area, and a social history of photography. Nearly every chapter consists of a verbal essay liberally interspersed with captioned photographs which carry their own sub-texts. The pages are laid out in two parallel columns of different widths, which thus allow for photographs of different sizes while emphasising the active part played by the visual dimension in this account (see Figure 28). The photographs contribute documentary material to the topic under discussion (Figure 28 shows a page from her Chapter 3, called 'Family Portraits'); while their symbolic significance and possible ideological influence is also debated. In this way, the ambiguity of the photographic image, which contains both documentary *and* symbolic meaning, becomes a central topic. A book in which the visual and verbal are more thoroughly integrated would surely be hard to find; and this visual/verbal, socio-historical format yields a wealth of material for social scientists who are interested in making cross-cultural comparisons.

Let us, for example, compare parts of her Chapter 3, 'Family Portraits', with a section entitled 'The Family' in *Gender Advertisements*. Goffman is concerned with the Western nuclear family. He remarks that

> . . . the nuclear family as a basic unit of social organization is well adapted to the requirements of pictorial representation. All of the members of almost any actual family can be contained easily within the same close picture, and, properly positioned, a visual representation of the members can nicely serve as a symbolization of the family's social structure.

(Goffman 1979: 37)

For her part, Graham-Brown notes that family portraits commissioned around 1900 by Middle Eastern families themselves (although inevitably only the fairly well-to-do) may seem startling in the sense that they so closely resemble Western family portraiture of roughly the same era. It appears that in the Middle East, the evolution of portrait photography followed a pattern similar to that in the West, except that it evolved more slowly. Thus, while Goffman observes that photographs of families in Western advertisements indicate more of an affinity between women and their daughters than between men and their sons, Graham-Brown notes – in a discussion of a Middle Eastern photograph of a family wedding group in 1952 from Turkey – that the formality is broken by the look of affection the bride is exchanging with her mother. And Goffman remarks that 'boys, as it were, have to push their way into manhood, which involves problematic effort' (Goffman 1979: 38), while Graham-Brown makes a similar observation in her discussion of a Middle Eastern photograph of a small boy and a small girl – Fathi and Aziza Radwan – at the time of the First World War. She comments that Fathi is 'here trying to look tall and proprietorial' (Graham-Brown 1988: 98) alongside his slightly older sister.

However, Graham-Brown notes that photographs of Middle Eastern family life made by *Europeans* are a very different matter. One taken in 1909 shows a 'family group' consisting of some members of the Turkish Imperial Harem, including two eunuchs. And Figure 28 reproduces a photograph entitled 'One Family' (top left) where the implication is that the single male in the picture has at least four wives. The figures stretch on and on, hardly fitting into the frame. Graham-Brown notes that the photographer of the

FAMILY PORTRAITS

18 'One Family'. Boesinger & Co, postcard, Baghdad, 1900s.

The photographer's presumed intention is to suggest that the single male in the picture has (at least) four wives. They could also be sisters, sisters-in-law, or other relatives – or not relations at all – simply people grouped together by the photographer. The fact that this can be regarded as a 'family' is presented as at best an oddity, or at worst, something which provokes disapproval in the viewer.

were more interested in patterns of kinship in the tribe and extended family, rather than in personal relationships within the family. Furthermore, their findings on family relationships were seldom evident from their photographic records. Even those women anthropologists, such as Hilma Granqvist, Winifred Blackman and Matthéa Gaudry, who were interested in these questions, rarely took photographs of family groups which included men and women. Their photographs tended to show only women relatives together, and occasionally brothers and sisters, or women with their sons. This reflected the sexual segregation which prevailed in most societies (see Chapter II), and therefore a marked reluctance on the part of many people to appear in a mixed photograph. On the rare occasions when photographs do show husbands and wives together, it seems likely that the anthropologist actually asked them to pose together.[11]

Mothers and Children

Among Western photographers, amateur and professional, the most common family theme was that of the mother and child. These images of motherhood sometimes had strong sexual overtones. Photographers were particularly attracted to scenes of women feeding their children in public which, especially among the poor of Egypt and North Africa, was a common practice allowing the photographer to create an image of earthy sensuality.

Many Western images of motherhood in the Middle East referred directly or indirectly to the iconography of the Madonna and Child, which had so coloured the portrayal of motherhood in the art and photography of the West itself. Sometimes the point was made simply by adding a caption to the photograph. For example, in a book published in 1910 describing women's role in missionary work from Palestine to China, entitled *Western Women in Eastern Lands*, there is a photograph of a woman, probably an Egyptian or Palestinian, with a child in her lap, with the caption 'A Muslim Madonna'.

19 Women of the Shammar tribe. Freya Stark, near Mosul, Iraq, 1930.

This photograph creates the impression that these women are quite at ease with the camera and its owner, and it also reflects something of Freya Stark's attraction to tribal life, a somewhat romanticized view perhaps, stressing the supportiveness and interdependence of the tribe as extended family. She wrote in a letter at that time: 'You would so love it here – the lovely free life of the tents, and pleasant family feeling of the tribe. I feel I should like to belong to a tribe, something so big and comfortable, and if you do come to grief you do it all together and there is none of the horrid petty bickering feeling of the towns.'[6]

106

Figure 28   Double-page spread from 'Family Portraits': *Images of Women: The Portrayal of Women in Photography of the Middle East 1860–1950* (S. Graham-Brown, 1988), pp. 106–7

20 'Arab Motherhood', Reiser, Egypt, turn of the century.

This photograph emphasizes the earthy, sensual quality of the relationship between mother and child, while also evoking the image of Madonna and Child. The age of the child still at the breast is not surprising – children were usually breast-fed until they were about two years old.

21 'Down Will Come Baby, Cradle and All – if Mama Trips!' – Published in National Geographic Magazine, *December 1938, in an article entitled 'Change Comes to Bible Lands'.*

The rest of the caption to this photograph of a woman from Nablus in Palestine stresses the irresponsibility and irrationality of this method of carrying children on the head, and compares the woman's attitude to her child unfavourably with an American mother. 'With her child sound asleep in the basket, this Arab woman of Nablus goes on her way with apparent indifference. Fancy a fond young American mother facing traffic with her first-born balanced on her head!'

harem picture had difficulty in getting the various members to pose at all, as a group, and without veils. This image was the result of the photographer's active intervention. And it seems that the members of 'One Family' were also assembled at the behest of the European photographer, who wanted to present his viewers with the strange social customs of the Orient.

Further contrasts emerge in the case of commercial photographs. While Goffman notes that in Western commercial photographs of the family, at least one girl and at least one boy are allocated to the 'mocked-up families in advertisements', ensuring 'that a symbolization of the full set of intrafamily relations can be effected' (Goffman 1979: 37), Graham-Brown shows that European commercial photographs depicting life in the Orient tend to exclude 'families' in favour of people who are shown in exotic dress and indolent pose. In sum, *Images of Women* indicates that although 'internally' commissioned photographs of Middle Eastern families resemble Western family photographs, many Western photographers of Middle Eastern family life were influenced by the cult of orientalism, and constructed a photographic vision of this ideology by arranging their Middle Eastern sitters in appropriate fashion.

However, *Images of Women* also shows that the flow of influences between Europe and the Middle East – which increasingly involved photographic images after 1850 – is not a simple matter. European photographs depicting 'exotic' aspects of Middle Eastern life were made for a European market, but these images were often emulated by Middle Eastern photographers wishing to make their own version of the exotic Orient in order to satisfy the demands of the growing Middle Eastern tourist industry. And while Western family portrait photography has clearly influenced the manner in which well-to-do Middle Eastern families wish to be portrayed, the social and personal relationships that lie behind those images are not easy to establish from the documentary information that photographs supply. What, for example, can we make of the photographic evidence of a bond between mother and daughter in both the Middle Eastern and the European family groups? Is it possible to establish that, in either case, this indicates an 'indigenous trait', or alternatively that the look of affection which the Middle Eastern mother and daughter are seen to exchange was 'influenced' by Western portraits of family groups, or even by advertisements which were beginning to include images of the Western nuclear family? Attempting to answer these kinds of question must, at the very least, take into account the degree of initiative retained by the photographer, and the purpose or purposes that the photograph was originally intended to serve. While photographs provide *documentary* evidence which may help to establish the historical order in which certain 'events' or categories of event have taken place, it is much harder, if not impossible, to pinpoint the influence that the *symbolic* significance of such a photograph may have had on the flow of a cultural influence in one particular direction or another. But on the other hand, photographs have clearly both reflected and helped to shape the complex character of the images that Westerners and Middle Easterners have and want to have of themselves, and of each other; and the particular value of Graham-Brown's socio-historical approach, using parallel texts with photographs, is that it allows her to discuss and partly unravel this complexity through a continual cross-referencing of general issues (including the part played by photography itself in constructing that complexity) with images of concrete instances which inform those issues.

In fact, the visual dimension penetrates this account at all levels, giving it a compactness – almost, as it were, a reflexive soundness or logic. Graham-Brown uses photographs as documentary evidence, and in this sense they contribute to the topic under discussion; she also analyses them in order to demonstrate the part which photography has played in creating images of women in the Middle East; and in addition, the page layout allows a flexibility in the relationship between text, image, caption and sub-text, which enables a continually changing series of visual and verbal emphases to be made throughout.[11] In other words, Graham-Brown's *subject matter* includes photographs, while photographs also contribute in various ways to her *analysis*, and at the same time the visual organisation of the page – which includes photographs presented in different sizes according to the significance of their contribution – is integral to the *methodology* which she carries out.

Creating formats for sociological knowledge which are reflexively compact and sound is one of the aims of *Health and Efficiency: A sociology of health economics* by Malcolm Ashmore, Michael Mulkay and Trevor Pinch (1989). The book's fourth chapter, entitled '"Fury over prof's kidney call": health economists in the media', is presented in an unconventional fashion; and, in fact, its sociological arguments can hardly be separated off from the manner in which the overall account is visually constructed. This is the last visually enriched social science text discussed in the present chapter, but at the same time it forms part of a wider project concerned with new literary forms for sociology. This project is examined in Chapter 6, where the implications of new literary forms for visual innovation in sociology are discussed.

The pages of Chapters 1–3 and 5–8 of *Health and Efficiency* are not eye-catchingly different from those in other social science texts, and the introduction to Chapter 4 is also written, typeset and laid out in an orthodox manner. In it, the authors explain that while they were researching the book, health economics, health economists and their invention, the QUALY (quality-adjusted life year – 'a technique for outcome measurement and resource allocation' [Ashmore, Mulkay and Pinch 1989: 58]) received a great

---

11 It is important to note the contribution made by Zelfa Hourani of Quartet Books: she spent a whole year laying out the pages of *Images of Women*.

the BMA on Monday which heard of evidence supplied by the Centre for Health Economics based at York University.

Pulse 6 Sept 86

'Stop the NHS cuts'

Pulse 6 Sept 86

The report was commissioned from York University's Centre for Health Economics by the Institute of Health Service Managers, the British Medical Association and the Royal College of Nursing.

Public Finance and Accountancy 5 Sept 86

Prepared by Prof Alan Maynard and Dr Nick Bosanquet, of York University's Centre for Health Economics, it endorses the findings of the first report published in October 1985.

The authors conclude that at least a two per cent increase in NHS funding is essential.

Doctor 11 Sept 86

DOCTORS, nurses and health managers claim to have provided Health Secretary Norman Fowler with the ammunition he needs to talk more money out of the Treasury.

Doctor 11 Sept 86

But the Government hit back in a statement from Health Minister, Mr. Norman Fowler.

He says spending in real terms under the Tories has increased by 24 per cent since 1978/79.

Savings

Mr Fowler said "In other words, the two per cent increase has already been achieved."

YE Press 2 Sept 86

Mr Bosanquet added: "The two per cent needed has not been achieved, even allowing for cost improvements in the key hospital and community health services.

"I must admit the Government response has been disappointing."

YE Press 2 Sept 86

But since recent rumours that political pressures were causing the Government to rethink its stance on NHS spending the debate took on another dimension.

HSJ 29 May 86

pay-out

Doctor 11 Sept 86

HEALTH SERVICE WELCOMES WINDFALL FROM MINISTERS

Nursing Times and Nursing Mirror 1 Nov 86

Mr Nick Bosanquet, senior research fellow at the York University centre for health economics and author of a recent report on NHS expenditure, said last night that Mr Fowler may have done enough to avert a serious crisis.

Guardian 2 June 86

Prof Alan Maynard: "Significant cash problems."

YE Press 3 June 86

Professor Maynard admitted there did seem to have been a real increase in National Health Service resources.

'But it is inadequate to meet the demands the government articulates each year in the public expenditure white paper.'

More money alone was not the answer. 'We have to divert resources to enable the service to perform more efficiently.'

HSJ 2 June 86

FROM AN IVORY TOWER

HSJ (Maynard column heading) 1987

Dimbleby: Professor Maynard is not an isolated voice. His team at York is financed by government and its work is given close attention by the DHSS.

'This Week', ITV, 16 Oct 86

Prof. Maynard told Social Services Secretary, Mr Norman Fowler, and Health Minister, Mr Barney Hayhoe, that university academic staff no longer have the security of jobs for life, so why should GPs?

YE Press 16 July 86

Ministers are known to favour the plan, originally drawn up by the York University health economist, Professor Alan Maynard. But it was considered too radical to be included in the green paper on GP services.

Guardian 19 June 86

But Maynard argues that the government frequently gets advice from York that it does *not* want to hear, and that the civil servants at least in the DHSS who commission research are open-minded about the answers.

THES 27 Feb 87

Health ministers have been careful to keep out of the debate. The DHSS has been equally wary.

Times 17 June 87

The professor's work is funded by government by the Department of Health. He guessed that his views were going to prevail in the debate.

Belfast Newsletter 13 Oct 86

Maynard's point is that the information is neutral: economics is simply a tool to understand what is happening. Policy

decisions on using that information are still in the hands of doctors and policy-makers.

THES 27 Feb 87

"What we essentially regard ourselves doing is informing policy-makers."

THES 27 Feb 87

Policy makers 'prefer ignorance and prejudice'

Hospital Doctor 12 June 86

"They do not wish to be confused by facts about the real world, preferring to remain in a dream world of ignorance and prejudice," he told the conference.

Hospital Doctor 12 June 86

Efficiency options are fudged by policymakers and politicians alike because they would involve such things as explicit prioritisation and confronting the monopoly power of provider groups, especially clinicians.

HSJ (Maynard) 3 Nov 87

This cowardice by policymakers is a major threat to the survival of the NHS.

HSJ (Maynard) 3 Nov 87

Sometimes we bring good news and sometimes we bring bad.

THES 27 Feb 87

Prof Maynard . . . failure.

Hospital Doctor 12 June 86

The pursuit of policies to equalise health-care expenditure is pathetic . . . .

Such action would be politically difficult because sectional interests would lose out . . . . Neither the present government nor the Labour opposition seems capable of confronting these problems as there are perhaps too many marginal constituencies at stake.

HSJ (Maynard) 3 Nov 87

"The government does lots of nice crude calculations, saying we need a 1 per cent increase in expenditure to meet the demands from more elderly.

"That's a very dangerous argument by the DHSS, because statistical basis is less than robust."

HSJ 2 June 86

"The Government spends a lot of money on collecting information for its Hospital Activity Analysis. But it's a joke. It only gives information on expenditure and on doing things. But no-one in the NHS knows the cost of anything and the data on outcomes is lousy."

Yorkshire Post 18 Jan 88

Health studies 'quick and dirty'

Laboratory News 26 June 87

Studies such as those to be carried on NHS pathology are described by Professor Maynard as "quick and dirty" appraisals for agencies requiring "instant wisdom."

Laboratory News 26 June 87

"But there's an increasing awareness of the power of very simple economic techniques in illuminating what's going on in the health service."

THES 27 Feb 87

---

are health economists a sufficient answer?

Nature 18 June 87

Professor Maynard believes that government should turn to the research community to provide answers to policy problems.

Laboratory News 26 June 87

The DHSS trains just six health economists a year to deal with a health care system that consumes £20 billion a year.

Laboratory News 26 June 87

"The government's attitude to health economics is a very simple one—that of cost containment. Economists take a much longer term view."

Laboratory News 26 June 87

'Be quick and dirty' researchers told

HSJ 31 Oct 85

Researchers are warned of perfectionism and urged towards 'quick and dirty' studies in a new discussion paper from Tony Culyer, professor at the Centre for Health Economics, York.

HSJ 31 Oct 85

The Centre for Health Economics has been commissioned by the IHSM to provide a detailed answer to the white paper (see page 96) which will probably be available in about a fortnight.

HSJ 23 Jan 86

Professor Culyer also urges health economists to adopt a higher profile. . . .

HSJ 31 Oct 85

But how could you seriously hope to measure—with the . . . conditions and social circumstances . . . possibly varying enormously—without invidious comparisons being made?

Yorkshire Post 18 Jan 88

"Yes, there is a chance you would get trial-by-media. So, we can either do what we do now and stay in ignorance, or work out a civilised means of assessing performance."

Yorkshire Post 18 Jan 88

THE OTHER YORK: HEALTH ECONOMICS UNDER THE MICROSCOPE

The sociologists at work

Ever wondered about the blue-suited pundits with the calculators, who want life and death decisions made on economic grounds? A new study of health economists reveals all.

Our reporters investigate

SOCIOLOGY STAR RISING

If York has a reputation in health economics it is also fast becoming known for its sociology of science. York Vice-Chancellor, Berrick Saul, in launching a recent appeal for more social science funding at York said: "The University Grants Committee has recognised York's achievement in the social sciences by awarding its elusive 'star rating' for out-standing work to two key departments, Economics and Social Policy, and also to the Sociology Department for its work on sociology of science". As yet largely unknown outside the academic community, York's sociologists of science are set to make a wider impact with their latest study of health economics.

And, to round it all off, Bobby rose again from the dead (*Dallas, BBC1*). Happily, this appears not yet to be available on the NHS. Goodness knows how many QALYs a resurrection scores.

Observer 12 Oct 86

Meanwhile at the other end of the University of York campus, away from the bright lights of the media . . .

Figure 29 Two double-page spreads from '"Fury over prof's kidney call": health economists in the media': *Health and Efficiency* (M. Ashmore, M. Mulkay and T. Pinch, 1989), pp. 78–9, 80–1

deal of media attention as a result of much public discussion of the future of the National Health Service. Therefore,

> In this chapter we try to convey a sense of what happens when health economists enter the world of mass communication. We show how their discourse is altered, fragmented and, from their own perspective, often distorted, as it is taken over, assessed and disseminated by the numerous conflicting voices of television and the press.
>
> (Ashmore, Mulkay and Pinch 1989: 58)

The introduction is followed by more than twenty pages of press-cuttings and excerpts from television and radio transcripts. These excerpts are grouped into categories, or sub-sections, displayed in double columns, and laid out in the manner of a newspaper article (see Figure 29). The majority of the category headings are actual media headlines or sub-headings. Occasionally the authors have invented one, but only when no appropriate headline already existed. Their story of the media coverage is thus presented via these grouped sequences of excerpts; and the idea is that the construction of this new, fictional 'press article' follows roughly the same procedure used by the media themselves when *they* selected, organised and dramatised their material relating to the practical application of the Qualy. Ashmore explains: 'Ideally it should tell our analytical story purely by the judicious ordering of the extracts' (Ashmore in Ashmore, Mulkay and Pinch 1989: 85). However, it is important to stress that the different typefaces and the 'newspaper' layout also make an important contribution to the analytical story. The typefaces do not correspond precisely with those used in the original media articles since the authors did not have access to an identical range of typefaces. This situation has obliged – or enabled – them to be visually creative. They have 'judiciously' selected a typeface for each excerpt which both visually *articulates* the relationship of that excerpt to those surrounding it and encourages a particular visual *interpretation* of that excerpt, whilst it contributes to the visual *enhancement* of the page as a whole. Large bold type lends emphasis and dramatic impact to short statements, while it also allows them to appear 'of a piece' with longer excerpts portrayed in smaller type, when both occupy the same amount of 'column inches'. In fact, this selective visual presentation demonstrates that typography and layout can play a major part in shaping and dramatising an analytical story, and that they therefore constitute an additional and powerful resource for social scientists to use. At the same time, the range of typefaces used in this piece indicates the choice available in desktop publishing – and the potential for visual innovation in sociology and other areas.

However, the final section of the chapter is somewhat different in appearance from the preceding twenty or so pages. It retains the journalistic style, double-column format and sub-headings which were deployed in the analysis constructed out of media excerpts; but it uses only one typeface for the narrative and one for sub-headings, and thus signals a return to a single account (see Figure 29, their page 81, starting with the headings 'Our reporters investigate', and 'Sociology star rising'). The section purports to be a newspaper article by journalists who have just returned from interviewing the three sociologist-authors. This journalists' story of the sociologists who constructed the 'newspaper article' analysis is, of course, like the rest of the book, written by Ashmore, Mulkay and Pinch themselves. It combines journalese with sociology, and is highly entertaining and at the same time very informative. In it, the authors' own methodological position is set out and justified, and the book's findings and conclusions are summarised. A central argument is that, in one sense, sociology is no different from health economics and media reports of it, in that a partial story is told, not an objective one. Elsewhere, Dorothy Smith has argued that 'If sociology cannot avoid being situated then it should take that as its beginning and build it into its methodological and theoretical strategies' (Smith 1974). *Health and Efficiency* does this. The book examines several different perspectives in addition to that of the health economists themselves, and it sometimes displays the existence of those alternative viewpoints by correspondingly varying the textual form of its presentation. Thus, its Chapter 4, which focuses on the media coverage of issues relating to health economics, is itself presented like the media present their stories, and is created out of material which actually originated in the media. Constructing one account roughly in the manner that the other is put together is not so far-fetched, the sociologists argue, since each is selective and each works to produce its own particular effect. However, Ashmore adds, 'and hopefully [our story] follows the conventions of good journalism' (Ashmore, Mulkay and Pinch 1989: 85). This suggests that relativism is not the end of the matter. If good journalism can be distinguished from bad, then – by extension – some sociological accounts or analyses are perhaps more informative, less morally questionable, more compelling, than others. Indeed, it even appears that *Health and Efficiency* may in some sense be superior to journalism or health economics. For in answer to a question from 'the reporters' about whether they would have liked some of the media limelight that the health economists attracted, 'the sociologists' are said to have answered that they would not, arguing 'that their book as a whole demonstrates its concern with much weightier issues' (Ashmore, Mulkay and Pinch 1989: 84). However, such is the level of complexity produced by this wheels-within-wheels story-within-a-story, that it is hard to tell whether the remark is intended to apply merely within the specific context in which it is uttered, or whether it signals a claim, however veiled, about the general superiority of the authors' account – or indeed, whether it is intended as a joke. In fact, the whole chapter presents would-be analysts of it with a slippery task because it operates on so many levels simultaneously, producing witty and shifting meanings which tend to evade attempts to pin them down. I suggest that although the methodology and manner of writing used in '"Fury over prof's kidney call"' are quite justified (for we know that there is no *one* truth and cannot expect to be able to pin down *a* meaning), indeed they are in some senses pioneering, this mass of interconnected shifting meanings also serves as a strategy to prevent other sociologists from gaining a firm analytical grasp on the work; it appears to be designed to leave the authors with the last word. . .

However, the relevance of Chapter 4 of *Health and Efficiency* to the present analysis lies in the fact that its narrative and its dramatic impact, and also its arguments and methodology, owe much to the unconventional use of typography and page layout. While all sociological texts are typographic-ally set and their page layouts are designed, typography and layout seldom make an active contribution to the meaning of a given text because the manner in which they are used has become conventionalised; they are merely treated as the vehicles by which meanings conjured up out of groups of words are conveyed. 'Ignore us' is what they usually signal. In '"Fury over prof's kidney call"', however, these conventions are broken. Media typo-graphical conventions and a newspaper layout actively interfere with – or shape – our interpretation of the meanings of the words, phrases and sentences we read, with the result that we cannot see a 'sociological message' separate from a 'media message'; and, at a more general level, we cannot grasp the arguments or the methodology deployed without taking into account the visual construction of the piece.

In the visually enriched social science texts examined in this chapter, there exists – perhaps inevitably – a relationship of some sort between the topic of analysis or subject matter and the fact that a piece of 'visual sociology' was carried out: in other words, the topic was connected with something of visual interest and/or importance. For example, Goffman analysed visual advertisements; anthropologists categorise ethnographic data from strange-looking places; my visual diary is a formal visual project like that of the visual artists I was studying. However, both *Images of Women* and *Health and Efficiency*, in their different ways, involve a more precise, systematic relationship between the type of visual representation which forms the topic of analysis or subject matter and the method used to conduct the sociological analysis. In the next chapter, I show that when form and content are systematically interrelated, sociology and visual innovation are also inseparable.

Chapter 6

Visual representation and new literary forms for sociology

Principal works discussed:

Susan Krieger, *The Mirror Dance: Identity in a Women's Community*, 1983.
Myra Bluebond-Langner, *The Private Worlds of Dying Children*, 1978
Michal McCall and Howard Becker, 'Performance Science', *Social Problems*, 37, 1, 1990
Michael Mulkay, 'Talking Together: An Analytical Dialogue', *The Word and the World: Explorations in the Form of Sociological Analysis*, 1985
Steve Woolgar, 'Reflexivity is the Ethnographer of the Text', *Knowledge and Reflexivity*, 1988
Anna Wynne, 'Accounting for Accounts of the Diagnosis of Multiple Sclerosis', *Knowledge and Reflexivity*, 1988
Michael Mulkay, 'Looking backward (1989)', *Sociology of Science: A Sociological Pilgrimage*, 1991
Trevor Pinch and Trevor Pinch, 'Reservations about Reflexivity and New Literary Forms or Why Let the Devil have All the Good Tunes?', *Knowledge and Reflexivity*, 1988
Bruno Latour, 'The Politics of Explanation: an Alternative', *Knowledge and Reflexivity*, 1988
Countervail project, 1990 – continuing

I would say that Mallarmé's work – in *Le Coup de dès*, for example – on the very space of the printed sheet, is an extremely important critical work insofar as it shows that the typographical space itself is one conquered on a plastic space, which resists it, which is suppressed by the space of discourse. And precisely in *Le Coup de dès*, this plastic space is suggested, restituted as the other of the discursive and textual space. They will surely say that this has no political impact whatsoever . . . but I am not sure they won't be wrong.

(Jean-François Lyotard, *Driftworks*, 1984)

It is time to understand that form and content are one, that the new content will inevitably be cramped in the old form, and that the old form has become for us a barrel organ on which you can play nothing but 'Farewell'.

(Nicolai Gorlov, *On Futurisms and Futurism*, 1924)[1]

---

1 This quotation is from Wood (1992, but not actually dated: 376).

It is not yet clear to what extent it is possible to escape the constraints of conventional academic discourse.

(Michael Lynch and Steve Woolgar, *Representation in Scientific Practice*, 1988)

In the seventeenth century, Holland had a visual culture (Alpers 1983). Its scientific researches were directed towards the development of optical instruments and the acquisition of visual knowledge which those instruments made possible. That visual knowledge enabled a small country to become very powerful, and it also provided the common sense upon which ordinary Dutch people were able to draw. However, our society today is rather different. Education is mainly concerned with literacy, and the result is that few educated people think easily or confidently in visual terms, apart from artists and some scientists and mathematicians. However, while social scientists – like most other intellectuals – generally assign privilege to verbal statements, we have seen that some have recently begun to take depictions seriously, and have subjected them to sociological analysis.[2] Bowker (1988), for example, has demonstrated that a scientific depiction does not mirror 'reality', but instead *represents* – or constructs a version of – that reality. And Fyfe and Law (1988) show that a depiction is never merely an illustration; while Woolgar (1988) suggests that the image always conspires with its frame, or – in the context of a book – with frame, caption, and verbal text, to produce an argument. In such cases where there is an array of images, they and their frames conspire together to produce an argument, or analysis, which is more clearly visual in character. Some of the works of social science discussed in the previous chapter contain visual analysis. That is to say, where several images are grouped together on the page (as in *Balinese Character*) the author has clearly been involved in making a series of linked visual choices in order to achieve a desired effect: images have been selected, judiciously cropped and framed, juxtaposed and grouped in such a way as to evoke a particular interpretation and to discourage alternatives.

However, not many social science texts contain depictions, because of the privileged status accorded to verbal statements and verbal understanding. But this does not mean to say that the visual dimension is absent from social science texts. Indeed, every one of them makes a visual contribution to social scientific knowledge, however weak, via its layout and typescript. In '"Fury over prof's kidney call": health economists in the media' (Ashmore, Mulkay and Pinch 1989), we saw that the unconventional visual layout of the text and choice of typescript actively contribute to the authors' sociological analysis. Furthermore, in cases where an account contains a great many depictions or where the verbal text is presented by means of unconventional layout and typography, these visual features also inevitably affect the formal structure of the account. For example, the socio-historical analysis offered in

---

2 That is, depictions outside the field of visual art. Visual art depictions have, of course, been subjected to sociological analysis for many years.

Images of Woman (Graham-Brown 1988) can hardly be 'separated off' from the book's unconventional structure, involving as it does the size and placement of photographic depictions, the judicious use of typography and the page layout of text in relation to the visual material. But the authors of '"Fury over prof's kidney call"' go further; they deliberately use non-standard typographical conventions and layout to help create the formal structure of the piece, to indicate their philosophical and methodological approach, and to imply that a sociological analysis cannot be couched in a form which is incompatible with the character of its own arguments.

Now, the standard form in which academic papers are presented has several distinguishing features which have become conventionalised. According to Taylor (1978), this form is recognisable by 'a certain sentence structure, vocabulary, the disposition to labour so as to make all arguments logically watertight' (Taylor 1978: 3), resulting in 'a courteous distancing of oneself from others'. Many such academic conventions, including those used in sociological texts, derive from a positivist conception of natural and social science. They include use of the third person passive to convey 'objective truths' in an impersonal manner, and either a marked absence of visual images (Stasz 1979) or photographs which are supposed to constitute windows on an objective world. These and other academic conventions have characterised the standard social science account. The authors of *Health and Efficiency*, together with other sociologists of scientific knowledge (SSK), have become dissatisfied that academic conventions deriving from a positivist conception of science should continue to influence the way in which sociological analysis is presented. But further than this, they argue that the structure of a sociological account should be consistent with and reinforce the epistemological status of that account. And they point out that sociological analysis, far from having the privileged epistemological status that positivism accords it, is *itself* a social activity just like the subject matter that sociologists study. Sociological analysis is therefore *reflexive* in character. SSKers argue that the structure of the sociological account, and hence its textual form, must therefore openly display the reflexive character of sociological analysis.[3] They have thus been concerned to experiment with new textual forms, more commonly known as new literary forms, which are compatible with the reflexive character of sociological analysis itself.

However, other sociologists, who are only indirectly concerned with the epistemological status of sociological knowledge, have also experimented with new literary forms. Without deriving their critique of standard academic form directly from a critique of positivism, they nevertheless argue that the constraints imposed by the conventions of academic writing prevent them from reaching new audiences, from talking with the reader, from saying what they want to say in the way they want to say it, and from generally

---

3 See Ashmore (1989).

having fun. These authors tend to make use of dialogue, drama and fiction and have, in effect, begun to bring sociology closer to the arts. In this context, Feyerabend (1975) has suggested that social science adopt a more playful attitude towards its subject matter and towards words; and the visual sociologist Nancy Rexroth has experimented with a soft-focus lens which produces photographic images 'that she believes are the equivalents of childhood dreams' (Harper 1988). Such authors may feel that new literary forms are more suited to some subject matters than to others. SSKers, however, could not take this attitude, since their central concern is that *all sociological* analyses are reflexive, and that this has in-built implications for the textual form that such analyses take. These implications are that the sociologist should make the form of his/her own account consistent with the fact that it is a social construct just like the social world it analyses. This form must therefore allow authors to make sociological proposals about the social world without hiding from view the socially constructed character of those proposals.

Altough '"Fury over prof's kidney call": health economists in the media' was included in Chapter 5 on account of the novel visual presentation of its subject matter, this piece also has a place in the present chapter, which examines the ways in which the visual dimension is implicated in socio-logical analyses whose literary forms are reflexively sound. This chapter also discusses some examples of unconventionally structured texts which repre-sent the 'liberatory' school of thought, since the visual dimension is also involved in the presentation of such texts and intrudes into the sociological understanding that they impart.

New literary forms are not new outside the field of sociology. There have been numerous attempts to break with the conventional form of the novel, one of the earliest being Cervantes' *Don Quixote* (1950) [1605]. Indeed, in novels of the 1750s there were many attempts at self-conscious narration, with a comically intrusive writer preoccupied by the problems of writing.[4] One of the best-known examples of this genre is Sterne's *The Life and Opinions of Tristram Shandy, Gentleman* (1985) [1759–67]. According to Christopher Ricks, 'Sterne's brilliant tactic was to bring out all the time how severe the limits of words are' (Ricks 1985: 16). This tactic is achieved in part by incorporating typographical oddities and unconventional layout, and by subverting depictive conventions. When Dr Slop crosses himself, a cross (+) suddenly pops up (as Sterne would say) in print. There are blank pages for chapters 'torn out' (Vol. IX, Chapters 18 and 19), and a very different kind of blank page upon which the reader is invited to depict the beauty of Widow Wadman. When Corporal Trim flourishes his stick, we are given not words but a twirling line on the page. Sterne emphasises the book as a physical object by having a large black rectangle on both sides of a page, when

---

4 See Booth (1992).

Parson Yorick dies.[5] And he frequently introduces different readers, and their opinions, into the text. Later works, such as James Joyce's *Finnegans Wake* (1939), Alain Robbe-Grillet's *Jealousy* (1959), William Faulker's *The Sound and the Fury* (1964) and Julian Barnes's *Flaubert's Parrot* (1984) all experiment with alternative ways of structuring the novel. Others have tested the constraints of the play format (Samuel Beckett), the autobiography (Gertrude Stein); and a few have deliberately crossed boundaries between visual and verbal domains (Tom Phillips) and the 'disciplines' of visual art and social science (Hans Haake, Lorraine Leeson and Peter Dunn, Stephen Willats).

In the case of *sociological* accounts which adopt new literary forms (both those that are generated out of a critique of positivism, and those which are chosen because they liberate authors from academic constraints), there are a number of ways in which the limitations of the conventional form can be demonstrated and the normalisation of textual strategies can be exposed. Authors may seek to emphasise the physical character of the account, in order to demolish the idea that it is a transparent vehicle for purveying knowledge. They may produce a multi-voice account in order to get rid of the single integrative narrative voice and thus the linearity and conventional temporality of a text. Some bring in the author and the reader, encouraging the reader to respond to the author's remarks and to explore alternative textual forms for what these might yield. And some authors use a multi-voice account in such a way as to suggest that the text is unresolved, uncertain; to de-privilege its epistemological status in relation to that of the topic under analysis. Fantasy and imagination may be brought into play; indeed, the division between social science and fiction is often problematised. Authors may also attempt to query the privileged status of the verbal text itself, although this is more often talked about than demonstrated.

Any new literary form involves the introduction of visual changes. By this I mean that the text will at least look mildly different, in terms of its page layout, and perhaps typography as well. Let us take *page layout* first (though the two are not necessarily easy to separate). In the quotation at the start of this chapter, Lyotard alludes to the political character of page layout. He seems to suggest that the 'plastic space' of the page competes with the space of discourse or printed text, which aims, as it were, to suppress that plastic space. One area of the plastic space of the page which has rarely been suppressed by sociology texts is the margin surrounding the text – except where footnotes are used in preference to endnotes; though this situation may change since the computerised setting of pages now makes such innovations far easier.[6] But sociological accounts which take an alternative

---

5 An edition of 1906 has additional illustrations by George Cruikshank. The subject matter of these illustrations indicates that at this date the emphasis was on *Tristram Shandy* as a narrative rather than as a work which explored the limits of the novel's form.

6 As an indication of this, see Squires (1990), where notes to the text are made in the left-hand margin.

literary form often draw our attention to the use they make of the plastic space of the page. These accounts are frequently multi-vocal, as in the script of a play, and the way such a script is visually presented is perhaps the first thing that strikes the reader. (Goffman [1959] talks of information 'given' and information 'given off'. This distinction can usefully be applied here. Layout and typographical information are usually given off.) The manner in which the lines of text are grouped, according to who is speaking, lends the whole work meaning as a play. Readers immediately associate the ideas being spelled out with the character who speaks them. Then a white space signals that someone else's ideas are about to be spoken instead. The look of the page – the play format – signals that these are personalised ideas, rather than timeless, objective truths. Another example of unconventional page layout occurs where the author places two texts side by side in parallel columns (see, for example, *Glas* by Jacques Derrida, 1986). This format, though not necessarily 'multi-vocal', offers more than one textual passage (usually about the same topic) simultaneously, and is frequently used to question assumptions about the linearity of the sociological account. I once used this format to convey that two sets of ideas had a shifting, speculative relationship to each other (Chaplin 1988: 9–13). Because I was writing about art works concerned with geometric proportions, I used a two to one layout (single-spacing in one column and double-spacing in the other). In general, sociologists who deploy alternative literary forms use unconventional layout to signal and reinforce underlying ideas and theoretical assumptions, and therefore to orientate or impose a layer of meaning on particular points which are being verbalised.

Typeface also contributes meaning to an analysis. The 'standard' typeface, consisting of slight variations on *Times 327*, itself a derivative of Janson's sixteenth-century typeface, has been used in newspapers and books in general circulation since the nineteenth century. Because it is commonplace, it has no special message of its own. However, authors and publishers may use an alternative typeface to inject a special message into a text; for example, to increase its credibility or to give it a sense of urgency. Routledge 'direct editions' of the mid-1970s looked typed,[7] signalling that the work was up to the minute and hot from the typewriter. (This was before the days of word-processing, which can – ironically – be printed out as a 'professional book'.) Typefaces can show social differentiation; for example upper-case is sometimes used in diagrams to give information about males, while lower-case is reserved for females (Ardener 1981). This type of visual discrimination may perhaps show unwitting prejudice on the part of the author. However, sociologists using new literary forms often make typefaces work to reinforce their chosen form, and thus the structure of their analysis. For example, in a multi-voice account, Pinch and Pinch emphasise the unequal relationship

---

7 See, for example, Barnes (1977).

between the two voices, by having the first 'speak' in bold and the second in weak type (Pinch and Pinch 1988). And, with an added twist, one of Woolgar and Ashmore's characters in 'The Next Step: an Introduction to the Reflexive Project' says, 'the use of UPPER-CASE makes it seem like you're shouting!' (Woolgar and Ashmore 1988: 3). Colour contrasts can be made to work in a similar fashion, though social scientists rarely get the opportunity to explore this area because of the expense involved.[8]

In the next section, I examine some examples of sociological accounts couched in unconventional literary form, noting the various contributions made by the visual dimension – whether these were conscious calculations on the part of the author or not. At the same time, I am aware that my own account is conventionally structured; and the reason for this is that I do not think that an alternative form is appropriate to its particular purpose. (I have already made reference to my own unconventionally structured work in Chapter 5.) This puts me in the camp of those who use new literary forms as a liberating alternative to the standard academic textual form, rather than as a direct critique of a non-reflexive sociology; a topic I will return to.

The Mirror Dance: Identity in a Women's Community by Susan Krieger (1983) was written before the SSK project became well established, and it does not clearly fall into either the SSK or the 'liberatory' camp. Nevertheless, Krieger's sociological researches are conceived, structured and presented in an unconventional manner. In the preface, she explains the book's origins. She participated as a member of a lesbian community while spending a year as a visiting assistant professor of sociology at an American university in a Midwestern town. At the same time, she made the community the topic of a sociological research project. However, when she subsequently came to order her research notes, she realised she was unhappy, and unclear, about the process of 'doing' sociology. This partly stemmed from her disinclination, indeed inability, to separate her personal involvement with the community (and feelings of ambivalence towards it) from her professional approach as a sociologist to the research project. But it also reflected her desire to treat her data in a more imaginative fashion than was customary in sociological accounts. After all, as she points out, presenting a hypothesis in social science involves the use of imagination; and since imagination does intervene between data and theorising, there is a case to be made that this should be brought into the open, rather than concealed.

Ultimately, then, she rejected a conventional sociological presentation, which would have forced a separation between the personal and the sociological, while it would also have entailed suppressing overtly imaginative writing. She began to construct the chapters of her book not as a linear

---

8 The *Observer* Colour Supplement once featured an article called 'The Art of Body Maintenance'. In it was a histogram depicting male deaths according to age-groups, with each bar in a different bright colour. Female deaths were shown as black shadows, behind them.

account but as a series of layers, to be read in any order. Each one gives a different vantage-point on the community, showing a different facet of it, and telling a different story about it which is basically true to her experience. She explains that this layering format allows her to be faithful to an interpretative whole whose construction of reality could not be realised either by an ethnographic or a heavily theory-informed approach; and she comments that the worlds we describe in social science too often reflect a limited set of currently fashionable theoretical views.

She says that in the process of writing up the research experience, she consciously avoided the use of the authorial voice, and absented herself as narrator. Instead, she saw herself as the orchestrator of the women's voices: 'I was "painting a picture" this time, and a modern abstraction at that, rather than "telling a story" as I had done before' (Krieger 1983: 191). This analogy with the visual, with painting, and indeed with a non-figurative painting,[9] is a fine example of a sociologist making use of a visual metaphor. It suggests to me that in the construction of non-linear composite accounts, the visual is never far away. *Health and Efficiency* (Ashmore, Mulkay and Pinch 1989) is another layered account; and one of its co-authors, Michael Mulkay, described it to me as a series of overlapping snapshots. A figurative image (such as a snapshot) suggests a context, and presents one moment and a particular view of it; whereas a series of overlapping figurative images allows a number of different views of that context within a limited timespan. And when the emphasis is on structure rather than on subject matter – as it is in the present context – the topic can indeed be expressed *as* a formal abstract spatial analysis. The Systematic Constructive artists, with whom I work, produce paintings whose purpose is to explore and accomplish formal visual analysis. In our exhibition *Countervail* (1992–3), my own visual contribution was geometrically structured in such a way as to show the eight women members as equal constituents of the Countervail Collective (see Figure 30). This reflects *their* (and my) concern with structure, while each of the eight strips is a documentary fragment from my daily visual diary.

Krieger explains that *The Private Worlds of Dying Children* by Myra Bluebond-Langner (1978) was one of the works which influenced her decision to adopt an unconventional textual form. Bluebond-Langner had spent time as a research sociologist in a hospital for terminally ill children. In the appendix to her account she observes that her original conventional approach to her 'data' did not quite survive her subsequent involvement with the participants. This was because:

> The children came to expect and even to demand my presence on various occasions, and became extremely angry if I could not be there when they wanted me. Although I was different things to different children, I was a definite part of

9 The work of Malcolm Hughes, in Figure 1, is also abstract; and, in addition, the concept of layering directly informs both pieces illustrated (a and b). Hughes has long been interested in layering, and recent work involves multiple computer plotting.

THE COUNTERVAIL COLLECTIVE

Figure 30 Elizabeth Chaplin. *The Countervail Collective.* Montage of photographs; 18.5 × 13.3 cms

their world of dying children. Of all the nonfamily persons, I was the only one who was always there, in a variety of situations, places, and roles.

(Bluebond-Langner 1978: 147)

Nevertheless, all but one of the chapters of her account are couched in fairly conventional academic form. But she breaks with the constraints of this form at one stage, in order to bring the participants into the text and play down her own authorial role. Chapter 2 is a play, entitled 'The World of Jeffrey Andrews'. She explains in Chapter 1 that first she wrote a play for each child from her notes. Then she assembled the plays to form the composite play, often creating a single character from two different children. Being terminally ill – living with dying – is an extended process, and the acts reflect the length of the various aspects of the disease. The longest act, Act IV, deals with a series of relapses and remissions, as this is the longest aspect of the process in actual time and the patients' view. Act V, the death, is the shortest. Each act represents a particular stage in the process; and each stage is discussed from a more theoretical perspective in another chapter.

Again, the structure of the play, in terms of the lengths of the acts, could have been represented visually, and another abstract painting made. Neither Krieger's nor Bluebond-Langner's work involving new literary forms makes use of depictions, although as women, both might have considered an alternative to the privileged discourse of the verbal. However,

Bluebond-Langner's chapter in play format transforms the world of dying children into an acutely visual experience for the reader. You can *see* the hospital wards, and the activities of the children, the parents, the nurses and the doctors in your mind's eye. It is a very moving experience. Sociological understanding, in this case, has a pronounced visual dimension to it.

Performance Science – text by sociologists Michal McCall and Howard Becker, stage direction by Paul Meshejian of the People's Light and Theatre Company (1990) – is a more recent multi-vocal work. Like 'The World of Jeffrey Andrews', it is in play format, though it was originally performed live by McCall and Becker, and the 'performance mode' is itself the object of the authors' attention. Since I did not attend the performance, I am instead obliged to read the script as a 'paper' (*Social Problems*, 1990, 37, 1). During the course of their dialogue, McCall explains that they are using the performance mode to present the results of fieldwork research on the social organisation of professional theatre in the United States. Thus, 'Performance Science' has in common with '"Fury over prof's kidney call"' that the textual form of the piece is the same as that used by the community being investigated by the sociologists. However, McCall and Becker suggest that the performance mode can be beneficially applied to a wide variety of research topics, that it has many advantages over the conventional academic textual form and that, moreover, it is fun. 'Performance Science' therefore represents the genre of new literary form designed to liberate authors and their data from the constraints of standard academic convention.

Although both Krieger and Bluebond-Langner use unusual textual forms to present their research findings, discussion of textual form, *per se*, takes place only in the introductions and appendices of their accounts. Almost a decade later, McCall and Becker put discussion of textual form centre-stage; and furthermore they enact this discussion. They explain that although their performances in the past have focused on the presentation of research data, this one is about performance science itself, and not about the theatre. During the performance, they discuss the history of their project, including previous performances of it. This allows them to bring out and demonstrate features of the performance mode itself, and to compare these with the constraints imposed on authors of conventional academic papers. As a result, the dialogue is notably self-conscious and inevitably somewhat introspective. In a final exchange, they rehearse the advantages of the performance mode:

> HOWIE: . . . Performance formats ought to make everyone realise – it made us see it – how much we take for granted when we write or read or hear conventional scholarly papers.
> MICHAL: The omniscient analyst.
> HOWIE: The dominance of the analytic voice.

MICHAL: Ignoring the richness of mood and emotion.
HOWIE: Hiding the facts of fieldwork.
MICHAL: Being alienated from our own work.
HOWIE: Since we are always editing reality, we might as well experiment.
(*They look at each other, walk to the center of the stage, join hands, and bow.*)

(McCall and Becker 1990: 132)

The stage directions play a central role in 'Performance Science'. These are closely keyed into the script and are very precise in their instructions to the performers. But, by the same token, they also instruct the reader. They allow us to *visualise* what is going on. They induce a clear mental view of the sequence of contextualised interactions. In this way, they give an extra layer of meaning to each utterance and action. We picture HOWIE and MICHAL moving around, picking up chairs, placing them elsewhere, looking at each other, looking away. We can envisage them talking to the audience, reading lines, exchanging views as they adopt various positions on the stage. In one of these exchanges, the performers note that audiences more or less automatically look to their left, perhaps because we read from left to right; and that consequently the performer on the right (stage-left) is in a relatively weak position. This is analogous to the use of bold and weak type to denote an uneven power relationship. Indeed, Becker notes that one of the problems with a live performance is that there are no typographical conventions to shape the text; for example, there are no indentations to denote quoted material, and no headings to indicate new sections. He suggests that 'Maybe staging is the performance science analogue of typography' (McCall and Becker 1990: 123). While these remarks reinforce the fact that typography does structure and give meaning to a text, the *text* of *their* performance contains stage directions, which are also, of course, typographically signalled, as are the players' lines. This allows the reader to do visual work on several levels. The look of the page signals 'playscript', with all that this implies; the stage directions induce a mental image of the actors as they move around the actual stage; and the precise performance of each personal utterance encourages us to visualise what the performer is talking about. All in all, this produces a far more visual sociological experience than is to be had from reading a conventional academic paper.

'Talking Together: An Analytical Dialogue' by Michael Mulkay (1985) also investigates – and demonstrates – an alternative approach to empirical research. Excerpts from an exchange of letters between Mulkay (a social scientist) and Spencer (a natural scientist) are followed by the transcribed tape-recording of an informal dialogue between these two participants. Here the authors are just themselves – two 'real people' talking together, in contrast to the situation where a script is performed. Their topic of conversation is patterns of communication in science; and they focus particularly on the idea of replacing the customary adversarial mode of communication with a more sympathetic and personal dialogue between participants. Mulkay suggests that if neither party proceeded by attempting to knock down his 'opponent's' position in order to defend his own, but instead collaborated courteously, acknowledging personal responsibility for the interpretative work on which his own texts and his claims about the natural world depend, whilst at the same time attempting to understand how the other party arrives at different conclusions, then this would be far more likely to lead to the modification of claims, and the eventual resolution of disputes – to the advantage of both participants. Indeed, he argues that if argument by refutation were to be replaced by dialogue along these lines, a different kind of knowledge would result.[10] It would be incompatible with certain basic features of technical discourse – such as the single right answer 'dictated' by the 'experimental facts' – and would instead be presented as the author's own account, thus embodying the assumption that scientists interpret nature, and that they do so in different ways. However, Mulkay observes that this alternative procedure involves trusting the other party to do as you do: trusting that he will not take advantage of your disinclination to defend your own position – an advantage which he could then use to argue that his position is the superior one. And Mulkay notes that perhaps the adversarial method is so prevalent because defending your own position is the surest way of minimalising your own losses.

In their dialogue, Spencer and Mulkay themselves demonstrate some of the positive features of the personal dialogic form. Neither hesitates to hesitate, to ask the other's views, to say he doesn't know the answer, to change his mind during the course of the discussion, and to bring up important new topics during the course of the discussion. For example, at one point Mulkay reveals an interest in communication in the *social* sciences. The participants begin to try to distinguish the structure of the informal dialogue from other forms of communication, such as an exchange of letters, and the formal scientific paper. Spencer suggests that for personal dialogue between natural scientists, it is important to spend time together, to have good food and congenial surroundings. He also observes that a conversation may seem more fruitful in retrospect than at the time it takes place. Mulkay, the social scientist, tends to emphasise the importance of words. At one point, he says:

---

10 Hegel's method of exposition, dialectics, bears a resemblance to this approach. To put the procedure in an everyday context, it often happens that in a discussion two people who at first present diametrically opposed points of view ultimately agree to reject their own partial views and to accept a new and broader view that does justice to the substance of each. Hegel believed that thinking always proceeds according to this pattern: positive thesis, antithesis, synthesis.

[In sociology] you're studying subjects who themselves are users of words. My increasing concern has been to try to understand how the people I'm studying use words . . . regarded . . . by other sociologists as mere semantics. But it's through the use of words that people create the world around them, give meaning to it.

(Mulkay 1985: 128)

Now, although verbal discourse *is* centrally important in social science, such an emphasis may lead to non-verbal factors – including visual ones – being ignored. And visual communication plays a significant part in the accomplishment of a successful cooperative project, as Spencer's remark about 'congenial surroundings' begins to suggest. Visual communication is intregrally implicated in the 'Talking Together' project. First, we are led to understand that it was a controversy between some biochemists which triggered the dialogue between Mulkay and Spencer in the first place; and that controversy would most probably have involved competing visual perceptions of nature. Second, the spoken collaborative dialogue, which Spencer and Mulkay both discuss and demonstrate, is interlaced with non-verbal communication. Third, as always, the look of the material page, which is what the reader has to go on, gives off specific signals.

To return to the first level: the subject matter of natural science is not originally verbal. And in Chapter 4, I indicated, with the help of a quotation from Einstein, that the initial processes in scientific problem-solving are often visual. Lynch (1990) shows how the various consecutive stages of scientific work transform raw, messy data into a more manageable set of figures, diagrams and text. Now, in the case of a disagreement between two or more biochemists, this may eventually involve competing verbal, diagrammatic or numerical formulations, but it will have originated in differing interpretations of natural scientific data, or in differing interpretations of visual representations of natural scientific data; that is to say, in differing visual perceptions, which in a linked interpretative process are transposed into verbal or diagrammatic form. Admittedly, social science is not like this. Social scientists focus on patterns of relationships between people whose principal mode of communication is verbal, as Mulkay emphasises. Yet to attend exclusively to verbal patterns of communication is to ignore other social factors, i.e. non-verbal communication and the physical context (the equivalent of the laboratory setting in natural science) which inform participants' talk. This surely bears on the distinction which anti-positivists like Mulkay make between the positivist and the post-positivist account. They emphasise that the positivist account uses *textual* strategies which make its author's knowledge claims appear impersonal, objective and true, while the anti-positivist account indicates the crucial part played by *social context* in accounting for varying interpretations of data. Verbal communication does not take place in a vacuum: it takes place in a social context which cannot be entirely verbal. Indeed, photographs show how visually rich and complex are the contexts in which verbal communication takes place.

This brings us to the second level: the character of personal dialogue itself. This form of communication, favoured by the authors of 'Talking Together', involves non-verbal communication, like smiling and physical proximity, as well as physical context. These non-verbal features surely account for much of what Mulkay terms the *ad hoc* nature of verbal dialogue – whether this be a social science conversation or one that social scientists may analyse. Non-verbal features continually intrude into conversation, helping to shape its characteristic pattern. The feminist methodological stance, which also advocates working *with* and *for* participants, rather than on them, also favours informal collaborative dialogue. My project *with* the Systematic Constructive artists involved learning to live their lives, and was admittedly a special case since they often communicate at the visual level, that is, through the production of art works in response to other art works. But no feminist research is just a matter of talk and text[11] (and even if it were, non-verbal and other contextual factors would always intrude themselves). Working with and for others tends to involve taking on a practical project together, in order to achieve change in the real world. This means that what you see and do are to the fore. I would suggest that the intrusion of non-verbal elements into the social situation constitutes one of the factors contributing to feminists' dissatisfaction with conventional forms of presenting their research.

At a third level, the *reader* is presented with an account laid out over consecutive pages of a book. In 'Talking Together', the look of the page differs slightly from that of a conventional social science text since a conversation is signalled: a block of text attributed to one speaker is followed by a gap and then by another block attributed to the other speaker; rather like in a play, but without the stage directions. At the least, this indicates that textual form is at issue. Further than this, the utterances are grouped according to who is speaking. Thus, ideas are personalised, which in turn persuades the reader to imagine the visual context in which they are uttered. In addition, each participant is signalled by the same typographical convention – *S* or *M*; and each participant's speech is displayed in the same typeface. This visually reinforces the equal, indeed shared, status of the participants.

'Talking Together' is associated with the SSK school of thought. It critiques positivist methodology, arguing that the social character of science – which is clearly displayed in transcripts of informal dialogue – should not be suppressed. Instead, it suggests that dialogue should be developed as a textual form, and investigated for the positive advantages it has to offer research participants. *Knowledge and Reflexivity: New Frontiers in the Sociology*

---

11 See Klein (1983: 88–104).

of Knowledge (Woolgar 1988) is a collection of essays about new literary forms which explore, demonstrate and in some cases *celebrate* the social and therefore reflexive character of sociological and anthropological analysis. In the second of these essays, 'Reflexivity is the Ethnographer of the Text', Woolgar discusses the strategies deployed in conventional anthropological accounts. He notes, for example, that such accounts 'exoticise' the world of the 'natives', and thus differentiate it from the 'normal' world of the 'researcher'. He also remarks that they frequently draw on the 'formidable authority' of photographs; formidable, because their captions enhance the idea of an objective world from which are chosen items for our consideration, while they purport merely to direct our attention to a pre-existing feature of the complex reality revealed by the frame. Woolgar argues that such strategies are textual accomplishments which buttress the anthropological account against reflexivity, privileging its status and giving its author control over his/her object of study. The social character of anthropological and sociological analyses is thus effectively disguised; and the fact that such analyses have the same epistemological status as the representations produced by their objects of study (although having a quite different aim and purpose) is concealed. Woolgar argues that reflexive texts should convey that sense of sameness deriving from the social character of both worlds; and that the analyst can attempt to achieve this by injecting uncertainty into his or her own account. That is to say, a continual questioning of his or her authority will reflect and sustain the uncertainty which always exists in the early stages of ethnographic inquiry, and should have the effect of making the methods adopted by social scientists seem less distinctively privileged.

This sense of uncertainty is undoubtedly achieved in the sixth essay in this collection: 'Accounting for Accounts of the Diagnosis of Multiple Sclerosis' by Anna Wynne (1988). Again, the account is multivocal, but in this case the two voices are both the author's own, though they are not named. One of these voices – the first – gives a straight account of her empirical project. Its overall purpose is to discover how lay people, or non-scientists, conceive of scientific knowledge as compared with common sense knowledge. The first voice explains that the non-scientists in her study are twelve people suffering from multiple sclerosis (MS), a disease which 'remains intensely difficult to establish with certainty' (Wynne 1988: 101); and that her empirical project involved interviewing each of the twelve, after diagnosis had finally been confirmed. This first-voice account draws on, quotes and analyses sections of the interview material which are concerned with the process of achieving a diagnosis of MS; for Wynne is trying to establish what counts for these sufferers as a correct as opposed to an incorrect diagnosis. Is a 'correct diagnosis' based on an idea of 'science' as the epitome of truth? Do lay people, in fact, accord scientific knowledge overwhelming legitimacy? For if they do, this would help to explain the commonly held belief that we live in a scientific age.

The 'second' voice is, in effect, an alter ego. While it does not 'talk' directly with the first voice, it weaves in and out of the first-voice account, articulating the analyst's doubts and anxieties about the implications of arguments and the accuracy of statements made in that account. The second voice thus brings up issues which might otherwise have remained hidden or been treated as unimportant. It raises to the surface many of the factors that seem essential to the integrity of the project, and yet are suppressed or distorted during the process of translation from the 'field' to the text – and, as a result, often produce a condition of self-doubt for the researcher which can be very debilitating. The second voice not only articulates these worries but talks them through from the point of view of an analyst whose 'theoretical auspices are an epistemological scepticism'. Sometimes this process ends in sheer bewilderment: 'Is it possible to say anything? What cannot be said?' (Wynne 1988: 113).

The relationship between the two voices is discussed in the short 'Reflexion on Wynne' which follows her account. The discussant concludes that these are better construed as one voice operating in two modes. This conclusion is strengthened by the fact that 'by contrast with what we shall see in Pinch and Pinch (see pp. 266–7 of this book), the "voices" are not differently weighted in their typescript' (Woolgar 1988: 123). Here is a clear example of the fact that typography contributes to the structure and semantic content of an analysis; for the discussant is obliged to attend to the typescript in order to try to establish the precise character of the relationship between the two voices, as part of his/her 'reflexion' on the piece. So how, exactly, is typography used to represent that relationship?

Figure 31 shows that the first voice is in conventional type (approximating to *Times 327*), indicating a 'standard' account. First-voice quotations are in smaller conventional type, and the names of people quoted are in italics of the same small-sized conventional type. This conforms with standard typographical procedure. In other words, the typography used to denote the first voice constituent parts conveys no special message. The second voice is typographically differentiated from the first by the use of a 'plainer' (*Optima*) sanserif type. The letters are very slightly smaller than those used to represent the first voice. This, in combination with the semantic content of the words themselves, gives the impression of a quietly persistent alter ego. However, second-voice quotations are in the *same*-sized plain sanserif typeface, with participants' names in plain italics. This appears to signal that the second voice and its quotations are *equal* in status (unlike the relationship between the first voice and *its* quotations). Endnotes are all in small conventional type, whether they refer to the first-voice text or to the second. Headings throughout the piece are in conventional first-voice type, though bold, and are always followed by passages in the first voice. This presumably indicates that the first voice/straight account dominates, since 'its' headings punctuate and overtly structure the piece. But while the conclusion (heading in bold conventional type) is commenced by the first voice, it is followed by a passage in the second voice, giving this the last word.

Whether the relationship between the first voice and its quotations is meant to be different from the relationship between the second voice and *its* quotations – as implied in the typescript – seems unclear. And what conclusion we may draw from the fact that the endnotes are all in small conventional type, regardless of whether they relate to the first voice text or the second, is not clear either. Drawing attention to such features may seem like carping about insignificant details, but it is not. SSKers rightly pay attention to typography since they want to emphasise that the medium is an integral part of the social science message, and is not merely the neutral means by which the message gets conveyed. In Wynne's essay, some of the distinctions between the typescripts are obviously intended; whereas others *may* be unintentional. If this is the case, then there are places in the text where conventional typographical practice is re-asserted. That is to say, there are places where the typeface temporarily poses as a passive vehicle for the conveyance of a message, giving the impression that it is not part of that message.

Yet the adoption of an inconsistent typographical format might be intentional. Wynne has perhaps used this as a way of injecting uncertainty into the text. She has certainly been successful in raising my doubts about its status. But on the other hand, the second voice is so questioning of everything the first voice takes for granted, and of the utterances that it makes, that we might have expected the second voice to discuss the reasons for the selection of the different typefaces. So is the uncertain status of the typographical schema in fact intended? And, if so, are this and a reflexively sound text compatible?

At one point, Wynne's second voice is concerned that data from the field are very seductive: the talk of others has the feel of the stuff of life, with the result that we, as researchers, tend to take this to be a document of reality, and to think that our analysis of it is engaging with the 'real world' outside the talk about it. The second voice goes on to argue that this is not so, and that we ourselves reflexively construct reality from what we take to be the documents of it, such as the talk of others! This means, as the 'Reflexion on Wynne' points out, that Wynne's reflective voice constitutes its *own* troubles, as opposed to pinpointing troubles which enjoy an objective pre-existence. The typographical distinctions which help to structure her script, and which were not there in the talk of others and of herself, clearly constitute a whole dimension of trouble. They draw our attention to one of the differences between the character of talk and the character of typescript, and constitute a reason why typescript can never directly refer to the 'document' of talk, let alone to the stuff of life to which that talk refers.

The second voice also speculates on what else there is besides talk which we may take to be documents of others.

remains fundamentally problematic. For the in-principle indexicality of documents (here, extracts of talk) is (only?) managed in practice through reference to context; context and extract reflexively producing meaning through their juxtaposition (Garfinkel, 1967). Extracts divorced from the contexts in which they originated and inserted into another – the context of my analysis – would seem to be particularly vulnerable to a radical distortion of their original meaning.

But to make this objection is to propose that they have *an* original meaning which is fixable – even if fleetingly and reflexively-tied-to-context; that there is, potentially, a crucial difference in meaning between the same words in their original context and in another.

Taking each quotation from its original site in each person's whole talk and re-placing it together with others in a common context – the context of analyst's topic – facilitates the interpretation that the quotations are, singly and together, about the topic: going to the doctor, for example.

But the in-principle flexibility of reinterpretation is not unlimited. For it would be difficult to select just any quotation and, by the same process of recontextualization, make it work as relevant to *any* (analyst's) topic. For example the extract:

> Meg: I do respond to cortisone very well so that I suppose my own sort of peculiar psychological defence is that every time I get it I'm going to have cortisone, I'm going to get better.

would not work as a convincing account of 'going to the doctor'. Why not?

One way for an analyst to discern what may be a noticeable absence (here the absence of reasons provided for going to the doctor) is through comparison with similar yet different instances. Patients referred in other parts of their talk to alternative medical practitioners, for example acupuncturists and faith healers. Was a different kind of account provided for going to these alternative resources?

The greater complexity of the accounting practices concerning recourse to 'alternative medicine' both requires and is demonstrated by the necessity for longer quotations from the data.

> George: Someone said try faith healing, I tried him and he did nothing. Mind you I had no faith in anything before I went so you know . . . and basically being scientifically-minded myself, I think that's the way it's [a cure] going to come . . . I went to an acupuncturist, not an acupuncturist, a faith healer. He moved me around and asked me you know he sort of twisted me in various directions and said what was the major problem and I told him and he said, sounds to me like MS. *Oh*, he was the one, thinking back now . . . yeah I think in the meantime I had decided that's what I had.
> AW: So you'd seen the television programme?
> George: I'd seen the television programme, *then* I went to him and he really confirmed my beliefs.

Figure 31 Double-page spread from 'Accounting for Accounts of the Diagnosis of Multiple Sclerosis' by Anna Wynne: *Knowledge and Reflexivity* (S. Woolgar, ed., 1988), pp. 106–7

Meg: From my own point of view the *most* difficult thing about having an illness
like this is that everybody has a cure for you [...] all of which sound fine
but if you, I mean if you can picture a situation where you've come out of
hospital, you're feeling fairly shattered, you you're not you definitely don't
feel as strong as you used to feel and you get this *barrage* of advice and you
must try my osteopath, you must try my this and and [...] and 'a' you find
it difficult to resist it but 'b', which is much worse, is that – now now whether
this is sort of conjectural or whether this is true, but I was left feeling that
if you don't do it, then it's your fault that you're so ill [*laughs*]. So I went
through a stage where I just thought, well, I had nothing to lose...
AW: Mm and how did that end then?
Meg: Oh well because I was talking to my neurologist about it and I said that
I found this quite a pressure and he said well fine, he said, well look, he said,
if you come across a faith healer or a homeopath or anybody else who can
cure this *please* ask them to get in touch with me because believe me, he said,
I'll go along with *anybody* who can cure you. And so then when people sort
of wanted to do things I just ask them if they would mind talking to my
neurologist, and that sort of stopped it all.

Meg provides an elaborate account for her resort to alternative medicine
– the grounds of social pressure from others combined with her initial
vulnerability to such pressures. By contrast, talking to her neurologist
appears the normal thing to do and requires no explanation. By appealing
to 'proper' medicine, she eventually managed to resist the pressure. Even
though her neurologist was clearly prepared to listen to any genuine alternative ('*any*body who can cure you') Meg implied that the people who
had pestered her were too afraid that their alternatives would not stand
up to scientific scrutiny to take up his eminently open-minded offer. The
implication is that should alternative medicine be endorsed by 'proper
medical knowledge' then Meg, like her neurologist, would have accepted
it; but it was unlikely. Real medicine is the natural and final arbiter.

The data also included an account of why an individual did *not* go to
alternative medicine:

Daniel: Yes the whole thing with that [the 'laying on of hands'] is you believe
in it. It may well have an effect for people who believe that whatever charlatan
offers them something is going to work. Maybe it will. But since I think they're
charlatans I'm not going to accept that they might work, and therefore they
won't work for me. Which leaves me a rationalist loser in an irrational
environment.

For both Daniel and George (quoted earlier), the efficacy of alternative
medicine depends on a person's belief in its power. They both invoke
'science' as the reason for their own lack of such belief. George's comment
suggests that being 'scientifically minded' is just one of his personal quirks,
a personal rather than a universal faith. Certain treatments are not considered either credible or effective because they are grounded in an alternative knowledge (not-science). It is not that he regards science as an

> The people on tape seem real because we are practised in the deduction of what people are from their talk, but there may be other documents too – bodies, gestures, smells, textures – but no medium that is any more direct; no way unmediated.
>
> (Wynne 1988: 115)

We can also, surely, become practised in the deduction of what people are from their appearance, their gestures and the character of the context in which we view them; and we can make our own visual documents, by photographing and filming them. But indeed, no document can *be* direct; there is 'no way unmediated', as this examination of typographical usage suggests. Figure 32 shows an art work by Jonathan Barnbrook and Tomoko Yoneda, from their series entitled 'Technology and Morality' (exhibited in *The Big Apple*).[12] It shows some oddly juxtaposed yet familiar messages, each one of which is laid out in an unfamiliar fashion across the centre of an 'old book', in a typescript which in several cases is notably idiosyncratic. This produces a conflict of meanings which emphasises that the medium through which an account is conveyed is *chosen*, even *constructed*, such that it shapes and enhances the message that the author intends. This art work serves to emphasise that a thorough sociological analysis of any printed message cannot discount the contribution made by typography and layout to its social character.

Wynne's text, like those of Krieger and Bluebond-Langner, is deeply serious, sensitive and somewhat hesitant in its discussion of methodology. I note that these authors are all women; and suggest that SSK authors who are men tend to display other qualities, notably panache and a certain jokiness. There is plenty of panache about Michael Mulkay's 'Looking backward (1989)' in his *Sociology of Science: A Sociological Pilgrimage* (1991b). This text purports to be a transcription made by the author of a tape which has recently come into his possession. In his introductory paragraph, Mulkay claims to have been 'given conclusive proof that it is genuine' (Mulkay 1991b: 204). He notes that on the original tape there is background noise and evidence of a live audience at some kind of academic conference, but that the transcription is of the voice of the main speaker, who is female. He believes it deserves a wide distribution.

Through the mouth of this imaginary female academic, and from the ninety-ninth year of the New Era (apparently more than a century hence), Mulkay then proceeds to tell the 'herstory' of the rise and fall of the bad old days of scientific–technological society, the 'discourteous' extended mono-logue which it favoured, and the subsequent transition to the New Era of women's dialogic discourse and multivocal accounts. The typography and layout of the text are standard. This is entirely justified since, as Mulkay explains in the Preface to *Sociology of Science*, the speaker's monologue

---

12 The series was first shown at the Zelda Cheatle Gallery (1992), and subsequently at The Studio, Beckenham, Kent (1993).

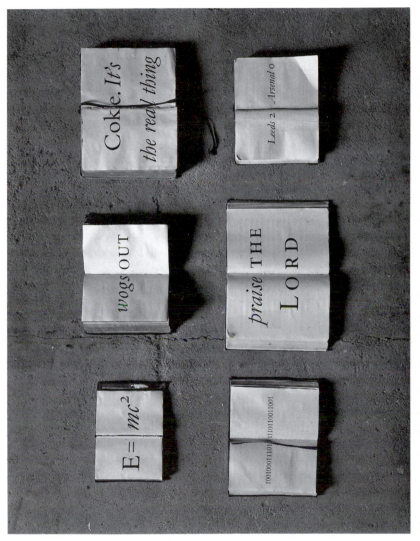

Figure 32 Jonathan Barnbrook and Tomoko Yoneda. Computer realisation from the series, 'Technology and Morality', exhibited in *The Big Apple*, 1993

speech is intended to demonstrate the 'now unfamiliar' unitary, anonymous, authorial voice which was customarily used in that scientific–technological society. The piece therefore comprises an ironic parody-as-critique, in which the author demonstrates, yet ultimately distances him/herself from, the monologic form. And it also indicates how Mulkay has extended new literary forms from the 'simple, multi-voice texts with which nlf's began' (Mulkay 1991a: xviii). However, there is an additional irony in the fact that the monologue, for which the author 'apologises', nevertheless provides him with a convenient opportunity to lay out an extended and linked set of ideas and arguments without having to attend to the tiresome methodological requirement of introducing other voices, which would presumably have questioned the coherence and comprehensiveness of the arguments, or at the very least diverted the monologic flow.

Towards the end of this monologue, the author links new literary forms with the women's movement. S/he says that its members eventually came to realise that both women and Nature had been exploited by men. They saw that just as the technical language of science had been used to exploit Nature, ordinary everyday language had been used to dominate and exploit women. Thus from the viewpoint of the women's movement ('which gave birth to the New Era') language is at the root of what went wrong. This is certainly a crucial point; but because it is being put by a man who himself impersonates a woman, a further irony is introduced. Leaving this particular irony aside for the moment, and stepping back out of Mulkay's fictional construction – though staying with the topic he has raised – I would draw attention to the observation, made by Lynch and Woolgar (1990: viii), that in science privilege has traditionally been assigned to the verbal statement or 'proposition'. In the same vein, Anna Wynne has noted that we are practised in the deduction of what people are from their talk, and that therefore this talk seduces us into thinking it *is* reality. Maybe the fact that we are practised in this way and tend to think that talk is reality is connected to the fact that patriarchy itself has been so seductive. Indeed, there is the suggestion in the work of some feminists that since language itself is a predominantly male construct, women's beliefs – and those of other minority groups whose cultures are 'muted'[13] – find authentic expression through ritual and art (Showalter 1981; Sulter 1989); while in a somewhat different context Lyotard (1984) argues that *all* verbal discourse is permeated by ideology, and that the potential for a truly radical critique lies with certain types of visual art practice. However, the fundamental problem for women and other minority groups is that they cannot step outside patriarchal society. While feminist dictionaries make us aware of the extent to which patriarchy creates standard English usage (the Queen's English?),[14] women cannot escape from the

---

13 Women are possibly the only majority (54 per cent of the population, 44 per cent of the workforce) to be classified as a minority.
14 For example, Kramarae and Treichler (1992).

primacy currently accorded to the verbal: indeed, they share the culture of the dominant group. This means that the idea of resorting to a purely visual form of communication is not realistic; and even if it were, its subordinate status would surely render it relatively ineffective – while reflecting and reinforcing the subordinate status of women themselves. Instead, women might explore gender-related, or gender-specific, ways of emphasising the visual aspects of and accompaniments to verbal language – unconventional layout, typography and imagery – which would thus help to shape the content and the structure of their work, setting it apart from conventional verbal texts and providing a position from which to critique them. *Typography Now: The Next Wave*, (Poynor and Booth-Clibborn 1991) contains examples of typography and layout which are suggestive for this project, although little work has yet been done in the specific area of gender.[15] But such a move should treat Mulkay's notion of 'New Era' discourse with circumspection. For, despite the scenario he outlines and anticipates, the women's movement has not yet gained precedence over our scientific–technological society, nor is there any guarantee that it will do so in future. To adopt new literary forms developed and advocated by SSKers like Mulkay is, yet again, to succumb to a man's programme of what women need.

And returning to 'Looking backward (1989)', I am uneasy about the fact that a man impersonating a woman, and invoking the women's movement, should be using this contrived situation, ultimately, to further his own career, even though this may in itself be devoted to furthering the careers of women. After all, Mulkay is credited with having written the book, despite his remark that publications in the formal literature demand an author – and thus he is obliged to put his name to this one.[16] Yet my unease is compounded by strong feelings of ambivalence, for Mulkay's preface to *Sociology of Science: A Sociological Pilgrimage* indicates that his underlying philosophy and methodology *are* close to those of many women colleagues. In the preface, he says that while he cannot condone the traditional form of sociology which privileges the author over the other participants, he nevertheless does not abandon the notion of sociological understanding itself; and in the quest for such understanding, he has 'come to use forms of analysis that move outside of science as it presently exists' (Mulkay 1991a: xviii). This surely describes the situation and encapsulates the attitudes of women who would be soci-

---

15 Such a project would, for example, at the very least have to combat the format, previously adopted in certain diagrams and graphs, that conveys information about men in black ink, bold type, or upper case; while showing comparative data relating to women in grey ink, weaker type or lower case (see Ardener 1986).

16 In the same vein, I would also criticise the final section of *Health and Efficiency*, where three different readings of the book are given from the perspectives of an economist, a sociologist and a lay person (Ashmore *et al.* 1989: 195–208). The layperson ('a textual device of the authors' making') is 'Mrs Jones'. How can male university academics know what it feels like to be lay person such as Mrs Jones? This section comes over as yet another instance of men patronising and manipulating women. Why not get a real woman to write this section? At least it would be more 'authentic', even if she didn't quite say what the authors wanted her to say.

ologists; except that they face the additional problem of finding a form of analysis which is generated by women's views of how they are structured into the social world – a form of analysis which seeks gender-informed sociological understanding.

The question of the authenticity of the voices in multivocal accounts is raised by Trevor Pinch and Trevor Pinch in the ninth essay in *Knowledge and Reflexivity* (Woolgar 1988.) This is called 'Reservations about Reflexivity and New Literary Forms or Why Let the Devil have All the Good Tunes?' . In 'their' opinion (and mine), when more than one voice is heard and each has equal rights, a kind of bogus democracy pervades the text and the voice behind the text is kept hidden. The text of 'Reservations about Reflexivity and New Literary Forms' is itself multivocal, but the two Pinches do not have equal rights. The typescript helps to construct this unequal relationship, and is rigorously consistent with the character of the relationship throughout. The 'senior' author's voice is in emphasised type, the 'junior' author's voice is in weak type, and the smaller type of the endnotes is either strong or weak, depending on which voice is being referenced. The complex interplay of typographical distinctions allows, or rather produces, a subtle exchange of messages between voices and endnotes. Despite typographical consistency, Pinch and Pinch also accomplish the SSK aim of injecting indeterminacy into their text. This is done by constructing the piece in such a way as to make the reader unsure of the Pinches' own relationship to the SSK school of thought. Its reflexively sound *form* leads us to surmise that this must be an 'internal' critique of the genre of multivocal text; yet the form in itself is flexible enough to allow arguments which, while compatible with it, subsequently persuade us that the Pinches come from outside the SSK camp. This flexibility derives from the unequal relationship which obtains between the two 'authors'. For towards the end of the piece, the senior author dispatches the junior author, thereby 'legitimately' altering the form; and this gives the senior author the opportunity to conduct an uninterrupted monologue, in which he summarises his views on new literary forms.

He says that they tend to irritate readers – and that their use can really only be justified if the text-as-a-whole works – that is, if the text doesn't get in the way of the reading of it. He observes that this is difficult to achieve because the argument must be more compelling in the unconventional form than in the conventional one; yet in cases where it is carried off, new literary forms are fun. He is not clear that they raise particularly important issues for sociology – they are a matter of the author's choice of style to suit the particular purpose at hand; furthermore, they can be used for other purposes in SSK than for displaying constitutive reflexivity. But his basic criticism, as indicated earlier, is that in multivoice texts which are used to stage a reflexive argument where the voices or authors deconstruct each other, the voice *behind* the text is kept hidden, and that therefore new literary forms do not serve the purpose of opening out the sociological text as a social process in itself. However, at the end of 'Reservations about Reflexivity and New Literary Forms', the junior author makes a brief, self-consciously jokey re-entrance into the text; and uncertainty is thereby re-injected into it.

The 'Reflexion on the Pinches', which follows, suggests that the text exemplifies some important and intriguing issues opened up by explorations in reflexivity. However, to the reader who is not fascinated with the intricacies of reflexivity to the exclusion of almost all else, it may seem that the social world *outside* is fast receding. This point is taken up by Bruno Latour in 'The Politics of Explanation: an Alternative', the eighth essay in *Knowledge and Reflexivity*. Latour criticises the SSKers' notion of reflexivity – their 'attempt to avoid a text being believed by its readers' – which he terms *meta*-reflexivity. While he agrees that social-science texts must draw attention to themselves as constructed texts, he argues for a quite different approach which deploys *infra*-reflexivity. I shall draw on Latour's ideas, as I do on those of the Pinches – in order to reinforce my own view that some serious objections can be made to SSK-generated new literary forms; while I nevertheless maintain that certain of these texts are important – not the least for their innovative use of the visual dimension. During the course of this section, I outline my understanding of the infrareflexive text, and compare some of its characteristics with features of a gender-specific project in social science – which I began to sketch earlier in this chapter.

Latour argues that meta-reflexive texts are ultimately no different from the less self-conscious texts they criticise, in that they are all talking about and thus transforming something else. From position A they seek to explain what happens in position B. Just as Malinowski explains what is going on in the Trobriand Islands, Woolgar explains what is going on in Stocking's account of Malinowski's account of the Trobriand Islanders; and photographs are no exception, since both text and photographs show things at a distance, and they both play with this distance. Yet, argues Latour, SSKers think that because of all the methodological precautions they build into their texts, their stories are somehow more than just stories. This means that 'in effect, they ignore the semiotic turn'. (That is to say, their texts, like those of the other story-tellers, are, from position A, transforming the meaning of B.) And in trying to reach the ultimate meta-level from which infra-languages can be evaluated, SSKers show that they share the same belief as the texts they criticise; which is that there is the possibility of a definitive way of representing 'over there' (position B) from 'here' (position A).

While I am reluctant to confront the issue of whether SSK-type new literary forms are basically flawed, I agree with Latour's observation that 'meta-reflexive' texts spend an enormous amount of energy on the side of the knowing and very little on the side of the known, and thus, as a genre, they could be said to have an inbuilt tendency towards sterility. In texts where this tendency is displayed in an acute form, and nothing very much about the outside world is said, I find it unacceptable;[17] as I do the inauthentic voices introduced into some of the multivocal texts. These represent my main reservations about SSK-related new literary forms. But some of these texts have important contributions to make. '"Fury over prof's kidney call"' makes exciting visual-sociological advances, as does Wynne's 'Accounting for Accounts of Multiple Sclerosis'. And these texts do not merely talk about their *own* talk, nor do they give off a kind of bogus democracy. Such texts can be loosely regrouped with those from the 'liberatory' genre which display similar positive features.

Latour sharply distinguishes the infra-reflexive text from a scientific explanation which 'merely' transforms the meaning of data into scientific terms, and from social scientific approaches, with their built-in methodological precautions. He explains that the infra-reflexive text 'just offers the lived world', as novelists do, and obtains its reflexivity from its style rather than from deploying any pre-conceived theoretical framework. The inevitable moving backwards and forwards between A and B is acknowledged by presenting the outside world to the reader in such a way that the text in itself becomes meaningful for the reader's own future course of action. Latour argues that this is what many of the Bible stories achieve. While Christ's parables do tell stories, the point is that they are told in such a way that the reader wants to re-create their meaning for his/her own life. However, infra-reflexive texts don't just tell parables; they use 'a multiplicity of genres' to explain the world: the novel, journalism, art, cartoon, philosophy, etc. Thus, as a whole, they obtain reflexivity by alerting the reader to the fact that there are many different, provisional, ways of representing the world; many different texts, and no privileged one. Latour argues that so much of the world is unknown, and that it needs to be 'brought to life'. Infra-reflexive texts tell of the fascinating detail of the world, and they draw attention to themselves by making what they say, in the ways that they say it, demonstrate their relevance for the reader's own future course of action. He or she thinks: here is a text I can use. The semiotic turn is thus acknowledged – and celebrated – in the many provisional meanings given to the world via a multiplicity of textual genres, and in the reader's deliberate transformation of such textual presentations into meaning for his/her own life.

It seems to me that some SSK new literary forms *do* achieve this kind of rapport with the reader. If we think of the particular multivoice device used in 'Accounting for Accounts of Multiple Sclerosis' as demonstrating a *style* of writing, rather than constituting a textual form generated from an SSK-derived stance, then this stylistic presentation of the content certainly

---

17 Latour compares the attitude of those who think social science can benefit from 'meta-reflexive' texts with 'the older idea that a sociological account full of statistics and methodological commitments can defend itself better than a '"plain" journalistic account' (Labour 1988: 169). I am, myself, vaguely reminded of some of the more 'abstract' work of the sociologist Talcott Parsons.

succeeds in making me identify with Wynne's dual-self, with the troubles generated by this literary form, with the problems associated with the original research project, and with the MS sufferers themselves. When I read that text, I begin to rethink my own life as a woman, as a sociologist and even as a potential sufferer from a disease which is difficult to diagnose. I want to know more because Wynne's way of writing makes what she says seem relevant for my future life.

Through their use of a multiplicity of textual genres, infra-reflexive texts ensure that disciplinary boundaries become blurred. Latour explains that such texts aim to cross over these boundaries: for if all we produced was work which formed a specific, distinct field of scholarship, then this would merely continue the process of convincing readers that A should be understood as B. Infra-reflexive texts also strive for equality with the discipline they study – and here, as with the idea of 'cross-over', Latour's vision is shared by many social scientists who are feminists: they strive to work *with* and *for* other women, rather than on them. For 'working on' merely generates material to be brought back for colleagues 'in the department' and added to the existing corpus of social science knowledge. Such women aim to work on joint projects which benefit as many other women as possible. Indeed, Latour's outline of an infra-reflexive text might be criticised on the grounds that ultimately he seems to be arguing for the type of sociological understanding which many feminists and other sociologists (for example, C. Wright Mills, 1959) strive to produce anyway. For example, one of the principal aims of a feminist social science text is to encourage women readers to use it to reinterpret and change their own lives. Yet *because* of this affinity with a feminist viewpoint, Latour's arguments and his concept of an infra-reflexive text provide a useful theoretical basis from which I shall eventually explore the idea of feminist texts which cross-over between visual and verbal domains.

However, at this point I want to return to Woolgar's 'Reflexivity is the Ethnographer of the Text' (Woolgar 1988) which was referred to earlier in the chapter. This essay may explain non-reflexive ethnographic texts in the same way that – semiotically speaking – those texts explain the exotic world of the natives. Nevertheless, Woolgar's text differs from those others in that he shows how ethnographers – including deconstructionists of earlier ethnographic studies – have used photographs to increase the authority of their texts. I have maintained that depictions cannot be considered as subsidiary to the verbal text. 'Reflexivity is the Ethnographer of the Text' makes an important contribution to this stance by showing very clearly the hidden semiotic work that is accomplished in the interplay between picture, frame, caption and text. In so doing, it has relevance for authors who would construct infra-reflexive texts which cross over between visual and verbal domains, as I shall show.

Woolgar suggests that anthropologists' photographs are used to convey pre-existing facts about the world, and that the frame enhances the credibility of the photograph. For the effect of the frame is to suggest that the depicted-object world continues on beyond its boundaries. It hints that if the frame were shifted, we would see more of the same. Photograph and frame conspire to persuade us to see the visible part as standing for the whole; to see it at once as part of a pre-existing reality which stretches on and on, coherently   and comprehensively. The caption further enhances this credibility-package, for it directs our attention to an item in that object world, while appearing to be neutral information of a different order from the photograph itself. Yet the image is given meaning by the caption while the caption draws on what is 'evident from' the image – in a mutually sustaining process of cross-reference. Finally, the verbal text creates distance between itself and this package of linked textual elements, by appearing to consist of yet another adjacent textual source. But it gives meaning to the captioned image at the same time as the latter, by the manner in which it has been crafted and orientated, reinforces the textual argument. In fact, when 'competently' used, the photograph/frame/caption/text package virtually disguises the fact that the text *is* a constructed text. Its arguments seem to enter our heads as reality; whereas the elements of photograph, frame, caption and text are in fact deeply implicated in one another, having been carefully crafted together by the author.

Infra-reflexive texts that cross over 'discipline areas' which deploy visual representation cannot comply with this conspiracy, this complex package of semiotic interplay between photograph, frame, caption and text. For if they did comply with it, the reader would be presented with an authoritative text whose arguments were strengthened by 'empirical evidence' – by illustrations of items in a 'pre-existing world'. The status of the text as one of a multiplicity of temporary explanations would thus be disguised; and its character *as* text would be hidden from readers, so that they might not think to create its meaning for their own lives. In other words, the text would not be reflexive: the picture/frame/caption/text relationship would be a positivist package. Yet once deconstructed, the photograph/frame/caption/text package can be reassembled differently.

And this project is well worth pursuing, for photographs are an excellent means of conveying the extraordinary detail of our world, as we saw in Chapter 5. In 'Reflexivity is the Ethnographer of the Text', Woolgar provides an SSK solution to the problem of producing a captioned, framed photograph which is at the same time reflexive. His text includes a photograph of himself, seated at a desk, writing a caption for that same photograph. (Shown on his desk are another copy of the photograph, some typed sheets of paper which are presumably the script of 'Reflexivity is the Ethnographer of the Text' and a copy of the book – *Knowledge and Reflexivity* – to which it forms a contribution.) The photograph is captioned: 'The author devising a caption for this photograph'. This certainly shows that SSK-derived nlfs concentrate on the knowing, while what it tells us about the world is limited by its theoretical frame of reference.[18] By contrast, an infra-reflexive text which makes active use of visual material depicts the world outside, and gains its reflexivity in other ways.

For example, if the 'caption' is superimposed *on* the image (as in Burgin's 'St Laurent demands a whole new lifestyle' [Figure 5]) rather than being placed underneath it in the conventional manner, readers are alerted to its *presence* and must speculate about its *function* in relation to the image. In effect, they are invited to treat the package more as a work of art, and to make their own interpretations of it.[19] There is indeed a marked contrast between the conventionally captioned, textually integrated photograph or diagram, which works well for positivists, and the unconventionally captioned image. For the latter tends to promote speculation, to suggest a range of interpretations, rather than to implant a feeling of certainty about what is depicted.

The frame–picture relationship can also be brought into question. Again, we may learn from visual art, for certain artists have been preoccupied with the function of the frame. For example, from 1887 onwards, Seurat would sometimes paint the frame surrounding a canvas using the same pointillist technique that he used on the canvas itself; so that the coloured dots continued from the depiction outwards to the edge of the frame. However, the dots on the frame are often in the same combination of colours all the way round, thus emphasising the framing function. This occurs in *The Eiffel Tower* (1889). Yet in that painting, the green, red and yellow dots round the frame merge with the foreground grass painted in the same combination of colours at the bottom of the picture, while they form a contrast with the blue and pink dots of the sky at the top. So Seurat makes us aware of the frame by giving it different functions in the same work, and by continually calling into question the distinction between frame and image.[20]

Finally, the relationship of the verbal text to the 'image package' (that is, the framed, captioned image) has to be rethought. Here we can learn from *Exploring Society Photographically* (Becker 1981), a work of social science whose unusually high-profile and high-status photographs disrupt the

---

18 I would argue that my own frontispiece to this book, which might seem rather similar to Woolgar's photograph, is actually quite different. In this particular and rather unusual situation, reflexivity is given by the presence of the author who is seen constructing the photograph. And although what is depicted of the world behind me is limited (computer, table, chair, wall, part of a plant, bottom part of a picture), I point my camera at you – and you can see me photographing each reader's world. I also draw attention to the semiotic work done by the 'frame' provided by the edges of the front of the book, by continuing the picture out beyond it – on to the spine and back cover (to the extent that Routledge 'house rules' will allow).

19 In the case of visual art works, titles and other accompanying verbal texts are often relatively open-ended and suggestive of a variety of interpretations, because visual artists want their work to be 'read' on several different levels.

20 Stephen Chaplin drew my attention to this dimension in some of Seurat's paintings.

conventional format of images-illustrating-the-text, and where some contributors use the early paragraphs of their verbal text to prepare us for the unconventional manner in which that text relates to the image-package in the rest of the piece.[21] In addition, the prominence of the photographs ensures that the page layout is unconventional. Though the contributors to *Exploring Society Photographically* are perhaps not particularly concerned with the ways in which typography can shape the meaning of a text, both non-standard typescript and unusual page layout also play a part in disrupting the conventional relationship between text and image-package.

In sum, an understanding of the ways in which image, frame, caption and text routinely conspire together to present an inevitability about the objective world allows us to re-order and reconstruct the relationship between these components, and thereby to contribute to the creation of an infra-reflexive text which crosses over between visual and verbal domains. *Balinese Character* (1942) corresponds with much that I have sketched out in the preceding paragraphs. It has many of the characteristics of an infra-reflexive text. In it, photographs, captions and verbal text are unconventionally related; and this relationship is discussed, thereby bringing the authors, the agents of representation, into the picture. Bateson describes the division of labour in which he took the photographs while Mead directed the process and simultaneously took notes on the content of each shot. He explains the process whereby a few of the thousands of photographs taken were selected for inclusion in the book. He draws attention to the way the photographs are arranged and grouped on the page, and accounts for the manner in which Mead's captions are laid out as a separate block on the facing page. He also explains the relationship of this predominantly visual part of the book to the more conventional written sections. All of this means that the work is presented as a *text* – which could have been otherwise. At the same time, *Balinese Character* portrays a world, and an ethos, which are very different from our own; and the *ways* in which this world is conveyed – for example, massed groups of photographs categorised according to various aspects of primary socialisation – encourage us to make comparisons with the ways in which we raise our children in the West.

This chapter has looked at the contribution made by the visual dimension to the structure of social science accounts. The visual dimension *always* makes a small contribution to such accounts, but in cases where a *new* structure, or

---

21 For example, Euan Duff says:

> The work became more personal and yet, I hoped, also more accessible to anyone wishing to look at it carefully. I thought about a text, about trying to explain to people what I was attempting to do, but realized that any linked text would interfere with the very photographic quality that I was trying to generate; so instead I wrote the following notes about the medium of photography itself.
>
> (Duff 1981: 74)

form of account is developed, visual changes are necessarily involved, and that contribution becomes more apparent. Typography, layout and depictions can be selectively deployed to help *create* the new structure. In the case of new *literary* forms, typography and layout can be made rigorously consistent with the character of the structure, so that they actually help to form it. At the same time, they visually shape the words and phrases which form the *content* of the piece. When the typescript and the manner in which that content is laid out are *unconventional,* the net effect is to help shape the *meaning* of that content. In other words, unconventional typescript and layout emphasise, enrich and make more subtle the essentially interactive relationship between structure and content. The semiotic work achieved by unconventional typography and layout would appear to be especially powerful in the case of SSK-derived new literary forms. For here the creative use of the visual dimension forms an integral part of a project generated from the methodological heart of sociology, since that project centres on the self-referential character of social science itself. However, there is a paradox – at any rate for me – in the fact that some SSK-derived new literary forms do not tell us much about the world; for this in turn makes their visual contribution seem less exciting. Yet if we think of such texts, not as a genre, but for the separate individual contributions that some of them offer, then these can be regrouped with the visually creative new literary forms whose purpose is the more general one of liberating an author from conventional academic constraints. In turn, a text within this broader group of nlfs can be regarded as exhibiting a distinctive *style.* Such a text is infra-reflexive when by its style it makes the reader see it as a text which has relevance for his or her own life, and when it crosses over other disciplines so as to produce knowledge for a wider range of participants. I would argue that some texts from within this broader group of new literary forms do achieve just that; and why I am particularly focusing on the idea of an infra-reflexive text is because this provides a theoretical basis from which to explore the cross-over between visual and verbal domains. And this *latter* project, in turn, has important implications for a gender-specific approach to sociological understanding. For although texts which cross over between visual and verbal are clearly not the preserve of minority groups, nevertheless, our dominant form of communication is verbal – or verbal-with-illustrations – and our dominant communicators are men. The idea of an unconventional text which crosses over between visual and verbal offers women the chance of exploring how typography, layout and depictions can be used in a gender-specific manner to structure the content of their work. Such a text would distance its author from the norm of male-dominated verbal discourse, would enable her to regard such normative texts with anthropological strangeness, and to critique them. Such a text aims to disperse authority between author(s), other participants in the project and readers; and to reach a wider audience of women and other feminists, or other minority group members.

But this is mere pie in the sky, I hear you say. The proof of the pudding
. . . The mere *idea* of a project that generates enough gender-specific visual/
verbal texts to allow the development of a coherent position from which to
regard conventional verbal texts with a certain anthropological strangeness
and to critique the norm of verbal textual argument (and linear progression)
is a tall order. However, this is to look at the visual/verbal cross-over from a
sociologist's viewpoint; scripto-visual feminist art practice is not dissimilar
from the proposal I have sketched out (see Chapter 3). In addition, I offer my
own experiences. I work with a group of artists who are women (the
Countervail Collective): and a situation where there are seven artists to one
sociologist means that we tend to operate more from a visual art perspective.
Our work is the result of group participation, and it focuses, in part, on
women's issues (in catalogue statements and essays, and in the visual work
itself), on the social use of space (much of the visual work is site-specific),
on the function of framing, and on the systematic use of colour and geometry
– as opposed to adopting an individualistic, 'inspirational' approach. The
artists produce paintings, sculpture and drawings, and I produce photographs (part-documentary) and written work; and we also write together.
We aim to reach beyond the group to other women. Exhibitions coincide
with a postgraduate course in sociology, to which I contribute. The
sociology students produce essays (not always conventional texts) about the
art works and their textual accompaniments, which explore and develop the
links between those works, feminist theory, social science methodology and
other social factors; and the two groups meet for discussion. Each feeds off
the other. This project is long-term, and the process of cross-fertilisation
between artists and sociologists and the link-up between women, though
small in scale and presently limited to those of an intellectual bent, has been
of undoubted mutual benefit.[22] The piece of writing reproduced in the
Appendix is intended to give a flavour of the benefit that I, for one, have
derived from our collaborative project. I think of it as a pilot study for
something larger.

22 I am aware that this project, concerned as it is with a liaison between Systematic Constructive
    artists and their work and sociology students at postgraduate level, is open to the same kind
    of criticism that I levelled at Pollock's project in Chapters 2 and 3. That is, the art is not very
    accessible to many women, and the postgraduate students are highly educated people. I
    regard our project as in one sense a blueprint for the future; but future projects should aim to
    focus on visual representation which is more accessible (preferably with a photographic
    component), and though sociologically informed, to involve women participants who
    represent a broader section of the population.

Chapter 7

A coming together

I shall not attempt to make a comprehensive summary of the material in this book; indeed, I very much hope to have stimulated readers to turn to some of the works discussed in previous chapters, and to pursue them in greater detail. Nor shall I come to any overall coherent theoretical conclusions. This would be quite inappropriate, for reasons that should become apparent. Rather, I am going to tell a story that draws fairly selectively on the previous chapters and their exploration of the relationship between visual representation and social science analysis.

Turning to analyses *of* visual representation first, this category of accounts for many years consisted largely of critical writings about visual art. In the critical paradigm, the history of the development of grand-scale theory, with its belief that certain forms of art have an emancipatory force, a potential to hasten the demise of capitalism, has been a long and fascinating one. However, from the vantage-point of today, this belief seems not only to have been over-optimistic, but somewhat misconceived. Over-optimistic, since art's contribution to the downfall of capitalism has not, even in the longer term, been particularly evident; indeed, analyses from within the empirical paradigm indicate that fine art, especially the kind of avant-garde art that critical theorists had in mind, is largely the preserve of the white, male establishment, and that its social status has been unjustifiably reified. Misconceived, since the downfall of many of the world's socialist states now makes the demise of capitalism itself seem a rather remote prospect, and indeed because early theorists could not know how complex and diverse in its aims and practices capitalism itself was to become; but also, and importantly, because their grand-scale theories ignored the different interests of minority groups which include vast numbers of people whose oppression cannot simply be reduced to economic and class-related factors.

Since the mid-1970s, critical theorists associated with the new, social art history have developed empirically orientated, local-level, minority-interest, group-specific approaches. These approaches have produced socio-political analyses of visual art works, photographs and writings about visual art within their historical contexts – analyses which are, at the same time, closely informed by broader critical concerns. These analyses are more informative and more compelling in their critique than previous grand-scale critical analyses. However, critical art practice – the visual arm of the critical paradigm – still has to face the problem of the thoroughly establishment character of the visual art world itself. Critical artists sometimes by-pass the gallery system and address a different public, or show their work in those few galleries devoted to minority group interests (e.g. the Pavilion), in their attempt to put critique to work. More often they choose to work within the gallery system, and let the work itself stand as critique. For example, scripto-visual works reject as fetishistic a fundamental distinction between 'visual' and 'verbal', and tend to focus attention on communication, and the interpenetration of visual and verbal codes; such works begin to blur distinctions between fine art (with its connotations of 'pure visibility' and special social status) and non-art forms of predominantly visual representation.

Outside the world of art, visual representation is becoming more prevalent; and there are theories of postmodernism that are centrally concerned with the visual character of present-day culture. While I have been writing this book, video-cameras have recorded crimes as they were being committed; and stills from these videos have featured prominently in the press. Comic books are becoming more popular; and fax, computer graphics and sophisticated layout and typescript produced by desk-top publishing are relatively commonplace. While all this points to the fact that people are developing a more wide-ranging and sophisticated visual literacy, the importance of visual representation 'on the page' is being recognised by a growing number of empirical sociologists. Their analyses show that a depiction is always more than an illustration because it is itself constructed, and then crafted into a particular interactive relationship with the other components of the text, in order to produce the author's desired argument. In addition, empirical sociological analyses have shown that depictive representations are capable of sending multiple messages, and of serving the social purpose of sustaining an ambiguous situation.

It is impossible to draw a clear line between sociologies *of* visual representation and sociologies which *use* visual representation. This is because the former use textual strategies which reshape the meaning of the object of their analysis (in this case, visual representation) so that, in the context of that analysis, it now conspires with their own analytical argument. However, at this point, I turn towards those texts which set out not just to analyse visual representation but unambiguously to use it in their own textual presentation. On the whole, sociology itself has been a thoroughly 'verbal' discipline – often with a penchant for statistical analysis – despite the evidence of photographs in very early publications; though anthropology, with its different intellectual problems, has not spurned the use of photographs. However, since the 1970s, some sociologists have incorporated depictions into their own work; and in the late 1980s and early 1990s, there has been evidence of a greater awareness of the visual potential of the printed page.

That awareness results, in part, from the fact that sociologists have begun to treat depictions outside the domain of visual art as analytical data, and have consequently thought that sociological analysis might put depictions to work on its own behalf. But this development in itself is probably linked to the fact that, during the past ten years, 'representation' has become a crucial concept in sociological discourse. For this concept prompts a consideration of the *variety* of ways in which we represent our realities, and an appreciation of the privileged status that our culture accords to written discourse, and more especially to the semantic content of words. The shift to a focus on 'representation' – and the process of representation – may, in part, have been influenced by new technological developments which now enable visual representations, in particular, to be constructed, manipulated and communicated quite easily and cheaply. For example, anyone who can operate an Apple Macintosh computer has the opportunity to design his or her own page layout and typographical format; while depictions can be reproduced in books far more cheaply than in former years. In addition, an awareness of the visual potential of the printed page may reflect an author's professional experience as a photographer. Social scientists who are also accomplished photographers have shown that photographs, both individually and in arrays, can contribute to sociological analysis things that words alone cannot. For example, while generalising about the social world is perhaps best accomplished with words, arrays of photographic images emphasise particular differences – and particularising is increasingly valued in both critical and empirical paradigms. Furthermore, works like *Exploring Society Photographically* (Becker 1981) have shown that the aesthetic quality of an image can give an analysis immediacy, vividness, poignancy – and therefore make it memorable, and on occasions ideologically hard-hitting. Photographs are particularly important, both as documentary evidence of people, places and events, and because they offer social scientists the opportunity to analyse the symbolic significance of their content. While at the same time, the process of photography allows the photographer a whole series of opportunities to shape the image, and thus the argument to which it contributes. However, in my view, the most interesting 'visual development' concerns the growing awareness that typography and page layout can make a positive contribution to the structure and content of a sociological analysis. Indeed SSKers have demonstrated that judiciously chosen typography and page layout can help to construct a reflexively sound text, and that they are thus an integral part of a project generated from the methodological heart of sociology; a project which stems from a critique of positivist philosophy and concerns the self-referential character of social science itself.

In the positivist era, sociologists used textual strategies to convince readers that the knowledge their accounts purveyed was objective and true. This, in turn, implied that an account that conveyed such 'truths' was definitive, and that the typescript and layout of such an account were merely aspects of the medium which conveyed the message. The post-positivist approach, however, maintains that there is no objective truth, therefore no definitive account, and in general terms no privileged form of account; but that instead each text is its author's interpretation of reality – indeed, its author's version of reality. This implies a situation in which there exists a plurality of social science accounts, and a plurality of realities. More recently, sociologists of scientific knowledge have argued that the structure of any sociological account must be reflexively sound, while other sociologists aim to produce a structure which liberates them from the constraints of conventional academic textual form. Both approaches, in turn, suggest the desirability of exploring new literary forms for social science, and both imply that the form of a social scientific account will actively contribute to its content. Adorno's epigrammatic, non-linear texts can perhaps be seen as a precursor to this way of thinking.

A somewhat similar approach is taken by feminists, who associate men with dogma, and men's texts with the purveying of philosophical, scientific and other truths. While some feminists associate their work with theories of postmodernism, others distance themselves from such theories. But all emphasise that there is no one feminist account, nor a specific feminist form of account, but that each woman contributes to the *diversity* of feminist accounts from her own position on the edge of patriarchal society. Feminist art practice, in particular, has produced a wealth of different kinds of critique of patriarchy; among these, scripto-visual works feature prominently. And although some feminist art practices have, perhaps, an overly intellectualist approach, others appeal – and are intended to appeal – directly to a much broader audience of women.

But not only is there a plurality of accounts (and authors' realities); each account is open to a different interpretation by the *reader*, and the manner in which some accounts are constructed actively encourages the reader to create his or her own interpretations of them. Burgin's critical visual/verbal works in *Between* (1986a), consisting of photographs with unconventionally placed textual passages, offer the viewer/reader a range of possible interpretations between certain limits. And in the empirical paradigm, authors have been experimenting with more open textual forms which are designed to encourage readers to recreate texts for themselves.

In addition, Michael Mulkay has said:

> As the empiricist tradition becomes aware of its own textuality and responds textually to that awareness, so the precarious character of its version of 'social reality' is accepted along with the need to recognise other ways of 'being in the world'. This implies, perhaps, a vision of a society in which difference is possible without oppression.
>
> (Mulkay 1993: personal communication)

There is thus an important sense in which the critical and empirical traditions seem to be drawing together; for while the critical paradigm has a vision of a more equitable society, the empirical paradigm seeks difference without oppression. There is also a tendency towards fragmentation in both paradigms: in the critical paradigm, through a refutation of grand theory and an emphasis on local, empirical, minority group-based projects in which a diversity of accounts are acknowledged and embraced; and in the empirical paradigm, through the fragmentation of the authorial voice which allows consideration of 'alternative realities'. Both approaches involve the active use of the visual dimension. While texts from within the empirical paradigm involve, at the least, an unfamiliar visual presentation in terms of layout and possibly typography as well, the critical paradigm, as represented by the work of Burgin in *Between* (1986a) and other similar visual/verbal texts, uses the latitude for interpretation which images (in conjuction with unconventionally positioned textual passages) allow.

I also brought my own parallel sections of the book together in the concluding parts of Chapters 3 and 6. Drawing them still closer together now, I want, tentatively, to advocate an approach which makes active use of both visual and verbal representation, and explores the possibility of gender-related or gender-specific layouts, typographical formats, and depictions which may themselves be unconventionally related to caption and text. Where depictions are concerned, photography is particularly appropriate. For it is on the whole affordable, it offers scope for creative work, and photographs can tell us much about the world that we did not already know. And recent developments in the field of typography may also have much to offer women and other minority groups. I am, of course, aware that many of the visual advances made in social science and the other areas that I have mentioned are not particularly associated with women, though they *are* generally associated with men who are sympathetic to women's positions. The approach I have sketched out is, therefore, not the preserve of women nor of other minority groups, yet it *does* distance itself from that composite cluster which has been accorded privileged status: the verbal text, truth about nature and society, and patriarchy. A text constructed according to this approach therefore constitutes a vantage-point from which to regard that composite cluster with anthropological strangeness. Such a text offers an alternative to the normative account, and countervails it. And in any case, I hope to have shown how a visually aware sociology is much richer than a merely conventional verbal one. Latour's (1988) notion of an infra-reflexive text is useful in this context (mirrored in one sense by the dialectical approach taken by many social art historians). For it provides a theoretical basis from which to cross over discipline boundaries and bridge visual (art) and verbal domains; and in many ways it parallels and would seem to strengthen the approach already taken by feminists who aim to reshape sociology through the collaborative projects in which they work with and for other women in areas outside social science.

Appendix

In January 1994, the participants in Countervail agreed that each of us should draft a paper or set of notes around the theme of 'what bugs me at the moment' and circulate it to the other participants before our next monthly meeting. This we did, and my offering is reproduced below. It tries to link up a particular triangle of concerns: sociology, SCAP (SCAP = Systematic Constructive Art Practice) and feminism, in order to clarify my own position in Countervail. What particularly bugged me at that time was the problem of what I should contribute to the Countervail 4 *exhibition, scheduled to take place at the King's Manor Gallery, University of York, in October 1994. The paper has significant inputs from sociology postgraduate students at York, and from Systematic Constructive artists. While it was provisional, revealing my stance as somewhat uncertain, I have set the paper out here because it shows a position reached as a result of a long-term programme of collaboration between sociologists and artists – plus our readings of certain sections of* Knowledge and Reflexivity *(Woolgar 1988).*

> The mode of vision I am trying to describe is also an epistemology; a different way of getting to know. The epistemology that is being tested here is based on relationality, or more precisely, on the model of friendship. Friendship requires getting to know other people in a dialogic mode. In the visual domain, this means a seeing radically different from the voyeuristic, assymetrical mode that has for too long been hegemonic.
>
> (Bal 1993: 400)

The positivist notion that there can be a definitive, true account of nature or of society seems to imply that the *text* of such an account is transparent, that it is merely the means by which a pure unadulterated morsel of nature or society is conveyed to readers. Although positivism was influential for many years, it has now been very largely discredited: both natural and social scientists have come to recognise that they *interpret* their data (represent rather than present it), and that they thus construct a textual account which could have been otherwise. While this stance raises problems, notably to do with value and relativism, scientists accept that there are competing textual accounts of nature and of society. For example, another social scientist would write a different account of the Systematic Constructive artists and their work from the one(s) I would write. In addition, interpretative social scientists have acknowledged that their work itself creates change in the *data* they study: they do not leave it as they find it. And feminist social scientists welcome this acknowledgement, because it indicates that social science methodology is becoming more compatible with the declared political and moral aims of feminism. For feminist social scientists want to enable their women research participants to *change* their lives, if they so wish; they want to work *with* and *for* women, rather than merely *on* them.

However, sociologists of scientific knowledge have recently observed that in social science texts – including those taking an interpretational approach – the authorial voice almost always has a superior epistemological status to that of the research subjects, or 'data'. Such texts distance the authorial standpoint from that of the research subjects by exoticising the culture of the research subjects while normalising that of the author. Yet, as SSKers point out, *both* researchers and the societal groups they investigate are engaged in *social* activity, and therefore sociologists' accounts actually have the *same* epistemological status as those produced by their research subjects. Sociology is *reflexive*: it is social discourse about social discourse. SSKers argue that sociologists cannot justify concealing the social character of their own work in their textual presentations. To be consistent with the aims of their discipline, they should reveal this social character. A textual analysis of the social character of another societal group should at the same time try to show how that analysis itself is also a social activity, by revealing the social processes involved in its own textual construction. This position is in complete contrast to the idea of the text as transparent, as a mere conduit. Such self-exemplifying texts could, as it were, almost be said to be opaque, or artefactual in character. However, the self-exemplifying text cannot necessarily be couched in the literary form taken by conventional sociology texts, since this is informed and moulded by the particular requirements of interpretative sociology. 'Reflexive sociologists' tend to experiment with alternative literary forms involving unconventional typographic arrangements and page-layout, such as the multivoice text which replaces the single authorial voice of the conventional format and brings the other research participants 'into the text', or the particular textual format adopted by the research subjects themselves in their own accounts. One result of such textual experiments has been to 'lessen the distance' between the two 'discipline areas', and to produce an intertwining, a cross-over between them. This development seems to indicate that the reflexive sociological project is even *more* compatible with the aims of feminist social scientists. For it could be argued that a sociology which is self-exemplifying is a sociology *for* people, because in showing its own processes as well as the outcome of these processes, it helps people to see the conventions by which it constructs itself, and in so doing, it allows people to understand how others construct meaning. In this sense, it gives people the tools to inquire how they themselves construct meaning. In helping people to see the conventions by which they are bound, it may enable them to change those conventions if they so wish.

The position reached thus far can be mapped on to the Countervail project. Barry Sandywell (postgraduate supervisor) noted at the last meeting (11 November 1993) between the York postgraduate students, you (Countervail artists) and myself that these meetings do reveal the reflexive character of sociology, because they display my work with the students in relation to SCAP as social activity (for the artists' inspection). However, when I contribute to our joint exhibitions, 'my work' is of a very different kind, because it is not discussion but artefact-in-a-group-exhibition. In what should this work consist? To start with, it should be generated from my own discipline, sociology, and not be an attempt at SCAP, nor a cosmetic application of SCAP to sociology. The argument in the paragraph above would seem to indicate that it might consist of a sociological analysis of SCAP in a visual-literary form which allows it to indicate its own social character through the display of its textual construction as social activity while at the same time being compatible with the character of the particular societal group (SCAP) being analysed. This would be working *on* you, and also *with* you in the sense that epistemological equality would be shown. I might argue that it would also be working *for* women in that by showing its own social processes, the work would aim to allow them to understand how meaning and conventions are constructed, and consequently might empower them to investigate and change their own. In addition, this work would also be congruent with several of the concerns which distinguish SCAP. For already, both projects, SCAP and sociology, are critical-theoretical, systematic in character, and acknowledge the social dimension to their own work. While I have already discussed this last point in relation to the reflexive sociological project, it is apparent – for example – in the site-specific character of many recent Systematic Constructive art works. Moreover, it is intriguing to explore a parallel between the current reflexive sociological project, and the reflexive SCAP project of the 1970s and early 1980s, when artists claimed to produce work that was self-exemplifying. However, while reflexivity in the case of sociology implies that its texts demonstrate that they are themselves socially constructed, reflexivity in the case of SCAP does not. It produces a different emphasis – on self-containedness, on features internal to the work (such as its system of colour and/or geometic relations), on the work as a constructed art object, on the relationship of system to structure. Systematic Constructive artists came to realise that their aim to produce *totally* self-exemplifying work is impossible, for the work cannot obliterate the unique subjectivity of the artist who produced it, though it can obscure it – which is worrying because this hardly constitutes an appropriate aim in the present context, presenting, as it does, parallels with positivist science. These artists also realised that self-exemplification is in no way a guarantee that the meanings that the viewer extracts from the work are those that the artist put in. This second difficulty also applies to self-exemplifying sociology texts, as SSKers acknowledge. For, ultimately, in both cases, the work constitutes its own 'troubles'. Nevertheless, an impulse towards self-exemplification does characterise both projects.

In fact, there are further 'difficulties' associated with self-exemplifying sociology texts. Bruno Latour has noted that these are usually 'inward-looking': they tend to tell us far more about the writer and his/her methodological problems than about the social world outside. Indeed, in extreme cases these texts seem to be almost entirely concerned with formalism, i.e. with the formal problems associated with the production of a self-exemplifying text. This can make for boring, irritating reading because – perhaps paradoxically – it seems to be the *author*'s work, work done by the 'I' of the author for the 'me' of the author (plus a very small group of similar thinkers) – to use G.H. Mead's terminology – rather than work for the 'me' of other recipients. A concern with formal problems may be appropriate, and indeed important, for the SCAP project – but it should surely not become a principal focus of *sociology*.

However, it is impossible to deny that a sociological analysis which conceals its own social character is untenable. Yet, to strive for a text which is formally self-exemplifying appears pointless because this is ultimately impossible to achieve, and because works whose chief preoccupation is formalism tend to be impoverished analyses of the social world. This indicates that epistemological parity between the sociologist-as-author and the group being studied must be brought out, yet in a manner which allows the former to tell the reader as much as possible about the latter, that is, in a manner which does not impoverish the description and analysis of the societal group in question. Here, clearly, is a challenge to be met.

But what does all this indicate for my proposed work-as-artefact in the *Countervail 4* exhibition? Could this piece of writing itself be that work? Perhaps not, but it certainly prepares the ground for it – that is for a work which consists of, or rather *arises out of* a social analysis of SCAP. And perhaps the way in which the analysis *manifests* its own social, feminist character and the way in which it engages with its audience – the way in which it 'arises' – is where the *visual* and the *art* come in, and consequently how the challenge may be met.

In more general terms, this piece of writing *and* my proposed work-as-artefact are intended to reach out into your world from mine and to contribute to the projects of both.

Bibliography

Adorno, T. W. (1984) *Aesthetic Theory*, trans. C. Lenhardt, ed. G. Adorno and R. Tiedmann, London and New York: Routledge and Kegan Paul.

Adorno, T. W., Albert, H., Dahrendorf, R., Habermas, J., Pilot, H. and Popper, K. R. (1976) *The Positivist Dispute in German Sociology*, trans. G. Adey and D. Frisby, London: Heinemann.

Alpers, S. (1983) *The Art of Describing: Dutch Art in the Seventeenth Century*, Chicago: University of Chicago Press.

Althusser, L. (1971) 'Cremonini, Painter of the Abstract', *Lenin and Philosophy and Other Essays*, trans. Ben Brewster, London: New Left Books.

—— (1984) 'Ideology and Ideological State Apparatuses (Notes towards an Investigation)', *Essays on Ideology*, London: Verso: 1–60.

Antal, F. (1948) *Florentine Painting and its Social Background*, London: Routledge and Kegan Paul.

Ardener, S. (1986) 'The Representation of Women in Academic Models', in L. Dube, E. Leacock and S. Ardener (eds) *Visibility and Power: Essays on Women in Society and Development*, Delhi: OUP: 3-14.

Ashmore, M. (1989) *The Reflexive Thesis: Wrighting Sociology of Scientific Knowledge*, Chicago: University of Chicago Press.

—— (1992) Review of Lynch, M. and Woolgar, S. (eds), 'Representation in Scientific Practice', *Sociology*, 26, 1: 155–6.

Ashmore, M., Mulkay, M., and Pinch, T. (1989) '"Fury over prof's kidney call": health economists in the media', *Health and Efficiency: A sociology of health economics*, Milton Keynes: Open University Press: 58–85.

Baines, G. (1990) 'Beams fuel the flames: television has been one of the key catalysts to change in Eastern Europe, particularly Romania', *Guardian*, 8 January 1990.

Bal, M. (1993) 'His Master's Eye' in D.M. Levin (ed.) *Modernity and the Hegemony of Vision*, Berkeley and Los Angeles: California University Press: 379–404.

Ball, M. S. and Smith, G. W. H. (1992) *Analysing Visual Data*, Newbury Park, London and New Delhi: Sage.

Barnes, B. (1977) *Interests and the Growth of Knowledge*, London: Routledge and Kegan Paul.

Barnes, J. (1984) *Flaubert's Parrot*, London: Jonathan Cape.

Bateson, G. and Mead, M. (1942) *Balinese Character: A Photographic Analysis*, New York: New York Academy of Sciences.

Battershill, N. (1990) *Learn to Paint Trees*, London: HarperCollins.

Baudrillard, J. (1975) *The Mirror of Production*, trans. M. Poster, St Louis: Telos Press.

—— (1983) *Simulations*, trans. P. Foss, P. Patton and P. Beitchman, New York: Semiotext(e).

Bauman, Z. (1992) Review of Wellmer, A., 'The Persistence of Modernity: Essays on Aesthetics, Ethics and Postmodernism', *Sociology*, 26, 1: 173–5.

Baxendall, M. (1972) *Painting and Experience in Fifteenth Century Italy*, Oxford: Oxford University Press.

Becker, H. (1981) 'Introduction' to H. Becker (ed.) *Exploring Society Photographically*, Mary and Leigh Block Gallery, Evanston: Northwestern University: 9–11.

—— (1982) *Art Worlds*, Berkeley, Los Angeles and London: University of California Press.

Benjamin, A. (ed.) (1989) *The Problems of Modernity: Adorno and Benjamin*, London: Routledge.

Benjamin, W. (1934) 'The Author as Producer', trans. J. Heckman, *New Left Review*, 62: 83–96.

—— (1973) 'The Work of Art in the Age of Mechanical Reproduction', *Illuminations*, London: Fontana: 219–53.

Berenson, B. (1948) *The Italian Painters of the Renaissance*, Oxford: Oxford University Press, London: Geoffrey Cumberlege.

Berger, J. (1972) *Ways of Seeing*, London: BBC, and Harmondsworth: Penguin.

Berger, J. and Mohr, M. (1967) *A Fortunate Man: The story of a country doctor*, London: Writers and Readers Publishing Cooperative in association with Allen Lane, Penguin.

Berman, M. (1982) *All That Is Solid Melts Into Air: The Experience of Modernity*, New York: Simon and Schuster.

Bernstein, J. (1992) *The Fate of Art: Aesthetic Alientation from Kant to Derrida*, Cambridge: Polity Press.

'Black Women in the Arts: 1992, Perspectives from Britain, Part I', (1992) *Feminist Art News*, 4, 1.

Blackmar, F. W. (1897) 'The Smoky Pilgrims', *American Journal of Sociology*, 2: 485–500.

Bloch, E., Lukács, G., Brecht, B., Benjamin, W., and Adorno, T. (1977) *Aesthetics and Politics: Debates between Bloch, Lukács, Brecht, Benjamin, Adorno*, London: New Left Books.

Bluebond-Langner, M. (1978) *The Private Worlds of Dying Children*, Princeton: Princeton University Press.

Boffin, T. and Fraser, J. (eds) (1991) *Stolen Glances: Lesbians take photographs*, London: Pandora Press.

Booth, W. (1992) 'The Self-Conscious Narrator in Comic Fiction before "Tristram Shandy"', in M. New (ed.) *Tristram Shandy: Contemporary Critical Essays*, Basingstoke: Macmillan: 36–59.

Bowker, G. (1988) 'Pictures from the Subsoil, 1939', in G. Fyfe and J. Law (eds), *Picturing Power: Visual Depiction and Social Relations*, London: Routledge: 221–54.

Bowlt, J. (1984) 'The Old New Wave', *New York Review*, 16 February 1984: 28.

Brighton, A. (1973) 'Museum Painters: Popular Painters', *Times Educational Supplement*, 9 March 1973.

—— (1977) 'Official Art and the Tate Gallery', *Studio International*, 1.

Brown, D. A. (1979) *Berenson and the Connoisseurship of Italian Painting*, Washington, DC: National Gallery of Art.

Burgin, V. (1977) 'An important tool of practice', in A. Brighton and L. Morris (eds), *Towards Another Picture*, Nottingham: Midland Group: 125–8.

—— (ed.) (1982) *Thinking Photography*, Basingstoke: Macmillan.

—— (1986a) *Between*, Oxford: Blackwell, in association with the Institute of Contemporary Arts, London.

—— (1986b) *The End of Art Theory: Criticism and Postmodernity*, Basingstoke: Macmillan.

—— (1991) 'Realising the Reverie', *Ten 8*, 2, 2: 5–15.

Bushnell, C. (1901a) 'Some social aspects of the Chicago stockyards, I', *American Journal of Sociology* 7: 145–70.

—— (1901b) 'Some social aspects of the Chicago stockyards, II', *American Journal of Sociology* 7, 3: 289–330.

—— (1902) 'Some social aspects of the Chicago stockyards III', *American Journal of Sociology* 7, 4: 433–74.

Cambridge Women's Studies Group (1981) *Women in Society: Interdisciplinary Essays*, London: Virago.

Cervantes (Saavedra), M. de (1950) *The Adventures of Don Quixote*, trans. J. M. Cohen, Harmondsworth: Penguin.

Chaplin, E. (1982) 'The Creation of Artistic Meaning: A Sociological Analysis of Responses to Visual Art with Reference to the Work of Jackson Pollock', unpublished D. Phil. thesis, University of York.

—— (1988) 'Feminism and Systematic Constructive Art', *Constructivist Forum*, 8: 4–19.

Clark, T. H. (1973a) *The Absolute Bourgeois; Artists and Politics in France 1848–1851*, London: Thames and Hudson.

—— (1973b) *Image of the People; Gustave Courbet and the 1848 Revolution*, London: Thames and Hudson.

—— (1974) 'The Conditions of Artistic Creation', *Times Literary Supplement*, 24 May 1974: 526.

—— (1984) *The Painting of Modern Life: Paris in the Art of Manet and his Followers*, London: Thames and Hudson.

Collier, J. Jnr (1967) *Visual anthropology: photography as a research method*, New York: Holt Rinehart and Winston.

—— (1979) 'Visual Anthropology', in J. Wagner (ed.) *Images of Information*, Beverly Hills and London: Sage: 271–81.

Collier, J. Jnr and Collier, M. (1986) *Visual Anthropology*, New Mexico: University of New Mexico Press.

'Colonizing Cyberspace' (1991) *BBC Horizon*, 22 April 1991.

Comte, A. (1936) *Cours de philosophie positive*, Paris: Larousse.

Connor, S. (1989) *Postmodernist Culture: An Introduction to Theories of the Contemporary*, Oxford: Blackwell.

Courtauld Institute of Art (1950) *Prospectus* [University of London].

Deepwell, K. (n.d.) 'In Defence of the Indefensible: Feminism, Painting and Post-Modernism', *Feminist Art News*, 2, 4: 9–12.

—— (1992) 'Time Ladies', *Women's Art Magazine*, 46, 1992: 6–7.

Denzin, N. (1991) *Images of Postmodern Society: Social Theory and Contemporary Cinema*, London and Newbury Park: Sage.

Derrida, J. (1986) *Glas*, English trans. J. P. Leavey Jnr, and R. Rand, Nebraska: University of Nebraska Press.

Dingwall, R., Tanaka, H. and Minamikata, S. (1991) 'Images of Parenthood in the United Kingdom and Japan', *Sociology*, 25, 3: 423–46.

Dormer, P. (1982) 'The Straw-Stuffed Artist-Person', *Art Monthly*, 54, 1982: 33–4.

Duff, E. (1981) 'Working World' in H. Becker (ed.) *Exploring Society Photographically*, Mary and Leigh Block Gallery, Evanston: Northwestern University: 74–9.

Eco, U. (1984) *Semiotics and the Philosophy of Language*, Basingstoke: Macmillan.

Evans, D. and Gohl, S. (1986) *Photomontage: a political weapon*, London and Bedford: Gordon Fraser Gallery.

Faulkner, W. (1964) *The Sound and the Fury*, Harmondsworth: Penguin.

Featherstone, M. (1988) 'In Pursuit of the Postmodern: An Introduction', *Theory, Culture and Society*, 5: 2–3; 195–215.

Feyerabend, P. (1975) *Against Method*, London: New Left Books.

Fisher, P. (1993) 'Serious suits get lost in space', *Guardian*, 7 January 1993.

Ford, C. and Steinorth, K. (eds) (1988) *You Press the Button, We Do the Rest: The Birth of Snapshot Photography*, London: Dirk Nishen.

Frascina, F. and Harrison, C. (eds) (1982) *Modern Art and Modernism: A Critical Anthology*, London: Harper and Row.

Fyfe, G. (1988) 'Art and its Objects: William Ivins and the reproduction of art', in G. Fyfe and J. Law (eds), *Picturing Power: Visual Depiction and Social Relations*, London: Routledge: 65–98.

—— and Law, J. (1988) 'On the invisibility of the visual: editors' introduction', in G. Fyfe and J. Law (eds), *Picturing Power: Visual Depiction and Social Relations*, London: Routledge: 1–14.

Gerrard, M. (1993) 'Electronic glue in the picture', *Guardian*, 19 August 1993.

Ghiberti, L. (1958) *I Commentarii*, trans. staff of Courtauld Institute of Art (based on J. Schlosser's edition of the original text, Berlin 1912), unpublished document, University of London.

Gilbert, G. N. and Mulkay, M. (1984) 'Working Conceptual Hallucinations', in *Opening Pandora's Box: A Sociological Analysis of Scientific Discourse*, Cambridge: Cambridge University Press: 141–71.

Goffman, E. (1959) *The Presentation of Self in Everyday Life*, New York: Doubleday Anchor.

—— (1974) *Frame Analysis*, New York: Harper and Row.

—— (1979) *Gender Advertisements*, London and Basingstoke: Macmillan.

Gombrich, E. H. (1960) *Art and Illusion*, New York: Pantheon Books.

—— (1966) *Norm and Form: studies in the art of the Renaissance I*, London and New York: Phaidon.

Graham, H. (1977) 'Images of Pregnancy in Antenatal Literature', in R. Dingwall, C. Heath, M. Reid, and M. Stacey (eds), *Health Care and Health Knowledge*, London: Croom Helm.

Graham-Brown, S. (1988) *Images of Women: The Portrayal of Women in Photography of the Middle East 1860–1950*, London: Quartet Books.

Gramsci, A. (1971) *Prison Notebooks (selections from)*, ed. and trans. Q. Hoare and G. Nowell Smith, London: Lawrence and Wishart.

Greenberg, C. (1984a) 'Conversation with Clement Greenberg 1', *Art Monthly*, 73: 3–9.

—— (1984b) 'Conversation with Clement Greenberg 2', *Art Monthly*, 74: 10–14.

—— (1984c) 'Conversation with Clement Greenberg 3', *Art Monthly*, 75: 4–6.

—— (1986) 'Towards a Newer Laocoon', in J. O'Brian (ed.), *The Collected Essays and Criticism*, Chicago and London: University of Chicago Press.

Gregory, R. L. and Gombrich, E. H. (eds) (1973) *Illusion in Nature and Art*, London: Duckworth.

Gutting, G. (1989) *Michel Foucault's Archaeology of Scientific Reason*, Cambridge: Cambridge University Press.

Hadamard, J. (1949) *The Psychology of Invention in the Mathematical Field*, New York: Dover Publications.

Hadjinicolaou, N. (1978) *Art History and Class Struggle*, London: Pluto Press.

Hall, J. (1992) 'Art is the loser in a photo-finish', *Guardian*, 13 May 1992.

Hall, S. (1987) 'When it's the only game in town, people play it', *Guardian*, 6 July 1987.

Harper, D. (1986) 'Meaning and Work: A Study in Photo Elicitation', *Current Sociology*, 34, 3: 24–46.

—— (1988) 'Visual Sociology: Expanding Sociological Vision', *The American Sociologist*, Spring 1988, 54–70.

Harris, N. (1976) 'Mao and Marx', *International Socialism*, 89: 16–21.

Harrison, C. and Orton, F. (1982) *A Provisional History of Art and Language*, Paris: Editions E. Fabre.

Harvey, D. (1989) *The Condition of Postmodernity: An Enquiry into the Origins of Cultural Change*, Oxford: Basil Blackwell.

Hauser, A. (1951) *The Social History of Art*, London: Routledge and Kegan Paul.

Hawkes, T. (1977) *Structuralism and Semiotics*, London: Methuen.

Hedges N. and Beynon, H. (1982) *Born to Work: Images of Factory Life*, London: Pluto Press.

Hegel, G. W. F. (1970) 'Encyclopaedia of the Philosophical Sciences in Outline', *Werke* (20 vols), ed. E. Moldenhauer and K. M. Michel, Frankfurt-am-Main.

—— (1975) *Aesthetics: Lectures on Fine Art*, trans. T. M. Knox, Oxford: Clarendon Press.

—— (1977) *Phenomenology of Spirit*, trans. A. V. Miller, analysis of text and foreword by J. N. Finlay, Oxford: Clarendon Press.

Heider, K. (1976) *Ethnographic Film*, Austin: University of Texas Press.

Henny, L. M. (1986) 'Trend Report: Theory and Practice of Visual Sociology', *Current Sociology*, 34, 3.

Hockney, D. (1991) 'On the lighter side in Bradford', interview with E. McCabe, *Guardian*, 6 June 1991.

Hoggart, R. (1988) *Life and Times, vol. 1: A Local Habitation 1918–40*, London: Chatto and Windus.

Holton, G. (1988) *Thematic Origins of Scientific Thought*, revised edn, Cambridge, Mass.: Harvard University Press.

Horkheimer, M. and Adorno, T. (eds) (1932–41) *Zeitschrift für Sozialforschung*, intro. by A. Schmidt, years 1–9, München: Kosel.

Iverson, M. (1979) 'Meyer Schapiro and the Semiotics of Visual Art', *Block*, 1: 50–2.

Ivins, W. (1953) *Prints and Visual Communication*, Harvard: Harvard University Press.

Jacobi, D. and Schiele, B. (1989) 'Scientific Imagery and Popularised Imagery: Differences and Similarities in the Photographic Portraits of Scientists', *Social Studies of Science*, 19, 4: 731–53.

Jameson, F. (1981) *The Political Unconscious*, Ithaca, NY: Cornell University Press.

—— (1985) 'Postmodernism and Consumer Society', in H. Foster (ed.), *Postmodern Culture*, London and Sydney: Pluto Press: 111–25.

—— (1987) 'Reading Without Interpretation: Postmodernism and the Video-Text', in D. Attridge, A. Durant, N. Fabb and C. McCabe (eds), *The Linguistics of Writing: Arguments Between Language and Literature*, Manchester: Manchester University Press: 198–223.

—— (1988) 'Cognitive Mapping', in C. Nelson and L. Grossberg (eds), *Marxism and the Interpretation of Culture*, Urbana: University of Illinois Press: 347–57.

—— (1991a) *Postmodernism or, The Cultural Logic of Late Capitalism*, London and New York: Verso.

—— (1991b) Interview, 'Third Ear', BBC Radio 3, 9 January 1991.

Jay, M. (1973) *The Dialectical Imagination: A History of the Frankfurt School and the Institute of Social Research 1923–50*, London: Heinemann.

Joyce, J. (1939) *Finnegans Wake*, London: Faber.

Kant, I. (1956) *The Critique of Practical Reason*, trans. L. W. Beck, Indianapolis and New York: Bobbs-Merrill.

—— (1961) *The Critique of Judgment*, trans. J. C. Meredith, Oxford: Clarendon Press.

—— (1986) *The Critique of Pure Reason*, trans. N. K. Smith, Basingstoke: Macmillan.

Keller, E. F. (1985) *Reflections on Gender and Science*, New Haven and London: Yale University Press.

Klee, P. (1964) *The Diaries of Paul Klee*, Berkeley: University of California Press.

Klein, R. D. (1983) 'How to do what we want to do: thoughts about feminist methodology', in G. Bowles and R. D. Klein (eds), *Theories of Women's Studies*, London and New York: Routledge and Kegan Paul: 88–104.

Kramarae, C. and Treichler, P. A. (1992) *A Feminist Dictionary: Amazons, Blue-stockings and Crones*, London: Pandora Press.

Krieger, S. (1983) *The Mirror Dance: Identity in a Women's Community*, Philadelphia: Temple University Press.

Kristeva, J. (1992) Series of four lectures on the philosophy and writings of Marcel Proust, University of Kent, 26–9 May 1992.

Kuhn, T. (1962) *The Structure of Scientific Revolutions*, Chicago: University of Chicago Press.

Landesman, C. (1992) 'Pagans at the church of culture', *Guardian*, 6 August 1992.

Lash, S. (1988) 'Discourse or Figure? Postmodernism as a "Regime of Signification"', *Theory, Culture and Society*, 5, 2–3: 311–36.

—— (1990) *Sociology of Postmodernism*, London and New York: Routledge.

Latour, B. (1987) *Science in Action*, Cambridge, Mass.: Harvard University Press.

—— (1988) 'The Politics of Explanation: an Alternative', in S. Woolgar (ed.), *Knowledge and Reflexivity: New Frontiers in the Sociology of Knowledge*, London: Sage: 155–76.

—— (1990) 'Drawing Things Together', in M. Lynch and S. Woolgar (eds), *Representation in Scientific Practice*, Cambridge, Mass., and London: The MIT Press: 19–68.

Law, J. and Lynch, M. (1990) 'Lists, field guides, and the descriptive organization of seeing: Birdwatching as an exemplary observational activity', in M. Lynch and S. Woolgar (eds), *Representation in Scientific Practice*, Cambridge, Mass., and London: The MIT Press: 267–300.

Livingstone, D. (1857) *Missionary Travels and Researches in South Africa*, London: John Murray.

Lodder, C. (1983) *Russian Constructivism*, New Haven and London: Yale University Press.

Lole, K. and Willats, S. (1975) 'Survey of Distance Models of Art', *Control Magazine*, 9: 16–17.

Lukács, G. (1950) *Studies in European Realism*, trans. E. Bone, London: Hallway.

—— (1971a) 'Reification and the Consciousness of the Proletariat', in *History and Class Consciousness. Studies in Marxist Dialectics*, London: Merlin Press.

Lynch, M. (1985) *Art and Artifact in Laboratory Science: A study of Shop Work and Shop Talk in a Research Laboratory*, London: Routledge and Kegan Paul.

—— (1990) 'The Externalized Retina: Selection and mathematization in the visual documentation of objects in the life sciences', in M. Lynch and S. Woolgar (eds), *Representation in Scientific Practice*, Cambridge, Mass., and London: The MIT Press: 153–86.

Lynch, M. and Woolgar, S. (1990) 'Introduction: Sociological orientations to representational practice in science', in M. Lynch and S. Woolgar (eds), *Representation in Scientific Practice*, Cambridge, Mass., and London: The MIT Press: 1–18.

Lyotard, J. F. (1984) *Driftworks*, New York, Columbia University: Semiotext(e).

McCall, M. and Becker, H. (1990) 'Performance Science', *Social Problems*, 37, 1: 117–32.

McCrone, D. (1992) *Places on the Margin*, London: Routledge.

McDowell, L. (1990) Review of D. Harvey, 'The Condition of Postmodernity', *Sociology*, 24, 3: 532–4.

McRobbie, A. (1991) *Feminism and Youth Culture: From Jackie to Just Seventeen*, Basingstoke: Macmillan.

Madge, C. and Weinberger, B. (1973) *Art Students Observed*, London: Faber and Faber.

Mandel, E. (1975) *Late Capitalism*, London: New Left Books.

Marcuse, H. (1955) *Eros and Civilization*, New York: The Beacon Press.

—— (1964) *One-dimensional Man*, London: Routledge and Kegan Paul.

Marx, K. (1968) 'Manifesto of the Communist Party', in *Karl Marx And Frederick Engels: Selected Works*, Moscow: Progress Publishers, and London: Lawrence and Wishart: 35–63.

—— (1968) 'Preface to A Contribution to the Critique of Political Economy', in *Karl Marx And Frederick Engels: Selected Works*, Moscow: Progress Publishers, and London: Lawrence and Wishart: 180–4.

—— (1968) 'Theses on Feuerbach', in *Karl Marx And Frederick Engels: Selected Works*, Moscow: Progress Publishers, and London: Lawrence and Wishart: 28–30.

Marx, K. and Engels, F. (1970) 'Introduction to A Contribution to the Critique of Political Economy', in *The German Ideology, Part One, with selections from Parts Two and Three, together with Marx's 'Introduction to a Critique of Political Economy'*, ed. and intro. C. H. Arthur, London: Lawrence and Wishart: 124–51.

Massey, D. (1984) *Spatial Divisions of Labour*, London and Basingstoke: Macmillan.

Maynard, M. (1990) 'The Re-Shaping of Sociology? Trends in the Study of Gender', *Sociology*, 24, 2: 269–90.

Mihill, C. (1992) 'New Man – still an old-style sexist', *Guardian*, 11 July 1992.

Mills, C. W. (1959) *The Sociological Imagination*, New York: Oxford University Press.

Millum, T. (1975) *Images of Women: Advertising in Women's Magazines*, London: Chatto.

Montag, W. (1988) 'What is at stake in the debate on postmodernism?', in E. A. Kaplan (ed.), *Postmodernism and its discontents: theories, practices*, London: Verso.

More, T. (1965) *Utopia*, trans. and intro. by P. Turner, Harmondsworth: Penguin.

Moreno, S. (1986) 'The light writing on the wall: the Leeds Pavilion Project', in S. Bezencenet and P. Corrigan (eds), *Photographic Practices: Towards a Different Image*, London: Comedia Publishing Group: 113–24.

Mulkay, M. (1979) *Science and the Sociology of Knowledge*, London: George Allen and Unwin.

—— (1985) 'Talking Together: An Analytical Dialogue', in *The Word and the World: Explorations in the Form of Sociological Analysis*, London: George Allen and Unwin: 103–29.

—— (1991a) 'Preface: The author as a sociological pilgrim', in *Sociology of Science: A Sociological Pilgrimage*, Milton Keynes: Open University Press: xiii–xiv.

—— (1991b) 'Looking backward (1989)', in *Sociology of Science: A Sociological Pilgrimage*, Milton Keynes: Open University Press: 204–16.

Muller, G. (1987) 'Washing the Linen', in L. Saunders (ed.), *Glancing Fires: An Investigation into Women's Creativity*, London: Women's Press: 130–40.

Mulvey, L. (1975) 'Visual Pleasure and Narrative Cinema', *Screen* 16, 3: 6–18.

Musello, C. (1979) 'Family Photography', in J. Wagner (ed.), *Images of Information*, Beverley Hills and London: Sage: 101–18.

Myers, G. (1990) 'Every picture tells a story: Illustrations in E. O. Wilson's "Sociobiology"', in M. Lynch and S. Woolgar (eds), *Representation in Scientific Practice*, Cambridge, Mass. and London: The MIT Press: 231–66.

National Council for Diplomas in Art and Design (1970) *Second Report of the*

National Council for Diplomas in Art and Design, London: The National Council for Diplomas in Art and Design.

Nelson, C. and Grossberg, L. (eds) (1988) *Marxism and the Interpretation of Culture*, Urbana: University of Illinois Press.

Nicholson, L. J. (1990) 'Introduction', in Nicholson, L. J. (ed.), *Feminism and Postmodernism*, New York and London: Routledge; 1–16.

Open University (1991) *Society and Social Science: A Foundation Course, D103*, Milton Keynes: Open University Press.

Orton, F. and Pollock, G. (1982) 'Les Données Bretonnantes: La Prairie de la Representation', in F. Frascina and C. Harrison (eds), *Modern Art And Modernism: A Critical Anthology*, London: Harper and Row: 285–304.

Osborne, P. (1989) 'Aesthetic Autonomy and the Crisis of Theory: Greenberg, Adorno, and the Problem of Postmodernism in the Visual Arts', *New Formations*, 9, Winter 1989: 31–50.

Overy, P. (1986) 'The New Art History and Art Criticism', in A. L. Rees and F. Borzello (eds), *The New Art History*, London: Camden Press: 133–45.

Owens, C. (1983) 'The Discourse of Others: Feminism and Postmodernism', in H. Foster (ed.), *Postmodern Culture*, London: Pluto Press: 57–82.

Painter, C. (1980) 'The Absent Public: A Report on a Pilot Survey of Objects Hanging on Walls in Households in Newcastle-upon-Tyne', *Art Monthly*, 29: 9–12.

Panofsky, E. (1939) *Studies in Iconology*, Oxford: Oxford University Press.

—— (1955) *Meaning in the Visual Arts: Papers in and on Art History*, New York: Doubleday Anchor.

Parker, R. and Pollock, G. (eds) (1987) *Framing Feminism: Art and the Women's Movement 1970–1985*, London: Pandora Press.

Partington, A. (1987) 'Feminist Art and Avant-gardism', in H. Robinson (ed.), *Visibly Female*, London: Camden Press: 228–49.

Peirce, C. (1955) *Philosophical Writings of Peirce*, selected, ed. and intro. by J. Buchler, New York: Dover Publications.

Penrose, B. and Freeman, S. (1986) *Conspiracy of Silence: The Secret Life of Anthony Blunt*, London: Grafton.

Pevsner, N. (1943) *An Outline of European Architecture*, Harmondsworth: Penguin.

Pinch T. and Pinch T. (1988) 'Reservations about Reflexivity and New Literary Forms or Why Let the Devil have All the Good Tunes?', in S. Woolgar (ed.), *Knowledge and Reflexivity: New Frontiers in the Sociology of Knowledge*, London: Sage: 178–97.

Pliny the Elder (1991) *Natural History*, selected, trans., intro. and notes by J. F. Healey, Harmondsworth: Penguin.

Plutarch (1972–3) *Vitae Parallelae* (selections), trans. R. Warner (1972), I. Scott-Kilvert (1972–3), Harmondsworth: Penguin.

Podro, M. (1982) *The Critical Historians of Art*, New Haven and London: Yale University Press.

Pollock, G. (1988) *Vision and Difference: Femininity, Feminism and the Histories of Art*, London: Routledge.

Poster, M. (1988) 'Introduction', in J. Baudrillard, *Selected Writings*, Cambridge: Polity Press: 1–9.

Poynor, R. and Booth-Clibborn, E. (eds) (1991) *Typography Now. The Next Wave*, London: Internos Books.

Raphael, M. (1933) *Proudhon, Marx, Picasso. Trois études sur la sociologie de l'art*, Paris: Editions Excelsior.

—— (1968) *The Demands of Art*, Princeton: Princeton University Press.

—— (1975) *Arbeiter, Kunst and Kunstler. Beitrage zu einer Marxistischen Kunstwissenschaft*, Frankfurt am Main: Fischer Verlag.

Ravetz, J. (1971) *Scientific Knowledge and Its Social Problems*, New York: Oxford University Press.

Read, H. (1933) *Art Now*, London: Faber and Faber.

—— (1937) *Art and Society*, London and Toronto: Heinemann.

—— (1943) *Education through Art*, London: Faber and Faber.

—— (1967) *Art and Alienation: the role of the artist in society*, London: Thames and Hudson.

Rees, A. L., and Borzello, F. (eds) (1986) *The New Art History*, London: Camden Press.

Renzio, T. del (1983) 'Works of art are produced by committees', *Art Monthly*, 63: 27–8.

Ricks, C. (1985) 'Introduction' to L. Sterne, *The Life and Opinions of Tristram Shandy, Gentleman*, Harmondsworth: Penguin.

Robbe-Grillet, A. (1959) *Jealousy*, London: John Calder.

Roberts, J. (1984) 'Rereading Adorno', *Art Monthly*, 81: 27–8.

—— (1990) *Postmodernism, politics and art*, Manchester: Manchester University Press.

—— (1992) 'Out of Our Heads', *Art Monthly*, 156: 11–17.

Robins, K. (1990) 'Global Local Times', in J. Anderson and M. Ricci (eds), *Society and Social Science*, Buckingham: Open University Press: 196–205.

Roskill, M. (1974) *What is Art History?*, London: Thames and Hudson.

Saussure, F. de (1974) *Course in General Linguistics*, C. Bally and A. Sechehaye (eds), in collaboration with A. Reidlinger, trans. W. Baskin, Glasgow: Fontana/Collins.

Sekula, A. (1982) 'On the Invention of Photographic Meaning', in V. Burgin (ed.), *Thinking Photography*, Basingstoke: Macmillan; 84–109.

Shanas, E. (1945) 'The AJS through Fifty Years', *American Journal of Sociology*, 50: 522–33.

Sherman, C. (1991) Interview, 'Third Ear', BBC Radio 3, 18 January 1991.

Showalter, E. (1981) 'Feminist Criticism in the Wilderness', *Critical Enquiry*, Winter 1981: 179–205.

Smith, D. E. (1974) 'Women's Perspective as a Radical Critique of Sociology', *Sociological Inquiry*, 44: 7–13.

Sollers, P. (1968) 'Ecriture et Révolution' in *Tel Quel: Théorie d'Ensemble*, Paris: Seuil.

Solomon, M. (1979) *Marxism and Art: Essays Classic and Contemporary*, Brighton: Harvester Press.

Sontag, S. (1967) *Against Interpretation*, London: Eyre and Spottiswoode.

Squires, C. (ed.) (1990) *The Critical Image: Essays on Contemporary Photography*, London: Lawrence and Wishart.

Stanley, L. and Morgan, D. (1993) 'Debates in Sociology: Some Thoughts on Editorship', paper distributed at British Sociological Association annual conference, University of Essex.

Stasz, C. (1979) 'The Early History of Visual Sociology', in J. Wagner (ed.), *Images of Information: Still Photography in the Social Sciences*, Beverly Hills and London: Sage: 119–36.

Stefano, C. di (1990) 'Dilemmas of Difference: Feminism, Modernity and Postmodernism', in L. J. Nicholson (ed.), *Feminism and Postmodernism*, New York and London: Routledge: 63–82.

Sterne, L. (1985) *The Life and Opinions of Tristram Shandy, Gentleman*, ed. G. Petrie, intro. by C. Ricks, Harmondsworth: Penguin.

Stoppard, M. (1985) *Pregnancy and Birth Book*, London: Dorling Kindersley.

Stummer, H. (1985) 'Photo-essay', *International Journal of Visual Sociology*, 2: 35–45.

Swinburne, A. J. (1896) *A Picture Logic*, London: Longmans, Green.

Sulter, M. (1989) (see under 'Artworks, Exhibitions and Films' – *Zabat*).

Tagg, J. (1975) 'The Method of Max Raphael: Art History Set Back on its Feet [Putting Art History on its Feet]', *Radical Philosophy*, 12, Winter 1975: 3–10.

—— (1980) 'The Method of Criticism and its Objects in Max Raphael's Theory of Art', *Block*, 2: 2–14.

—— (1986) 'Art History and Difference', in A. L. Rees and F. Borzello (eds), *The New Art History*, London: Camden Press: 164–71.

—— (1988) *The Burden of Representation: Essays on Photographies and Histories*, Basingstoke: Macmillan.

Taylor, R. (1978) *Art, An Enemy of the People*, Brighton: Harvester Press.

Thucydides (1972) *History of the Peloponnesian War*, trans. R. Warner, intro. and notes by M. I. Finlay, Harmondsworth: Penguin.

Tisdall, S. (1992) 'Perot beams himself straight to voters as polls push him towards a declaration', *Guardian*, 6 January 1992.

Vasari, G. (1927) *The Lives of the Painters, Sculptors and Architects*, trans. A. B. Hinds (4 vols), London: J. M. Dent and Sons Ltd, and New York: E. P. Dutton.

Villani, *De Famosis Civibus*, continued as *Quatuor Uomini Famosi* ([1955]) MS. notes from lecture 'Masaccio/Vasari' [Vasari's possible sources] by J. Wilde, 9 November 1955.

Walker, J. A. (1979) Introduction to M. Iverson, 'Meyer Schapiro and the Semiotics of Visual Art', *Block*, 1: 50.

Watson, J. D. (1974) *The Double Helix: a personal account of the discovery of the structure of DNA*, Harmondsworth: Penguin.

Williamson, J. (1978) *Decoding Advertisements: Ideology and Meaning in Advertising*, London: Marion Boyars.

Wilson, E. (1992) 'Art at the cutting edge of politics', *Guardian*, 30 July 1992.

Wolff, J. (1981) *The Social Production of Art*, London and Basingstoke: Macmillan.

—— (1990) 'Postmodern Theory and Feminist Art Practice', in R. Boyne and A. Rattansi (eds), *Postmodernism and Society*, London: Macmillan: 187–208.

—— (1993) *The Social Production of Art* (2nd rev. edn), London and Basingstoke: Macmillan.

Wölfflin, H. (1950) *Principles of Art History*, trans. M. D. Hottinger, New York: Dover Publications.

—— (1953) *Classic Art*, trans. P. and L. Murray, London: Phaidon.

Wood, P. (1985) 'Art and Politics in a Workers' State', *Art History*, 8, 1: 105–24.

—— ([1992]) 'The Politics of the Avantgarde', in *The Great Utopia: Russian Avantgarde, 1915-1932*, Stedelijk Museum, Amsterdam: 353–82.

Woolgar, S. (1988) 'Reflexivity is the Ethnographer of the Text', in S. Woolgar (ed.), *Knowledge and Reflexivity: New Frontiers in the Sociology of Knowledge*, London: Sage: 14–34.

Woolgar, S. and Ashmore, M. (1988) 'The Next Step: an Introduction to the Reflexive Project', in S. Woolgar (ed.), *Knowledge and Reflexivity: New Frontiers in the Sociology of Knowledge*, London: Sage: 1–11.

Worth, S. and Adair, J. (1972) *Through Navajo Eyes: An Exploration in Film Communication and Anthropology*, Bloomington: Indiana University Press.

Wynne, A. (1988) 'Accounting for Accounts of the Diagnosis of Multiple Sclerosis', in S. Woolgar (ed.), *Knowledge and Reflexivity: New Frontiers in the Sociology of Knowledge*, London: Sage: 101–22.

Young, H. (1992) 'The Medium is the Massage', *Guardian*, 16 March 1992.

Zube, E. (1979) 'Pedestrians and Wind', in J. Wagner (ed.), *Images of Information*, Beverly Hills and London: Sage: 69–84.

ART WORKS, EXHIBITIONS AND FILMS CITED

A Diary for Dewsbury (1991), an exhibition of photographs and drawings by Elizabeth and Stephen Chaplin at Dewsbury Museum.

Along the Lines of Resistance: An Exhibition of Contemporary Feminist Art (1988) at the Cooper Gallery, Barnsley, and subsequent venues.

Approaches to Realism (1990), an exhibition curated and catalogued by J. Roberts, at the Bluecoat Gallery, Liverpool and subsequent venues.

Countervail (1992–3), an exhibition of Systematic Constructive art at the Mappin Art Gallery, Sheffield, and subsequently at the Mead Gallery, University of Warwick.

Fabled Territories: New Asian Photography in Britain (1989–90), an exhibition at Leeds City Art Gallery, and subsequent venues.

Film Diary (1972–82) by David Perlov, broadcast on *ITV Channel 4*, 29 October 1988 and on consecutive nights through the following week.

[Five Women] 5 Women (1988–9), an exhibition of photographs at The Pavilion, Leeds. (The Pavilion, Leeds is sometimes cited as The Pavilion Women's Photography and Visual Arts Centre, Leeds.)

Herbert Read: A British Vision of World Art (1993–4), an exhibition and catalogue publication, Leeds City Art Galleries, in conjunction with the Henry Moore Foundation and Lund Humphries Ltd.

Looking for Sheba (1990), an exhibition at The Pavilion, Leeds.

'Nature Wheel' (1986), an artwork by Chris Drury exhibited in Leeds City Art Gallery.

Paintings, Paul Winstanley (1992), an exhibition at Kettle's Yard, Cambridge, and subsequent venues.

Photography Now (1989), an exhibition curated by M. Haworth-Booth, at the Victoria & Albert Museum, London.

Post-Impressionism: Cross-Currents in European Painting (1979–80), an exhibition at the Royal Academy of Arts, London.

Real Lemon: Broadening Out (1991), an exhibition of paintings by Rachael Field at Rochdale Art Gallery, and subsequently at The Pavilion, Leeds.

Stolen Glances: Lesbians take photographs (1991–3), an exhibition at the Cambridge Darkroom, and subsequent venues.

Systems (1972–3), an Arts Council exhibition at Whitechapel Art Gallery, London, and subsequent venues.

'Technology and Morality' (1992–3), a series of computer realisations by J. Barnbrook and T. Yoneda, exhibited in *The Big Apple*, at the Zelda Cheatle Gallery, London, and subsequently at The Studio, Beckenham.

Testimony (1986), an exhibition at The Pavilion, Leeds.

That's Action Women (1988–9), an exhibition of photomontage at The Pavilion, Leeds, and subsequent venues.

The Art of Photography (1989), an exhibition at the Royal Academy of Arts, London.

The Everyday Creative Process (1988), a series of photographs by G. Muller; illustrated in 'Washing the Linen', in L. Saunders (ed.) *Glancing Fires: An Investigation into Women's Creativity*, London: Women's Press; facing p. 118.

The Pre-Raphaelites (1984), an exhibition at the Tate Gallery, London.

Through the Looking Glass: Photographic Art in Britain 1945–89 (1989), an exhibition at the Barbican Art Gallery, London, and subsequently at Manchester City Art Gallery.

Visual Diary (1988), an exhibition of photographs by Elizabeth Chaplin at Leeds University Art Gallery, and subsequent venues.

Zabat: Poetics of a Family Tree (1989), an exhibition of photographs by Maud Sulter at Rochdale Art Gallery, and subsequent venues.

Name index

Subject index

account: competing 280; informal 223–30; injecting uncertainty into 231, 257–62, 266; structure of 244–5, 249, 250, 272; *see also* multi-voice account

advertisement 107, 142–3, 212–18, 233, 237

aesthetics 22–4, 25–8, 36–9, 40, 52, 68–72, 126, 170; bourgeois, as consensus 170–1; critique of 75; and photography 179, 218–222, 229, 277

aestheticisation 42, 141–5, 155

analysis: of postmodernity 139; secondary 192, 201–7; structural 97; textual 75–7; visual 47, 81, 89–92, 244; *see also* class analysis; critical analysis; empiricism; feminism; Marxism; social analysis; verbal analysis

anomie 164–5, 179

anthropology 257; and photography 199–212, *203*, 208–9, 276; method and anthropological strangeness 192, 200, 211, 273–4; visual 203, 212, 270, 276

art 103, 124; abstract 9, 10, 57, 250; academic 172; avant-garde 36, 119; black women's 103, 116, 119; as collective action 169/74; critical 29, 30, 31; critical practice 91–2, 104–11, 264, 276; demand for 41; figurative 10, 11, 48, 89, 125; form 38–9, 43, 69, 75, 125; good/bad 43, 46, 49, 54–5, 163–4; 'high' 36, 39, 126, 168–9; innovation in 126, 173–4; knowledge 6, 7, 45, 53; liberatory potential of 27–8, 31, 36–9, 40–1, 64, 69, 110, 122, 125; and Marxism 27, 28–47, 173; modern/contemporary 35, 44–5, 48, 167; and morals 23; and nature 45–6; and objectivity 7–8, 46, 50, 51, 56; personnel 68, 161, 170; and philosophy 22–4, 27, 170; and photography 41, 80–1, 104–11, 114, 225, 229; and politics 141, 173; popular 39, 62, 167–9; production of 68, 168, 169; and reproduction 41, 50, 167, 177–80; and science 8, 46, 51–2, 189, 218; and semiotics 68–9, 80–1, 96–100; and social class 167–9; and sociology 10, 87–92, 132, 170, 228; students 150, 162–7, *166*, style 21, 22, 42, 63, 74; teaching 163–7; theory 22, 26, 36, 39, 40, 44–5, 70; and truth 46; uniqueness of 41, 124, 179; and utopianism 39, 46, 110, 140; as universal 167; work of 32, 34–5, 37–9, 40–2, 47–50, 60, 70, 76, 78, 124, 125, 179; world 165, 169–74; *see also* art criticism; art education; art history; audience for art; autonomy of art; feminist art theory/ practice; ideology and art; modernism in art; value judgement of art; visual art

art criticism 32–3, 40, 92

art education 162–7, 169; existing system of 78, 89–90, 150, 244; through photographic projects 113, 121, 150

art history 21, 24, 32–3, 173–4; bourgeois/dominant/conventional 63, 65, 72, 77, 82; connoisseurial 22, 49–50, 51–2, 62; Courtald 53–7; feminist 93–104; Marxist 28, 29–44, 63–72; modernist 72–4, 95; 'New'/social/critical 2, 51, 57, 58–63, 72–9, 194, 275–6; science of 63–6; *see also* method, problems in art history

artefact, image and text as 106, 109, 110; sociology as 282, 283; and subjectivity 47, 50, 55; work of art as 40, 78, 124, 125

artist 6, 31, 52, 124, 201, 274; eye of 69; famous 21–2, 167; individuality of 49; men 95, 165; radical/critical 36, 38–9, 41, 45, 60–2, 66, 276; 'special status' of 67–8, 73, 163, 169; as subject 71; subjectivity of 282; visual 72, 125, 210; *see also* Constructivism, Systematic

artwork *see* art, work of

audience 283; for art 36, 61–2, 70, 74, 101, 151, 171, 276; for art writing 57; characteristics of 87, 146, 153, 195; for drama 253; female 102–3, 109, 119–20, 121, 122, 278; male 100; reaction 155, 207; *see also* reader; viewer